Thomas Bog Slade and Female Education in Early Georgia, 1800–1882

Thomas Bog Slade and Female Education in Early Georgia, 1800–1882

One Mass of Crimson Beauty

Timothy E. Miller

HAMILTON BOOKS

HAMILTON BOOKS
Bloomsbury Publishing Inc, 1359 Broadway, New York, NY 10018, USA
Bloomsbury Publishing Plc, 50 Bedford Square, London, WC1B 3DP, UK
Bloomsbury Publishing Ireland, 29 Earlsfort Terrace, Dublin 2, D02 AY28, Ireland

BLOOMSBURY and the Diana logo are trademarks of Bloomsbury Publishing Plc

First published in the United States of America 2026

Copyright © Bloomsbury Publishing, 2026

Cover image by the author

All rights reserved. No part of this publication may be: i) reproduced or transmitted in any form, electronic or mechanical, including photocopying, recording or by means of any information storage or retrieval system without prior permission in writing from the publishers; or ii) used or reproduced in any way for the training, development or operation of artificial intelligence (AI) technologies, including generative AI technologies. The rights holders expressly reserve this publication from the text and data mining exception as per Article 4(3) of the Digital Single Market Directive (EU) 2019/790.

Bloomsbury Publishing Inc does not have any control over, or responsibility for, any third-party websites referred to or in this book. All internet addresses given in this book were correct at the time of going to press. The author and publisher regret any inconvenience caused if addresses have changed or sites have ceased to exist, but can accept no responsibility for any such changes.

Library of Congress Cataloging-in-Publication Data

ISBN: HB: 978-0-7618-9208-3
PB: 978-0-7618-7474-4
ePDF: 978-0-7618-8037-0
eBook: 978-0-7618-7909-1

Typeset by Deanta Global Publishing Services, Chennai, India

For product safety related questions contact productsafety@bloomsbury.com.

To find out more about our authors and books visit www.bloomsbury.com and sign up for our newsletters.

For Kristina Peavy

Contents

Acknowledgments		viii
Introduction		1
1	North Carolina	9
2	Clinton	37
3	The Journey North	101
4	Macon and Wesleyan	141
5	Penfield	197
6	Columbus	211
Conclusion		257
Bibliography		259
Index		278
About the Author		287

Acknowledgments

While the content of this work originated with me and all errors herein are my responsibility, a work such as this is not possible without the several contributions of mentors, colleagues, friends, and family.

I came to this project while working with Kristina Peavy, Virginia Blake, and Rhiannon Bruner, all librarians at Wesleyan College, Macon, Georgia, and Dr. Brandi Simpson Miller, Wesleyan assistant professor of history, to research and revise the history of that college which was attempting to understand its origins and early history within the complicated context of slavery. Peavy is the library director at the Willet Memorial Library on the campus and she initially contracted me to be the "outside" member of the team in 2021. Blake is the archivist/public services librarian, and Bruner is the electronic resource manager. I could not have contemplated this project without each of these valuable people. The book is, therefore, dedicated to Peavy because it was she who, when we were deep in the early records of Wesleyan, even though she may now deny it, said, "You'll never get a book out of Slade," just because she doubted there was enough material available about this man of whom so little was known. He was, indeed, quite mysterious, and almost invisible at the time, although he was one of Wesleyan's first four professors. Her challenge inspired me, however, to try and the quest began. Now, all are amazed at how much material has been uncovered and how someone so well known and respected during the early nineteenth century could have been forgotten in the records. As it turns out, this was the second time I had raised a man from the dead, historically speaking. I cannot express my gratitude to Rhiannon, who is one of the most brilliantly qualified records researchers in the world. She made her help available by email and consistently came up with appropriate material every time I wrote to ask her for help on any topic, even the most obscure and unusual questions, usually responding within minutes.

I first produced an article, "One Mass of Crimson Beauty: Thomas Bog Slade and Early Female Education in Georgia, 1800–1882," which was presented and positively reviewed by professional historians at the 2024 Annual Florida Conference of Historians in Melbourne, Florida. The article came to the attention of this publisher, and further research began to turn the article into a book. Every door led to a hallway full of doors and soon the problem was more about how to limit the story and, sadly, what to leave out. Whereas the topic of female education and the history of nineteenth-century Georgia are more fully known, I chose to focus on Thomas Bog Slade, the man, and his role in these wider topics. He was a major character in both, and to understand him, his vision, motives, and faith, is to more clearly understand the history of public education more generally.

I am grateful to the staff of the David M. Rubenstein Library at Duke University in Durham, North Carolina, where the Slade Family Papers are housed. J. Andrew Armacost, Jennifer Baker, Molly Bragg, Kate Collins, Hillary Gatlin, Valerie Gillispie, Brooke Guthrie, Kate Henningsen, Tracy Jackson, Naomi L. Nelson, Megan O'Connell, Rebecca Patillo, Alice Poffinberger, and Neal Shipe were all equally helpful over several full days of research. Fully 2,781 items have been preserved, all dating from the period 1751 to 1929 and directly related, if not created, by members of the Slade Family. These are financial records, the affairs of an early American plantation, student letters, deeds, lists of enslaved persons, notes of relations with the Tuscarora Indians, and other legal papers. Personal letters and reports discuss fisheries, timber, hog farming, horse breeding, tobacco, and cotton. They move seamlessly through the Mexican-American and Civil War.

I am grateful for Helen M. Prescott, a granddaughter of Slade living in Atlanta, who donated a copy of Slade's journal to the Southern Historical Collection of the University of North Carolina, but I am puzzled as to why she destroyed the original. Surely, having the journal in Slade's own hand would have provided far more detail regarding his 1837 journey north. Mrs. Broadus E. Willingham Jr. of Macon, Georgia, later donated another copy but, sadly, it was a copy of Prescott's typed version.[1] In the Southern Historical Collection of the university are found the Alfred M. Slade Receipts, 1822–7, Cabarrus and Slade Family Papers, 1794–1932, and the Helen M. Blount Prescott Papers, 1835–1944, in addition to the papers of Slade.[2]

Also in North Carolina, the staff of the B-H-M Regional Library in Williamston, North Carolina (Martin County), director Kimberly Davenport, and especially the curator of special collections Stephen Farrell at the George H. and Laura E. Brown Library in Washington, North Carolina, were helpful.

In Columbus, Georgia, the staff of the Columbus Public Library and Columbus State University Special Collections Library contributed to the research used to produce this record of Slade and his role in early nineteenth-century female education.

Finally, I want to thank the living descendants of Slade for their kind permission to use Slade family historical material.[3] Kirsten Slade Schmitt was the administrator of her father Thomas Bog Slade III's estate and spoke for her siblings who agreed to support this work. She kindly contacted her extended Slade family, including Sarah Boone Slade, wife of James Jeremiah Slade and their three children, Richard Kirven Slade II, Dorothy Slade Mann, and Blanche Slade Hancock. Kirsten supplied obituaries and photos which were invaluable. The immediate family and contributors to this work included her siblings, Vivian Slade Burr and Bowen Slade. William Martin Stewart, a son of Rose Gignilliat Willingham and descendant of Janet Elizabeth Slade (1825–1914), living in Houston, Texas, provided much enthusiasm for the project and original letters from members of the family. He shared one letter from his ancestor Janet, pronounced *Jenette*, about her wedding and one from the comrades of John Henry Slade (1843–62) about his Civil War death at Sharpsburg. Further, Stewart directed me to Richard Read Gignilliat of Marietta, Georgia, a descendant of William Robert Gignilliat, Sr. and his first wife, who quickly sent forty-one newspaper clippings from his personal research archives.

Notes

1 *Autobiography of Thomas Bog Slade*, typed copy, 1837, and family tree added May 1944, Thomas Bog Slade Papers, 1837–1846, 2683, Southern Historical Collection, University of North Carolina (Chapel Hill).
2 Helen M. Blount Prescott Papers, 1835–1944, 1509, OCLC 25754121, Southern Historical Collection, University of North Carolina (Chapel Hill).
3 Sunya Kirsten Slade Schmitt, email, August 8, 2024.

Introduction

Whatever honor, therefore, Georgia is entitled to for her other great work . . ., let this still be at the top, the fitting and crowning point of her glory, that she took and holds the lead of all the world in female education.

Alexander H. Stephens, 1859

In early nineteenth-century America as Georgia was pushing its territorial claim northwestward from Savannah, Thomas Bog (pronounced *Bōwg* according to his descendants) Slade was born in Martin County, North Carolina.[1] He died eighty-two years later in Columbus, Georgia but in the meantime, graduated from the University of North Carolina (UNC) Chapel Hill at the top of his class, passed the bar exams of both North Carolina and Georgia, started six schools, four of them exclusively for females, and served as both an inferior court judge and president of the Georgia Teachers Association.[2] The leading contemporary educators of nineteenth-century America knew Slade as a promoter of public education in general and female education in particular, corresponded with him and spoke highly of him in personal letters, public speeches, and when quoted in the newspapers of their time. He was "gifted in oratory" according to one, detested hypocrisy, and possessed a "love of learning" according to others.[3] A lawyer, judge, Baptist minister, teacher, school founder and administrator, Slade was an expert botanist and taught himself French when he was fifty years old.[4] At UNC, Slade never received a demerit, never missed a recitation, and according to one historian, "never failed a single duty."[5] In fact, he became a comparative proof on campus for those who wanted to guarantee the certainty of any possibility after one student said, "I am as sure to hit that marble as Tom Slade is to know his lessons."[6] Slade later claimed that his conduct at North Carolina had been so "remarkable" the president of "Chapel Hill" made it public at the time of his graduation.[7]

Numerous educated women of the late nineteenth-century era of reform were educated in Slade's early nineteenth-century schools, inspired by his progressive vision and motivated to complete his work as they participated in the nationwide movements for abolition of slavery, universal suffrage, mental health reform, temperance, and a system of government-funded public schools. An uncompromising insistence on a classical education on the Georgia frontier lay at the heart of the Slade enterprise and yet Slade's own valuable contribution to this movement has disappeared from the modern history of education in America.[8] Slade supported a broad-based, rigorous liberal arts curriculum which included classical languages and the fine arts along with the humanities and hard science. There was no place for subjects such as business or psychology which have become the most popular undergraduate majors today. The educated graduates of Slade's schools were more than proficient in biology, chemistry, debate, English, history, Latin, literature, mathematics, physics, and rhetoric.

The argument of this volume is driven by two contrasting lacunae in the historical literature. Firstly, the existing historiography of the establishment of public education in the State of Georgia is largely silent on the Slade projects, although Slade worked diligently for six decades to support education expansion and female intellectual improvement.[9] Conversely, the thin literature regarding the Slade family, including that on key colleagues of Thomas, has almost completely ignored the significance of his educational interests and activities, concentrating instead on his work and connections in law, politics, or religion. As shown throughout this work, however, Slade regularly corresponded with colleagues as well as community, state, denominational leaders, and others regarding the improvement of education in Georgia and America, recorded his personal thoughts on related topics in his letters to his family, and often spoke with government officials about issues connected to his educational projects.

As a licensed attorney who became a county judge in Jones County, Georgia, and having originated from a wealthy landowning pioneer family of eastern North Carolina, Slade enjoyed a comfortable and prosperous life before he turned to education. Although his original wealth came to him from a slave-based plantation economy, he acted out of a genuine concern for education when he voluntarily gave up the lucrative practice of law and accepted the far less profitable position of headmaster of the Clinton (Georgia) Boys Academy in 1824. This was not his original plan. According to his own account, he had "no fondness for books" until he was fifteen years old.[10] As an adolescent, Slade consistently chose rather to hunt and fish than study. Teachers were not well paid in the early nineteenth century, especially those who founded new schools. Slade owned slaves; however, and his family owned more slaves, but he also had eleven children of his own, eight of them girls. An ordained Baptist minister, Slade did not allow his denominational preference to prevent him from joining the original faculty of the Georgia Female College (Wesleyan Female College after 1842), a Methodist institution, in Macon, Georgia. He committed his life to education and continued until the last days of his life.

Although Slade came from a wealthy family, he abandoned much of this wealth. Then, when he moved to Georgia in 1824, he married Anne Jacqueline Blount, who came to the marriage with resources of her own, including a classical education.[11] She was a graduate of the Moravian Seminary in Salem, NC. She was also related to Slade, being his second cousin on his mother's Blount side of the family.[12] Anne's sister was Lavinia E. Blount, the wife of Simi Rose of Ft. Hawkins, Georgia, editor of the Macon newspaper that became the *Telegraph* and namesake of Macon's Rose Hill Cemetery. Slade struggled financially for sixty years, starting and developing schools for boys and girls.[13] It was said he never turned a student away due to their lack of ability to pay. Partly because of this benevolent policy, however, there was always a lingering financial deficit since all the schools' income came from tuition. So, Slade's mission was meant to benefit children, primarily girls, of all social and economic classes as well as from neighboring states. A product of the early nineteenth century, however, it must be understood that these students were primarily the white, privileged upper-class daughters of planters living all along the Georgia fall line from Columbus to Augusta. They were educated, in most cases, not for their own careers but to be the supporting wives of young aspiring Georgia men who became the economic, political, and religious leaders of Georgia in the late nineteenth century. There were exceptions, however, and some of their stories are included here.

As Francis M. Manning and W. H. Booker wrote in the *Martin County History*, "The Slades were a prolific group, their numbers running well into the hundreds."[14] Without including the students, their numbers now run into the thousands and they live all around the world. This work is primarily about the life of one Thomas Bog Slade, but because of the Slade family's preference to reuse a small number of names for children of every generation, there are, for example, at least eight different individuals in this same family named Thomas Bog Slade and this has caused much confusion in the family history. The present subject is the oldest and first known to have the name, born in 1800 and named for his maternal grandfather Thomas Bog (1740–77). Thomas Bog Slade (1816–35), however, was a first cousin to the subject and was likely named for the same. This second Thomas Bog Slade was a son of Henry Blount Slade (1762–1821) and Elizabeth Bennett (b. 1780) and died young, at the age of nineteen. He never married and he fathered no children. Thomas Bog Slade (1834–1926), the son of subject Thomas Bog Slade, is logically known as Thomas Bog Slade, Jr., but that seems to ignore Thomas Bog Slade, the son of Henry Blount Slade who might logically be Thomas Bog Slade II. Thomas Bog Slade, Jr. married Almarine Cowdrey (1848–1926), raised six children, and became a school teacher in Carrollton, GA. Thomas Bog Slade, Sr. (1845–1929) was a son of William Slade, an uncle of our subject Thomas Bog Slade and should be known as Thomas Bog Slade IV. He lived and died in Martin County, North Carolina, thereby creating the North Carolina line of Thomas Bog Slades. Thomas Bog Slade (1863–1942), also known as Thomas Bog Slade, Sr. but who logically ought to be Thomas Bog Slade V, was a nephew of the subject Thomas Bog Slade, a son of the subject's brother James Jeremiah Slade, Sr. (1831–1917) and therefore first cousin of Thomas Bog Slade, son of the subject. To confuse the research further, he was born in Columbus, Georgia but migrated to Florida, thereby creating the Florida line of Thomas Bog Slades. The first Thomas Bog Slade, Jr. (1891–1956), who ought logically to be known as Thomas Bog Slade VI, was the son of Thomas Bog Slade, Sr. (1845–1929) and, like his father, spent his entire life in Martin County, NC. The second Thomas Bog Slade, Jr. (1906–71) was a son of Thomas Bog Slade, Sr. (1863–1942) and grandson of Jeremiah Slade, Sr. (1831–1917) and ought logically to be known as Thomas Bog Slade VII. He was born in Mexico but lived in Jacksonville, Florida. Thomas Bog Slade III (1915–78) was a son of Thomas Bog Slade, Jr. (1891–1956) and ought logically to be known as Thomas Bog Slade VIII. He lived in North Carolina, married Myrtle Matthews, and had two daughters but, mercifully, no sons. Thus, the first daughter is, believe it or not, named Thomasine Bog Slade (b. 1952). Finally, Thomas Bog Slade III (1931–2021) was a son of Thomas Bog Slade, Jr. (1906–71) and ought logically to be known as Thomas Bog Slade IX. He looked remarkably like actor Patrick Stewart and was the father of three children, two girls and one boy who he named . . . Dewitt Bowen Slade (b. 1961). For now, both lines of the Thomas Bog Slade name have come to an end. All of this to demonstrate how careful a student of Slade family history must be. They did almost as much with names such as Ebenezer, Henry, Jeremiah, William, and every conceivable combination thereof for the boys. As for the Slade girls, every family has their share of Elizabeth, Mary, and Anne.

The Slades also seemed to have an unwritten rule that few members of the family were allowed to be called by their legal name. Some are understandable as "Annie" is preferred for Anne, "Willie" for William, or "Jere" for Jeremiah, yet Emma Jacqueline Slade was consistently addressed in the correspondence only as "Coon" and "Nettie" was used for Mary Janet Slade, the daughter of James Jeremiah, Sr. (1831–1917). The explanation for the latter is understood when pronunciations for Slade names are properly grasped. Just as "Bog" was pronounced *Bōwg*, "Janet" was pronounced *Jeanette*. The subject Thomas Bog Slade's mother and daughter were both, at one point, known as "Jeanette," spelled Janet, Slade. There were loads more and thus more cause for concern in navigating the Slade family correspondence.

In conclusion, Thomas Bog Slade was a son, brother, husband, and father. He was also a lawyer, educator, administrator, and minister. A native of North Carolina, he became one of Georgia's leading education advocates and one of its most esteemed nineteenth-century Baptist preachers. "In every Southern state there may be found some ladies, in almost every station in life, who, under his instruction and that of his lifelong companion, received that stamp of cultivation and refinement which so distinguishes the daughters of the South."[15] Without interruption, Slade organized, led, and taught in female academies, colleges, institutes, and seminaries for fifty years. "Thousands of ladies in the land are indebted to him for their education," Georgia Baptists proclaimed in tribute.

Notes

1. Slade Family Papers, 1751–1929, David M. Rubenstein Rare Book & Manuscript Library, Duke University; The National Archives in Washington D.C., Records of the US Bureau of the Census, 1840, Howards, Bibb, Georgia; roll 37, p. 81; 1850, Columbus, Muscogee, Georgia, roll 79, p. 337a; 1860, Columbus, Muscogee, Georgia, roll M653_132, p. 156; and 1880, Enumeration District 092, Columbus, Muscogee, Georgia, roll 159, p. 670a. See also Jean E. Friedman and Rachel Mordecai Lazarus, *Ways of Wisdom: Moral Education in the Early National Period* (University of Georgia, 2001); Jennifer L. Goloboy, *Charleston and the Emergence of Middle-Class Culture in the Revolutionary Era* in the Early American Places Series (Univ. of Georgia, 2016); Keri Holt, *Reading These United States: Federal Literacy in the Early Republic, 1776–1830* (Univ. of Georgia, 2019); Natalie R. Inman, *Brothers and Friends: Kinship in Early America* in the Early American Places Series (Univ. of Georgia, 2017); Robert C. Jones, *History of Georgia Railroads* (History Press, 2017); Susan E. Klepp, *Revolutionary Conceptions: Women, Fertility, and Family Limitation in America, 1760–1820* (Univ. of North Carolina, 2009); John E. Lamar and Ben Yarborough, *Reminiscences of John E. Lamar: Early History of Columbus, Georgia* (Sunshine, 2013); John Lauritz Larson, *Internal Improvement: National Public Works and the Promise of Popular Government in the Early United States* (Univ. of North Carolina, 2001); S. Emmett Lucas, *The Third or 1820 Land Lottery of Georgia* (Southern Historical Press, 2005); Buddy Sullivan, *Georgia: A State History* (Arcadia, 2010); and Gordon S. Wood, *Empire of Liberty: A History of the Early Republic, 1789–1815* (Oxford, 2011).
2. "Rail Road Meeting in Jones County," *The Macon Advertiser & Agricultural & Mercantile Intelligencer* (August 23, 1831), p. 3. See also Thomas Bog Slade, *Autobiography of Thomas Bog Slade*, Southern Historical Collection 1837–1846, 2683-z, University of North Carolina, p. 2.
3. W. C. Woodall, "The First of the Slades," in *Jones-Muscogee Counties, GA Biographies* (Columbus Ledger, Mon., January 6, 1964), p. 13.

4 Dorothy Orr, *The History of Public Education in Georgia* (n.p., 1950). See also Thomas Bog Slade, *Autobiography of Thomas Bog Slade*, Southern Historical Collection 1837–1846, 2683-z, University of North Carolina, p. 1.

5 Carolyn White Williams, *The History of Jones County, Georgia 1807–1907* (Macon: J. W. Burke, 1957), pp. 423–5.

6 Dorothy Orr, *The History of Public Education in Georgia* (n.p., 1950).

7 Thomas Bog Slade, *Autobiography of Thomas Bog Slade*, Southern Historical Collection 1837-1846, 2683-z, University of North Carolina, p. 1. See also Dorothy Orr, *History of Public Education in Georgia*.

8 James O'Neil Spady, *Education and the Racial Dynamics of Settler Colonialism in Early America: Georgia and South Carolina, ca. 1700-c.a. 1820* (Routledge, 2020).

9 See Dana Goldstein, *The Teacher Wars: A History of America's Most Embattled Profession* (Anchor, 2015); Edward McInnis, "The Spartan Woman: Symbol for an Age?," *American Educational History Journal* 43:1/2 (2016): 195–210; Johann N. Neem, *Democracy's Schools: The Rise of Public Education in America* (Johns Hopkins, 2017); John D. Pulliam and James J. van Patten, *History of Education in America*, 9th ed. (Pearson, 2006); Barbara Miller Solomon, *In the Company of Educated Women: A History of Women and Higher Education in America* (Yale, 1986); Rebecca Weissman, "The Role of White Supremacy Amongst Opponents and Proponents of Mass Schooling in the South during the Common School Era," *Paedagogica Historica* 55:5 (October 2019): 703–23.

10 Thomas Bog Slade, *Autobiography of Thomas Bog Slade*, Southern Historical Collection 1837–1846, 2683-z, University of North Carolina, p. 1.

11 Marriage Records from Select Counties, 1811-1828, Georgia Archives, Morrow, GA; County Marriage Records, Jones County, Book 11, p. 244 and Thomas Bog Slade, *Autobiography of Thomas Bog Slade*, Southern Historical Collection 1837–1846, 2683-z, University of North Carolina, p. 2.

12 Thomas Bog Slade, *Autobiography of Thomas Bog Slade*, Southern Historical Collection 1837–1846, 2683-z, University of North Carolina, p. 1.

13 Thomas Bog Slade, Letter to Elizabeth Slade, undated, Slade Family Papers, Box 2 (1821–1824).

14 Francis M. Manning and W. H. Booker, *Martin County History*, vol. I (Williamston: Enterprise Publishing Co., 1977), p. 231.

15 *History of the Baptist Denomination in Georgia: With Biographical Compendium and Portrait Gallery of Baptist Ministers and other Georgia Baptists* (Atlanta: J. P. Harrison & Co., 1881), p. 188.

1

North Carolina

Litterae sunt ornamenta et hominum solatia.

Thomas Bog Slade

Thomas Bog Slade was the son of General James Jeremiah Slade (1775–1824) and Janet Bog (1774–1831).[1] He graduated first in his university class at the University of North Carolina (UNC) Chapel Hill and joined his father's Williamston, NC, law practice in 1815.[2] Jeremiah had been born in 1775, also in Martin County, NC, and had been a member of the early American North Carolina House of Commons (1797–1800), a state senator (1809–15), commissioner to the affairs of the Tuscarora Indians in 1803, and brigadier general in the War of 1812.[3] General Slade was the son of William Slade (1745–91) and Nancy Ann Gainor (1735–78). William was a member from Martin County to the colonial meeting of North Carolina deputies in Hillsboro, North Carolina, in 1775. He was a member of the General Assembly in 1777 and then served in the American Revolution rising to the level of first lieutenant by 1778. His name appears on the prestigious list of members of the *Society of Cincinnati*, which is an organization founded for and by the officers of the Continental Army, including General George Washington, who served as the first president of the United States.

The Slades are described as "white plantation owners and businessmen in Martin County, NC."[4] Their surviving papers include family and business correspondence, account books, memoranda books, daybooks, time books, court records, and more. In the Rubenstein Library of Duke University, they have left over 2,781 manuscripts dating from 1751 until 1929. These are the family and financial documentation of an eastern North Carolina plantation mixed with deeds, lists of enslaved persons, the Tuscarora Nation, and letters to and from children who attended the University of North Carolina, Trinity College (Duke University), North Carolina State University, the Normal College at Greensboro, and others. Because Jeremiah was a trustee at the University of North Carolina, all the early Slade men who went to college, eleven of them by 1889, studied there. This included all four of Jeremiah's surviving sons. Alfred, the oldest, graduated in 1815 and later became a United States consul to Buenos Aires, Argentina. Thomas Bog finished with an A.B. (Bachelor of Arts) in 1820 and A.M. (Master of Arts) in 1823, James graduated in 1822 with his A.B. and went on to earn his MD (Doctor of Medicine) at the University of Pennsylvania in 1826, and William dropped out of the Class of 1824. Grandsons James Jeremiah, Thomas Bog's son completed his studies at Chapel Hill in 1852 and William's sons Jeremiah (1855) and Thomas Bog Jr. (1856) also finished there. Finally, William Bonner Slade, a great grandson of Jeremiah, graduated from the University of North Carolina in 1879. Others, including the females who went to college, graduated from Duke University, originally known as Trinity College, North Carolina State University, and the Normal College at Greensboro, NC. Their correspondence passed through the War of 1812, the Mexican-American War, and the American Civil War. Among reports of legal work and intimate family details of affection are other valuable historical details of fisheries, logging, farming of hogs, tobacco, and cotton, and horse breeding.

The North Carolina part of the Slade story is focused on Thomas Bog Slade's father Jeremiah Slade (1775–1824), his grandfather William Slade (1745–91), and his great grandfather Ebenezer Slade (1715–87). These are the men who built one of the largest plantations in North Carolina, finally to be the largest slave owners in Martin County. They owned thousands of acres spread across several plantations, yet they were, like many other planters, also politicians and soldiers. Jeremiah served in the state legislature of the young state, was appointed commissioner of Indian affairs, was promoted to brigadier general, maintained a successful law practice, was a trustee for the University of North Carolina, and still managed to increase the wealth bequeathed to him before passing it on to his children. The Slades were prolific. Ebenezer raised six children, William fathered five, and Jeremiah had nine. This is thus the story of a politically and economically powerful planter class family from which came one who selfishly promoted education for girls, often at his own expense, to his own poverty, in his private home, in the neighboring State of Georgia.

The Slades had been in the New World since 1671 when General Slade's great great grandfather, Henry Wickman Slade (1655–1730), immigrated to Virginia from Dorset in England.[5] Henry married Hannah Loveridge in England but lived in America on the Pungo River near "the mouth a creek known as Slade's Creek in Hyde County." The original settlement has survived "and is known today as the village of Sladesville."[6] This is where Henry and Hannah Slade raised four surviving sons: John, William, Samuel, and Benjamin. William married Frances Abigail Sylvester, the daughter of Richard William and Hannah Leonard Sylvester. They were married in 1709 and raised six children: William, Henry John, Ebenezer, Jemima, Daniel Samuel, and Dorcas. They lived in both Hyde and Albemarle Counties, North Carolina.

Ebenezer Slade (1715–87) married Agnes McNare (1720–1800) and raised six children, including William Slade (1745–91) the father of Jeremiah Slade (1775–1824). In 1742, Ebenezer, of the planter class operating in the early modern plantation economy of the American South, received a grant of land from the state in what was Tyrell, now Martin, County, North Carolina. He created generational wealth on the labor of involuntary servitude, as many planters did in the seventeenth century. While the lands of the Slade family were never among the largest plantations in the state, they were nevertheless significant, whereas the entire plantation class, also known as the planter aristocracy, represented less than three percent of the state's total population. While planters held disproportional but significant political power and wealth, they were always a numerically limited class due to the amount of property required to be a planter. Beginning with Ebenezer, land-based wealth was created that was passed down through multiple generations of the Slade family. He was a planter and politician. He represented Tyrell County in the North Carolina Colonial Assembly in October 1769.[7] Ebenezer, along with others, was appointed a commissioner of the newly chartered Martin County and the parish of St. Martin. He assisted in establishing the boundaries of the county in 1774. When Ebenezer died in 1787, he owned only one enslaved person, thus indicating the Slade estate was established by Ebenezer but first grew exponentially into a commercial enterprise that was passed down through multiple generations under his son William.[8]

William Slade (1745–91) married Nancy Ann Gainor (also spelled Gainer) in 1761. They raised five children in Tyrell/Martin County. Ann, as she was called, was the daughter of Benjamin Gainer who was also from the area.[9] Gainer served in the North Carolina Colonial Assembly from 1769 until 1773, meeting in New Bern, the capital of the colony and state until 1794 when the government was moved to Raleigh. There, he worked to create a new county from Halifax and Tyrell Counties, introducing bills in 1769, 1770, and 1771.[10] The legislation passed the assembly each time but never received the support of Royal Governor William Tryon (1729–88). Tryon was a British Army officer, Lt. Gen., who served as governor during 1765–71 before being appointed colonial governor of New York (1771–7). He was a key figure in the buildup to the American Revolution by suspending the meeting of the state assembly for eighteen months in 1765–6 to prevent the delegates from passing a resolution in opposition to the Stamp Act. At the same time, he built a governor's mansion that was considered one of the finest examples of Georgian architecture in America at the time and was thus critically known as "Tryon's Palace" to the working class of North Carolina. Tryon was from Surrey in England and may have had historical connections to the Slades who also originated there. He expanded the Anglican Church in North Carolina, and he created the first North Carolina state postal service but he opposed the creation of Martin County. He is known in history as a fair and able administrator but was also ruthless with ambition. He raised taxes to build his "palace" and then suppressed the Regulator Movement 1768–71, which was a revolt against taxes. The state militia defeated two thousand regulators in the *Battle of Alamance* after which several leaders of the regulators were hanged on the order of Tryon. The palace burned in 1798, was later paved over, but then was rebuilt in its original design according to the architect's plans and is now open to the public.

Martin County was thus created on March 2, 1774, three years after Tryon moved to New York and one year after Benjamin Gainer lost his bid for reelection on December 10, 1773. As he had proposed, however, land was taken from Halifax and Tyrrell Counties and named for the then current and final colonial governor of the colony, Josiah Martin (1737–86).

On his maternal side, Jeremiah Slade's great great grandmother Elisabeth Eldred (1642–94) was descended from the Puritans in Cambridge, MA. She was the daughter of Samuel Eldred and Elisabeth Miller.[11] They were married in England in 1641 and, like many other English couples, then took a permanent honeymoon to the New World. A shoemaker, he joined the Ancient and Honorable Artillery of Boston in the same year. Friends with Edward Hutchinson, the Eldreds moved to Rhode Island and joined the Baptist church shortly after the banishment of Roger Williams and Anne Hutchinson from Massachusetts.[12] He was one of only two signers, making "his mark," of the 1660 treaty by which the Narragansett Indians "sold" their land to the Colony of Rhode Island and Providence Plantations.[13] Elisabeth Eldred, therefore, was married to Samuel William Gainer, Sr. (1640–97). Samuel Jr. (166–1751) was the father of Benjamin, the father of William Slade's wife Nancy Ann Gainor.

William Slade won election in 1775 to the provincial congress meeting in Hillsboro, NC, which adopted the *Mecklenburg Declaration of Independence* that had previously been adopted in Charlotte, North Carolina, on May 25, 1775. Fourteen months before the American Declaration of Independence, therefore, and while the same was being debated by members of the Second Continental Congress in Philadelphia, the *Hillsboro Resolves* called for a complete separation of the colonies from the government of Britain.[14]

William Slade subsequently served in the American Revolution, first as an ensign, beginning May 1, 1777, but then was promoted to lieutenant, adjutant, and first lieutenant. He resigned his commission February 18, 1780, nineteen months before the *Battle of Yorktown* and three years before the signing of the *Treaty of Paris 1783* which officially ended the war. He became one of the first six town commissioners of Williamston, the newly designated county seat of Martin County in 1799. He was one of twenty-two appointed to be a Justice of the Peace by Governor Richard Caswell (1729–89) and he was elected to the newly formed North Carolina House of Representatives in 1777.[15]

William Slade and Ann Gainor raised four sons and one daughter; Mary Ann known as "Polly," who never married. The boys were Henry Blount Slade (1762–1821), William Henry Slade, Jr. (b. 1768), Jeremiah Slade, and Ebenezer Slade (1775–1847). According to his will, William was working as a merchant as well as serving as a politician while owning a sawmill and another "mill." He owned a "vessel," and it apparently ran between North Carolina and the West Indies.[16] In the will of William Slade, he was also the first member in the family to have owned the Marsh Plantation and the land in the Conoho Islands, which he purchased from James Glases and Benjamin Gainor, respectively. He, therefore, bequeathed lands inherited from his father Ebenezer, bought from his father-in-law Benjamin Gainor, and purchased himself to his sons. William bought the Manner Plantation but mentions other "land given my father south of the Little Conehoe," which he gave to son Ebenezer, along with enslaved Sam, Poshpatt, and her three children. According to Jeremiah's unpublished journal, this land amounted to 1,220 acres. Son William received the Little Conoho Plantation along with other "land given by my father," along with enslaved Tom, Leander, Dave, Lewis, and Joe. Henry was given the Turkey Swamp Plantation and the enslaved Liz, Princess, James, Isaac, Pinder, and Jaeol. Finally, Jeremiah inherited the Marsh and Kelley Plantations along with the Conoho Islands Plantation, which William had purchased from his father-in-law. Jeremiah received ownership of the enslaved Liz, Ponfy, Moses, Jack, Chere, and Jude. Altogether, twenty-four enslaved persons are mentioned in the will of William Slade, son of Ebenezer.[17] This is confirmed by the North Carolina state census taken between 1784 and 1787 that records twenty-three slaves.[18]

The Matin Architectural Heritage clarifies these various properties and how they were used by the Slades. The family built a "Georgian-style plantation house" on the Marsh Point Plantation.[19] Poplar Point, Conoho, and the other farms were used exclusively for "farmlands and workers' quarters." One of the last remaining slave quarters remains on the Poplar Point Plantation because it was converted after the Civil War to a tenant home. Near this house is an antebellum cotton house that was owned by the Slades. Twenty-seven slave dwellings were recorded in the 1860 US Census but only five of these houses survive. Fourteen were standing as recently as the late 1980s. Jeremiah Slade's main house was demolished in the early 1990s.[20] This work also supports that the Slades were growing cotton until the 1920s when Thomas Bog Slade (1845–1929), son of William Slade (1807–52) switched cotton for tobacco. There is also a Slade-Gainer House on Slade Farm Road built c. 1875. This plain farmhouse was built for Dawson Slade, a formerly enslaved person, on land given to him by the aforementioned Thomas Bog Slade. When the property was foreclosed, it was purchased by Edward Gainer (1878–1941), an African American farmer, and his wife Lena (1876–1973).[21]

Although the will fairly distributed the property of William Slade to his four sons, Jeremiah, the third son, came to own most of his father's property as the oldest son, Henry Blount Slade, moved to Alabama with his wife. William, the second son, married but seems to have died soon after his father (date unknown) and childless, and Ebenezer the fourth son, married, had children, but moved to Georgia before his death in Dooly County, Georgia in 1847.[22] Jeremiah, therefore, was as least as wealthy as his father and likely more because he increased the value of the estate by adding additional property between 1791 and 1824. According to one Georgia tax digest, he also owned land in Bulloch and Baldwin Co., GA.[23] In 1809 he paid $1.50 property tax on more than two hundred acres valued at $500.

Jeremiah Slade was, in turn, the father of nine children with Janet Bog, whose own family had been in America since the early seventeenth century and in North Carolina before 1700 on both her paternal and maternal sides. She was the daughter of Thomas Bog (1740–77) and Hannah Blount (1750–1805). Little is known of Thomas Bog, but General Jeremiah's great-granddaughter Helen Malvina Prescott (1861–1946), a historian of the family, claimed he was born in Edinburgh, Scotland, and immigrated to North Carolina to marry Hannah Blount. A loyalist, he left the colonies during the American Revolution for his personal safety and rather than take up arms against King George III. He died in Scotland, where he is buried.[24] Nothing more is known of his ancestry, but it is his surname that lives on in the Slade line. Family historian Virgil T. Bogue has an extensive explanation of the origin and spelling of this family name in his work *Bogue and Allied Families*. On the maternal side, Janet was a granddaughter of Henry Benjamin Blount, Jr., who served as a captain and colonel during the colonial wars, then as a legislator to the state assembly from Tyrrell County, North Carolina. Janet Bog was born there. She and General Jeremiah were married in Martin County, NC, on June 10, 1798.[25] He was serving at the time in the North Carolina House of Commons (1787–1800, 1802). He was also a state senator from 1809 until 1815.[26]

Jeremiah and Janet Bog Slade appear in the 1800 census living in Martin Co., NC. At that time, they were twenty-six and twenty-seven years old, respectively, and had only two children, Alfred M. Slade, two years old, and newborn Thomas Bog Slade.[27] In 1810, they were living next to Jeremiah's oldest brother Henry Blount Slade (1762–1821) who was married and had seven children. By that time, Jeremiah and Janet had eight of their own: Alfred, twelve, Thomas Bog, ten, Mary Ann, nine, James Bog, seven, Elizabeth, six, Jeremiah Jr., four, William, three, and newborn Henry. This completed their family except for Hannah, who died at birth in 1817.[28]

In 1803, Jeremiah was appointed a commissioner of Indian Affairs by Henry Dearborn, who was then Secretary of War under President Thomas Jefferson. His primary responsibility was to assist in the removal of the Tuscaroras from North Carolina to New York State. They were then living primarily in Bertie County, North Carolina. The Tuscarora became the sixth tribe of the Iroquois Confederacy after conflicts with white settlers pushed them out of the Tar Heel state. Many Tuscarora had already fled to New York from North Carolina during the Tuscarora War of 1711–13. The tribe remains tied to a surviving reservation in New York until today. Although some Tuscarora remained in North Carolina after 1803, they were thereafter no longer recognized as members of the tribe by the federally recognized tribe located in New York. Ironically, the northern tribe was led in the Tuscarora War by Chief Tom Blunt. He seems to have adopted this surname because of his close friendship with the Blount family in and around Bertie County. This, of course, is the family of Janet Bog Slade and may partially explain Jeremiah's nineteenth-century appointment. When the Tuscarora split into two tribes, like the Muscogee of Georgia and Alabama, and the southern tribe, led by Chief Hancock, a merged title was offered to Blunt. Hancock was leading a confederacy of tribes to attack settlers in and around New Bern. They were, particularly, attacking planters along the Pamlico, Roanoke, Neuse, and Trent rivers. On the other hand, Blunt refused to join in the hostilities. The Southern Tuscarora were defeated when more than three hundred were killed and more than one hundred were captured. Many of these were subsequently sold into slavery. The peaceful southern tribe was allowed to remain in Bertie County because of their neutrality and signed a treaty with the colonial government in 1718, which promised them 56,000 acres.[29] Undoubtedly much of this conflict was rooted in a clash of cultures and a misunderstanding of goals and objectives. Gentleman John Lawson, the surveyor general of North Carolina, traveled to eastern North Carolina before the Tuscarora War and attempted to unravel many of the issues which ultimately led to the removal of the tribe in the nineteenth century.[30] He despaired that most English immigrants to America were of the working class and thus less educated and more insensitive to cultural differences. He wrote:

> TIS a great Misfortune, that most of our Travellers, who go to this vast Continent in America, are Persons of the meaner Sort, and generally of a very slender Education; who being hir'd by the Merchants, to trade amongst the Indians, in which Voyages they often spend several Years, are yet, at their Return, uncapable of giving any reasonable Account of what they met withal in those remote Parts; tho' the Country abounds with Curiosities worthy a nice Observation. In this Point, I think, the French outstrip us.[31]

Lawson promoted having the missionaries, generally of a broader education, and working for their denominations, to study the Indians as well as evangelize them so that they might, upon their return, give the needed reasonable account of what they encountered in the country. In words that cut the heart of every Englishman, Lawson suggested their being more like the French who kept detailed journals and gained a "good correspondence with the Indians."[32] The wisdom of Lawson proved true in the French and Indian War when far more Native Americans allied with France against the British and in the American Revolution when more Indians fought with the British against the Americans. Lawson's journal, however, was an attempt to improve British-Native relations just before the Tuscarora War. In more than 200 pages, Lawson highly detailed the agriculture, architecture, classes, clothing, entertainment, faith, festivals, food, death rituals, gender roles, government, language, marriage ceremonies, music, and sports of the Tuscarora. His work is valuable for understanding the tribe's history and anthropology until today. "They have good Store of Rabbits, Quails, and Fish and you see at the poor Peoples Doors great Heaps of Perriwinkle-shells, those Fish being a great Part of their Food," he wrote.[33] Although he consistently referred to the Tuscarora as "heathen," he obviously did not intend that label to be derogatory because he also wrote:

They are really better to us, than we are to them; they always give us Victuals at their Quarters, and take care we are arm'd against Hunger and Thirst: We do not so by them (generally speaking) but let them walk by our Doors Hungry, and do not often relieve them. We look upon them with Scorn and Disdain, and think them little better than Beasts in Humane Shape, though if well examined, we shall find that, for all our Religion and Education, we possess more Moral Deformities, and Evils than these Savages do, or are acquainted withal.[34]

In 1805, Jeremiah received a land grant from the State of North Carolina in Martin County for an additional 640 acres, land situated between Thomas Pollock and Jeremiah's brother Ebenezer.[35] A survey was ordered by Jeremiah's brother William indicating the land may have been part of his inheritance then being transferred to Jeremiah. William died two years later, married but without children. Furthermore, Henry Slade bought the remaining three hundred acres of William's land in 1806.[36] It may be that after Henry migrated to Washington Co., Alabama in 1805 and established Ravenswood Plantation there, allowing Jeremiah to end up with all these lands in eastern North Carolina.[37] Henry married Elizabeth Bennett and had seven children.

In the middle of the War of 1812 as Jeremiah Slade was serving with the state militia, he was "ordered" as a trustee of the University of North Carolina to attend the annual seven-day examination of students.[38] Governor William Hawkins was also a trustee of the university. The nephew of Indian agent Benjamin Hawkins, the governor, just three years younger, was also a lawyer and, it is reasonable to assume, a friend of Jeremiah Slade. This commencement was eleven years before Thomas Bog Slade's graduation in 1820 but only two years before Alfred's graduation in 1815.[39]

Although Jeremiah is now commonly known as "General" Slade, early records of his service in the War of 1812 indicate he was a Lieutenant Colonel Commandant during his active duty.[40] He was the commander of the Third Regiment as detached militia from the Fifth Brigade in August 1814, which was composed of eight companies of 626 men. The regiment names from which these companies were detached indicate the area from which the soldiers were enlisted. They include Halifax, Northampton, Edgecombe, Martin, Nash,

Warren, and Franklin, as would be expected. He was promoted to brigadier general during the war, December 1812.

The War of 1812 was a bit of a rematch of the American Revolution. It began when the United States declared war on Britain on June 18, 1812. The war ignited because of several lingering unresolved issues left out of the *Treaty of Paris* in *1783*. American expansion in the Old Northwest (the Midwest today) and the British alliance with Tecumseh's Confederacy led to increased tension. Britain began to interfere with America's trade with France, and the British Navy began to "impress" captured Americans into involuntary service. Their claim was that these individuals had previously been British subjects and were only being reclaimed by their sovereign king, who was, technically, still George III. Napoleon's abdication in France allowed the British to concentrate their navy and army in the West, and they established a very effective blockade of American trade. As peace talks began in 1814, the British burned the White House. The war officially ended with the *Treaty of Ghent* in *1814* and the end of fighting that lingered after the signing of the peace.[41]

The war in the southern states involved fighting against an anti-American tribe of the Muscogee (Creek) Indians, including the *Battle of Horseshoe Bend* in Alabama and the *Battle of New Orleans* under the command of General Andrew Jackson. Slade's regiment, however, was sent in September 1814 with others to Norfolk, Virginia, to participate in the conflict around Chesapeake Bay, which was a target for the British. Some regiments were sent home, but others from Halifax, Northampton, and Martin County gathered at Gates Court House. Fortunately for the North Carolina troops, this was primarily a theater of naval battles and explains why there were only eighteen casualties for the entire North Carolina contingent.

Many Americans and British perceived the fighting in the northern states to be a completely different conflict than the war in the southern states because the enemies in the North were British and the enemies in the South were the Muscogee. The Southern Creeks wanted peace with the United States, but the Northern Creeks, the so-called Redsticks because of their red war clubs, allied with the Tecumseh Confederacy and indirectly with Britain. Although there was fighting as far east as Georgia, most of the fighting occurred in Alabama, although most of the soldiers came from Georgia and Tennessee. During the

War of 1812, North Carolina supplied over 14,000 soldiers to the American side. Major General Thomas Brown was the high command of these two brigades, which were to ultimately march to Canada, but the war ended while they were en route.

Jeremiah Slade appears in a US Army Register of Enlistments as a brigadier general at the end of the war, documenting his return of the militia to Raleigh between December 1, 1815 and December 1, 1816. Several years later, one Eugene Bogue Wiggins Bryan left an antique desk in his will that he claimed belonged to his great grandfather General James Jeremiah and was carried by him through the American Revolution and War of 1812. While Bryan was likely a descendant of Jeremiah through his daughter Elizabeth Slade Wiggins, and he undoubtedly had a desk which may have been carried in the Revolutionary War of 1812, it was certainly not carried in the American Revolution by Jeremiah. He was born in 1774.

In 1817 Jeremiah Slade claimed another land grant for two hundred acres, this time, along with Thomas B. Houghton in Bertie County on Huff's Island.[42] This was in the Roanoke River which forms the border between Martin and Bertie Counties. The grant states that this plot began on the river "opposite the mouth of Welch's Creek thence down the courses of Roanoke River to the easternmost river thirteen hundred poles to the mouth of the Horse throughfare thence along the throughfare," and so on. It was surveyed on October 15, 1918, by Bertie County.

In 1819 Jeremiah Slade, who had been appointed Commissioner of the Affairs of the Tuscarora Indians in 1803, traveled from Williamston to Nashville, TN, on "Indian" business. He kept a journal of his journey as he was negotiating and representing the Tuscarora in relation to money owed to them by the State of North Carolina.[43] Shades of Jeremiah's stoic personality come through in this unpublished journal. He wrote, for example, that he felt the capital city of Raleigh was "bristling with class feeling" and "distasteful to a man of republican simplicity." When he met with the deputy clerk of the federal court, he recorded that he "was ushered into his office with all the hauteur of a French exciseman, and treated with every mark of supercilious pride and haughty arrogance, and finally dismissed with contempt."[44] Jeremiah also recorded his experience in finding accommodation as he traveled west across the state. He complained that he was treated no better than a "northerner." He wrote that even a "casual acquaintance" was "money mad," providing hospitality that included "every demonstration of unalloyed friendship and almost relative affection" but then charging an "exorbitant bill of eighty cents for breakfast, dinner, and horses' feed."[45]

Finally, in 1820, Jeremiah and Janet appear in Tattnall County, Georgia, but because they were back in Martin County, North Carolina, by 1824, it appears they were only visiting relatives. Perhaps they considered moving to Georgia in 1820 because Henry Slade left the state in that direction and eventually died in Washington County, Alabama, in 1821 but their son Jeremiah Jr. died in Hawkinsville, Pulaski County, Georgia, in 1822, four hundred miles to the west and toward Alabama. This happened after they had already lost two children within three years 1817–19, Hannah and Henry, in Martin County, North Carolina. This may have been some of the motivation for Thomas Bog Slade to have relocated on his own to Georgia in 1824 even after the rest of his family returned to North Carolina.

At least some of the Slades were Baptist in their faith, others Methodist. William Slade (1841–1919), the son of William Slade (1807–52), and his wife Cordelia Hassell (1849–1915) are buried at the Skewarkey Primitive Baptist Church near Williamston, NC. The church was located on NC 1420 south of Hwy. 125, was active between 1785 and 1950, and formerly situated on the property of the Slade Plantation.[46] Some of the enslaved persons are also buried there, designated in the record as "(col.)" or "servant of" such as Milly, Primus, and Flora Slade, who died in March 1890. Primus died in 1803 but the other named individuals all passed after the Civil War.[47] Further, Cordelia was the daughter of Cushing Biggs Hassell (1809–80) who was the leading primitive Baptist minister in the State of North Carolina during the mid-nineteenth century. His mother, Martha Biggs Hassell, was very devout and encouraged his conversion in 1828. He joined the Skewarkey Church, became a deacon in 1833, and an ordained minister of the Gospel in 1842. In 1859 he was moderator of the Kehokee Association which is the oldest primitive Baptist association in America. He was a trustee and member of the Board of Examiners for the University of North Carolina. He founded and was the secretary-treasurer of the Williamston Library Association. He became a trustee of the Williamston

Academy and published his own history of the Kehokee Primitive Baptist Association.[48] His son-in-law, William Slade, served as a deacon and assistant clerk of the association.[49] Representative of his denomination and time, Hassell wrote and spoke in his time about many things, but his *History of the Church of God* is, among other things, a defense of slavery. He documented the existence of slavery through the ages from the most ancient times down through the history of Ancient Greece, Israel, Rome, and the Muslim World. In the modern history of his work, he identifies the issue of slavery to explain why the Presbyterians, "New Baptists," and Methodists split North and South. Finally, he was critical of the Quakers for many things such as being "weak," "dark," and for opposing the institution of slavery.

Of Jeremiah and Janet's other children, Alfred served in the North Carolina House of Representatives in 1821 and 1834–5. He was a Justice of the Peace and the first Worshipful Master of the Skewarkey Masonic Lodge, No. 90, in 1826.[50] He was later appointed consul to Buenos Aires, Argentina in the 1830s and died there in 1840. He married Elizabeth Ann Sutton in 1821 and had one daughter, Agnes (b. 1824), who married Benjamin R. Duval. Thomas Bog Slade's relationship with him was usually positive, but Alfred was "inflexible," according to Thomas, when following the will of their father regarding the distribution of the slaves after Jeremiah's death. In a letter from Thomas in Georgia, this "matter of chief gave Ma more concern than every thing else connected with the estate." Having resolved the matter, however, "It will no doubt be a source of great consolation to her," he wrote to William. Thomas was "particularly pleased" to hear of the agreement and that the final settlement of the estate was "nearly brought to a close." It was "a great gratification to know that [William] has made such arrangements as will secure to Ma her property."[51]

Mary Ann married William Franklin Henderson in 1820 and had six children. He died in Martin County in 1838, then she is found living as a widow with three of her grown children, William, Maurice/Morris, and Jeanette, in Martin County next to her brother William in 1850. In Clinton, Georgia, Thomas thought the Hendersons were living in Waynesboro, Georgia, only 105 miles from Clinton, and intended to write Mary Ann there but wanted confirmation in 1827 from William in Williamston, North Carolina.[52] They may have been there, but it must have been a short period because it seems, in the records, she remained in North Carolina until she migrated as a widow to Carroll County, Louisiana, in 1860 with three of her children, Jeanette and Mary, "instructresses," and Maurice who was farming.[53] Perhaps this is the "error of his ways" Thomas meant in his letter to William. While Thomas thought it was a mistake for Henderson to move them to Waynesboro, "it would not be more strange than agreeable for me to know that such was the fact," he wrote. In Louisiana, Mary Ann and her children lived next door to Thomas Bog Slade's son James Jeremiah Slade (1831–1917) who was working there as both an attorney and planter. On the other side of "Jere" lived Charles and Sarah C. Blount with their three young children. Charles was also a planter but owned a plantation appraised at $40,000 compared to Jere's $6,000. Mary Ann died in 1873 and is buried in Bastrop, Louisiana.

James Bog Slade graduated from the University of North Carolina in 1818, the school of medicine at the University of Pennsylvania in 1826, became a physician in New Orleans, Louisiana, and was a charter member of the American Medical Association.[54] He had a daughter, Amelia, born in 1830. He served as a surgeon in the Mexican-American War, attached to the fifteenth US Infantry, which was activated on February 11, 1847, for service in Mexico. As described in some of James' letters from Mexico, they first arrived in Vera Cruz but then marched inland to join General Winfield Scott. Of James, General Gideon J. Pillow wrote on August 24, 1847, to the Third Division, US Army, headquarters, just three months before he was killed in action, "My medical staff (particularly Surgeon Jordon and Surgeon Slade) distinguished themselves by their great activity and energy in keeping with the column throughout the action, and attending to the wounded and dying on the spot where they fell, as did also the entire medical staff of my division."[55]

The 15th Infantry fought in the battles of Contreras, also known as the *Battle of Padierna* August 19–20, 1847, and Churubusco on the next day before capturing and garrisoning Mexico City. Both were overwhelming victories for the United States even though neither battle received much attention in the American media at the time, perhaps because the aftermath of these battles included the largest mass executions in US history. This happened because, previously, so many US troops, known as the San Patricio Battalion, had deserted to the Mexican side. James was killed in Mexico City just two months later and only nine months before the regiment returned to the United States. These were some of the last battles fought in the Mexican-American War. The obituary appearing in the *New Orleans Times-Picayune* read:

> Funeral of Dr. Slade, The remains of the late Dr. JAMES B. SLADE, Surgeon to the 15th Regiment U. S. Infantry, having arrived from Mexico, will be interred THIS EVENING at the Protestant Cemetery. The funeral will take place from the residence of Dr. Fenner, No. 5 Carondelet Street, at half past 1 o'clock. The friends of the deceased are invited to attend without further notice.[56]

James was later reburied in the National Cemetery at Vicksburg, Mississippi. He was forty-four years old.

Elizabeth married Mason Lee Wiggins in 1826, her first and his second, who was a graduate of Randolph Mason College and who owned the Woodlawn Plantation in Halifax County, later appraised at $4,000 in 1850 and $6,000 in 1860.[57] By the later date, Wiggins' personal estate was valued to be $108,625.[58] Further, "Eliza," as she was called, was working along with several of the daughters and a female boarder as a seamstress, indicating they were also operating a home "factory" in textiles. They had been members of the Methodist Episcopal Church since 1836, but Wiggins, who attended the Methodist Randolph Mason College, was likely Methodist historically. Woodlawn is not to be confused with the plantation of the same name in Wakefield, Virginia. In 1839, Wiggins served as a trustee for the La Valle Female Seminary located in Halifax County, midway between the towns of Halifax and Warrenton. The school was under the administration of "two ladies from the North."[59] Like the female seminaries operated by Thomas Bog Slade, La Valle focused on the classical liberal arts of history, mathematics, and science but also stressed language, French and Latin, and music classes, preparing the daughters of the planter class for their roles as wives and mothers.

Elizabeth kept a detailed record of their enslaved property, including parentage and dates of birth on a list in the family Bible she titled "A Register of Births in Our Family" between 1826 and 1841.[60] The page is dated 1852, but the detail of the record proves the information was recorded through the years.

Elizabeth was forty-eight years old then and had twelve biological children of her own. The list, however, hides the fact that, according to the 1860 Slave Schedule, Wiggins and Eliza owned a total of sixty-seven enslaved persons.[61] Apparently, some were considered part of the family while most were not. There were fifteen slave houses constructed on the property to shelter thirty-nine females and twenty-nine males ranging in age from four months to one hundred years old. Among them were three "mulattos," all of them likely the children of Wiggins, who was, in 1860, sixty-two years old; one woman, thirty, and two teenage boys, thirteen and fourteen. Wiggins supported the South in the Civil War but then received a personal pardon signed by President Andrew Johnson and Secretary of State William H. Seward.[62] Most of the Wiggins slaves survived the war and were emancipated in 1865. When Eliza died on November 23, 1876, at home, notice appeared in the Wilmington Morning Star, "She was a lady of rare intelligence and of the highest Christian worth. She died as she had lived, trusting humbly and confidently in the merits of Jesus Christ for a life of blessedness in heaven. Her life was beautiful; her end was peace."[63] Wiggins died in 1880. Both he and Eliza are buried in the Woodlawn Cemetery.

Jeremiah Jr., son of Jeremiah Sr., went to Pulaski County, Georgia, with his parents at the age of sixteen and died there in Hawkinsville in 1822.

William stayed in Williamston, North Carolina, where he married Penelope Williams (1811–90) and was the father of eleven children. Penelope was the daughter of Col. William Williams, the one for whom the Martin County seat town was named.[64] Also a planter, William owned the Marsh Point Plantation, appraised to be worth $12,000, the home of his parents known as the Jeremiah Slade House west of Williamston, and twenty-three enslaved persons according to the 1850 slave schedule for Martin County, North Carolina, fifteen males and eight females. He was "among the largest slave owners and cotton planters in the country" according to one 2005 study.[65] William also served as the assistant clerk of court for Martin County in 1825. He was later practicing law 1834–1837 in Williamston. His sons, James Bog Slade and Richard William Slade, and daughter Ann moved to Columbus, Georgia, after the Civil War to be near their uncle Thomas Bog Slade and remained there until his death. James Bog's and Ann's marriage ceremonies were conducted by Thomas. James

Bog married Mary E. Denson of Harris County, Georgia, and Ann married J.A. Maultsby of Columbus. James Bog died in 1886, "Annie" in 1901, and Richard in 1920 of Pulmonary Tuberculosis.[66] The remaining seven children stayed in North Carolina, five in Martin County. William Jr., known as "Buck," became a successful merchant in Williamston. Unmarried daughters Elizabeth and Francis Penelope continued to live in the ancestral home until they died there in 1914 and 1940, respectively. By 1976, the house was abandoned and fell into ruin. Besides having eleven children of his own, William Sr. was guardian for at least one orphan, Peter P. Perkins, in 1832. William died in 1852 and is buried in Martin County. He left the plantation to his wife Penelope.[67] Henry Williams and Asa Biggs (1811–78) were appointed executors of his estate. Biggs, whose home in Williamston remains, was a very prominent figure in North Carolina history serving in both chambers of the US Congress and as a US district judge. William is buried in the Slade Family Cemetery on his father's Marsh Point Plantation.[68] William's six sons, Confederate soldiers all, left their mother and five sisters to manage the plantation during the war.[69]

The last two children of Jeremiah Slade Sr and Janet Bog died young. Henry died at the age of nine in 1819, and Hannah died the day she was born. Both are buried in the Slade Family Cemetery on the Marsh Point Plantation.

Thomas Bog Slade (1800–82) was faithful to write home from college in Chapel Hill, and some of these letters have survived. Several of those were addressed to his brother Alfred and are filled with details of his activities on campus and questions about life in Martin County. Many of them were found in 1897 among some other papers in the Bertie County Courthouse, seventy-eight years after they were penned. A certain Kemp Battle sent them to James Jeremiah Slade, through whom they came to the archives of Columbus State University. In a letter of February 24, 1819, for example, Thomas was troubled by Alfred's letter of February 19. It seems that their brother Henry was ill, and Thomas expected the worst. "The tidings of your letter," he responded:

> has wracked my mind with uneasiness throughout the day, my night's repose I expect will be disturbed by disagreeable visions and tomorrow's sun will find me in the same situation. In vain I have sought a refuge from uneasiness in my studies, they are slighted and my mind still tortured, I shall anxiously wait for every mail to bring me an alleviation.[70]

He went on to give thanks for Alfred returning safely from discharging his "cargo with satisfaction" having ploughed "the watery element." With no further details given, Thomas may have been referring to another successful trade mission to the West Indies by Alfred. Just eleven days later, he wrote again to Alfred. This series demonstrates that letters were moving quickly between Chapel Hill and Williamston, taking no more than six days to travel these 132 miles. Thomas was relieved to learn that Henry was recovering. He was faithful to write but claimed he had, due to the rigor of his studies, "no time to idle."[71] He wrote, however, that his junior year at the university "formerly considered the most difficult is now, I believe, the easiest, for the two lower classes recite three times a day and their lessons are now much longer than when I passed through the same classes." He reported that the Class of 1820 had lost eighteen members and had fallen to only thirty-two, some of whom he expected to also soon leave their studies before the end of the year. Thomas gave Alfred a summary update of students at the university who were friends of both: Davis W. Stone, apparently Thomas' dearest friend, and William H. Haywood, the "old friend" of Alfred. He further mentioned Walker Anderson, Owen Holms, Martin Armstrong, Clement Read, James Chalmers, John M. Starke of South Carolina, and others. The letters range from two pages to four but each, one obviously so precious that they were written carefully, read and re-read, and preserved over a century later.

Thomas also wrote to his mother, Janet Bog Slade, assuring her that he was studying diligently at college so that he and James could return home soon in August 1819.[72] By 1821, however, he was writing to his brother William, in Hillsborough [sic], from Marsh Point Plantation. Then, on June 27, 1823, M. D. Slade informed William from Raleigh that "Thomas has been gone 20 days to visit/pay his duty to Ann Blount in GA who is a cousin."[73] The letter seems to communicate an expectation that Thomas would soon return, but soon Ann Blount became more than a cousin and Thomas only returned to visit North Carolina with his newlywed bride. His mother wrote to William on May 29, 1824, "Your brother Thomas Slade leaves us today for Georgia in good health." This may have been the last time Thomas saw his mother, who died in 1831, years before he passed through Martin County on his way to the north.

All of this, therefore, is given to create a complete profile of Thomas Bog Slade's immediate family of origin and to illustrate what he gave up in 1824 when he moved to Georgia and married Anne Jacqueline Blount. In his youth he was physically described as

> a stout, round-limbed, healthy man, about five feet nine inches high, with a dark complexion, remarkable for his early rising, purity of morals, intense application to books, temperateness in all its forms, and when a lawyer, for untiring diligence and industry in the interests of his clients. In oratory he was not gifted. Hypocrisy he detested. From boyhood he rejected tobacco in all its forms; nor did he ever use spirituous liquors, after the first temperance movement in Georgia, except as a medication. Uniformly polite to rich and poor alike, he has never, even under excitement, been betrayed into an expression stronger than "Bless my life!"[74]

He loved keeping up correspondence with family, friends, and colleagues. He found solace in scientific studies, doing research with scientific instruments, and reading works of natural history. In many of his books was written his adopted life motto *Litterae sunt ornamenta et hominum solatia* or letters are an ornament and comfort for people. By *Litterae* he obviously meant all the works of his studies and by *hominum* he also meant himself.[75]

He might have remained in Martin County and increased the property and wealth of his father, but he gave it up for a life of financial struggle as an educator. He even passed on an opportunity to come back to Williamston even after spending almost one year in Jones County, Georgia. His father Jeremiah, fifty, made his will in August 1824 and died the first day of September, in the same year. The will was witnessed by a Henry Slade, but it is not certain who this relation was. His brother Henry died in 1821, his uncle Henry had been dead since 1782, and his son Henry died in 1819. The will was probated within a month of Jeremiah's death and reveals that he owned more than twenty-nine enslaved persons, whereas that many are named, but he added the "residue of my negroes," indicating there were others.[76] Jeremiah owned several plantations totaling more than 1,220 acres of land at the time of his death. At least nine tracts are mentioned in the will, at least two of them named plantations, Manner and Conoho Islands, which he left to his wife Janet and his son Alfred respectively. He was buried on the Marsh Point Plantation, which is not mentioned in the will, but the James Cobb Purchase, Spring Branch, Beaver-dam, Turkey Swamp, "the grant from the state to me," and two tracts on Hunter Ponds are. This much property, if being cultivated, would certainly necessitate labor greater than members of the family, and twenty-nine slaves might have provided.

In the will, Jeremiah named his second son, Thomas Bog, executor of the estate, with others, even though he was living nine months, by then, out of state, 487 miles away in the age of horse transportation. Thomas inherited slaves Sampson, Dick, Harry, Hariot and her child Madison, Poll, Sophronia, and Ellen but allowed his sister Mary Ann Henderson, the wife of William Franklin Henderson, to take possession of them "until she died" which occurred fifty-two years later in 1876 when she was seventy-two and he was seventy-three years old.[77] Thomas found out about the death of his father days after Jeremiah had already been buried in the Slade Family Cemetery on the Marsh Point Plantation near Williamston, North Carolina, in Martin County.[78]

The cemetery, established so beautifully in a large field and clearly demarcated with a cast iron fence around, is now so neglected and overgrown that access beyond the fence, though headstones can be seen through the vines, is now impossible. The plot contains grave markers which span from the eighteenth to twentieth centuries, more than 150 years. Few other cemeteries in the area compare to the Slade Cemetery in their age or pattern of development. Thus, remarkably, the cemetery was rejected in 2005 for listing as a historic site on the National Register of Historic Places.[79] A thorough study was completed on several sites which were impacted by the construction of the NC 125 Bypass of Williamston. Although the cemetery was initially determined to be "eligible" because of "its association with the growth and development of plantation family-burials in Martin County," the North Carolina Department of Cultural Resources ultimately ruled it was "not eligible."[80] The report concluded that Jeremiah Slade was not a man of "transcendent importance" despite being a wealthy landowner, member of the North Carolina colonial House of Commons, a state senator, commissioner of Indian affairs, agent and attorney for the Tuscarora tribe, trustee of the University of North Carolina, "a superior classical and mathematical scholar," and brigadier general in the War of 1812, dismissively concluding that he was not a trustee at the time of death and that

Figure 1.1 The Slade Family Cemetery, Williamston, North Carolina (photo by author).

"the university had many trustees—54 in 1821."[81] Fortunately, the cemetery was not destroyed by the highway construction, which ultimately ran well east of the site, and remains, however overgrown and neglected. Extensive cleaning is desperately needed to preserve this valuable site.

There are nineteen marked graves in the Slade Cemetery ranging from Mary, the first burial there in August 1780, to William Slade Rhodes, buried August 26, 1945. Jeremiah and Janet are the sixth and eighth oldest graves. Of their children, it is interesting to note five who are not buried in the Slade Cemetery with their parents. Alfred, the firstborn, is buried in Argentina, Thomas is in Columbus, Georgia, Mary Ann is in Louisiana, James is in Vicksburg, Mississippi, and Elizabeth is in Halifax County. There is no marker for the last-born Hannah but she is likely buried, nonetheless, in the Slade Cemetery. Jeremiah Jr., William, and Henry are there and have marked graves. Six of William's eleven children are buried in the Slade Cemetery. The most ornate tomb is that of Bessie Rhodes Maultsby (1872–1909), who was a granddaughter of William and daughter of Helen Bog Slade who married Franklin A. Rhodes.

"Our dear father had suffered much in his illness," older brother Alfred wrote, "[he] constantly asked for death as his relief."[82] After the general's death, there were several members of the family who assumed Thomas would return to North Carolina and assume control of the family businesses since he was serving as executor of his father's estate. No one pressured him more than his sister Elizabeth Slade Wiggins, who struggled to understand why he would choose to remain in Georgia. As an illustration of his firm commitment to both his wife and career, Thomas wrote several letters, which ended in a final correspondence of uncharacteristically strong rebuke to the twenty-year-old Elizabeth in 1824. With loving words to soften his decisive conclusion, he explained that even though he had been in Georgia less than one year, returning would create "a thousand difficulties."[83] He wrote that he did not have money to move his family even temporarily to North Carolina and that his only income had come from "the hire of three or four negroes."[84] Seemingly frustrated after several letters of back and forth about the matter, he expressed his determination and offered to resign his position as executor rather than leave his responsibilities in Clinton.

Notes

1 Richard Taylor Slade, "Slade Family," in Francis M. Manning and W. H. Booker, *Martin County History*, vol. I (Williamston Enterprise Publishing Co., 1977), p. 564.
2 Thomas Bog Slade, Letter to Mrs. James Slade, August 23, 1819, Slade Family Papers, Box 1 (1803–1820). See also Thomas Bog Slade, *Autobiography of Thomas Bog Slade*, Southern Historical Collection 1837–1846, 2683-z, University of North Carolina, p. 1; and Florence Fleming Corley, "The Presbyterian Quest: Higher Education for Georgia Women," *American Presbyterians* 69:2 (Summer 1991): 83–96.
3 Slade Family Papers, 1751–1929, Rubenstein Library (Durham, NC).
4 Ibid.
5 U.S. and Canada, Passenger and Immigration Lists Index, 1500s-1900s, VA, 1671, p. 100. See also Francis M. Manning and W. H. Booker, *Martin County History*, vol. I (Williamston Enterprise Publishing Co., 1977), 564.
6 Richard Taylor Slade, "Slade Family," in Francis M. Manning and W. H. Booker, *Martin County History*, vol. I (Williamston Enterprise Publishing Co., 1977), 564.
7 Ibid.
8 North Carolina, US, State Census, 1784–1787.

9 *Wills, 1774–1867*, County Court of Pleas and Quarter Sessions (Martin County, NC) Book 1, p. 72.
10 Richard Taylor Slade, "Slade Family," in Francis M. Manning and W. H. Booker, *Martin County History*, vol. I (Williamston Enterprise Publishing Co., 1977), 564.
11 Marston Watson, "Royal Families: Americans of Royal and Noble Ancestry," vol. 2. *Reverend Francis Marbury and Five Generations of the Descendants Through Anne (Marbury) Hutchinson and Katherine (Marbury) Scott*. (Baltimore, MD: Genealogical Publishing Co., 2004), p. 25; Charles Edward Banks and Elijah Ellsworth Brownell, *Topographical Dictionary of 2885 English Emigrants to New England, 1620–1650* (Philadelphia, PA: The Bertram Press, 1937), p. 157; and Clarence A. Torrey, *New England Marriages Prior to 1700* (Baltimore, MD: Genealogical Publishing Co., 2004).
12 Richard V. Simpson, *Historic Tales of Colonial Rhode Island: Aquidneck Island and the Founding of the Ocean State* in American Chronicles, series (The History Press, 2012).
13 Robert A. Gaeke, *A History of the Narragansett Tribe of Rhode Island: Keepers of the Bay in American Chronicles*, series (The History Press, 2011).
14 See George Washington Graham, *The Mecklenburg Declaration of Independence, May 20, 1775, and Lives of its Signers* (University of Michigan, 1905) and Richard Plumer, *Charlotte and the American Revolution: Reverend Alexander Craighead, the Mecklenburg Declaration and the Foothills Fight for Independence* (The History Press, 2014).
15 Richard Taylor Slade, "Slade Family," in Francis M. Manning and W. H. Booker, *Martin County History*, vol. I (Williamston Enterprise Publishing Co., 1977), p. 564.
16 *Wills, 1774–1867*, County Court of Pleas and Quarter Sessions (Martin County, NC), Book 1, p. 74.
17 Ibid.
18 North Carolina, US, State Census, 1784–1787.
19 Thomas Russell Butchko, "Slade Tenant Houses," in *Martin Architectural Heritage: The Historic Structures of a Rural North Carolina County* (Martin County Historical Society, 1998), p. 259.
20 Ibid.
21 Ibid., p. 258.
22 Original Will Records (Mobile County, Alabama), Ca. 1813–1961; Index, 1813–1957; Author: Alabama. Probate Court (Mobile County); Probate Place: Mobile, Alabama.

23 *Georgia, US, Property Tax Digests, 1793–1892* [1809]. 140 volumes. Morrow, Georgia: Georgia Archives.
24 Virgil T. Bogue, *Bogue and Allied Families* (Virgil T. Bogue, 1944), p. 22.
25 Flora Myers Gillentine, ed., Lineage Book, vol. 110 (National Society of the Daughters of the American Revolution, 1929), p. 204.
26 Richard Taylor Slade, "Slade Family," in Francis M. Manning and W. H. Booker, *Martin County History*, vol. I (Williamston Enterprise Publishing Co., 1977), 564.
27 U.S. Census Bureau, *Second Census of the United States*, Year: 1800; Census Place: Hallifax, Martin, North Carolina; Series: M32; Roll: 34, p. 408; Image: 54; Family History Library Film: 337910.
28 Ibid., Year: 1810; Census Place: Martin, North Carolina; Roll: 41; p. 439; Image: Ncm252_41-0020; FHL Roll: 0337914.
29 Patrick Keith, *Through Colonialism and Imperialism: The Struggle for Tuscarora Nationhood in Southeastern North Carolina*, M.A. Thesis (University of Arizona, 2005). See also John R. Swanton, "The Indians of the Southeastern United States," Smithsonian Institution, Bureau of American Ethnology Bulletin 137 (Washington, D.C., 1946); Bruce G. Trigger, ed., *Northeast*, vol. 15 of *Handbook of North American Indians*, ed. William C. Sturtevant (Washington: Smithsonian Institution, 1978); Anthony F. C. Wallace, "The Modal Personality Structure of the Tuscarora Indians," Smithsonian Institution, *Bureau of American Ethnology Bulletin 150* (Washington, D.C., 1952) and *Tuscarora: A History* (Albany: SUNY Press, 2012).
30 John Lawson, *A New Voyage to Carolina; Containing the Exact Description and Natural History of that Country: Together with the Present State thereof and a Journal of a Thousand Miles Traveled through Several Nations of Indians, Giving a Particular Account of their Customs, Manners, etc.* (London, 1709).
31 Ibid., p. iv.
32 Ibid.
33 Ibid., p. 1.
34 Ibid., p. 235.
35 North Carolina, US, Land Grant Files, 1693–1960.
36 Bureau of Land Management, General Land Office Records; Washington D.C., USA; Federal Land Patents, State Volumes.
37 John Bennett Pierson, *A Journey of Slades: From England to Ravenswood Plantation, Washington County, Alabama* (2015).
38 "University," *The Raleigh Minerva* 17:887 (April 2, 1813): 2.

39 *A Catalogue of the Members of the Dialectic Society, Instituted in the University of North Carolina, June the Third 1795* (Raleigh: North Carolina Standard, 1841), p. 7.
40 *Muster Rolls of the Soldiers of the War of 1812: Detached from the Militia of North Carolina in 1812 and 1814* (Raleigh: C. Raboteau, 1851).
41 See Pierre Berton, *War of 1812* (Anchor Canada, 2011); Walter R. Borneman, *1812: The War that Forged a Nation* (Harper Perennial, 2005); George C. Daughan, *1812: The Navy's War* (Basic Books, 2011); Donald R. Hickey, *The War of 1812: A Forgotten Conflict* (University of Illinois Press, 2012); Willard Sterne Randall, *Unshackling America: How the War of 1812 Truly Ended the American Revolution* (St. Martin's Press, 2017); Theodore Roosevelt, *The Naval War of 1812* (G. P. Putnam's Sons, 1882); and Alan Taylor, *The Civil War of 1812: American Citizens, British Subjects, Irish Rebels, and Indian Allies* (Vintage, 2011).
42 North Carolina Land Grants. Microfilm publication, 770 rolls. North Carolina State Archives, Raleigh, North Carolina.
43 Stephen B. Weeks, ed., *Index to the Colonial and State Records of North Carolina* (Goldsboro, NC: Nash Brothers, 1909).
44 Jeremiah Slade, *Journal of a Trip to Tennessee*, unpublished journal, Trinity College Historical Papers, VI (1906), p. 38.
45 Ibid., pp., 40–1.
46 Skewarkey Primitive Baptist Church Records, 1785–1950, Martin Co., NC Church Records, p. 43.
47 Ibid., pp. 29, 40–1.
48 Cushing Biggs Hassell, *History of the Church of God, From the Creation to A.D. 1885: Including Especially the History of the Kehukee Primitive Baptist Association* (Middleton, NY: Gilbert Beebe's Sons, Publishers, 1886).
49 Ibid., pp. 822, 871.
50 Skewarkee Lodge, *Minutes*, 1873–1895, Williamston, NC and Richard Taylor Slade, "Slade Family," in Francis M. Manning and W. H. Booker, *Martin County History*, vol. I (Enterprise Publishing Co., 1977), pp. 232, 565.
51 Thomas Bog Slade to William Slade, personal letter (May 13, 1827), *Slade Family Papers*, Rubenstein Library, Duke University.
52 Ibid., p. 3.
53 The National Archives in Washington D.C.; Record Group: Records of the Bureau of the Census; Record Group Number: 29; Series Number: M653; Residence Date: 1860; Home in 1860: Ward 7, Carroll, Louisiana; Roll: M653_409; Page: 325.

54 Richard Taylor Slade, "Slade Family," in Francis M. Manning and W. H. Booker, *Martin County History*, vol. I (Enterprise Publishing Co., 1977), p. 565.
55 Linda Arnold, *The Mexican-American War and the Media, 1845–1848* (Virginia Tech University, 2003).
56 *Obituary*, Dr. James B Slade, MD, *New Orleans Times-Picayune*, March 3, 1848.
57 The National Archives in Washington, DC; Record Group: Records of the Bureau of the Census; Record Group Number: 29; Series Number: M432; Residence Date: 1850; Home in 1850: Halifax, North Carolina; Roll: 633; Page: 63a.
58 The National Archives in Washington D.C.; Record Group: Records of the Bureau of the Census; Record Group Number: 29; Series Number: M653; Residence Date: 1860; Home in 1860: Western District, Halifax, North Carolina; Roll: M653_899; Page: 453; Family Hist.
59 *The Weekly Standard*; Publication Date: January 2, 1839; Publication Place: Raleigh, North Carolina, USA.
60 Elizabeth Slade Wiggins, *Family Bible*.
61 *1850 US Federal Census*—Slave Schedules, The National Archives in Washington DC; Washington, DC; NARA Microform Publication: M432; Title: Seventh Census of the United States, 1850; Record Group: Records of the Bureau of the Census; Record Group Number: 29.
62 U.S., *Pardons Under Amnesty Proclamations, 1865–1869* (Washington, DC: The National Archives).
63 *The Wilmington Morning Star*; November 28, 1876; newspaper (Wilmington, NC).
64 Richard Taylor Slade, "Slade Family," in Francis M. Manning and W. H. Booker, *Martin County History*, vol. I (Enterprise Publishing Co., 1977), p. 565.
65 Peter Sandbeck, Administrator, North Carolina Department of Cultural Resources, State Historic Preservation Office, to Gregory Thorpe, PhD., Director of Project Development and Environmental Analysis Branch NCDOT Division of Highways, letter, June 23, 2005, p. 52.
66 Georgia Department of Health and Vital Statistics; Atlanta, Georgia.
67 *Wills, 1774–1963*; North Carolina. Superior Court (Martin County); Martin, North Carolina.
68 Donna Dodenhoff, "Jeremiah Slade Plantation" Survey Form and File (MT-415), North Carolina State Historic Preservation Office, Raleigh, NC, 1992.
69 Richard Taylor Slade, "Slade Family," in Francis M. Manning and W. H. Booker, *Martin County History*, vol. I (Enterprise Publishing Co., 1977), p. 565.

70 Thomas Bog Slade to Alfred M. Slade, letter, February 24, 1819, Columbus State University Archives, Columbus, GA, donated by Seymour Slade Dozier, October 15, 1933.
71 Ibid., March 7, 1819.
72 Thomas Bog Slade to Mrs. Janet Slade, letter, August 23, 1819, Slade Papers, Box 1, 1803–1820, Rubenstein Library, Duke University.
73 M. D. Slade to William Slade, letter, June 27, 1823.
74 Richard Newton Smith, Jr, *Slade Family Roots in North Carolina and Georgia* (Columbus, GA, 1880), p. 2.
75 *History of the Baptist Denomination in Georgia: with Biographical Compendium and Portrait Gallery of Baptist Ministers and other Georgia Baptists* (Atlanta: J. P. Harrison & Co., 1881), p. 484.
76 *Wills, 1774–1867*, County Court of Pleas and Quarter Sessions (Martin County, NC) Book 2, p. 100 and *History of the Baptist Denomination in Georgia: with Biographical Compendium and Portrait Gallery of Baptist Ministers and other Georgia Baptists* (Atlanta: J. P. Harrison & Co., 1881), p. 483.
77 *Wills, 1774–1867*, County Court of Pleas and Quarter Sessions (Martin County, NC) Book 2, p. 100.
78 Richard Taylor Slade, "Slade Family," in Francis M. Manning and W. H. Booker, *Martin County History*, vol. I (Enterprise Publishing Co., 1977), p. 231.
79 Peter Sandbeck, Administrator, North Carolina Department of Cultural Resources, State Historic Preservation Office, to Gregory Thorpe, PhD., Director of Project Development and Environmental Analysis Branch NCDOT Division of Highways, letter, June 23, 2005.
80 Ibid.
81 Richard Newton Smith, Jr, *Slade Family Roots in North Carolina and Georgia* (Columbus, GA, 1880) and Peter Sandbeck, Administrator, North Carolina Department of Cultural Resources, State Historic Preservation Office, to Gregory Thorpe, PhD., Director of Project Development and Environmental Analysis Branch NCDOT Division of Highways, letter, June 23, 2005, p. 53.
82 Alfred M. Slade, Letter to William Slade, September 2, 1824, Slade Family Papers, Box 2 (1821–1824).
83 Thomas Bog Slade, Letter to Elizabeth Slade, undated, Slade Family Papers, Box 2 (1821–1824).
84 Ibid.

2

Clinton

> To an unusual degree it maintains the ambience of an early nineteenth century American town.
>
> Anonymous

Abraham Baldwin is credited by many for initiating "an educational program in Georgia," but for the state's focus on economics, growth, Indian removal, political conflict, and war, his early efforts, other than those toward establishing the university in Athens, produced little of lasting impact.[1] Like so many early Georgia industrialists, Baldwin was from Connecticut. He was also a graduate of Yale College who migrated to Georgia in 1783. With Baldwin's lobbying in the Georgia legislature, the state set aside 40,000 acres "for the endowment of a college, or seminary, of learning." In 1785 they passed another act for "the full and more complete establishment of a public seat of learning in Georgia." Baldwin copied Yale in planning the structure and organization for the University of Georgia. When he addressed the first trustees, who included the governor, speaker of the state house, and chief justice of the state supreme court, he declared that "riches and prosperity without training and culture were causes of war," that property and wealth were nothing unless they could be possessed in "security and enjoyment." The only path to these goals, he affirmed, passed through "religion and education."[2]

Baldwin argued for the Piedmont as the best location for the university, not Savannah or Augusta, the most populated Georgia cities during his time. The state Constitution of 1777 called for a public school in every Georgia county, and this was further supported by an act of the state legislature in 1783. By 1789, five male academies had been established. The university opened in 1801. The initiative struggled and by that time no schoolmasters were found

Figure 2.1 Thomas Bog Slade and Anne Jacqueline Blount (public domain, courtesy of Old Clinton Historical Society, 412 Pulaski St., Gray, GA 31032).

outside of Savannah and Augusta. Soon thereafter, however, several schools opened throughout the state, all private schools for boys and all teaching either primary subjects or preparation for college. Just before Slade migrated to Georgia, Duncan G. Campbell sponsored new legislation in the capital which created a committee to establish a public educational system. Georgia Governor John Clark mentioned the need for education in a speech of 1822 and Campbell, brother-in-law of the governor, was encouraged and soon introduced "a bill to establish and endow a public seat of learning in the state for the education of females."³ Campbell was calling for a full college dedicated solely to the education of women comparable to the University of Georgia. A board of trustees was appointed to supervise female education in Georgia and plans were made to support the college financially with proceeds from stock in the Bank of the State of Georgia. Ultimately the act failed in the Senate and female education fell back to the private schools, most of which were of the primary level.

Also in 1822, a state Committee on Public Education and Free Schools was created to investigate the possibility of starting "common schools" throughout Georgia. More than $12,000 of bank dividends were to be proportionally divided by Georgia's fifty-six counties based on population. As this initiative also stumbled, several counties began to create their own local schools. Glynn County started a system of schools in 1823 for all children of parents who paid less than two dollars in state tax per year. In 1826, Elbert County and Jackson County took steps to start academies for girls. There was no female college in Georgia, but teachers were being hired from the north to teach the lower levels of education to girls.⁴ This was the situation when Slade decided to quit his legal partnership with his father in North Carolina and migrate to Georgia where he opened a new legal partnership in Clinton. When he changed professions to education it was, first, to take over a male academy. It was only after three more years and the birth of his first three daughters that Slade finally crafted his lifetime mission of educating young women.

Although the prevailing view has been that public schools began in Georgia with the legislation of 1867, Early Twentieth Century Historian George Slappey argued that the history is better grounded in looking back to 1783 when provisions were made for the establishment of an academy in each county of the state. While Slappey does not contend that the academies were public schools, they were common schools and as the state directed, perhaps invited, individuals to establish a common school in each county. Slappey counted this network as the foundation for Georgia's system for public school education. "By 1829," he wrote, "the number of academies in the state had increased to ninety."⁵

According to a letter received by brother William Slade in Martin County, North Carolina, Thomas Bog Slade made at least one trip to visit and "pay his duty" to Anne Jacqueline Blount in Georgia, "who is a cousin," wrote Marmaduke Johnson Slade in 1823, also a cousin. Slade was taken by her blue eyes but was undoubtedly also captivated by her intelligence and ability to be a supportive partner. They were a power couple since she was also highly educated. She was described as "brilliant," "elastic," and had a "solid mind."[6]

"Thomas has been gone 20 days," he added, on June 27, 1824.[7] Marmaduke, known as "Duke" or "Cousin Marma," also a graduate of the University of North Carolina, was the son of Thomas Bog Slade's Uncle Ebenezer and within two years he too followed in his cousin's footsteps to Georgia. He also married a Blount girl from Georgia, Ann Gray Blount, who was not related to Anne Jacqueline Blount despite much confusion among historians and family genealogists.[8] Because Anne had two brothers named Thomas, there have been contradictory conclusions in the sources about the relationship between her and Marmaduke's wife.[9] If she was a relative, the common ancestor was more than five generations away, back to the seventeenth century. They may not have been related at all. Anne Jacqueline Blount descended from North Carolina Blunts, including John William Blount (1670–1725) who owned the Mulberry Plantation in Chowan County, North Carolina, while Ann Gray Blount descended from Surry County, Virginia Blounts, including her father Thomas Blount Jr. (1768–1840) who came directly to Jones County, Georgia from Virginia and was among the first sixty-three settlers. Marmaduke was a newspaper man, however, and settled in Macon, Georgia, to become the junior editor of that city's *Georgia Journal and Messenger* before migrating further to Tuscaloosa, Alabama, where he spent the rest of his life.[10] Thomas Bog Slade chose to settle "permanently" in Jones County, Georgia, after Marmaduke's report to William and just before his wedding to Anne Jacqueline Blount. By all accounts, he was content to remain there until 1838.

Slade's father, Jeremiah, died September 1, 1824, just three months after Slade moved to Georgia. It took some time for Slade to receive notice of his father's death even though he was named executor of the estate. His older brother Alfred wrote to his younger brother William, who was away at school in Chapel Hill, on September 2 in Martin County, North Carolina, to tell him "our dear father had suffered much in his illness, and constantly asked for death as his relief; the messenger came, welcome to him, but the bearer of despair and pain to us."[11] Alfred was at home with other members of the family who were not expecting William or Thomas to come home for a funeral due to the distance and the difficulty of travel in those days. "Our mother stands with fortitude," he added. They buried Jeremiah the same day in the Slade Family Cemetery next to his son Jeremiah Jr. who had died two years earlier at the age of sixteen. Jeremiah Sr. was only forty-nine years old, six years more than the average life expectancy in 1824.

According to Slade, no one wrote to him from North Carolina for nine and one-half months after he arrived in Clinton, Georgia. The first "intelligence" he received was from his brother William, he wrote, on March 14, 1825.[12] William had interviewed the "Nation's Guest," the Marquis de Lafayette, and subsequently inquired of his brother about the passage of the same through Clinton. One letter addressed to Slade lingered in the post office at Ft. Hawkins in April 1824, two months before he left North Carolina, but he had no reason to know that and failed to receive it for months. It had been there long enough; it was finally published in the *Georgia Messenger* by Postmaster Charles Bullock in a list of fifty-five other unclaimed letters. It is not clear who sent this letter to Slade, but it was either not from North Carolina or Slade did not receive it until thirteen months later.[13]

"Your brother Thomas B. Slade leaves us today for Georgia in good health," his mother Janet wrote on May 29.[14] Besides his family, Slade left his horse at his mother's house. The next year he instructed Marmaduke to "dispose" of it "as he might think best in his judgment."[15] The Georgia town of Clinton was five hundred miles away and was Anne's home in 1824. There is no record of how Slade traveled without his horse so he must have taken a stagecoach. Upon arrival, he first practiced law in all the courts of the Ocmulgee Circuit and in the counties of Monroe, Pike, Upson, Crawford, Bibb, and Houston in the Flint Circuit successfully with his partner Wiley Williams from then until 1827, traveling regularly on horseback. When he resigned his legal partnership to accept an offer to become a schoolmaster, he called it "rector" of the Clinton Male Academy.[16] Slade taught several students who progressed to make their own mark on Georgia history but one, for example, was Thomas H. Murphy from Wilkes County. The son of William Murphy, Thomas became a lawyer in Harris County, Georgia, and by 1837 was elected to the Georgia State Senate.

In 1843, he resigned from law and politics to become a Baptist minister. Before his retirement in 1876, he pastored twenty-four churches and baptized over one thousand people.[17]

The Academy post came with an annual salary of $1,000 per year, which may seem modest to a modern reader, but it had the same purchasing power in 1824 as $32,536 in 2025.[18] The salary further depended, however, Slade explained, on the price of cotton which, of course, was highly volatile in the early eighteenth century but was averaging between ten and thirteen cents per pound in 1824. At least once in 1825, before Slade took over the Clinton Academy, he reported that cotton had been as high as thirty and thirty-one cents. In that year, he worried that the great profits earned in growing cotton threatened to destroy the timber "on our land" in North Carolina.[19] If the price fell too low, many of Slade's tuition-paying planters would not have been able to maintain their child as a student. His decision to accept the offer was likely prompted partially by "the astonishing hordes of attorneys," he complained about to his brother, "who are daily flocking to this land."

Slade may have changed professions, but his marriage lasted fifty-eight years until his death in 1882. His tenure at the male academy lasted only three, however, before Slade decided to start his own school, a school for girls and not for boys. In his own words, he reasoned that if he were going to teach his own children, then three daughters, he might as well accept tuition to teach other children.[20] The eventual father of eight daughters confessed he "was necessarily *forced*" to found the Clinton Female Seminary in 1832, which became one of the most successful academies for females in the entire State of Georgia and, arguably, in the southern states. One Frances Lord may have come to Clinton from New York City just to attend the seminary.[21]

Before the Muscogee (Creek) cession of lands in 1805, the area that became Jones County, Georgia, was temporarily on the frontier of English-speaking settlement because of the Treaty of Fort Wilkinson in 1802 which transferred a narrow strip of land on the west bank of the Oconee and east of the Ocmulgee rivers from the Muscogee (Creek) tribe to the State of Georgia. Benjamin Hawkins, then acting as the sole United States commissioner to the Indians of the Southern states, negotiated and concluded another treaty with Chief Hopoie Micco on November 3, 1804, in Crawford County, Georgia.[22] The treaty was ratified by the United States Senate eleven days later and signed in Washington, DC, on June 2, 1805, by Secretary of War Henry Dearborn and six Muscogee chiefs including William McIntosh.[23] Most of the land, two million acres, between the Oconee and the Ocmulgee rivers was transferred in this 1805 treaty to the State of Georgia. The Muscogee received $206,000 or ten cents per acre (price of a pound of cotton).[24] Founded in 1809, Clinton, Georgia was created on part of this land, as was Jasper, Twiggs, Bleckley, Dodge, Telfair, and Wheeler counties, half of Morgan and Laurens, and portions of Putnam, Newton, Bibb, Wilkinson, and Pulaski. More importantly for the future of newly founded Clinton, a military outpost named Fort Hawkins was built ten miles south near the Ocmulgee River on the federal road from Augusta, Georgia to Mobile, Alabama. This federal road was originally built for mail delivery but was widened in 1811 for use by the militia.

Immediately after the Treaty of 1805, the land that became Jones County was part of Baldwin County. Thirty-eight districts were created from the newly acquired land, and the state legislature authorized a land lottery on June 26, 1806, to begin the process of a legal, fair, and organized settlement based on chance. All free white males age twenty-one or over who were citizens and residents of Georgia for at least three years were eligible to draw a number on a piece of paper from a large, rotating wooden drum. Not all papers in the drum had a number, but all the land lots available for distribution were included, and hundreds of citizens in the state qualified and drew. Married men were allowed two draws, giving them a better chance; widows received one draw, as did unmarried free white women over the age of twenty-one. The lottery took place at the statehouse, then in Louisville, Georgia, between August 10 and September 23, 1807. Winners paid six dollars per one hundred acres or six cents per acre.[25] The winners who, unknowingly at the time, drew the lots that became Clinton, and as an example of the much larger group of original white owners of the land from the 1805 treaty, included Thomas Johnston of Baldwin County, John Shackleford of Jackson, Sarah Granberry of Jefferson, George Michael Troup, later governor of Georgia, and David Emanuel of Burke County, who was once thought to be the first Jewish governor in America. A leader in the American Revolution, Emanuel is one of Georgia's least known governors because of the scarcity of records surviving him and his administration. Georgia's Emanuel County is named for him, but more recent research has proven he was not Jewish.[26] He was, however, the father of Mary Martha Emanuel (1768–1827) who was the mother of Ann Gray Blount.

The capital of Georgia was moved to Milledgeville in 1807, Thomas Jefferson was president of the United States, and Lewis and Clark were on their journey west to explore the Louisiana Purchase. Settlers arrived quickly thereafter in Jones County and chose the site for a town settlement because it was the geographic center of the new county, was on Tom's Path, a trail that paralleled the federal road following the Fall Line, there were several freshwater springs flowing in the area, and it was described as "a healthy and pleasant village" over four decades by outsiders who visited there.[27] The town was founded on land lots four, five, twenty, and twenty-one in the ninth district, each lot composed of 202.5 acres. The first residents called the place Albany. Historian William Lamar Cawthon argued this name was chosen by Roger McCarthy, one of the first residents, because he was from New York and Albany is the capital of that state. McCarthy worked as a merchant and served as postmaster in Clinton during 1809–21. Postmasters usually exerted a disproportional influence on the names of places during the nineteenth century. Others claim the legislature chose the name Clinton rather than Albany to honor George Clinton who was then vice president of the United States, a hero of the American Revolution, and who was subsequently elected governor of New York for seven consecutive terms. Still others argue the town was named for DeWitt Clinton who was the mayor of New York City during 1803–6 and arguably the most powerful figure in the state at that time. He was a scientific and literary man and a strong proponent of states' rights, a position always popular in Georgia. Despite the early indecision, the name was permanently established to be Clinton by December 22, 1808, when 1,327 residents voted and the permanent name was used. This was the name when the first twenty-two lots were sold for $500 each raising $7,153.50 for construction of the first courthouse, a county jail, and other county expenses. The new town commissioners bought Thomas Johnston's entire lot number four for $2,000. Four acres of this land were reserved in the center of the town for the location of the courthouse and other public buildings. The private home of William Jones was designated a temporary courthouse until the actual first courthouse was built. When it was finished, the courthouse was small, hastily and poorly constructed, and proved to be inadequate for its purpose within one year. Inferior court judges acted as the first town commissioners and these were William Jones, Hugh Moss Comer, and John McKenzie.

By 1909, the grand jury determined the first courthouse was untenable so the commissioners contracted James Thompson to build the second courthouse that year for $1,797, paid to him in three unequal installments.[28] They also paid Surveyor John Rosser $30 to lay out the town lots. Thompson's brick courthouse was completed in the Georgian style in 1818 and the town limits of Clinton thereafter extended in a one-half mile radius from the spire of this centrally located building. There were eighty-nine lots within this small circle and forty-eight of them had been "taken up" by May 1, 1808, eleven more within one year, and seventy-eight by January 1, 1810, when there were eighty-five residents living within the limits of Clinton including "Indian fighter" and Southern frontiersman Sam Dale (1772–1841). At the age of thirty-eight, Dale was yet to fight with Andrew Jackson and become a brigadier general in the US Army. He left Clinton by 1811 and spent the rest of his life in Alabama.

The first houses in Clinton were originally built with logs. Three of the houses built during the first year have survived. The first frame house built "stood on the spot now covered by an elegant three-story brick building on the N.W. corner of the Public Square."[29] They were generally constructed on lots of one-half acre though some were as large as five acres. The jail was completed September 3, 1810, for $490. Clinton was legally incorporated by the state legislature on December 2, 1809. In 1810 four merchants reported annual sales of $1,260 but by the next year this rose to $16,900, most of which was earned by Edmund Cox who rang up $10,000 in 1811.

Construction began in 1808 on a 22-mile road from Clinton to Milledgeville. This road is today known as Georgia Highway 22, and when it was first completed, a once daily stagecoach journey cost three dollars. Eventually, the road was extended 115 miles to Columbus, Georgia, on which a twenty-two-hour journey cost travelers $10 in 1830. The names of Clinton's streets reflect the list of heroes from the period and include Hawkins, Jackson, Jefferson, Madison, Pinckney, Pulaski, Randolph, and Washington. Of course, there is also Liberty Street and Walnut.[30] Those running southwest to northeast, such as Liberty, Madison, and Pulaski, were made 60 feet wide, while those running northwest to southeast, such as Randolph, Hawkins, and Washington, were made 30 feet wide.[31] Despite its rich history, "few Georgians are aware of Clinton today."[32]

Only slightly more Georgians are aware of the fall line and its significance to the geography, climate, and economy of central Georgia. Running all along the Atlantic and Gulf coasts, the fall line passes through Georgia from Augusta to Macon and Columbus. It is literally the ancient coastline of the southeastern corner of North America and marks the place of a dramatic rise in elevation as one travels from the southeast to the northwest, and it determines the northernmost navigational point on Georgia's major rivers such as the Savannah, Ocmulgee, and Chattahoochee. Although cotton was grown north and south of the fall line, the line itself marks the "sweet spot" for Georgia's cotton plantation economy. Too far south of the line and the soil becomes too sandy, draining well but having few minerals, and too far north of the line the soil becomes too rocky with increasing hills and mountains, having an abundance of minerals and better suited to small-scale farming, but more difficult to conduct large-scale plantation agriculture. As the fall line runs slightly south of Clinton, Jones County was ideal for this type of farming, lying on the southern edge of the upcountry plantation belt.

Those who drew in the land lotteries were often wealthy speculators who earned enormous profits subdividing and selling the land they drew for much higher prices per acre. Shackleford, who drew lot five, for example, sold his portion within ten days of the lottery for $700 to William Butler, who settled on it before the founding of Clinton, where he was appointed Justice of the Peace in 1808. Sarah Granberry sold lot twenty, which she drew, in April 1810 for $1,500, a 12,500 percent increase! These increases reflect the rapidly increasing demand for property in Jones County and the growing desire to settle in Clinton during its earliest days.

By 1820 Jones County was the second most populated county in the state with 1,341 residents, including the enslaved, and larger than long-settled Washington County. Sixteen free blacks were living in Clinton in 1820. There were thirty-two merchants and thirty-nine manufacturers. Only Savannah, Augusta, and Milledgeville were larger towns than Clinton at the time. Clinton was larger than Washington, Georgia, Louisville, Madison, and Athens, even with all the students.[33] Jones County and the thirteen other "upcountry plantation counties were as densely settled as New Jersey and Delaware" in the 1820s. With 43.5 persons per square mile, Jones County was Georgia's most densely settled county and was more dense than New York, Pennsylvania, New Hampshire, or Vermont at the time.[34]

Whereas Macon was still no more than Ft. Hawkins, Clinton quickly became the most important town west of the state capital in Milledgeville. Just as early Georgians were drawn to Macon in the 1830s, Clinton was one of Georgia's fastest-growing centers of trade and culture as settlers were drawn to Jones County in the 1820s. Many of them arrived from Milledgeville, such as Charles J. McDonald (1793–1860) who was born in Charleston, SC, studied law in Georgia's capital, and then opened his office in Clinton in 1818. He was later elected governor of Georgia during 1839–3 but not before he served as a trustee for the Clinton Academy.

In 1820, Clinton had ten manufacturing establishments producing $14,000 worth of merchandise annually, employing thirty people who made furniture, carriages, hats, and tinware including buckets, bake pans, and cooking utensils. On the streets downtown, there was a tannery, saddlery, millinery, and a shop selling shoes and boots.[35] There were three hotels including The Globe Tavern, the Eagle Tavern, and The Clinton Hotel, and at least eight lawyers including Slade's partner James Webb, who had also been partners with Samuel Lowther. There were four doctors by 1819, including Thomas Hamilton, who was a trustee of the Medical Academy of Georgia and a state senator. Doctors were not licensed in Georgia until 1825. Death certificates were not required until 1919. Two doctors were known for studying "the stars with telescopes, often at the 'Literary Rocks,' two granite boulders northwest of Clinton where they discussed scientific subjects."[36] This is the type of activity Slade would have looked for after he moved to Clinton in 1824, more especially in 1827 when he shifted from law to education.[37] He was, however, always a scientist. He was not a dramatist, but he appreciated the fine arts. In 1818, a Clinton Thespian Society presented *Hamlet* in the Jones County courthouse.[38]

Clinton quickly became an agricultural and manufacturing center exporting cotton, cotton gins, peaches, and pepper. The most successful industrialist in

Clinton was Samuel Griswold, who built a factory in 1820 to manufacture cotton gins after migrating to Jones County from Connecticut. The small hand crank gin had only been invented twenty-seven years earlier and patented by Eli Whitney in 1794. This simple machine immediately led to a 30 percent increase in the amount of cotton produced and the corresponding increase in the demand for labor, that is, the number of enslaved workers imported from Africa. Picking the seeds out of the fibers by hand had always been the bottleneck in the cotton producing process, and this necessarily suppressed the number of acres committed to cotton before 1794. Griswold became the first manufacturer in the county to make gin his primary product on a large scale. As one of the best gin manufacturers in the South, Griswold shipped these large horse and water-powered gins to towns throughout Georgia and South Carolina, delivered on large wagons pulled by six mules each. Soon, almost every town of the smallest size in and outside the cotton belt had its own gin, many of them made in Clinton. The first great industrialist of Alabama, Daniel Pratt, who migrated south from Temple, New Hampshire, began as a foreman at Griswold's Clinton gin factory in 1831. He later supplied cotton gins to Alabama and Mississippi from his own factory just as Griswold had done in the East. Joseph Winship (1800–78) of New Salem, Massachusetts, who later made cotton gins and railroad cars in his Atlanta foundry, also first learned his skills in Clinton working for Griswold. Winship and his descendants did so well in manufacturing and gave so much to charitable, non-profit institutions that their name is associated throughout Georgia with many associations, institutes, centers, foundations, etc., many of them Methodist, due to their affiliation with the First Methodist Church of Atlanta, such as the Winship Cancer Institute of Emory University. The Winship foundry was located on Forsyth Street and the Western & Atlantic Railroad in Atlanta, where several federal buildings are located today. Joseph's son George Winship, Sr. (1835–1916) was born in Clinton and is buried in Atlanta's Historic Oakland Cemetery. George Winship Jr.'s home, built in 1925 on Brookwood Drive in Atlanta, is listed on the National Register of Historic Places.[39]

The Marquis de Lafayette was to have visited Clinton in 1825 as he passed through America, and Slade expressed his disappointment that he was unable to meet "the nation's guest."[40] Lafayette could not have lingered in Jones County because there is no mention of any stops in Auguste Levasseur's account between Milledgeville and Macon. According to Slade, Lafayette bypassed Georgia's fourth largest town. He wrote, as the residents of Clinton awaited his arrival, "our ears were saluted by the quick firing of the cannon by his arrival at Fort Hawkins, having passed only a few miles below us."[41] Slade wanted to rush to the fort "but the firing of the cannon announced his departure from that place." By the time Slade wrote to his brother on April 3, Lafayette had departed the state and was heading toward New Orleans. Incidentally, Lafayette did visit Emma Hart Willard in Troy, New York, at the Troy Female Seminary in 1826, which helped Willard access other influential supporters of female education. In 1837, Willard helped Slade, who visited her and the seminary as part of his educational trip north.[42]

Clinton had twelve factories by that time producing hides, farm tools, lumber, cornmeal, flour, wagons, ox carts, and more cotton gins. There were three large taverns, two hotels, a photograph gallery, a silversmith, saloons, other stores, and shops. The Clinton Methodist Church is one of the oldest Methodist churches in the State of Georgia, dating to 1810 and is the oldest church, of any denomination, in Jones County. Clinton was a booming town that appeared to be the promising municipality in Georgia. Year over year through the 1820s, Clinton's population grew, the number of commercial enterprises increased, and the positive trade balance was going up as fast as the New York Stock Exchange in early 1929. Clinton was Georgia's most economically prosperous town and was in the process of becoming a "seat of culture and learning."[43] Political, commercial, industrial, and educational leaders such as Slade had big plans for their little town. No one anticipated the impact of a new Indian treaty and what it would mean for Clinton's future.

By 1829, Clinton had fifty-six houses, ten stores, four taverns, five law offices, three medical doctors, and eight mechanic shops. The stagecoach ran through Clinton on its way between Milledgeville and Macon. There were few farms in Jones County over one hundred acres and, therefore, fewer slaves than in many surrounding counties. In 1810 there were thirteen enslaved persons in Clinton among a total population of eighty-five. In 1811, Planter Thomas Hill, who lived four miles from Clinton, owned nineteen slaves. Later Anne Jacqueline Blount's brother Thomas owned forty-four. Other early planters included Samuel Cook who also, with Robert Beasley, owned an 1811 hotel in Clinton. Jonathan Parrish, Zachariah Pope, Julius Caesar Bonaparte Mitchell, and William Flewellen were the other large planters in the county and among those who sent their daughters to Slade's new school.[44] No one else owned thirty slaves or more. Only 11 of 173 white males over the age of 21 were listed as planters, a designation which required ownership of at least twenty enslaved persons.[45] Besides cotton and corn, these plantations were producing significant harvests of wheat and tobacco. They included orchards of peach and apple trees. The 1820 Jones County census listed 505 slaves and this amounted to 40 percent of the population. Sixty-two percent of these enslaved persons were female, many of whom were domestic servants. There were sixteen free blacks in 1820, half of them under fourteen years of age and four who were more than forty-five years.[46] Slade wrote in 1825 that a man could make more money with "ten negroes" in Georgia than he could with twenty in North Carolina.[47]

During the 1820s, horse racing was a popular sport in Clinton. Thomas Blount owned a half interest in a racehorse named Diomed, "a beautiful Bay eight years old." The horse was reported to be sixteen hands, two and three-quarters "high" and "equaled by few and surpassed by none in America."[48] Residents also partook in shooting contests, animal shows, and traveling performers including a magician. It was illegal to sell alcohol on "the Sabbath," which was Sunday, or gamble, but several presentments were made in court for both. For example, one early complaint read:

> We present as a grievance the violation of the Sabbath by the immoral and disorderly practices of gaming drinking and nocturnal reveling as well as the practice of firing Guns on that day in the Town of Clinton and pursuing other amusements of an irregular and immoral nature . . . and request that the magistrates of this District will be vigilant in checking these improprieties and cause a greater respect to be paid to the Lords Day.[49]

Cauthen has argued that many southern humorists have given the impression that places like Clinton on the early Georgia frontier were rough, uncultured places, deficient in morals and manners, but that the history does not support this conclusion. To be fair, there were some rough characters found in the records of Clinton and described in Cauthen's work, but the truth is that most of the individuals who lived in the town during the 1820s were honest, hardworking Christians who lived by moral principles that were only "strict" by modern comparisons. The percentage of Clinton residents who were church members was no different than every comparable town in America during the same time. There were eight churches in Jones County by 1821, some of them Baptist churches of 705 members who were affiliated with the newly organized Ocmulgee Baptist Association. Lorenzo Dow, a well-known evangelist of the period, preached in Clinton in 1810, passing through Georgia on his way from Louisiana to North Carolina as he often did. Besides being an eccentric itinerant preacher, Dow was an abolitionist fifty years before emancipation.

> With his long hair, his flowing beard, his harsh voice, and his wild gesticulation, he was so rude and unkempt as to startle all conservative hearers. Said one of his opponents: "His manners (are) clownish in the extreme; his habit and appearance more filthy than a savage Indian, his public discourses a mere rhapsody, the substance often an insult upon the gospel."[50]

His sermon, nonetheless, on "strictly puritanical morality and his concern for religion" was well received in Clinton.[51] On the other hand, when Englishman Henry Champion, then a resident of Connecticut, visited Clinton with his highly cultured British sensibilities, he wrote that the "planters spent too much time enjoying leisurely pursuits." This was only possible, he explained, because of the institution of slavery, who, he confessed, also "enjoyed numerous diversions" such as hunting and horse racing.[52]

The frequent mistake made today in attempting to understand the early frontier settlers of Georgia is to conclude they were uneducated, morally decadent, and possessing little sophistication because of their log homes, slavery, and rural way of life. As demonstrated here, there are far too many exceptions to justify any such conclusions. Social occasions such as barn raisings, corn shuckings, quilting bees, and dances provided residents of Clinton and Jones County opportunities to build relationships with one another, to teach and be taught, while developing a sophisticated culture and enforcing a Christian morality while having a good, safe time with friends and family. The church may have discouraged games of chance, but in the 1820s drinking alcohol was almost universal. The taverns in Clinton were the most popular places for residents as well as travelers to eat, drink, visit, and rest.[53] Slade, however, supported the Sons of Temperance and was never known to have tasted alcohol. He was rather an "earnest, solemn" man who prioritized his work and responsibilities.

By 1830, Clinton's population had fallen dramatically to 6,471 as the border of Georgia had been suddenly pushed west of the Ocmulgee River by a new treaty extracted from the Muscogee (Creek) Indians.[54] As a frontier town, Clinton prospered but once the frontier moved west, this thriving community went into a fatal decline from which it never recovered.

As a young man, newly arrived in Georgia, Slade was described as "physically, a stout, round-limbed, healthy man, about 5 feet 9 inches high, with a dark complexion" and blue eyes.[55] He was "remarkable for early rising, purity of morals, intense application to books, temperateness in all its forms." As a lawyer he was known for his "untiring diligence and industry in the interests of his clients." As an educator, he was a pioneer of female education in Georgia. "He paid his own way, put up his own buildings, hired and always paid his teachers, bought pianos, and supplied amply and fully all apparatus illustrating the natural sciences." He was "excelled by few as a botanist." As a minister "he ever preferred the gentle and soul-saving themes of the Gospel—the love of God in Christ, faith and salvation. Christ and him crucified—mingled with earnest and pointed appeals to both saint and sinner in regard to personal duty." He was a popular speaker, much loved and in demand, although no one thought he was a great orator. "He was earnest and devout," they said, "permitting no speculative theology." He "preached entirely without notes" because he "made the Bible a constant study."[56]

Anne Jacqueline Blount (1805–91) was the daughter of James Blount (1780–1820) and Elizabeth Gregoire De Roulhac (1786–1834). She was the oldest of six children, born in Washington County, North Carolina, before her family moved to Blountsville, Jones County, Georgia in c. 1815 after James served in the War of 1812 as an ensign with Latham's Beaufort Regt., North Carolina, militia. He and Elizabeth were married in Beaufort County, North Carolina on May 14, 1803. He was the son of Edmund Blount (1755–1822) and Judith

Rhodes (1756–90). Elizabeth's parents were Psalmet Gregoire De Roulhac (1752–1808) and Anne Hare Maule (1765–94). Psalmet was born in France and came to America as the agent of the Beaumarchais Bank of Paris during the American Revolution. When the bank fell, Psalmet chose to remain in the New World but was found in Beaufort and in poverty before the end of the war. James Blount lived and died in Blountsville which was named for his family. The town was a stop on the stagecoach line and site of a strong Baptist church and the Blountsville Academy, chartered in 1834. A state historical marker for this site is today found on US Hwy. 129 at the Damascus Church Road. John and Benjamin Milner were two of the most well-known pastors of this early church. As stated, Janet Bog and James Blount were first cousins, making Thomas and Anne second cousins, by virtue of their common ancestor Henry Benjamin Blount, Jr. (1728–88) being the father of both Hannah Blount, who married Thomas Bog, and Edmund Blount.

Thomas and Ann built their own house in 1824 on 5 acres they bought from Elias Bliss of Savannah for $600.[57] The lot was in the south end of Clinton "On the hillside back of Lowther Hall and south toward Macon," a spot that is today on the south side of Georgia Highway 18 near the intersection with Lite-N-Tie Road.[58] The house has long been demolished but was near the present site of the Exchange Bank of Gray and the Piedmont Animal Hospital. The home has been described as "the usual architecture of that period."[59] It was described in greater detail by S. H. Griswold in 1908 in a letter to the editor of the *Jones County News*. He wrote, "a large two-story frame building . . . it faced toward the courthouse square and its front yard was nicely terraced and planted with beautiful flowers. The school room was on the ground floor and the sleeping rooms were on the upper floor. The back yard and grounds were planted in fruit trees and were well kept."[60]

Seven of Thomas and Anne's eleven children were born on the upper floor of their Clinton home. Janet Elizabeth Slade, pronounced "Jenette," was born eleven months after their wedding on May 5, 1825, and Mary Lavania Slade followed on December 11, 1826, while Thomas was working in Clinton as a lawyer and inferior court judge. By the time Anne Louisa Slade, called "Annie," was born on August 21, 1829, Thomas was director of the Clinton Academy for boys. His firstborn son, however, was born on April 28, 1831, after he had resigned from the academy post and founded the Clinton Female Seminary. He informed his brother William he "was necessarily forced to have a school of my own," implying this was so because of the number of daughters in his family and proving that he was not forced to resign from the Clinton Academy. For a Baptist minister such as Slade explaining such a decision in 1832, it is remarkable he made no mention to William about the force of Providence or the call of God. In December 1832, however, he had only joined the Elim Baptist Church in Clinton two months earlier, but with his wife Anne's assistance, Slade was confident the female seminary would be a success. "Anne will assist me in teaching the department of music and painting—She has been for some time past devoting her time to the study of music and I would not want a more competent assistant in every branch of English education."[61]

By that time, Janet was only six years old, Mary was five, but Slade was already teaching them the basics of reading and writing. Emma Jacqueline Slade, called "Coon" by her siblings, arrived January 10, 1833; Thomas Bog Slade, Jr. on December 16, 1834; and Martha Bog Slade on December 3, 1837. Janet Elizabeth was named for her two grandmothers, Janet Bog and Elizabeth Gregoire De Roulhac. Mary Lavinia was named for two aunts, one on each side of the family: Thomas' sister, Mary Ann Slade, and Anne's sister, Lavania Elizabeth Blount. Anne Louisa was named for her mother Anne Jacqueline Blount and her mother's first cousin Anne Louisa Ely, the daughter of Mary Jane Dumas De Roulhac. James Jeremiah was named for his late paternal grandfather and Emma Jacqueline for her mother. It is not clear from where Thomas or Anne chose the name Emma since neither had anyone in their family who previously had that name, and it is not a biblical name. Emma Winbush, fifty-one, was living in Clinton at the time, and despite this being a common nineteenth-century female name, she was apparently the only Emma in Clinton until the birth of "Coon." Little else is known about Emma Winbush or her relationship with the Slades, but her relationship with the Slades may have been so close it necessitated the need for the nickname. Thomas Bog Jr.'s name is obvious, and finally, Martha Bog was given Martha along with Bog, but like Emma, it is not clear from whence the first name was chosen. Martha, like Emma, was a common female name in the nineteenth century, but only distant in laws of Slade cousins had the name in 1837. Cordelia Hassel's mother and

Marmaduke Slade's mother-in-law were Marthas. At least four Marthas lived in Clinton in 1837, including Martha Jones, Martha Blow, twenty-five, Martha Duncan, fifty-six, and Widow Martha M. Harris. Any of these could have been the namesake. At least one of these may have served as a midwife.

In Slade's first Georgia years, he was a lawyer and inferior court judge, and as an attorney was representing the residents of Jones County and his family in all manner of suits, petitions, registrations, and other legal transactions. Before becoming an educator, he enjoyed a life supported by the practice of law in one of Georgia's largest towns. In the September term of 1824, for example, he dismissed Stephen Ventress on September 6, in Jones County court, as the executor of the estate of Anne's cousin William Roulhac and who had "completed the administration on said estate, and prays to be dismissed from the same."[62] One month later, he appointed John and William Gay administrators for the estate of their mother Amelia Castleberry Gay on October 19.[63]

The most famous legal trial that took place in Clinton occurred in December 1837 just as Slade was beginning to transition from Jones County to Macon and ten years after he had given up the full-time profession of an attorney and judge. Slade was very much aware of the trial and followed its development from the seminary as he had conducted the wedding ceremony of William Dawson Bunkley, Jr., brother of the defendant, and his wife, Miss Camilla Dorinda Sanford, both of Jones County, in 1829.[64] As it was the talk of the nation, it was certainly the most frequent topic of casual conversation in Clinton during those days. The case involved a man who claimed to be Jesse Lucas Bunkley, son of William Dawson Bunkley, Sr., and Elizabeth Flewellen Slatter, one of the wealthiest families in the county, and one who was talented but both wild and rude in his youth.[65] His intellect gained admission to the University of Georgia in 1822, but his character earned him expulsion from the same.[66] After a fight with his uncle regarding his unauthorized use of a horse, Bunkley decided to leave home and go west. He traveled to Natchez, Mississippi, and then to New Orleans, where most residents of Clinton believed he had died August 31, 1825. He wrote to his mother, however, in 1833 from a New Orleans prison pleading with her to believe that he was her son.[67] A few years later, a man appeared in Clinton claiming to be Bunkley and demanding his share of his family's inheritance. By then, his father had been dead since 1812 but had owned a house, store, over three hundred acres spread over three counties, and sixteen enslaved persons worth more than $5,000. He also operated as a private banker, profiting from loaning money to locals for interest. In a time when many could afford few luxuries, William Dawson Bunkley, Sr. owned thirty rare books in his private library, including a treasured dictionary. Elizabeth Bunkley invited the suspect to stay in her home and although she testified that she "begged him to satisfy me that he was my son but he has never done so."[68] She said his handwriting and the scars on his body were different from those on the body of her son. He did not know the middle name of his father.

Other witnesses confirmed that the man had similar features to Bunkley, who was about 5' 9¾" tall, with a "dark" complexion, dark hair, and gray eyes.[69] There were several significant inconsistencies in his story, however, and serious lapses in his memory, so he was ultimately indicted for cheating and swindling. More than 130 witnesses testified in this sensational 1837–8 trial of the man who claimed to be Bunkley, held before Clinton Judge John G. Polhill. Large crowds gathered in and around the courthouse daily, larger in the winter months because of the season of the year when agricultural activities were largely dormant. Though some continued to believe through the spring that the man was, in fact, Jesse Bunkley, the claimant, he was later positively identified as Elijah Barber, was convicted, and sentenced in Superior Court to five years in prison for impersonating another for personal financial gain.[70] Barber only survived nine months in prison, however, and died July 5, 1839. He was thirty-two years old. Others discovered after the trial that Barber had been imprisoned with Bunkley in a New Orleans jail and learned about Jesse's life in Georgia through lengthy conversations about his family, friends, and experiences. When Bunkley died, Barber determined to go to Georgia, take possession of Bunkley's inheritance by impersonating him, and then flee the area to a life of leisure. Polhill later profited from producing a book detailing the trial, which was thereafter included in a larger work cataloging the most famous criminal trials in America over a three-hundred-year period.[71]

The Bunkleys were a wealthy family, but in the 1820s, Anne Jacqueline Blount's brother was the largest planter in the Clinton area, which had doubled its population despite so many residents already migrating to both Macon and Alabama. Blount owned over 1,123 acres in Jones County, another 572 in Burke County, and held 44 enslaved persons. Anne was an 1820 graduate of the Moravian Seminary in Salem, North Carolina.

Slade remained in law for only three years before accepting the responsibility for the Clinton Academy, a school exclusively for boys, in 1827 which had been in operation since shortly after the state legislature of Georgia "had passed an act in 1792 appropriating $1,000 for the endowment of an Academy in each county."[72] In 1817, $250,000 was appropriated by the state for "poor schools" and, in 1821, an additional $250,000 was set aside for the county academies.[73] The Clinton Academy, first known as the Academy in Jones County or Jones County Academy since 1810, was the first such educational institution but there seems to have been interruptions in activities over the next six years. Its name appeared in the Georgia Journal in 1816 when Peter Clower and Samuel Cook advertised, "An Academy is now open in Clinton to receive students, where good attention will be given to their education and moral rules."[74] Subscribers held a meeting at the courthouse in Clinton to build a school building in 1818. This project was led by Thomas Blount, Samuel Cook, Isaac Harvey, William Williams, and Thomas Hamilton.[75] The effort must have failed because in 1819 there was no academy in Clinton. Only in October of that year did Orray Ticknor, father of Poet Francis Orray Ticknor, announce that the Clinton Academy would open on the second Monday of November with "a female department in the care of Mrs. Ticknor."[76] The Ticknors were originally from Columbia, Connecticut where Orray had been a physician. Mrs. Ticknor was Harriot Coolidge from Norwich Town, Connecticut. They first migrated to Savannah in 1815 but soon arrived in Jones County where their children were born. Orray had a medical office open in Clinton since 1816 where he saw patients in addition to his work supporting the Clinton Academy. This school was reorganized yet again in 1821, incorporated, because of Governor John Clarke's signature on the bill December 15, 1821. The trustees of this 1810 school were Abner Biddle, Reuben Cole, Worly Rose, David White, and Thomas White. Girls attended the school before 1821 which charged both genders $3.75 tuition per four and one-half month semester.[77] In 1818, the *Georgia Journal* reported construction of a building for this early academy which consisted of 200,000 bricks.[78] Surely this was used for the 1821 rechartered academy and the organization simply continued under a new legal status.

Rufus Huntington, "a young gentleman from New England" and an 1817 graduate of Yale, was hired to be the teacher of the Clinton Academy in 1820 after having arrived in Georgia in 1819. According to two local newspapers he was known as being "eminent for his morality." Having placed the school in highly qualified hands, Ticknor resumed his medical practice. Successful and well-loved in the community, Huntington died suddenly in 1825.[79] J. L. Hyde was found to replace Huntington, and his wife took charge of the female department. They recruited a young lady from New York to teach music. The curriculum was segregated by gender with the boys taking English grammar, arithmetic, geography, Virgil, natural philosophy, rhetoric, Cicero, Homer, composition, and elocution. Even before Slade's arrival, the girls of the Clinton Academy were given English grammar, geography, the grammar of philosophy, rhetoric, chemistry, moral philosophy, history, logic, and music.[80]

Along with James Smith, Samuel Lowther, lawyer, US senator, and owner of Lowther Hall, Charles J. McDonald, lawyer, Governor of Georgia, and Gustaves Hendrick, one of the first trustees of the 1821 school, was Henry Graybill Lamar (1798–1861) who later became the original and long-serving chairman of the first board of trustees for the Georgia Female College which became Wesleyan College in Macon.[81] These same trustees hired Slade to be the administrator and main teacher of the Clinton Academy in early April 1827. Slade informed his brother William six weeks after accepting the offer, "Since I wrote you last I have engaged in a new employment."[82] The connection, therefore, between the Clinton schools and Wesleyan has proven to be much stronger than previously understood, and the role of Slade, working with Lamar for at least nine years previously (1827–36), cannot now be underestimated. These trustees were authorized to control "the property, gifts, donation, and grants of the institution."[83] They elected new members of the board and were authorized to use a legal seal. Slade likely assisted in the legal work required for this charter before becoming the school's administrator, and the trustees of the boys' academy assisted Slade in founding the seminary for girls.[84] Some of their daughters became his students. The academy for boys, sometimes called the Day's Boys' School, was located on "a triangle in front of the Methodist Church and was in the north end of Clinton." It is often confused in the history with the girls' Clinton Female Seminary because resident S. H. Griswold was elderly when he wrote his memories of Clinton for the *Jones County News* in 1909 and occasionally confused the two. This was repeated in Williams' *History of Jones County* and has caused more than a little misunderstanding about the two schools, partly because Slade was the administrator for both and the names are similar. Because of their different locations, body of students, and histories, the two schools are very different. One was almost for boys only; one was exclusively for girls. The Clinton Academy began twenty years before Slade's Clinton Female Seminary, lasted years after the seminary moved to Macon, and was still in operation until the Civil War. By that time, Slade was teaching in Columbus, Georgia.

Lamar was born in Clinton and married Mary Ann Davis, a cousin of Confederate States president Jefferson Davis, in 1823. They lived in Clinton until Lamar began to practice law in the newly founded town of Macon, where he became a Superior Court judge. When Ambrose Baber was elected to represent Macon in the Georgia Senate in 1827, Lamar was elected to the Georgia House of Representatives. In 1828, the Macon town commissioners were John T. Lamar, Robert Birdsong, John Corbitt, John S. Childers, and Marmaduke Johnson Slade.[85] Henry G. Lamar went on to the US Congress (1829–33) when he won a special election, as a Jacksonian Democrat, in 1828 to fill the unexpired term of George Rockingham Gilmer. Reelected in 1830, Lamar served until he was defeated in his second reelection in 1832. He was also defeated in his 1857 unsuccessful campaign to be governor of Georgia. He died in Macon in 1861 and is buried in the Rose Hill Cemetery, but for at least four decades he was one of the leading men of Bibb County. Known as a jurist and politician, he is not as well known for the extensive work he did as a trustee, adviser, and philanthropist for education in both Clinton and Macon. In 1821, however, as the Academy was founded and Clinton was at its peak, Macon was still an outpost called Fort Hawkins.

The Clinton Academy was funded by the state, county, and tuition from the students. Trustees, therefore, were annually accountable for reporting all receipts and expenditures made to the grand jury. Besides the initial appropriation from the state legislature, academies across the state collectively received the benefit of fines and forfeitures collected by the state from criminal prosecutions, given annually on Christmas Day as if it were a gift. The academy continued after Slade's resignation because it was still receiving funds from an act of the state legislature after 1827. B. W. Kellog was hired from Windham, MA, a "well educated and quite capable man" who "conducted the academy very efficiently and had a large patronage."[86] Although he was popular with students and the community, he died of tuberculosis one day after delivering, to the students, a farewell lecture in 1835. The residents of Clinton paid for his wife to return "to her people in the north." His music teacher, a certain Miss Ripley, settled in Clinton as a governess for the family of Samuel Griswold. Kellog, who seems to have admitted girls after the Clinton Female Seminary moved to Macon, was replaced by Joseph M. Waterman of Belfast, Maine, as the trustees of the Clinton Academy attempted to keep the school functional. Waterman was said to have "conducted it successfully for several years," but by 1860 he had moved to Macon with his wife Caroline and their four children.[87] Waterman owned three slaves in 1850 and five in 1860 who likely worked at the school. A teacher for about twenty years in Clinton, Waterman was listed as a retired merchant in 1860 and retired druggist in 1870 by the time he had migrated further to Talbotton, Georgia. He voted there in 1867.[88] His pattern followed Slade, but it is not clear if they were in communication through those years, whereas no letters between them have been found. It is not likely Waterman was involved in the Georgia Teacher's Association once he left Clinton and the educational profession. The female seminary, however, prospered under Slade's leadership.

The Clinton Academy for boys was one of many buildings, approximately one-third of the town, burned by troops under the command of Gen. William T. Sherman who passed through Clinton during his March to the Sea during November 19–23, 1864. It was said that it "would" have burned if it had not been saved by "several slaves and young boys" who "put it out."[89] The federal troops involved camped four days outside the town, according to *The Telegraph and Confederate* of Macon, were Maj. Gen. Hugh Judson Kilpatrick's cavalry and the 15th Army Corps under Gen. Oliver Otis Howard (1830–1909) who commanded the right wing of Sherman's army. Kilpatrick was praised by northerners for his victories but hated by Southerners for the destruction of property. Sherman said of him in 1864, "I know that Kilpatrick is a hell of a damned fool, but I want just that sort of man to command my cavalry on this expedition."[90] Kilpatrick delighted in destroying property. On the other hand, Howard was known as "The Christian General" for his evangelical piety. Sherman praised him for "the utmost skill, nicety and precision."[91] Of those four days in 1864, seven-year-old William Wiley Barron of Clinton remembered in 1930, "Soldiers were all over town. They were passing constantly down the road by our house.... I remember while I was sitting on a gate post, watching 'em pass, one of the soldiers pinched my ear," and "Gen. Kilpatrick gave each house a guard, but supplies of every kind were taken. We didn't have anything left but a few jars of lard which my mother had hid under the bed."[92] Finally, according to Griswold, "A few years after the war Henry Greaves bought the academy building and tore it down and used the lumber to construct a dwelling on his plantation. This house is still standing [1909] and is about five miles from Clinton on the road to Macon."[93]

Between 1821 and 1826, three additional academies were founded in Jones County. These included Farmers (1822), Fortville (1822), and Flat Shoals (1826). Of these, the Clinton Academy was the best known and most successful. It is not surprising, however, that Slade resigned the boys' school after four years and founded the Clinton Female Seminary in his Clinton home in 1931. The word "seminary" was not used to describe a graduate school for theological training in the 1820s but was a more general term synonymous with "academy" or "college" whereas the Clinton Female Seminary was a secondary and tertiary grade institution specifically for girls in the town of Clinton, Georgia, and the surrounding area. Slade was never known to recruit pupils other than advertising his seminary's enrollment period. He was known for never rejecting an applicant due to her family's inability to pay tuition. His purpose "was to give the southern girl adequate educational facilities."[94] In 1836, Slade was the legal guardian for Francis Harris, who was likely one of his students at the seminary.[95] This "orphan" female is found in a later US census able to read and write and living in a house she owned. This illustrates the intersection of Slade's work as educator and minister and the difference his work made in the lives of young women.

In one 1830s paid announcement found in the *Macon* Messenger, Slade described his vision for the seminary:

> This school is conducted on the most improved plan. It is our business to give to it an intellectual character.... To induce the pupils rather to cultivate their minds, than to lumber them with words. We are provided with a Chemical, Philosophical, and Geometrical apparatus, geological specimens, and other facilities for illustrating the various branches of Sciences. It is located at the Subscriber's house, in a retired and pleasant part of town. The exercises of the School commence at sunrise, and continue during the day, with suitable intervals for recreation. Branches of education taught, are Reading, Writing, English Grammar, Geography, with the drawing of maps, Arithmetic, Algebra, Geometry, Natural and Moral Philosophy, Chemistry, Geology, Rhetoric, Botany, Music, Drawing, Painting, Embroidery.[96]

Clearly the school was in his home rather than him living in the school as some have stated. He built the home in 1824 and lived there as a lawyer and judge, then administrator of the Clinton Academy before creating a seminary classroom in his house in 1832. Many of the boarding students were distributed throughout Clinton, but it is interesting how his large family adjusted to accommodate so many in the residence. It was "well adapted for a family [of eight] and twenty-five boarders," according to Slade. By 1832, the seminary enrollment never fell below sixty students, ages eight to fourteen, thereafter until the relocation in 1838.

For those who were able to pay, the base rate of tuition, including instruction in language and science, was $32 per year.[97] For a girl who lived out of the area and required boarding at the seminary, Slade charged $100 per year, and this did not include candles or laundry. Several students came from Hancock, Putnam, Twiggs, and "various parts of the state."[98] Some enrolled from out of state. A professor of science, Slade asked for $10 extra per year for "Chemical Lectures" and $50 per year for a student to take vocal and/or instrumental music with Maria Lord of Boston and Anne, his wife, not including $6 per year for use of a piano. Drawing and painting classes were $20. Because each dorm room had a fireplace for heat, students paid $4 per year for firewood, which came with a "servant" to manage the fire and keep the fireplace clean. Only a few students registered for all these classes and services, but doing so amounted to only $222 annually as late as 1837, an amount, accounting for inflation, which would equal the purchasing power of $3,286 in 2024. Whereas the least expensive colleges and universities in the twenty-first century charge at least, on average, $36,000, it becomes evident how reasonable the rates were at the Clinton Female Seminary, especially when one considers the quality of instruction received under the teaching of the highly qualified Slade. The rates prove that Slade was genuinely interested in promoting education, not in profiteering from the need of early Georgia families to educate their daughters. For those who enrolled, they knew inexpensive did not mean "cheap" when it came to the Clinton Female Seminary. For paying students, half of the total due was required before matriculation, the commencement of classes, and the other half was collected over the course of the term. Students were only accepted for a full term, meaning no student was allowed to knowingly enroll for less than one full academic year at a time. The Clinton Female Seminary was an "excellent school" that had not been given the "notoriety it merits," according to the group of Macon businessmen who visited Slade and the seminary in 1835. This they accounted to Slade's aversion to attracting publicity, which they believed was an injustice done to the public. They concluded that more parents would have enrolled their daughters in the seminary if they had known how good the Clinton school was. The observers were impressed by how "practical" the instruction was in the seminary and wrote, "We have observed that young girls are quicker in their perceptions than boys of the same age, they memorize with greater facility . . . by rote with more readiness but with less apprehension of their meaning."[99] Slade had the ability to make the hard topics of science easy to understand.

There were no other schools for girls in the United States offering more or charging less than Slade's school where, in early nineteenth-century Jones County, Georgia, girls were learning chemistry, biology, botany, geometry, Greek, Latin, and physics. By 1835, they were also learning the fine arts of drawing, music, and painting but not as "ornamental" subjects being taught in most other female academies. Students were also allowed use of "all necessary apparatus" such as globes, microscopes, telescopes, etc.[100] In advance of his trip North in 1937, Slade advertised his intention of visiting some of the best female academies of the northern states to guarantee the quality of his own school and to purchase additional and higher quality necessary apparatus.

The academic term of the Clinton Female Seminary began on the second Monday of October each year between 1833 and 1838. It ended on the Friday before the second Monday in July, roughly pausing for a two-and-a-half month summer break. Academic and moral integrity rules were strict for the students of the seminary under Slade's administration. These rules reflected Slade's own moral views but also the desire of parents to ensure the good behavior and safety of their daughters who were away from home and the protection of their parents. Girls were, therefore, not allowed to attend "balls and parties" during the academic term. Slade himself clarified that his purpose in having and enforcing these rules was "to impart practical and substantial knowledge, and to inculcate those principles of integrity, and habits of industry, which will lay the foundation of future usefulness."[101] The last three days of the term were always the most public and challenging for the students, whereas these were the examination days when parents and the public were invited to come to the seminary and witness the examination of students. Although this event concluded with a graduation ceremony, much like Slade experienced at the University of North Carolina, all grade levels of students were publicly examined, not only those graduating. This ensured invested and otherwise interested persons of the school's quality and supported future enrollment and the seminary's enduring sustainability. Every year the students ended the public examinations and the school term by singing for those in attendance. In 1835, the song was an anonymous prayer addressed to God, thankful for His blessings, petitioning for instruction from "above" and interceding on behalf of their teachers and the graduates:

> To Thee we come, (a favoured band,)
> With thanks, for blessings from thy hand;
> Still may we in thy bounty share—
> Assist us to deserve they care.
> We for our teachers humbly pray,
> Be thou their guide, their guard, their stay;
> Prolong their useful lives, and give
> Thy choicest blessings while they live.
> And she who leaves our little band,
> To journey to her native land—

Be thou her shield, by day and night—
Make her health precious in thy sight.
Almighty Maker, condescend
To be the pupil's constant friend:
Grant us the teachings of they love,
And give us lessons from above.
And if we leave these walls awhile;
To go where friends and kindred smile,
May we return, with mind and heart,
Prepared to choose the better part.
Eternal Power, 'tis thee we owe,
Life and its blessings here below:
In thee we trust thro' Jesus' love,
To bring us to thy home above.

The young men of the town established a tradition of sponsoring a celebratory "grand ball" for the students at the Gibson Hotel in Clinton with music provided by the enslaved Jack Weathers once the term had ended.[102] Little is known of Weathers; he was never "famous" as an entertainer. He was living in Heard and Troup counties after the war and employed by farmers David C. Gentry and J. B. Savill along with other freedmen.[103] He voted in Heard County in the 1867 election.[104] While the young men were, no doubt, sincere in their praise for a successful academic year, one can easily imagine how this event was an opportunity for them to become better acquainted with the young women of their otherwise gender-segregated community. The seminary rule against attending balls was thus suspended once commencement was concluded.

Lest Slade come across as a strict, lifeless Puritan or one who equated all things fun to unnecessary, silly, or sinful behavior, he was known to attend the annual Fourth of July celebrations, as the head of the seminary, in Clinton. Both he and Marmaduke were listed among the notable men who took part in the festivities.[105] "Cousin Marma" was living with the Slades in 1825 but was alternating in his plans about whether he would go to North Carolina in May or June, or go "to Alabama to see his relations."[106] In the same letter, Slade was being tempted to go on a hunting "expedition . . . to kill deer, bears, turkeys, etc." with Maurice Henderson and expressed his desire that William or their brother James, both in North Carolina, could go with him. By June, Marmaduke had decided to go to North Carolina to visit his own sister and offer that if Slade's sister would come to Warrenton, Georgia, Slade would pay for her expenses of travel.[107] Apparently, Elizabeth declined the offer.

Slade's brother William quit school in 1825 at the age of eighteen, and it became an occasion, before he became an educator, for Slade to express his opinion of this decision. The disadvantages that a lack of education causes, in his letter to William, could impede someone's progress through life and were a thing that would need to be remedied only by "individual exertions." He, therefore, encouraged his brother to continue his studies even if he were not enrolled in school. Then Slade admitted that his family's wealth would lessen the disadvantages for William but would have concluded that most people did not have that same luxury and that most others should not quit school.[108]

As early as 1825, William F. Henderson, Slade's brother-in-law, and the husband of Mary Ann Slade, was expressing his desire to join Slade in Georgia. They remained in North Carolina, however, due to Mary Ann's desire to remain near her mother. Henderson shared with Slade that he was "tired of Carolina." Slade, on the other hand, told his brother William, "if I was to express my opinion I should say he hated anything like work and the unfortunate consequence is sister [Mary Ann] must be his eternal slave."[109] Mary Ann did eventually come to Washington, Georgia, but not until both her mother and husband had died in 1831 and 1838, respectively. Mary Ann was still in Martin County, North Carolina, in 1850, but by 1860 she was living in Carroll County, Louisiana, opposed to allowing her children to leave her.

Slade's other sister was Elizabeth Jane Slade (1804–76) who married Mason Lee Wiggins (1798–1880). She never left or even considered leaving North Carolina. She moved to Halifax County with Mason after their wedding and lived there for the rest of their lives. The distance, however, did not diminish the pressure Elizabeth put upon her brother regarding his responsibilities, as she saw them, to their family. This spilled over into their political differences and their communications reveal much about their relationship and tension in the immediate family. Elizabeth sent a letter to Slade criticizing the State of Georgia, particularly its disgrace in opposing the US president on the issue of the Muscogee (Creek) Indians. She may have been attempting to undermine Slade's presence in Georgia, but she undoubtedly felt that it was inappropriate for Georgia's governor to oppose the US government which was defending the rights of the Native Americans against the state. "My head still runs on politics," Slade wrote to her, "and more probably than it ought."[110] Then he proceeded to undermine her supposed knowledge of the issue and in unusually stern language, explained the facts as he saw them to his sister. She was normally called "Eliza" by everyone, especially Slade, but here Slade addressed her, "What is it you say Elizabeth?" Slade suggested her deficiency lay in not reading the Georgia newspapers which might have provided her a better picture of "a crying shame and a most disgraceful outrage on a free and independent people that a standing army should be ordered out to prevent the exercise of their unquestionable rights," referring to the right of the state to possess the Indian lands within its borders. "Even children," he wrote, "listen with indignation to the injustice of the general government and I wonder that the stones do not rise up and speak."

Most residents of Georgia agreed with Slade and that Slade was likely biased by the hope of possessing Indian land. Slade told William in 1825, "Tell [Uncle Henry] he may shortly have an opportunity to purchase that handsome tract of land on the Chattahoochee which I have often heard him speak of. If I had the money I could soon make a fortune by speculating on those lands lately acquired from the Indians."[111] The *Second Treaty of Indian Springs* helped Governor Troup (1780–1856) win reelection in 1825. He ignored the *Treaty of Washington* which would have preserved some land for the Muscogee and avoided their complete removal. Troup ordered a survey of this land and prepared for a land distribution by lottery for the residents of the state. He began removing the Lower Creeks (those Muscogee in Georgia) by force. Many in the nation, like Elizabeth, saw Troup as being unreasonable but the federal handling of the incident alienated Georgians who favored immediate Indian removal. US president John Quincy Adams, who favored a gradual assimilation of Indians, threatened federal intervention but he backed down when Troup mobilized the Georgia Militia. When General Edmund P. Gaines confronted the governor, that both should be obedient, Slade asked Elizabeth, "Obedience to whom?" He asserted that obedience to the president on this issue would be "more like the cringing syncopation of a court," implying that Adams was acting in the manner of a monarch.[112] Slade questioned Gaines' patriotism despite his being called an "American patriot" on a 1957 Georgia historical marker on Washington Street in the town of Fort Gaines. He was one of the army's senior commanders with experience in the War of 1812, the Seminole Indian War, the Black Hawk War, the Mexican-American War, and he had arrested Aaron Burr for the murder of Alexander Hamilton and then testified at the trial. Adams had no support in the South, it seemed, other than Gaines and Slade's sister. Andrew Jackson was a hero in the South and when he was elected US president three years after Slade's confrontation with his sister, the tables were turned. Elizabeth and Gaines opposed Jackson for his Indian removal policy. The general's hard stance on obedience evaporated and in 1846 he was court-martialed for overstepping his authority.

Jane Thigpen (1823–1914) was a student of the Clinton Female Seminary and became both a Clinton and Rome, Georgia teacher and a poet after completing her studies. Several of her poems were published in one antebellum magazine under the name of Jessie Linn. A collection of her works appeared in 1876 as *The Lover's Revenge*.[113] Thigpen's home in Clinton has not survived but was described as a one-story house also used as a school for many years after her death.[114] She taught into her eighties, at least as late as 1900 according to the US census.[115] When she died at the age of ninety, *The Houston Home Journal* commented, "Miss Thigpen was indeed a remarkable woman, not physically robust but of exceeding great mental and spiritual strength."[116] Although she never married, Thigpen wrote of many things, including romantic love. For example, from her poem also titled *The Lover's Revenge*, she wrote:

> Once, again, among the flowers,
> Mantling o'er my own fair bowers,
> On a pleasant eve in May,
> I wandered, happy, light and gay;
> Soon a footstep that I knew,
> Brought my wayward friend to view,
> Who, on graceful knee low-bended,
> Kissed the hand I had extended.[117]

Thigpen did not attend Wesleyan, neither did seminary students Carrie Billingslea, Corinne Drewry, or Carrie Etheridge. At least, they did not graduate. Most likely, they came along too early to have participated in the relocation. One who did, however, was Catherine Lucinda Drewry, called "Lizzie" by her family and friends. She was described to be a "very serious-minded young lady" who was "petite and small of physique."[118] There is no greater example of the impact that a Clinton Female Seminary and Georgia Female College education made on the world through one exceptional student. Lizzie was born in Sparta, Hancock County, Georgia on November 11, 1823. When she was young, her family moved to Clinton and Lizzie was enrolled in Slade's seminary. She was there in 1838 when the school moved to Macon and was one of the thirty who formed the core and foundation of the new female college. She graduated with the A.B. degree on her eighteenth birthday in the second Georgia Female College commencement as part of the twenty-member Class of 1841.[119] She was later given an honorary MA degree by the college, then called Wesleyan. Her granddaughter Sallie Comer Lathrop, who also went to Wesleyan in 1888, claimed, one hundred years after the fact, that her grandmother had graduated in 1838, but Wesleyan classes did not begin until January 1839 and the first commencement was held in 1840.[120] According to college records, Lizzie graduated in 1841.[121] Several issues of *The Watchtower* say 1842 but this contradicts the earlier records. She married November 11 of the same year. She was united with a Jones County man named John Fletcher Comer who soon migrated with his bride to Barbour County, Alabama where he established the Old Spring Hill Plantation which eventually grew to over 32,000 acres and included its own sawmill, cotton gin, grist mill, and distillery which produced apple and peach brandy. John was elected to the Alabama state legislature in 1856 but died suddenly in 1857, leaving Lizzie as the thirty-four-year-old mother of six young boys. The Comers had eight children but Lizzie lost two daughters, each passing in their second years.

Demonstrating the fortitude that only comes from a serious, solid confidence based on faith and proper training, Lizzie managed to successfully develop her plantation, supervising their enslaved labor, and raising her six sons. Based on the success achieved by all six of these young men, Lizzie, without a doubt, poured her love and knowledge into each of them. Their lives are an emphatic testimony of the education a single mother received in both Clinton and Macon and passed on to her fatherless boys. In reviewing some of the greatest women in Alabama history in 1949, C. M. Stanley, editor of the

Alabama Journal, included Lizzie but was forced to admit she was a product of Georgia. "She was great through her own achievements as a plantation manager," he wrote, "but she was greater through the distinguished sons she brought into the world."[122] Arguably, it was not so much that "she brought [them] into the world" but that she brought them into the academy as she educated and inspired them with her intellect, vision, faith, and knowledge of the world to be bold, confident, and ambitious in humility and gratitude with poise and grace.

Her oldest son was Hugh Moss Comer (1842–1900) who became president of the Central Georgia Railroad and the Ocean Steamship Company, president of the Cotton Exchange in Savannah, director of the Banking Company of Georgia, co-founder of the Bibb Manufacturing Company, owner of the Old Town Plantation near Atlanta, and senior owner of the Comer, Hull, and Company, a manufacturer of fertilizer. His daughter Annie married Clark Howell, the longtime editor of *The Atlanta Constitution*.[123]

The second son, John Wallace Comer (1845–1900) was a civil war sergeant attached to the 27th and 57th Alabama Infantry Regiments, C.S.A. He was wounded in the *Battle of Atlanta* but was removed from the battlefield by his body servant Burrell, who saved his life. John consistently maintained that Burrell, sixteen, was a slave and not a soldier; yet after the war, Burrell received a soldier's pension from the State of Alabama. During Reconstruction, John and his brother Bragg were involved in the Barbour County, Alabama Election Riots of 1874. Old Spring Hill was used as a polling site, and after the Civil War, formerly enslaved persons, Republicans, were newly voting and winning elections because, one, they were the majority in the area, and two, most unreconstructed whites, Democrats, were not yet allowed to vote. The White League was formed and attacked the Old Spring Hill polling site on election day and destroyed the ballot box. They forcefully removed all Barbour County Republicans in public office and illegally installed Democrats by force. The local white judge, Elias M. Kells, was the target of the League, but his life was ultimately spared because he, John, and Bragg Comer were members of the local lodge of Free and Accepted Masons. Thus, besides being a white supremacist resistant to the changes brought on by the Civil War and Reconstruction, John was also one of the most successful Savannah cotton brokers, owner of the Eureka Iron Works, and president of the Cowikee Mills in Eufaula, Alabama.

George Legare Comer (1847–1933) was a law school graduate of the University of Georgia, one of Alabama's most prominent lawyers, a politician, director of the Eufaula Cotton Mills, part owner of the Bluff City Mills, owner and proprietor of the New St. Julien Hotel, and mayor of Eufaula, Alabama, 1882–84. During his term as mayor, George brought in the first public schools. He was also a Mason and a leader in his local Baptist church, serving as deacon and moderator of the association for several years.

Braxton Bragg Comer (1848–1927) attended the University of Alabama until it was burned during the Civil War. He continued to the University of Georgia and Emory Henry College in Virginia. Bragg was president of the City National Bank in Birmingham, AL, grain broker, planter, president of Avondale Mills, 1897–1927, a textile manufacturing company operating ten mills near Birmingham which, at the insistence of Bragg, employed women as well as men. He apparently also endorsed hiring children, whereas hundreds of them were also employed threading spindles throughout the Avondale Mills. He assisted his family in managing the Old Spring Hill Plantation before being elected, as a Democrat, governor of Alabama, 1907–11, and appointed US senator, 1920–5. Although Bragg lost votes in his election for governor due to his opposition to child labor laws, he proved to be the better candidate, especially in public speaking, than his opponent, Lt. Gov. Russell M. Cunningham. His commitment to reform railroads and education was popular, and he won the election with more than 85 percent of the vote.

Lizzie obviously thought much of Wesleyan even years after living in Alabama. "Wesleyan was the best school in the South," Sallie Comer Lathrop wrote, "Papa [Bragg Comer] always intended to send me there. He would not have considered sending me north of the Mason and Dixon line."[124] Today buildings at both the University of Alabama and Auburn University, a bridge in Scottsboro, AL, and various other locations and schools are named for Bragg.[125]

John Fletcher Comer was a planter in Midway, Alabama, and was the long-serving postmaster of James, Alabama.

Finally, Lizzie's "baby" was Edward Trippe Comer (1856–1927) who became president of the Bibb Manufacturing Company with plants in Macon, Columbus, and Porterdale, Georgia, and was a cattle broker in San Angelo, Texas. Edward owned the "beautiful and historic" Millhaven Plantation in Screven County, Georgia.[126] He was a good accountant and was thus immensely successful in accumulating wealth. In 1919, Edward gave Wesleyan College $50,000 in Liberty Bonds to establish the Comer Loan Fund in honor of his mother, then deceased about twenty years. This was followed by a second gift of $25,000 in 1926 to enhance the fund.[127] On the centennial anniversary of Lizzie's graduation in 1941, fourteen years after the death of Edward, interest earned from the Comer Loan Fund was used to endow a chair at the college known as the Catherine L. Comer Chair of Fine Arts.[128] By 1959, the Comer Loan Fund had grown to $77,818 despite funding the chair and giving scholarships to Wesleyan students.[129] By 1960, the fund was $80,447 and trustees added a second Catherine L. Comer Chair, this one of Painting and Drawing.[130]

In his will, Edward left fully one-third of his estate to a variety of educational charities in both Georgia and Alabama.[131] As his mother grew older, she gave the plantation to a granddaughter and began to visit her six sons in rotation. She died in Savannah, at the home of her oldest son, Hugh, March 7, 1898, in the "Comer" house which has survived at 2 Taylor Street East on Monterey Square and Bull Street, directly facing the monument and gravesite of Casimir Pulaski. "She was the highest type of the brave, resourceful women of the south," one wrote of Lizzie, "whose circumstances were so changed by the fortunes of war. No one can ever pay too much honor to the self-sacrificing widows who by sheer will power and love kept their families together after the death of their husbands."[132] She left many legacies and, not to be lost in the many, it is remarkable how many of her descendants as well as non-relatives attended Wesleyan through the years because of her influence, especially for an alumna who raised only boys. Her body was returned to Old Spring Hill on one of her son's trains and was buried next to her long-deceased husband. Several years after Lizzie's death and burial, a copy of *Elements of Logick, and Summary of General Principles of Different Modes of Reasoning* was found in the attic of her Old Spring Hill home.[133] On the inside cover is written, "Catharine L. Drewry, Georgia Female College, Jan. 4th, 1840."[134]

Henry Graybill Lamar also made the transition from Clinton to Macon. He was likely drawn to Macon, instead of Alabama, after 1823, as were so many others, when the frontier was pushed west, the city was organized, and businessmen began to relocate there from Clinton, only 13 miles away. In fact, a large portion of Jones County was taken by the state legislature to create Bibb County. Once the railroad came to Macon in the 1830s, the decline of Clinton was certain and the prospects in Bibb County's seat were far more promising. Macon had the river and the railroad; Clinton had neither. "A treaty having been executed," Macon Historian John Campbell Butler wrote, "by which the lands between the Flint and Chattahoochee rivers were ceded, the bridge over the Ocmulgee presented a stirring scene in the passage of large numbers of immigrants with wagons, stocks, and all their household effects, prospecting for a new settlement."[135] An area this small could not support two towns so large and Macon, at the geographic center of the state, had claimed the superior site. When the railroad did finally reach Jones County in 1886, it bypassed Clinton by two miles and gave rise to a new county seat town, the City of Gray founded in the 1850s. As the Jones County courthouse deteriorated in Clinton, it was rebuilt in 1905 in Gray which, with a population of 3,436, has not until today exceeded the 1825 population of Clinton. Samuel Griswold relocated his factory away from Clinton, as well, moving to a location, still in Jones County, but just ten miles east of Macon, on the railroad, and nearer the Ocmulgee River to a new settlement that came to be called Griswoldville. There, he built a new three-story, twenty-four room mansion, a church, houses for laborers (both slave and free), a sawmill, gristmill, and brickworks. In addition to making his famous cotton gins, he also built factories to produce furniture, candles, soap, and various other products. The "town" continues as an unincorporated community but was largely destroyed in the *Battle of Griswoldville* during the Civil War because Griswold had been making arms, primarily 3,700 revolvers, and ammunition for the Confederate Army.[136] The town was not rebuilt after the war.

Others were drawn in a significant migration of residents to the "New Purchase" in Butler County, Alabama, many before 1820 from Clinton, including Col. William Lee, a veteran of the Creek Wars and a retired state legislator, James O'Kelly Garrett, clerk of the inferior court, Attorney Absalom

Carter, Jesse Womack, Butler County's first sheriff, and several others. After the migration, Clinton was described as an unsustainable aristocratic enclave "surrounded by the estates of wealthy planters."[137] By 1888, Clinton had but one store.[138] By then, most people in Bibb County and the City of Macon were unaware that the tiny county seat next door in Jones County was the remaining artifact of such a rich early Georgia history.

The Atlanta Journal and Constitution recognized Clinton in 1975 as a pioneer Georgia town; however, in the education of women, it recognized its schoolmaster, whom they lost to Macon. They wrote, "On the frontier belt of Georgia, while the prints of the Indian's moccasins were still fresh in the soil, a far-sighted scholar who, with the ken of a prophet, could read the signs of the future, here opened an academy in the year 1828 [sic] and started a movement for women's intellectual emancipation."[139]

Perhaps this was prompted, and Slade made known in Macon, by an 1831 report by "some individuals who attended the examination of the Clinton Male Academy" to the *Macon Advertiser*.[140] The review was flattering to Slade and exalted the success of his seminary based on the proficiency of the students and the qualifications of their principal. "The method of teaching," they wrote, "is radically correct, and upon the most improved plan." They were confirming that they had seen pupils induced to cultivate their own minds rather than students who were lumbered with words, as was rarely seen in schools of the period but which had been the intended method of Slade. Practically, this meant that rather than making heavy use of lectures, students at the Clinton Female Seminary had been led to a curiosity about various subjects, it drove them to investigate the unknown, discovering truths for themselves as much as possible under Slade's guidance. The accomplishments of the academy caused the *Advertiser* to praise "our neighboring village" and "Mr. Slade" for his generosity to the "child of poverty" in Clinton.

The success at Clinton and the report initiated by the *Macon Advertiser* contributed to a decision of the University of Georgia trustees to grant Slade the degree of Master of Arts (now PhD) in August 1831 *ad eundem gradum*, or granting a degree to someone now living in the area who completed work elsewhere.[141] This early American frontier practice recognized a qualification

Slade already had but gave him the academic credentials he needed from the oldest and largest university in the state.

In December 1831, the Georgia Teachers Convention was organized in Milledgeville to establish a "system of education" in Georgia.[142] The idea that resulted in this organization originated with the faculty of Franklin College, the oldest and largest college in the University of Georgia. Named for American Founding Father Benjamin Franklin, this college includes the arts and sciences. Three leading advocates for education in Georgia, Rev. Dr. Alonzo Church, Rev. James Shannon, and William Letcher Mitchell gave the inaugural "Committee Address" in Milledgeville. The newly written constitution of the Teachers Convention was printed in several major newspapers throughout Georgia including *The Macon Advertiser* and *The Georgia Constitutionalist* of Augusta, and featured Slade's signature as treasurer of the organization.[143] Nineteen attended the first meeting in person and ten others sent their apologies for their absence "signaling" their intent to join the convention and attend as soon as possible, giving a total charter membership of twenty-nine. Besides Church, Shannon, Mitchell, and Slade, those in attendance included Gardner Kellogg (1730–1814), Rev. Dr. Carlisle Pollock Beman (b. 1797), and Rev. Dr. Robert C. Brown. Georgia Governor Wilson Lumpkin was made an honorary member with his permission. This prestigious assembly included Beman, the first president, who was the founder of Oglethorpe University, Church, the first vice president, who was the president of the University of Georgia, and Rev. George White, the second vice president, who was a historian and archaeologist from Savannah. Arguably, none were more significant in Georgia history than Mitchell who came to the meeting as the math tutor at the University of Georgia. He had, however, been involved in two previous educational movements in Georgia, the Presbyterian Educational Society, and the Athens and Clarke County Lyceum. He was close friends with the university president, Church, and he was secretary of the faculty there. An educator, lawyer, and engineer, Mitchell went on to serve as president of the UGA law school, 1867–82, after having been chairman of the Prudential Committee on the Board of Trustees for the university.[144] Mitchell later wrote his wife in 1850, "The longer I live the more I see the importance of education."[145] If Slade, thirty-two years old, had not met all these men before, he certainly impressed them in 1832 at the first meeting because they elected him treasurer and invited him to make the second annual convention speech.

Baptists eventually grew to become the largest Christian denomination in Georgia, and the Methodists were close behind, leading the Baptists with their educational programs. The Presbyterians, however, though the smaller denomination of the three, valued education most and demonstrated their convictions by promoting both male and female education.[146] Of course, all three denominations eventually had their colleges and universities throughout the state. Some of them, such as Mercer, Emory, and Oglethorpe, for example, were founded in this period, but Presbyterians were always an educated people, placing a high priority not only on an educated clergy but also on primary, secondary, and college education for their children, male and female. Col. Duncan Green Campbell, the Scots Highlander from North Carolina who started his own school for girls and then lobbied the Georgia legislature in the interest of female education, was a Presbyterian. Some criticized the tendency of wealthy philanthropists for endowing colleges and universities "while neglecting common school education" and charged this to be "a relic of British aristocracy."[147]

The founding members of the Teachers Association were a diverse though educated assembly. They were not all wealthy, but they were respected men of their far-flung communities. Article four of the constitution established the application fee to be one dollar and annual dues to be two dollars thereafter.[148] White traveled to Milledgeville from Savannah, Smith from Powelton, James Gordon Waddel of Augusta, F. D. Cummins from Macon, A. L. Lewis of Madison, and George P. Cooper from Twiggs County. Article three of the constitution declared the convention was for "all the teachers now in the State of Georgia."[149] They were a deeply religious group even though they were the leading educators in the State of Georgia at the time. Most of them were Presbyterians, including Beman, Mitchell, Waddel, and Church.[150] White was Episcopalian, Slade and Smith were Baptists, and Shannon was Methodist. Several were men who were born in the northern states but who had moved to Georgia at various times for various reasons, most looking to take advantage of newly opened lands and rapidly growing populations. Kellogg came from Hadley, Massachusetts, Beman was from Hampton, New York, and Church was from Vermont. Shannon was born in Ireland and migrated to Liberty County, Georgia in 1820. Both Beman and Church had graduated from Middlebury College in Middlebury, Vermont.

Beman was the first president of the Teachers Association, Slade was elected treasurer, and Brown served as secretary. The eight vice presidents were Church, White, Smith, Waddel, Cummins, Cooper, Lewis, and Alexander. There were also censors appointed, according to article six of the constitution whose responsibility was to "examine all candidates for membership and grant certificates of their moral and literary qualifications to teach."[151] Slade served as one of these censors who were granting Georgia's earliest form of teacher certification. If the censors found a member, once certified, guilty of dishonorable or immoral conduct, their task was to report the member to the regular annual meeting where the member faced the possibility of being removed from membership and loss of certification by a vote of two-thirds of those members present, according to article eight of the constitution.[152]

In the inaugural address, Church, Shannon, and Mitchell focused on the knowledge acquired by an individual through education and the difference it makes for that person and for civilization in general. "Knowledge is power," they said, "The slaves of ignorance ever have been, and they must continue to be, the slaves of tyrants. The strongholds of despotism are still the abodes of mental darkness, the dreary dungeons where the cheering beams of knowledge have not been permitted to enter."[153] They argued that even though the technology of the early nineteenth century was progressing rapidly, the benefits of new labor-saving machines were not benefiting uneducated people, yet the greatest luxury was an education itself. "What has been done," they asked, "to diffuse the richer blessings of knowledge, and to bring, to every man's door, the luxuries of a well cultivated mind?" The trio of speakers described the process of education as climbing a steep mountainside, which is itself littered with formidable obstacles, which led to knowledge at the summit. They claimed that the challenge was so daunting that most people simply refused to try. Only the wealthy with their social privileges, which they described as "golden ladders," were able to spend the necessary time to achieve this power known as knowledge. Speaking for society in general, they proclaimed, "We seem to consider the light of science as too bright for vulgar eyes, and her paths too devious and leading and too far away from the beaten track of common life to be trodden by the feet of the ignoble." Clearly, the Teachers Convention agreed that the light of science was not too bright for any eyes. Because too many working-class people labored in specialized tasks, many of the period had concluded that "a very moderate share of information is sufficient for the man who is to engage in the common pursuits of life." The members of the convention agreed that even the mechanics, farmers, and laborers deserved a chance at education and an opportunity to achieve knowledge. This was a minority opinion in Georgia at the time, but the leading teachers of 1831 were determined to change the expectations. Calling upon a spiritual context, and speaking to a significant number of ecumenical ministers, they declared, "Many pass through life unconscious of those powers that ally them to angels, and which, under prouder culture, would raise them to a proud height among their fellow men."

Church, Shannon, and Mitchell not only advocated the right of a "mechanic" to receive an education, they also spoke passionately about what the mechanics can teach everyone else. Imitating the seventeenth-century scholars of the Hartlib Circle, they explained, "The mechanics know things and this knowledge must be shared, known, and thus preserved. Should not every mechanic be able to illumine his shop with a torch lighted from the altar of science?" We can only assume these highly educated men of the nineteenth century were aware of and had read Milton, Boyle, or Hartlib. Gabriel Plattes, who wrote for the circle and Hartlib in particular, declared in 1641:

> Well, doe you know any man that hath any secrets, or good experiments? I will give him gold for them, or others as good in exchange, that is all the trade I have driven a long time, those riches are free from Customes and Impositions, and I have travelled through many Kingdomes, and paid neither fraight nor Custome for my wares, though I valued them above all the riches in the Kingdome.[154]

Based on several common themes and multiple parallels in presuppositions, logic, analysis, and conclusions, it seems that not only did the seventeenth-century empiricists leave a legacy of universal education for the common good and improvement of land, trades, and life in general, but there is undoubtedly a link between those scholars of the seventeenth century and these organized educators of early nineteenth-century Georgia. Both groups were committed evangelical Christians who saw no conflict between faith and science, religion and empiricism. All of them were affirming that not all education happens in the classroom. The "mechanic" is a student and a teacher simultaneously and may have more to teach a student about the sciences than many so-called teachers. Men who were forced to charge tuition for an education did so reluctantly because those who were passionately concerned about raising the level of knowledge in the population advocated universal public education made available to all with government appropriation in purpose-built schoolhouses staffed by trained and certified teachers. Georgia, however, was not ready for the state to build schoolhouses with tax money that was, widely considered, better spent on developing the land with infrastructure. One newspaper in Augusta declared, "It is no more the right nor duty of the state to set up schoolhouses and license teachers than it is to build factories and determine the qualifications of workmen."[155] Others were particularly opposed to education for women. "No, I will not give a dollar," one wealthy Georgian told a solicitor, "All a woman needs to know is how to read the New Testament, and to spin and weave clothing for her family."[156] Another responded to the possibility of marrying an educated woman and said, "I will not give you a cent for any such object. I would not have one of your graduates for a wife, for I could never even build a pig-pen without her criticizing it and saying it was not put up on mathematical principles." Convincing Georgians to support public education was one thing, recruiting them to sponsor a school for girls was another thing altogether.

The leaders of the Teachers Association knew Francis Bacon because they had read his *New Atlantis* just as most of them had a copy of *Utopia* by Thomas More on their library shelves. They knew, like their predecessors, that a utopia was not an impossible imagined society of an educated society exploring, discovering, inventing, understanding, and sharing knowledge, but was an achievable reality if only enough public support could be gathered. Science, rather than questioning God or the principles of his Word, was the empirical investigation of God's creation for the purpose of finding those secrets that could improve life for all people regardless of class, gender, occupation, or location. Sadly, nothing was said of the slaves of economic slavery who labored as property beneath the yoke of ownership. Many of the Teachers Convention members were slave owners themselves, and if they had thoughts about educating the enslaved, there was no mention of it in the 1831 inaugural address.

"How many sons and daughters of free born Americans are unable to read their native language!" they marveled in a time when the national literacy rate was approximately seventy-five percent but far lower in Georgia. Then Church, Shannon, and Mitchell linked illiteracy and lack of education to unfavorable results in public elections. "How many," they continued, "by their votes, elect men to legislate upon the dearest interests, which they themselves are unable to read even the proceedings of those legislators whom they have empowered to act for them!" In rousing the teachers to remedy this tragedy, they admitted, "Little has yet been effectually done." They declared that Georgia was behind its "sister states" before investigating in the speech for the responsible party. The Georgia legislature had made appropriations, usually against the will of the majority in the state, but the money had been spent on unqualified teachers who failed their students. Most voters of Georgia did not believe the taxpayers of Georgia were responsible for the education of children. "It was no more the duty of the state to regulate education," historian E. Merton Coulter wrote, "than it was to determine the number of stripes that should go into a yard of calico."[157] Yet even with the managed appropriation, according to the speakers at the Teachers Convention, those strongly in favor of public schools, "The idle, and the profane, and the drunken, and the ignorant are employed to impart to our children the first elements of knowledge." The precious funding was being wasted. Fundamental changes, therefore, had to be made in the primary schools before the convention could honestly lobby the state legislature for more funding. With the passion of an eighteenth-century Georgia revival preacher, and using the best oratory skills they themselves possessed, they concluded that the profession of teaching, which should be among the most admirable, honorable, and respected, "is but too often a term of reproach." Many "teachers" were incompetent, unqualified to teach but Georgia had no rules about who could teach and many communities, desperate to have a school for their children, had hired imposters, pretenders, and outright criminals who took the state's money with no accountability and spent it on their pleasures while leaving the children in their miserable pool of ignorance.

"Some more systematic plan should be adopted for the establishment and support of common schools, is a truth acknowledged by all," they said, and only a minority advocated that the advantages of an education should not be available to every child. Poor men could not afford to send their children to the private academies. Even though Slade agreed with almost everything in this inaugural address and although he often accepted students unable to pay, it was not fiscally possible for the Clinton Female Seminary or any other school to operate without paying students or public funds. So, the charter members of the Teachers Convention agreed that while teachers must be trained, certified, and subject to periodic review, teachers must be "sufficiently rewarded" or the best candidates would continue to avoid the profession for other more lucrative occupations. Secondly, "The opposition on the part of the parents to the exercise of salutary discipline over their children, is, without doubt, a cause that operates extensively in making the common schools generally as worthless as they are."[158] There followed a dramatic pause before sixteen teachers gave a generous applause. It seems the academics were "speaking to the choir," so to speak, selling universal public education to the citizens of the State of Georgia proved to be a far more difficult challenge. Georgians had little regard for education. It was "little more than a commodity," Coulter wrote, "a latest corn cure or some kind of Yankee notion—to be peddled around and hawked about by wandering nondescripts, often referred to as pedagogues."[159] This being true, it did not help that several of the founding members of the Georgia Teachers Convention were from the northern states including Kellogg, Beman, and Church. The problem was worse, however, because *The Augusta Chronicle* pointed out that even when public schools were available, free of charge for students of poor citizens, many poor but proud Georgians refused to send their children to school, counting education as charity. "Parents laboring under the mortifying affliction of genteel poverty would not send their children to a public school for fear of their being counted as charity scholars," they said.[160]

This same group was known in June 1832 as the Teacher's Society or Board of Education of the State of Georgia in the *Macon Messenger*, which reported the stated purpose of this organization was "to promote a diffusion of knowledge, especially among Teachers; to promote harmony and cooperation in their efforts, and uniformity in their modes of Teaching."[161] The members of this convention recognized Slade's qualifications and elected him their first treasurer and appointed him to deliver the keynote address to their first semi-annual state meeting, to be held six months later in Macon.[162] Slade was already one of nine censors appointed to examine teachers throughout Georgia who voluntarily requested certification. Slade's philosophy of education is revealed in the speech he delivered on June 11 at the Macon meeting. "Hence we find in every nation removed from a state of barbarism," he proclaimed, "and free from the debasing yoke of tyranny, education holds a prominent station, and may with truth and reason be considered the groundwork of every temporal blessing we enjoy."[163] Later, just before assuming his chair at the Georgia Female College, he added, "Classical studies and mathematical science are resorted to as the best method of training the mind."[164] He was affirming and expanding on the points made in Milledgeville by Church, Shannon, and Mitchell and promoting the Liberal Arts model that became the foundation of a meaningful degree earned by students nationwide until today.

Slade compared the standards of living in Ireland and Scotland for his American audience and concluded that education along with the "withering touch of superstition and popery" was the explanation for the "degraded and miserable condition of the lower class of the Irish" when compared to the "same ranks in Scotland."[165] Slade was a conservative evangelical Baptist minister living and ministering in early Georgia, so he was certainly not including any Bible-based Protestant faith in his "superstition and popery." Like the early modern fathers of modern science such as Hartlib and Boyle, Slade saw no contradictions between faith and science or empiricism and the Bible. He, also like the fathers, however, had no tolerance for superstitious beliefs that could not be supported by the scientific method or Catholic theology, which valued interpretation equal to Scripture itself. As for the difference between Ireland and Scotland, Slade did not mention, however, over six hundred years of English imperialism, plantation, and extirpation of the Emerald Isle or that Scots settlers had been used to colonize the Irish space created by the confiscation of land and systematic removal of the Irish people. "Ignorance is not bliss," he said, equating education with civilization. "Man is destined for nobler purposes," he said as he advocated for all manner of improvement through education. He gave his assessment of conditions in Georgia, including his opinions regarding the contemporary state of education in the state. "Knowledge is power," he said, as he called for statewide common standards and rigorous minimum qualifications for teachers. "We cannot accomplish everything at once," he admitted, "more than probable we may not live to witness the harvest of our labors." A prophet tested by time; he was correct.

As early as August 1831, as director of the Clinton Academy, Slade led a committee of five inferior court justices who called a meeting in Clinton as the first step in bringing the railroad to their town. The meeting was held on August 31 and delegates from Clinton were appointed to attend a "convention" in Eatonton, Georgia on the topic of "Internal Improvement."[166] Although the effort was ultimately not successful because it took so long to bring the railroad to central Georgia, it did prove that several forward-looking residents of Clinton realized the importance of this transportation and communications link to the future of their town. This and other records prove Slade was still serving as an inferior court judge while he was director of the academy.[167] The other justices were T. H. D. Weaver, Peter Northern, John R. Moore, and Batt Peterson, but Slade was consistently listed first in a non-alphabetical list.

Anne joined the Elim Baptist Church of Blountsville in April 1832; Slade followed six months later, was baptized by immersion outdoors, and was soon thereafter ordained to the ministry.[168] He was baptized and mentored by the pastor of Elim, Rev. Jesse Harrison Campbell, who remained in Jones County several years and was among those Georgia Baptists who assisted in forming the Southern Baptist Convention (SBC). Campbell later served on the newly organized Foreign Mission Board of the SBC.[169] Campbell's only daughter, Martha Jane, "Mattie," was another of Slade's students who transferred to the Georgia Female College. Furthermore, Slade performed Mattie's 1851 wedding in Stewart County when she married another Baptist minister, Robert G. Bennett.[170] Campbell was also a scholar. He authored a Baptist history entitled *Georgia Baptists: Historical and Biographical* in 1874.[171] Slade was first ordained a deacon and then as a minister. He explained his decision to his brother William, who he expected, along with "all of our relations," to "appear strange." "Four years past," he wrote, "it would have been highly incredible to me but thanks and praise to a good and gracious God that our minds have been so enlightened as to see our corrupt and depraved situation by nature and can utter insufficiency to escape the wrath of an angry God but by and through the merits of his beloved Son, Christ Jesus."[172] Slade reasoned with William as he reasoned within himself that he had considered himself a good, having the best morals before his conversion experience, and happy person, believing this to be the "best security" one can have. "But when I examined and scrutinized my heart by the holy and pure law of God," he added, "I discovered I had often transgressed it in thought and in deed and was therefore already in a state of condemnation." There is no record of what effect, if any, Slade's testimony had on William or any of their other relations in North Carolina, but here is an example of a good, moral person realizing, as the Bible says, sinners are saved by grace and not by their works.[173] "The question then arose," he continued, "in my mind how am I to escape the storm of wrath which ultimately awaits all the impenitent." The language indicated that Slade had been attending church with his wife since before April 1832, perhaps up to one year before his own commitment. He confessed it was his own obstinacy that kept him from joining the church with Anne and delayed for six months as he wrestled with "much anxiety and disquietude of mind." He recalled times of weeping and mourning in which he could only find relief in the "Gospel hope and comfort in believing that Christ had died for such a poor wretch as I was," he concluded.

As Anne had prayed for him, Slade committed in writing to pray for William. His wife's decision to join the church six months earlier is a testimony of her independence and her patience to wait for him is proof of her faith; her love for God and for her husband. As stated, this entire episode further explains Slade's philosophy of education and his peace with the compatibility of faith and science in education which, granted, may have been more culturally acceptable in the early eighteenth century but also so culturally objectionable to so many in the twenty-first century. Arguably, honestly comparing the accomplishments of Slade's students to those of today, it is difficult to make a successful argument that a modern faith-neutral philosophy has been an improvement in academic achievement.

As a highly educated man, Slade grew spiritually in discipleship within a short time. He was ordained to the Gospel ministry in Clinton, although he never pastored a church. He was, however, frequently invited to speak in churches across the region without remuneration. He supplied for absent pastors, and this gave him an opportunity to hear from Georgians across the state and speak to them, before and after his sermons, about general, public education. When the Clinton Baptist Church was incorporated in 1836, Slade, then a lawyer, deacon, and schoolmaster, handled the legal work, registering the church with the state. As a minister, Slade was not known as a great orator but was known to have preached throughout the area with effectiveness, earning the well-deserved respect of most who heard him. If he preached the way he taught, Slade was practical and methodical in his explanation of Scripture, making complicated theology simple for the listeners of all educational levels in the congregations. He conducted weddings and funerals as a judge in Jones County and as a minister in Muscogee County, but he was always, after 1832, a source of Christian encouragement to people of all denominations.[174] On January 30, 1830, he joined Caleb Elliot and Mrs. Mary King in marriage, and on November 27, 1831, he performed the ceremony for John Perry and Mrs. Susan Bowen, in their forties, and on November 1, 1832, he united Thomas H. Bray and Martha W. Smith.[175] Perry was originally from North Carolina, and by 1850 he had moved to Laurens County, Georgia, where he was a farmer, still married to Susan, and 63-year-old father of 17-year-old Teral Perry. Slade never sought to have his own church, and he never asked for money for anything he did as a minister. He supported the church with his tithing and attendance whenever he was at home and not speaking somewhere out of town.

Giving further insight into Slade's philosophy of education, in a letter to his brother in 1832, Slade declared, "If I may have but ten years of the life of a man of seventy to form his character, give me the first ten. This is the period when those impressions are to be made which are to determine his future welfare."[176] In the same letter, he announced that he had resigned his "situation in the Clinton Academy and have concluded to establish a female seminary upon my own footing and upon my own lot. While I was attending to a male school [The Clinton Academy], I discovered that my own daughters were shamefully neglected."[177] In acknowledging the birth of his brother William's son James,

Slade wrote he was "pleased to heart it, but time alone can determine whether he is to be a blessing or a curse" in words modern ears might think rude or offensive. "One thing, however, is certain," Slade explained, "a wise Providence has designed all our children for our peace, comfort, and happiness, and a failure in these respects is attributable to a defective education."[178] Slade may have been talking about all his "children," biological, adopted, or enrolled students, but the child in question was William's oldest child James Bog Slade who was born twenty-two months earlier in North Carolina who ultimately graduated from the University of North Carolina with his A.B. degree in 1852, came to Georgia to assist his uncle in the ministry of education, and married a student of the Slade Academy in Columbus, Mary Elizabeth Denson.[179] Slade performed their wedding ceremony "at the residence of the bride's father" December 16, 1856, and must have concluded William's son, having been educated, was a "blessing" to many including his parents, his wife, their five children as well as his friends and extended family.[180]

At the writing of this correspondence, Slade had exactly three daughters aged seven, six, and three. The Clinton Female Seminary opened the following January 1833 for girls eight and older with Slade as teacher and principal and Anne teaching music and painting. Anticipating financial needs and feeling the pressure of little funds, Slade concluded his letter to William with an appeal for his brother to pay what he owed to his older brother in Georgia. William did not respond to this gentle request, so Slade followed up with a stronger appeal in 1834 when the need was dire.[181] "The chief object of this communication is money," he began emphatically. "I should not," he continued, heretofore or at present make this request if I did not need it." "A check upon any good house whether in the Southern or Northern cities would answer my purpose," he concluded before announcing the birth of his sixth child, Thomas Bog Slade Jr., born on December 16 at Clinton. He later reported the seminary was prospering and that he expected a "considerable increase" in the 1835 term. He had completed a large building for accommodation, but clearly increased enrollment did not equate to greater financial stability, and he continued to struggle. As early as 1824, his first year in Georgia, Slade explained to his sister Elizabeth that he did not have enough money to travel back to North Carolina. "Eliza" was only twenty in 1824 and seemed to have been against Slade's leaving home. He would not consider "such an expensive journey."[182]

Anne's mother, Elizabeth Blount, who had moved to Clinton after the death of her husband in Blountsville, died on February 17, 1834, at the Slade home, and Slade served as a witness to her will along with Anne.[183] Assuming she had been living with the Slades since 1820, Elizabeth had thus also been living upstairs at the school for the last fourteen years of her life. She was forty-seven years old.[184]

In June 1835 at the end of the spring term, another "group" visited the Clinton Female Seminary identified in their report and in the subsequent *Georgia Messenger* article printed on the eighteenth only as "We." This was likely those residents of Macon, local businessmen, interested in starting a school for girls in their city. Perhaps they came, invited by Henry G. Lamar, to learn from Slade's organization, instruction, and requirements. It is more logical that this meeting was to recruit Slade as a consultant for founding the Georgia Female College of Macon. They must have offered to send him north on an exploratory mission to visit female institutions in the northern states and then relocate his successful seminary to Macon where it would become the foundation of the new college. The detailed financial accounting he provided after the trip and the scarcity of funds he proclaimed to possess before his departure indicate that his travel must have been funded by the wealthy local businessmen of Macon who became the original trustees of the college. There is no other obvious source from which Slade could have drawn the funds for which he kept a highly detailed accounting. No transcripts of these meetings have been found because the college was only an idea being discussed by a few city leaders in early 1835. It was not chartered in June 1835 and "the group" was not yet authorized to act as trustees of the same. Unless a personal correspondence supporting this theory is found, the specifics of how the Clinton Female Seminary became Wesleyan College will continue to be controversial with some discounting the role of Slade and the importance of the seminary but considering this research, far more likely and more difficult for the skeptics to dismiss.

Besides the notoriety Slade achieved through the Georgia Teachers Convention and previous press coverage in Macon and Athens, the unnamed visitors concluded that the seminary and Slade were deserving of greater commendation. They explained the discrepancy by noting Slade's aversion to "display and the popular resorts which are used [by some] to attract publicity."[185] They declared that while this was a worthy characteristic of Slade, he had done the public an injustice to keep so many residents ignorant of the fact that "one of the best schools for the instruction of females is to be found in the pleasant and healthy village of Clinton." The anonymous visitors counted sixty young girls between eight and fourteen years of age having mastered a variety of subjects, including science and music, above their expectations. They praised his practical methods of instruction and, in the author's opinion, decided to wholly incorporate the Clinton Seminary into their new Macon college because of this visit to Clinton in 1835, despite the fact there was already another female seminary operating in Macon. The Macon Female Seminary was not merged into the Georgia Female College and no faculty came to the new school from there. Perhaps that was the school they meant when they said "display and the popular resorts which are used [by some] to attract publicity." The "Wesleyan" trustees, did, however, recruit faculty, staff, administration, and students of the Clinton Female Seminary wholesale to relocate to Macon and become the foundation of the Georgia Female Academy, which soon became Wesleyan College. There was a divergence of academic rigor and integrity and these men were wise enough to know the difference.

The Georgia Female Academy was chartered December 23, 1836, but classes did not begin until January 9, 1839, so Slade continued operations of the Clinton Female Seminary for three and one-half years, seven full semesters more, until Fall 1838, knowing, along with everyone else, that they were moving to Macon for Spring 1839 when classes began there. In the meantime, a board of trustees formed and Slade traveled to New England for the benefit of both schools, learning from the best educators in New York, Massachusetts, and Connecticut and purchasing books, maps, and scientific instruments he intended to use in Clinton as well as Macon. Construction began and Slade, along with his family, staff, and thirty students, packed their wagons during Christmas 1838. They were joined by three other faculty members and thirty other students, and the next chapter of Slade's career began. Incidentally, Slade left these instruments, purchased in New York during his exploratory fact-finding trip to the north, at Wesleyan when he resigned even though he was going directly to Penfield, Georgia, to start a new school, because they were not his to keep; they belonged to Wesleyan and remain there to this day on public display in the Monroe Science Center precisely because they were paid for by the Wesleyan trustees.

The Clinton Female Seminary was not without controversy. At the end of the Fall term, 1836, Slade was accused by some parents of neglecting the character of his pupils and of an instance of wanton cruelty. Rumors had reached the neighboring counties and had the potential of ruining Slade's reputation and undermining enrollment at the seminary. One anonymous student was identified as the principal accuser. A "respectable portion of the citizens of the town of Clinton" attended a public meeting which Slade organized to voice his explanations and statement of facts in response to these charges on November 28. Dr. Abner H. Flewellen was "called to the chair" of this meeting. An investigation was made to confirm Slade's statements and, as a result, resolutions were adopted to affirm Slade and dismiss the charges. The charges were found to be "untrue" to the satisfaction of all, and Slade's abilities and "faithfulness as an instructor" were affirmed with the "utmost confidence." As this episode was resolved, he was commended by the assembly of parents and residents of the town for his "ability and faithfulness as an instructor." Flewellen signed his name to the report of the meeting, which was thereafter published in the *Georgia Messenger*. [186]

There is some limited evidence of a new school for girls formed in Clinton after the departure of Slade and the Clinton Female Seminary, founded to educate the younger girls of the area and act, in today's language, as a "feeder" school for the Georgia Female Academy. The known students all came from Jones and Twiggs counties. Nothing else is known of how long this school lasted or when it ceased to offer classes, but for the record, that school is not a continuation of the Clinton Female Seminary, which Slade closed absolutely at the end of 1838. He sold the building and moved everything to Macon, including part of his staff and half his students. Any new girls' school in Clinton after 1838 was a new foundation and, by any account, did not last more than a few years. As Clinton declined, the need for a school and the ability of the area to support it was reduced.

In conclusion, there were 14,000 Creek Indians living in Georgia in 1837 and Indian removal became an occasion for Slade to inadvertently explain his later move to Columbus even before he migrated to Macon and Penfield. "The State of Georgia has lately by treaty with the Creek Indians," he wrote, "acquired a vast extent of territory lying between the Flint and Chattahoochee Rivers and have now completely extinguished the Indian title to all the land which they possessed within the limits of this state."[187] He further revealed his political ideologies when he rebuked his sister for being on the "wrong side of politics," of people outside of Georgia not properly understanding the views of Georgians, and praising Governor Troup for successfully standing up to US president John Quincy Adams over the issue of Indian removal.[188] Troup threatened to use the Georgia Militia to prevent the president from interfering with the removal of the Creeks, prompting Slade to write, "I am more and more pleased with Georgia."[189] The *Second Treaty of Indian Springs* was, in fact, popular in Georgia and Troup was re-elected in Georgia's first popular election for governor in 1825. Not without significant controversy, however, including the murder of Creek Chief William McIntosh, the treaty was signed by six Creek chiefs. Troup also supported public education and, perhaps because of these issues, Slade supported Troup.

Notes

1 L. E. Roberts, "Educational Reform in Ante-Bellum Georgia," *The Georgia Review*, 16:1 (Spring 1962): 68.
2 Ibid., 69.
3 Ibid., 72.
4 *The Macon Telegraph* (December 11, 1830).
5 George H. Slappey, "Early Foundations of Georgia's System of Common School Education," *The Georgia Historical Quarterly* 14:2 (June 1930): 139.
6 *History of the Baptist Denomination in Georgia: With Biographical Compendium and Portrait Gallery of Baptist Ministers and other Georgia Baptists* (Atlanta: J. P. Harrison & Co., 1881), p. 483.
7 M. D. Slade, Letter to William Slade, June 27, 1823, Slade Family Papers, Box 2 (1821–1824).

8 *Georgia Marriages, 1699-1944*.
9 Georgia, US, *County Marriage Records, 1828-1978*, Jones County (August 10, 1826), Morrow, GA: Georgia Archives.
10 Alabama Department of Archives and History; Montgomery, AL; Alabama Surname Files; Box or Film Number: M87-0733.
11 Alfred M. Slade to William Slade, personal letter (September 2, 1824), *Slade Family Papers*.
12 Thomas Bog Slade to William Slade, personal letter (April 3, 1825), *Slade Family Papers, 1751-1929*, David M. Rubenstein Rare Book and Manuscript Library, Duke University, p. 1.
13 *The Georgia Messenger*, newspaper (Macon, GA), April 7, 1824, p. 3 and April 14, 1824, p. 1.
14 Janet Slade, Letter to William Slade, May 29, 1824, *Slade Family Papers*, Box 2 (1821-1824).
15 Thomas Bog Slade to William Slade (June 23, 1825), *Slade Family Papers*.
16 Thomas Bog Slade, Letter to William Slade, May 13, 1827, *Slade Family Papers*, Rubenstein Library, Duke University. See also *The Georgia Messenger* (May 17, May 24, June 7, June 14, June 28, July 5, July 11, July 18, August 8, and August 15, 1826), p. 4. Thomas Bog Slade, Letter to William Slade, December 22, 1832, Slade Family Papers.
17 *History of the Baptist denomination in Georgia: With Biographical Compendium and Portrait Gallery of Baptist Ministers and other Georgia Baptists* (Atlanta: J. P. Harrison & Co., 1881), p. 188.
18 CPI Inflation Calculator.
19 Thomas Bog Slade to William Slade, personal letter (June 23, 1825), *Slade Family Papers*.
20 Thomas Bog Slade, Letter to William Slade, December 22, 1832, *Slade Family Papers*.
21 Thomas Bog Slade, *Autobiography of Thomas Bog Slade*, Southern Historical Collection 1837-1846, 2683-z, University of North Carolina, p. 3.
22 Kevin Kokomoor, "Creeks, Federalists, and the Idea of Coexistence in the Early Republic," *Journal of Southern History* 81:4 (2015): 803-42.
23 William Lamar Cawthon, *Clinton: County Seat on the Georgia Frontier 1808-1821*, MA Thesis (University of Georgia, 1984), p. 4.
24 Ibid., p. 5.
25 Ibid., p. 9.

26 Russell Brown, "David Emanuel," *New Georgia Encyclopedia* (September 2, 2016). See also Kenneth Coleman and Charles Stephen Gurr, eds., "David Emanuel," *Dictionary of Georgia Biography* (Univ. of GA Press, 1983); James F. Cook, *The Governors of Georgia, 1754–2004*, 3rd ed. (Mercer Univ. Press, 2005); Albert M. Hillhouse, *A History of Burke County, Georgia, 1777–1950* (Spartanburg, 1950); Lucian Lamar Knight, *Georgia's Landmarks, Memorials, and Legends* (Atlanta: Byrd Printing, 1913); William J. Northern, *Men of Mark in Georgia*, 7 vols. (Spartanburg, 1907); and George White, *Historical Collections of Georgia* (Danielsville, GA: Heritage Papers, 1854).

27 William Lamar Cawthon, *Clinton: County Seat on the Georgia Frontier 1808–1821*, MA Thesis (University of Georgia, 1984), p. 11. See also *The Georgia Messenger* (June 18, 1835), p. 3.

28 Ibid., pp. 18–19.

29 *An Historical Guide to Clinton, Georgia: An Early Nineteenth Century County Seat* (Old Clinton Historical Society, 1975), p. 1.

30 Ibid.

31 William Lamar Cawthon, *Clinton: County Seat on the Georgia Frontier 1808–1821*, MA Thesis (University of Georgia, 1984), p. 22.

32 Ibid., p. v.

33 Ibid., p. 145.

34 Ibid., p. 152.

35 Ibid., pp. 87–8.

36 Ibid., p. 104.

37 Thomas Bog Slade to William Slade, personal letter (May 13, 1827), *Slade Family Papers*, Rubenstein Library, Duke University.

38 William Lamar Cawthon, *Clinton: County Seat on the Georgia Frontier 1808–1821*, MA Thesis (University of Georgia, 1984), p. 125.

39 William Bartram, *Travels of William Bartram* (New Haven, 1958); Kenneth Coleman, ed., *A History of Georgia* (Univ. of GA, 1977); Augustin Smith Clayton, *A Compilation of the Laws of the State of Georgia, 1800–1810* (Adams and Duyckinck, 1813); James C. Bonner, *Milledgeville: Georgia's Antebellum Capital* (Athens, 1978); US Congress, Senate and House of Representatives, *American State Papers, Indian Affairs* (Washington: Gales and Seaton, 1832); *Augusta Chronicle and Sentinel*, 1837–1838, newspaper (Augusta, GA); John Goff, *Placenames in Georgia* (Univ. of GA, 1975); and Kenneth Coleman and Charles Stephen Gurr, *Dictionary of Georgia Biography* (Univ. of GA, 1983).

40 Thomas Bog Slade, Letter to William Slade, April 3, 1825, Slade Family Papers, Box 3 (1825). See also Auguste Levasseur, *Lafayette in America: 1824 and 1825*, Alan R. Hoffman, trans. (Manchester, NH: Lafayette Press, Inc., 2006).
41 Thomas Bog Slade, Letter to William Slade, April 3, 1825, Slade Family Papers, Box 3 (1825).
42 Anne Firor Scott, "What, Then, is the American: This New Woman?" *The Journal of American History* 65:3 (December 1978): 692.
43 Carolyn White Williams, *The History of Jones County, Georgia 1807–1907* (Macon: J.W. Burke, 1957), p. 236.
44 *The Georgia Journal*, newspaper (Milledgeville, 1812).
45 William Lamar Cawthon, *Clinton: County Seat on the Georgia Frontier 1808–1821*, MA Thesis (University of Georgia, 1984), p. 78.
46 1820 US Census, Clinton, Jones County.
47 Thomas Bog Slade to William Slade, personal letter (April 3, 1825), *Slade Family Papers*.
48 William Lamar Cawthon, Clinton: County Seat on the Georgia Frontier 1808–1821, MA Thesis (University of Georgia, 1984), p. 135.
49 Second Minute Book, Jones Superior Court (February 1808–October 1809), Office of the Clerk of the Superior Court, Jones County Courthouse.
50 Benjamin Brawley, "Lorenzo Dow," *The Journal of Negro History* I (1916): 265.
51 *The Georgia Journal*, newspaper (November 28, 1810).
52 Francis Bacon Throwbridge, *The Champion Genealogy: A History of the Descendants of Henry Champion of Saybrook and Lyme, CT Together with Some Account of Other Families of the Name*, vol. I (1891), p. 3.
53 William Lamar Cawthon, Clinton: County Seat on the Georgia Frontier 1808–1821, MA Thesis (University of Georgia, 1984), p. 139.
54 Carolyn White Williams, *The History of Jones County, Georgia 1807–1907* (Macon: J.W. Burke, 1957) and William Bragg, "Jones County," in the *New Georgia Encyclopedia*.
55 Richard Newton Smith, Jr, *Slade Family Roots In North Carolina and Georgia* (New Bern, NC, 2008).
56 Ibid.
57 Deed Book N, Jones Co., GA, p. 44. See also Thomas Bog Slade to Elizabeth Slade, personal letter (1824–1825), *Slade Family Papers*.
58 Carolyn White Williams, The History of Jones County, Georgia 1807–1907 (Macon: J.W. Burke, 1957), p. 286.

59 Ibid., p. 287.
60 S. H. Griswold, *Jones County News*, September 10, 1908.
61 Thomas Bog Slade to William Slade, personal letter (December 22, 1832), p. 2.
62 Carolyn White Williams, *The History of Jones County, Georgia 1807–1907* (Macon: J.W. Burke, 1957), p. 860.
63 Ibid., p. 961.
64 Georgia, US *Marriage Records from Select Counties, 1828–1978*, Jones County, Book B, 1821–1936.
65 Bunkley Family Bible, Tallahassee, FL and *An Historical Guide to Clinton, Georgia: An Early Nineteenth Century County Seat* (Old Clinton Historical Society, 1975), p. 2.
66 A. L. Hull, *A Historical Sketch of the University of Georgia* (Atlanta: The Foote and Davies Co., 1894), p. 227; *The Athenian* (August 9, 1831), p. 2; and *The Macon Advertiser* (June 28, 1831), p. 3, and (August 12, 1831), p. 3.
67 *Chronicle and Sentinel, 1838–1838* (Augusta, GA, 20 Jan 1838), p. 2.
68 Ibid.
69 *Central Register of Convicts*, 1817–1976. Series 21/3/27. Georgia State Archives, Morrow, Georgia, p. 33.
70 Ibid., p. 35.
71 John G. Polhill, "Pleadings and Evidence in The Trial of Elijah Barber, Otherwise Called Jesse L. Bunkley, for Cheating and Swindling," in *The Making of the Modern Law: Trials, 1600–1926* (Milledgeville, GA: The Federal Union Office, 1838).
72 Carolyn White Williams, *The History of Jones County, Georgia 1807–1907* (Macon: J.W. Burke, 1957), p. 285.
73 William E. Dawson, *Compilation of the Laws of the State of Georgia Passed by the General Assembly Since the Year 1819 to the Year 1829 Inclusive*, no. 10 (Milledgeville, GA: Grantland and Orme, 1831), pp. 7–8.
74 *The Georgia Journal*, newspaper (March 27, 1816).
75 William Lamar Cawthon, *Clinton: County Seat on the Georgia Frontier 1808–1821*, MA Thesis (University of Georgia, 1984), pp. 131–2.
76 Ibid., pp. 132.
77 Record Book A, *Inventory and Appraisement of Estates, 1809–1818*, Estate of Eliza Hooten, Office of the Probate Judge, Jones County Courthouse, p. 196.
78 William Lamar Cawthon, *Clinton: County Seat on the Georgia Frontier 1808–1821*, MA Thesis (University of Georgia, 1984), p. 60.

79 *The Georgia Journal*, newspaper (July 4, 1820) and *The Georgia Statesman*, newspaper (January 3, 1826).
80 William Lamar Cawthon, *Clinton: County Seat on the Georgia Frontier 1808–1821*, MA Thesis (University of Georgia, 1984), p. 135.
81 *William E. Dawson, Compilation of the Laws of the State of Georgia Passed by the General Assembly Since the Year 1819 to the Year 1829 Inclusive, no. 10* (Milledgeville, GA: Grantland and Orme, 1831), pp. 7–8.
82 Thomas Bog Slade to William Slade, personal letter (May 13, 1827), *Slade Family Papers*, Rubenstein Library, Duke University.
83 Carolyn White Williams, *The History of Jones County, Georgia 1807–1907* (Macon: J.W. Burke, 1957), p. 285.
84 Georgia Historical Commission, "Clinton Female Seminary," 1956, Bronze Plaque, Clinton, GA.
85 John Campbell Butler, *Historical Record of Macon and Central Georgia*, vol. IV (J. W. Burke, 1958), p. 95.
86 Newspaper Extractions from the Northeast, 1704–1930, *Columbian Centinel*, 1790–1840, newspaper (Boston, MA) and S. H. Griswold, *Jones County News*, September 10, 1908, p. 2.
87 1860 US Census and Carolyn White Williams, *The History of Jones County, Georgia 1807–1907* (Macon: J.W. Burke, 1957), p. 291.
88 Georgia, Office of the Governor. Returns of qualified voters under the Reconstruction Act, 1867. Georgia State Archives, Morrow, Georgia.
89 S. H. Griswold, *Jones County News*, September 10, 1908.
90 John C. Fredriksen, *American Military Leaders*, vol. 1. (Bloomsbury, 1999), p. 403.
91 Allen C. Guelzo, *Gettysburg: The Last Invasion* (Vintage/ Random House, 2014), pp. 207–8.
92 *An Historical Guide to Clinton, Georgia: An Early Nineteenth Century County Seat* (Old Clinton Historical Society, 1975), p. 4.
93 S. H. Griswold, *Jones County News*, September 10, 1908.
94 Carolyn White Williams, *The History of Jones County, Georgia 1807–1907* (Macon: J.W. Burke, 1957), p. 285.
95 *History of the People of Jones County, Georgia*, Alphabetized 1836 Tax Digest, p. 61.
96 Thomas Bog Slade, *The Macon Messenger*, 1830s, in *An Historical Guide to Clinton, Georgia: An Early Nineteenth Century County Seat* (Old Clinton Historical Society, 1975), p. 4.

97 *The Georgia Messenger*, newspaper (December 1, 1836), p. 3.
98 *The Georgia Messenger*, newspaper (June 18, 1835), p. 3.
99 *The Georgia Messenger*, newspaper (June 18, 1835), p. 3.
100 Thomas Bog Slade, *The Macon Messenger*, 1830s, in *An Historical Guide to Clinton, Georgia: An Early Nineteenth Century County Seat* (Old Clinton Historical Society, 1975), p. 289.
101 Handbill, Office of the Ordinary of Jones County, 1837.
102 S. H. Griswold, *Jones County News*, September 10, 1908.
103 *The Newnan Herald*, newspaper, 1865–1887 (May 12, 1885), p. 3. See also Georgia, US, *Property Tax Digests, 1793–1892* and *Freedman Tax List, 1881–1887*, Heard and Troup counties, GA (Morrow, GA: The Georgia Archives).
104 Georgia, US, *Returns of Qualified Voters and Reconstruction Oath Books, 1867–1869* (The Georgia Archives), p. 438.
105 *The Georgia Messenger*, newspaper (July 17, 1834).
106 Thomas Bog Slade to William Slade, personal letter (April 3, 1825), *Slade Family Papers*.
107 Thomas Bog Slade to William Slade, personal letter (June 23, 1825), *Slade Family Papers*.
108 Ibid.
109 Thomas Bog Slade to William Slade, personal letter (April 3, 1825), *Slade Family Papers*.
110 Thomas Bog Slade to Elizabeth Jane Slade, personal letter (April 25, 1825), *Slade Family Papers*.
111 Thomas Bog Slade to William Slade, personal letter (June 23, 1825), *Slade Family Papers*.
112 Thomas Bog Slade to Elizabeth Jane Slade, personal letter (April 25, 1825), *Slade Family Papers*.
113 Jane Thigpen, *The Lover's Revenge and Other Poems* (Macon: J.W. Burke & Company Publishers, 1876).
114 *An Historical Guide to Clinton, Georgia: An Early Nineteenth Century County Seat* (Old Clinton Historical Society, 1975), p. 4.
115 1900 US Census, Davidson, Jones Co., GA, roll 207, Enumeration Dist. 63, p. 141.
116 *The Houston Home Journal*, newspaper (February 12, 1914).
117 Jane Thigpen, *The Lover's Revenge and Other Poems* (Macon: J.W. Burke & Company Publishers, 1876), p. 14.

118 C. M. Stanley, "The Petite Mother of Six Distinguished Sons," *The Alabama Journal* (Montgomery, 1949).

119 "Class Notes," *The Wesleyan Alumnae* (Wesleyan College, 1941), p. 17.

120 Sallie B. Comer Lathrop, *The Comer Family Goes to Town* (Birmingham Printing Co., 1942), p. 59.

121 *Catalogue of the Trustees, Faculty, Alumni and Students of the Wesleyan Female College Macon, GA, 1850–1915*, annual eds. (Benjamin F. Griffin, 1851–1915).

122 C. M. Stanley, "The Petite Mother of Six Distinguished Sons," *The Alabama Journal* (Montgomery, 1949).

123 "Clark Howell Married: Wedded to a Daughter of the Late President Comer of the Georgia Central," *New York Times* (July 13, 1900).

124 Sallie B. Comer Lathrop, *The Comer Family Goes to Town* (Birmingham Printing Co., 1942), p. 59.

125 Anne Kendrick Walker, *Braxton Bragg Comer: His Family Tree* (Richmond: The Dietz Press, 1947).

126 C. M. Stanley, "The Petite Mother of Six Distinguished Sons," *The Alabama Journal* (Montgomery, 1949).

127 "Alumnae Notes," *The Watchtower* 1:15 (Wesleyan College, 1924): 2; "Fund in Honor of His Mother Received Here," *The Watchtower* 4:3 (Wesleyan College, 1926): 1; and "Student Loan Funds Help College Girls: Money Given for This Purpose Throughout Year," *The Watchtower* 13:18 (Wesleyan College, 1936): 8. See also "The Catharine L. Comer Chair of Fine Arts," *The Wesleyan Alumnae* (Wesleyan College, 1941): 3.

128 Sallie B. Comer Lathrop, *The Comer Family Goes to Town* (Birmingham Printing Co., 1942), p. 59.

129 "Loan Funds," *Bulletin of Wesleyan College, Macon, Georgia: The Liberal Arts College and the School of Fine Arts* (Wesleyan College, 1959), p. 100.

130 "Endowment and Aid Funds," *Bulletin of Wesleyan College, Macon, Georgia: The Liberal Arts College and the School of Fine Arts* (Wesleyan College, 1959), pp. 102, 108.

131 "The Catharine L. Comer Chair of Fine Arts," *The Wesleyan Alumnae* (Wesleyan College, 1941), p. 3.

132 Anne Kendrick Walker, *Backtracking in Barbour County: A Narrative of the Last Alabama Frontier* (Richmond: The Dietz Press, 1941).

133 Levi Hedge, *Elements of Logick, and Summary of General Principles of Different Modes of Reasoning* (Kessinger, 1824).

134 C. M. Stanley, "The Petite Mother of Six Distinguished Sons," *The Alabama Journal* (Montgomery, 1949).

135 John Campbell Butler, *Historical Record of Macon and Central Georgia*, vol. IV (J. W. Burke, 1958), p. 95.

136 Kenneth K. Krakow, *Georgia Place-Names: Their History and Origins* (Macon, GA: Winship Press, 1975), p. 98.

137 *An Historical Guide to Clinton, Georgia: An Early Nineteenth Century County Seat* (Old Clinton Historical Society, 1975), p. 2.

138 William Lamar Cawthon, *Clinton: County Seat on the Georgia Frontier 1808–1821*, MA Thesis (University of Georgia, 1984), p. v.

139 Lucian Lamar Knight, "A Town Progress Passed By," *The Atlanta Journal & Constitution* (June 22, 1975), pp. 12–14 and 19–20.

140 "Education," *Macon Advertiser* (June 28, 1831), p. 3.

141 "Athens, Aug. 9, 1831," *The Athenian* (August 9, 1831), p. 2 and "Georgia University," *The Macon Advertiser* (August 12, 1831), p. 3.

142 *Macon Advertiser* (May 11, 1832), p. 3.

143 Ibid and The Georgia Constitutionalist, v. xi, no. 9 (January 10, 1834), p. 1.

144 J. Patrick McCarthy, Jr., "Commercial Development and University Reform in Antebellum Athens: William Mitchell as Entrepreneur, Engineer, and Educator," *The Georgia Historical Quarterly* 83:1 (Spring 1999): 1–28.

145 William Mitchell to Sarah Mitchell, Athens, 17 Mar 1850, *William Letcher Mitchell Papers*, Southern Historical Collection, University of North Carolina Library, Chapel Hill, NC.

146 Florence Fleming Corley, "The Presbyterian Quest: Higher Education for Georgia Women," *American Presbyterians* 69:2 (Summer 1991): 83.

147 George H. Slappey, "Early Foundations of Georgia's System of Common School Education," *The Georgia Historical Quarterly* 14:2 (June 1930): 144.

148 Macon Advertiser (May 11, 1832), p. 3 and The Georgia Constitutionalist, v. xi, no. 9 (January 10, 1834), p. 1.

149 Ibid.

150 James Stacy, *A History of the Presbyterian Church in Georgia* (Elberton, 1912).

151 *Macon Advertiser* (May 11, 1832), p. 3 and The Georgia Constitutionalist, v. xi, no. 9 (January 10, 1834), p. 1.

152 Ibid.

153 Ibid.

154 Gabriel Plattes, Printed Pamphlet, *A Description of the Famous Kingdome of Macaria* (Samuel Hartlib, 1641).
155 *The Southern Eclectic*, newspaper (February 1854).
156 Frances Rees, "A History of Wesleyan Female College from 1836 to 1874" (M.A. thesis, Emory Univ., 1935), p. 11.
157 E. Merton Coulter, "A Georgia Educational Movement During the Eighteen Hundred Fifties," *The Georgia Historical Quarterly* 9:1 (March 1925): 1.
158 *Macon Advertiser* (May 11, 1832), p. 3 and The Georgia Constitutionalist, v. xi, no. 9 (Janury 10, 1834), p. 1.
159 E. Merton Coulter, "A Georgia Educational Movement During the Eighteen Hundred Fifties," *The Georgia Historical Quarterly* 9:1 (March 1925): 1.
160 George H. Slappey, "Early Foundations of Georgia's System of Common School Education," *The Georgia Historical Quarterly* 14:2 (June 1930): 147.
161 *The Georgia Messenger* (June 2, 1832), p. 3.
162 *Georgia Courier* (January 5, 1832), p. 2; "Teacher's Convention," *Georgia Messenger* (June 2, 1832), p. 3; and *Macon Advertiser* (December 30, 1831), p. 3.
163 "An Address," *Georgia Messenger* (June 21, 1832).
164 Thomas Bog Slade, *Autobiography of Thomas Bog Slade*, Southern Historical Collection 1837–1846, 2683-z, University of North Carolina, p. 6.
165 Ibid.
166 *The Macon Advertiser and Agricultural and Mercantile Intelligencer*, newspaper (August 23, 1831), p. 3.
167 *The Georgia Messenger*, newspaper (August 20, 1831).
168 Thomas Bog Slade, Letter to William Slade, December 22, 1832, Slade Family Papers and Thomas Bog Slade, *Autobiography of Thomas Bog Slade*, Southern Historical Collection 1837–1846, 2683-z, University of North Carolina, p. 2.
169 *History of the Baptist Denomination in Georgia: With Biographical Compendium and Portrait Gallery of Baptist Ministers and other Georgia Baptists* (Atlanta: J. P. Harrison & Co., 1881), pp. 206, 484.
170 County Marriage Records, 1828–1978. The Georgia Archives, Morrow, Georgia.
171 Jesse H. Campbell, *Georgia Baptists: Historical and Biographical* (Macon: J. W. Burke & Co., 1874).
172 Thomas Bog Slade, Letter to William Slade, December 22, 1832, Slade Family Papers, p. 3.
173 *Ephesians* 2:8-9 and *Romans* 6:23.

174 Thomas Bog Slade, Letter to William Slade, December 22, 1832, Slade Family Papers.
175 Georgia, US, *Marriage Records from Select Counties, 1828–1978*, p. 860.
176 Thomas Bog Slade, Letter to William Slade, December 22, 1832, Slade Family Papers, pp. 1–2.
177 Ibid., p. 2.
178 Ibid., p. 1.
179 1850 US Census.
180 *Daily Columbus Enquirer* (December 18, 1856), p. 3.
181 Thomas Bog Slade, Letter to William Slade, December 24, 1834, Slade Family Papers.
182 Thomas Bog Slade, Letter to Elizabeth Slade, 1824–1825, Slade Family Papers.
183 *The Georgia Messenger*, newspaper (February 20, 1834).
184 Jones County Extracts, vol. II, 1832–1888.
185 *The Georgia Messenger*, newspaper (June 18, 1835), p. 3.
186 "Communicated," *Georgia Messenger* (December 1, 1836), p. 3.
187 Thomas Bog Slade, Letter to William Slade, April 3, 1825, Slade Family Papers, Box 3 (1825) and Thomas Bog Slade, *Autobiography of Thomas Bog Slade*, Southern Historical Collection 1837–1846, 2683-z, University of North Carolina, p. 2.
188 Thomas Bog Slade, Letter to Elizabeth Slade, April 25, 1825, Slade Family Papers, Box 3 (1825).
189 Thomas Bog Slade, Letter to William Slade, April 3, 1825, Slade Family Papers, Box 3 (1825).

3

The Journey North

> The pleasure of traveling consists in the obstacles, the fatigue, and even the danger.
>
> Théophile Gautier

As late as June 1, 1837, Slade was advertising his Clinton Female Seminary in the *Georgia Messenger*, but on the same day, he was announcing that his Principal Music Teacher, Miss Maria T. Lord, would be teaching at the Female Academy in Macon.[1] Less than two months later, July 26, Slade left Plymouth, North Carolina, on a fact-finding trip to New England with the purpose of visiting and learning from established female colleges of the northern states. It is proven by this research that Slade was already in conversation with those residents of Macon, Georgia, who were in the process, from 1836, of organizing Georgia Female College and that he did not take the trip of his own initiative but for the benefit of the college. He may have continued classes in Clinton for two additional years, and the trip probably improved the program there, but he knew, as did the organizers in Macon, that he was in a long, gradual transition, as early as 1835, to merge his seminary with their idea and create the college. He announced the trip in an advertisement of the Clinton Female Seminary on May 12, which recruited students for the 1837–1838 academic year.[2] He was not required to be resident in Macon until January 1839 and, for continuing the educational program of his students and for his own family's financial standing, he kept the seminary going. This proves he planned the trip after accepting the offer of the trustees. The fact that he had so little money, before and after the trip, that he kept extremely detailed financial records of the journey, and that he bought instruments in

New York which belonged to the college, is conclusive evidence to prove his trip was paid for by the founders of the college. Slade met several significant individuals during his journey, many of whom were the national leaders in US female education in New York, Massachusetts, and Connecticut. He took copious notes and was then officially employed by the founders within a year of his return.[3]

In 1837, Slade was thirty-seven years old and had been in Clinton for just thirteen years. He had been a member of the Elim Baptist Church for five years and an ordained minister for two. When he embarked on his trip north, he left his wife Anne, thirty-two, four months pregnant with their seventh child, Martha Bog Slade, who was born five months later in December. Anne was at home with Janet, twelve, Mary, ten, "Annie," seven, "Jery," six, "Coon," four, and Thomas, Jr., two. Various relatives and seminary employees lived with the Slades at times, so it is reasonable to assume Anne had one or more other persons in the home to help with the children and her summer duties of the home and school. The seminary was between semesters, so all the students were at their homes and classes were suspended.

Although Slade mentioned no traveling companion in the journal of his trip, he nevertheless recorded his prayers in the first-person plural:

Into thy hands, O Lord! *we* [emphasis added] commit *ourselves*. *We* humbly pray Thy guidance and protecting care. Give *us* safety. *We* are upon the deep and darkness all

> around, but unto Thee light and darkness are the same. Praise and gratitude for favors past. Thy mercy *we* ask for Christ's sake. Lord, be pleased to bless Thy servant's companion and children, and, if consistent with Thy blessed will, suffer *us* to meet again in health and happiness.[4]

The plurals may have been Slade's formality in writing a prayer, but it may also have been his awareness that he was going north as the representative of those Macon businessmen who paid his expenses. In effect, they and the future success of the college were going with him, personified in his person. When contemplating the state of education in Georgia during the 1830s, the prayer may as well have been about the campaign to secure government-sponsored public schools in early nineteenth-century Georgia.

Slade traveled on the *S. S. Fox* to Baltimore, Maryland, where he toured the *S. S. George Washington*, a Philadelphia steamboat. The *Fox* was an old schooner, built well before 1822 when it was purchased in Baltimore and commissioned fourteen years before Slade came on board. It had been assigned to patrol for pirates in the Caribbean until it returned to Norfolk, Virginia, in 1826 as a "receiving" ship. The *Fox* had been part of the *Mosquito Fleet* and was engaged in several battles at sea, including one incident in which the commanding officer had been killed. The Fox was decommissioned December 8, 1837, barely four months after Slade's passage. It was sold and disappeared from the historical record. The *George Washington*, on the other hand, was not the more famous ship of the same name, which was not completed until 1838 in Ashtabula, Ohio. At least six ships have been named for America's first president. Slade seems to have seen the fourth *George Washington*, a ship of the line which served from 1815 to 1843. The ship had spent most of its early career in the Mediterranean engaged fighting Barbary pirates. The *George Washington*'s ninety guns had been tied up in New York since 1820 as Commodore Isaac Chauncey's flagship and remained there six more years after Slade's 1837 tour when it was finally broken up.

Noting he saw two hundred passengers but was acquainted with none, Slade took a train, just seven years after the first passenger service on trains began in the United States, from Frenchtown on the Susquehanna going a noteworthy 30 miles an hour. Frenchtown, located near modern Wysox, Pennsylvania, was a planned settlement in Bradford County established since 1793 for royalist French refugees of the French Revolution and of the slave revolts in San Domingue (Haiti). The refuge was founded by the Asylum Company which was led by two Frenchmen and one Irish-born Englishman.[5] Louis Marie the Vicomte de Noailles was known as "the most exquisite dancer in the gay court of Louis XVI and Marie Antoinette" and was also the brother-in-law of the Marquis de Lafayette. Like Lafayette, Noailles also fought in the American Revolution and was present at the *Battle of Yorktown*. Before her execution, residents planned for the arrival of French Queen Marie Antoinette in 1793. Slade referred to the place as Frenchtown but to the fifty aristocratic French families who were residents, it was known as French *Azilum*. Slade's route was one of the first commuter train lines of the period and the corridor had become the main passage for north-south travel during the 1830s. In 1837 the Newcastle and Frenchtown Railroad was advertising daily service, departing at "about 10:30" or whenever the steamboat arrived from Philadelphia.[6] The town had begun to decline by the 1790s when many of the residents migrated south or returned, with assurances from Napoleon, to France. The rail line declined after Slade's trip and by 1858 the track bed was abandoned.[7] New lines offered passengers more direct connections which did not require links to steamships and stagecoaches and, consequentially, little remains of this historic town today other than a small footprint and a history somewhat like Clinton, Georgia.

Another steamboat, unnamed by Slade, took him up the Delaware River to Philadelphia. He was annoyed during the night by the noise of the city at the Mount Vernon House on North Second Street. The following day he toured the market and the Fairmount Waterworks, which he credited for the good health of "The Philadelphians."[8] Fairmount was Philadelphia's second municipal waterworks, operating on the Schuylkill River from 1815 until 1909. Besides Slade, the waterworks was visited by Charles Dickens and Fanny Trollope, who described the place in her 1832 book:

> There is one spot, however, about a mile from the town, which presents a lovely scene. The water-works of Philadelphia have not yet perhaps as wide extended fame as those of Marley, but they are not less deserving it. At a most beautiful point of the Schuylkill River the water has been forced up into a magnificent reservoir, ample and elevated enough to send it through the whole city. The vast yet simple machinery by which this is achieved is open to the public, who resort in such numbers to see it, that several evening stages run from Philadelphia to Fair Mount for their accommodation.[9]

Slade was being a tourist. The waterworks and other sites he visited in Philadelphia and New York were not directly related to the purpose of his trip, but layovers between legs of the journey afforded him time to visit sites open to the public that were also of interest to him. Slade visited Joseph Bonaparte's home and noted the owner "was once proclaimed King of Spain." Napoleon's older brother (1768–1844) was, in fact, king of Naples and Spain and was considered the legitimate king of France in 1832 after the death of

Napoleon's only son.[10] His rented home in Philadelphia is located at 260 South Ninth Street and is not the mansion the modern reader might imagine. The house had been, however, a popular gathering place for Bonapartist refugees and French nationals after Joseph arrived there in 1815. In addition to this Philadelphia home, Joseph purchased another house in Bordertown, New Jersey, in 1816 on the Delaware River, which he called *Point Breeze*. Whereas the Philadelphia home was a crowded zero lot line row house, Point Breeze was located on an 1,800-acre estate and included gardens along with the mansion. Joseph lived there until 1839, five years before his death in Florence, Italy. The Philadelphia house, therefore, seems to have been his one-year residence before moving to New Jersey twenty years before Slade's visit. Perhaps Slade's interest was captured after his having been to Frenchtown. It is not certain how Slade traveled from his boarding house on North Second Street to Joseph Bonaparte's house on South Ninth, but the logical route would have taken him past Independence Hall and other historically significant sites, which are not mentioned, however, in Slade's travel journal.

A second train, this one "of elegant cars crowded with passengers," transported Slade to Amboy, New Jersey, before he passed Rattan Bay, Staten Island Sound, Newark Bay, and New York Bay. Arriving there forty-nine years before the Statue of Liberty, the first thing to attract his attention was "a number of vessels lying at quarantine" and the number of Dutch immigrants arriving thereon from Europe. Slade lodged in New York at 161 Broadway and wrote that the noise was "much worse" than Philadelphia.[11] He found a letter from his wife Anne at the post office but blamed "General Jackson" for the high price of the postage.[12] He visited Niblo's Garden, a theater on Broadway and Crosby Street established in 1823 as Columbia Garden, but he did not say whether he attended a performance.[13] The garden was twenty-one blocks north of Slade's lodging, but stagecoaches were running regularly each evening from his block out to Niblo's Theatre, which was built by William Niblo in 1834 and featured an open-air "saloon" in the center that, at night, was illuminated by hundreds of colored glass lanterns. Admission to the garden in 1829 was fifty cents. In 1835, Niblo's hosted P. T. Barnum's first public show, and in 1837, while Slade was in New York, it featured a vaudeville company that was performing farces such as *Promotion of the General's Hat* and *Meg Young Wife and Old Umbrella*.

These bawdy comedies were not the kind of production where we might have expected to find Slade, with their drunken behavior and sexual jokes, but Niblo's Theatre was considered New York's most fashionable theater at the time and may have thus earned only a daytime sightseeing visit from Slade. The final performance at Niblo's Garden was in 1895, after which it was torn down by Henry O. Havemeyer and replaced by modern commercial buildings.[14]

Walking to the battery, up and down Broadway, down Maiden Lane, Slade recorded the "unwholesome air and bad water."[15] Leaving New York City by steamboat, Slade passed by the Palisades, steep cliffs 300 feet high and increasing to 500 feet along the west bank of the Hudson River. Stretching for twenty miles between Jersey City, New Jersey, and Nyack, New York, where the river widens, the Palisades are among the most impressive geological features in the country. As an educator with a keen interest in science, Slade would have been impressed and must have spent this part of his trip inspecting the rocks. As a teacher with his knowledge of history, Slade must have been aware that the Palisades were also home to at least eighteen documented duels, including the well-known Aaron Burr and Alexander Hamilton duel of July 11, 1804, just thirty-three years before his passing.

Only forty miles upriver, Slade's boat stopped at the village of Sing Sing (Ossining, NY) in Westchester County, and he visited a former pupil, Miss Frances Lord. "We conversed upon scenes and days that were past," he wrote, "I feel as I trust I always shall, an affectionate regard for all my pupils. May the good Lord make her the object of gracious care."[16] While research has not revealed further information about this student, since the seminary only held its first graduation five years earlier, Lord could not have been more than about twenty-three years old in 1837 or away from the school more than five years. It is also not yet known her relation, if any, with Miss Maria T. Lord who taught music for Slade in Clinton and then transferred with him to the Georgia Female College in Macon. The New York State prison, however, named for the village had been built there since 1826, just eleven years prior to Slade's visit. Although he made no mention of the prison or Miss Lord's reason for being in Sing Sing, the institution was a model correctional institution. The name for both the village and the prison was taken from the Wappinger Native American tribe's word for "stone upon stone."[17]

Back onboard toward Albany, Slade stopped 35 miles further north at Stoney Point and thought about its role in the American Revolutionary War, just forty-four years before. The town was named for its location on a rocky point jutting out into the Hudson River, and it was the local ferry that was strategic to the movements of Washington's Continental Army during the American Revolution. The French utilized this King's Ferry in 1781 on their way to the *Battle of Yorktown*. Due to the ferry's logistical value and its proximity to West Point, it was defended carefully by the Americans throughout the war. Major Henry Lee and General Anthony Wayne were specifically assigned this duty by Washington, and this led to the *Battle of Stoney Point*. The Stoney Point Lighthouse was completed there in 1826.

Slade also visited the West Point Military Academy on the next stop, twenty-nine miles further toward Albany above Stoney Point. Established as an American Revolutionary fort during the war, the academy had been established there since 1802, thirty-five years before Slade's visit.[18] By 1835 there was pressure from Jacksonian Democrats to close the academy since supporters of the president were suspicious that America's oldest military academy was at work building an aristocracy in the young republic. This popular conspiracy was based on the fact that there were only three generals in the army when the Second Seminole Indian War began and the only successful way for an army officer to reach the rank of general, during the 1830s, was to have graduated from West Point.[19] The superintendent in 1837 was René Edward De Russy (1789–1865) who was, himself, a French emigre of San Domingue at the age of two years. An 1812 graduate of West Point who finished last in his class, De Russy nonetheless became superintendent in 1833 and served five years based on his proven service as a military engineer. He built several forts, including Fort Montgomery on the Canadian border and fortified several harbors, including New York. Slade made no mention of De Russy in his journal but he did record meeting with Edward Bishop Dudley (1789–1855), the twenty-eighth Governor of North Carolina, and Ashton Alexander (1772–1855), the provost; Slade called him "president" of Baltimore College (now the University of Maryland) founded in 1807. Dudley, a Whig, had been elected governor in 1836 and was only eight months in office in July 1837.[20] He was previously a member of the US House of Representatives 1829–31. Like Slade's father,

Dudley was a veteran of the War of 1812. He was also a major investor, then president, in the Wilmington—Raleigh Railroad which began construction in 1836, a major transportation link connecting his home region of the state to North Carolina's capital city. An early supporter of Andrew Jackson, Dudley had joined the Whigs almost as quickly as the party had been organized.[21] As for Alexander, there was no office of president for the university in 1837, the provost was the chief executive of the institution. Alexander, a former resident of North Carolina, thus his relationship with Dudley, became the provost at Baltimore in 1837 but had been affiliated with the university since 1796. Incidentally, Alexander had only recently been named provost at the time of his meeting with Slade and was yet in the process of replacing the previous and fifth provost, Roger B. Taney, who was the recently appointed fifth chief justice of the US Supreme Court, appointed by Jackson and successor of Chief Justice John Marshall.[22] There is no explanation in Slade's journal as to why these gentlemen were present at West Point that day, whether he met with them together or separately, for how long, for what purpose, or whether his meeting was scheduled or coincidental. While this information would be valuable for understanding Slade's journey, it speaks to his reputation to have received the attention of such influential leaders as Dudley, forty-eight, and Alexander, sixty-five. It is quite possible both men had been friends of Slade's father, Jeremiah Slade.

Having departed West Point and resuming his steamboat journey, Slade finally came to Albany then Troy, New York, where he toured his first northern female school, Emma Hart Willard's, which was in session.[23] Troy is located on the Hudson River in the westernmost part of Rensselaer County and is the county seat. It is, however, only eight miles northeast of Albany. Clearly Emma Hart Willard's Troy Female Academy, along with Sarah Pierce's Litchfield Female Academy in Connecticut, were the primary destinations of Slade's mission north, but Troy was also home to the Rensselaer Polytechnic Institute, an engineering school founded in 1824, where Slade may have known Amos Eaton (1776–1842), a botanist who was building a science curriculum at the institute and was a dedicated Pestalozzian. A co-founder of the institute and famous for his books on teaching science as well as his laboratory, Slade would have found him hard to ignore. Eaton willingly admitted women to his classes, including Willard and the students of her female seminary who qualified for dual enrollment.[24] Almira Hart Lincoln, Willard's sister, a student of Eaton and, perhaps, more well known as A. Phelps, was also teaching there since 1824. She was conducting teaching experiments with inductive methods applied to empirical science.[25] Eaton and Hart were the first science teachers in America to allow students to conduct their own experiments. A botanist in her own right, Lincoln published several works including *Lectures to Young Ladies, Comprising Outlines and Applications of the Different Branches of Female Education for the Use of Female Schools, and Private Libraries.*[26] As Lincoln wrote books on science, Willard wrote geography and history. In Troy, there was also the 1834 Troy Academy, St. Peter's College, the Provincial Seminary (Catholic), and a successful public school system which was organized into four "grades," primary, intermediate, grammar, and high school. These public schools were free to all residents of Troy between the ages of five and twenty-one years. There was a school for "colored" children. There were 109 teachers living in Troy and staffing this variety of educational institutions which recorded an average daily attendance of 4,690.[27] There were fourteen school buildings in Troy, and all but one were made of brick. Troy was a very prosperous city, especially after the completion of the Erie Canal in 1825, which begins directly across the Hudson River.[28] Due to the number of educational institutions and the diversity of their missions, Troy was a center of educational research and applied innovations.

A very destructive landslide occurred in Troy in January 1837, five months prior to Slade's arrival. Chronicler Hamilton Child best described the slide that struck Troy on New Year's Day:

> A large mass of the clayey earth from the hill east of the head of Washington Street, and extending for some distance each way, slid rapidly down, overwhelming everything in its course, covering several acres of ground and accompanied by a torrent of water. The mass carried with it two stables and three dwellings, crushing them into a thousand pieces. The stables and horses were moved over two hundred feet, into a hollow on the corner of Washington and Fourth Streets. A brick kiln was also destroyed by the avalanche. One of the dwellings was unoccupied, another occupied by Mr. John Grace, wife, and little boy. The parents were both killed but the

boy escaped. Mrs. Leavensworth and her children occupied another of the houses; she was so badly injured that she survived but a short time. Her two children were crushed to a jelly. There were 22 horses in the stables, sixteen of which were killed. The earth was piled up in the street from ten to forty feet deep.[29]

The next day, the local newspaper reported, "The scene that presented itself in the early part of the evening was awful in the highest degree. The horrors of an earthquake could not have presented a more dreadful spectacle."[30]

The pastor of the local Troy Baptist Church became Slade's companion although Slade failed to mention his name or the name of the church. The parsonage was, apparently, where Slade found accommodation while in Troy. As there were four or five Baptist churches at Troy in 1837, it is not clear whether Slade meant the Baptist Church of Christ (founded 1787), Millis Memorial Church (founded 1803), the Baptist Church on Third Street (founded 1805), the Particular Baptist Church (founded 1810), or the Second Baptist Church (founded 1834). There were forty churches of all denominations in Troy.

The Troy Female Seminary was founded on Second Street next to a beautiful park. Emma Hart Willard started this school in Middlebury, Vermont, in 1814, moved it to Waterford, New York in 1819, and finally to Troy in 1821.[31] It was incorporated only two months before Slade's arrival. Willard has been described as "one of the most important pioneer advocates of higher academic education for women" in American history, so Slade's connection with her is absolutely essential in supporting his own legacy as an early nineteenth-century educator of women.[32] The seminary was found to be much to Slade's expectations. Willard, however, was "very different from what I had anticipated," he wrote. "She is considerably above the ordinary size of females, quite corpulent, but dignified and commanding, easy and pleasant in her manners; in her conversation shrewd and intelligent, but fond of adulation and self-esteem. Her dress was more gaudy than my 'beau ideal' of a literary lady and instructress of youth."[33]

Far from a flattering description of this esteemed lady, this quote is also nothing like historian Anne Firor Scott's citation of Slade as the father who said she was "the most attractive woman" he had ever met.[34] Neither quote is consistent with Slade's character, but the first one above, written for himself in his personal notes and thereby not having been meant for public knowledge, is documented as authentic. Because none of Slade's daughters are known to have attended the Troy Female Seminary as Scott implied, the author appears to have been confusing Slade, who she refers to as "the father of one pupil," with someone else. There is no explanation given of Slade's own work in female education by Scott or reference to his visit in Troy during 1837.[35]

As historian Florence Fleming Corley has documented, "Early in the nineteenth century, male champions of higher education for white women in Georgia rose from the congregations and schools of Presbyterians," but it was not only the Presbyterians as Slade, a Baptist, and others bear witness.[36] Several Georgia educators, according to Corley, were influenced by Willard's writings and her school. Georgia students are found in the records of the Troy Female Seminary's enrollment.[37] Unlike Slade's enrollment, which was less diverse due to his location, the Troy Female Seminary counted Baptists, Congregationalists, Episcopalians, Lutherans, Methodists, Presbyterians, Quakers, and Unitarians among its denominationally diverse student body.[38] As her reputation was well established throughout the nation and among all denominations, Slade made his way to Troy.

Willard, herself, was Congregational. Her father was one of the founders of Hartford, Connecticut. At twenty-two years old, she married Dr. John Willard, a physician and friend of female education who was thirty years older.[39] He was an encouragement to her in the work. Emma Willard was raised in a household full of books, but she taught herself classical and scientific subjects, which she later offered, first in Middlebury, Vermont.[40] For Willard, much of her success was based on timing.[41] She was born in the year of the constitutional convention and was, thus, fifteen years old when Thomas Jefferson secured the Louisiana Purchase.

The early years of the United States were a time of furious founding and building of institutions of all types: political, economic, social, religious, and educational. In New England especially, and as observed by the French traveler Alexis de Tocqueville, Americans were remarkable in working together toward common goals. According to de Tocqueville, they had carried "this new science" to its ultimate purpose.[42] The early nineteenth century was a period of founding various associations dedicated to the improvement of American society. Many of these were dedicated to the relief of disadvantaged persons such as widows and orphans, but many others were more progressive movements to achieve societal reforms such as abolitionist, temperance, and educational organizations. Most of these were founded and led by women, who also made up the bulk of organizational memberships. As the women worked to improve society, they grew in leadership skills.[43] Most of these organizations were led by groups of women, but some institutions, like seminaries and academies, were often led by a single, usually highly talented individual similar to Willard. While there were a multitude of male-led institutions in various sectors of society, many female seminaries and academies were led by women. Willard was a "force of nature" and between 1821 and 1872, her Troy Female Seminary educated more than twelve thousand female students. The Scottish phrenologist George Combe described Willard as "the most powerful individual at present acting upon the condition of the American people of the next generation."[44] Some women were members of several organizations. Willard, for example, in 1837 specifically, was a member of the *American Colonization Society of the City of New York*, which was one of several such American societies seeking, in the early nineteenth century, to transplant enslaved Americans to Africa to end slavery without freeing blacks to be assimilated into the white society of the United States.[45] According to Scott, Willard was an abolitionist but was more than "willing to make concessions to the South in order to avoid war," which she saw as a greater evil than slavery.[46] Remarkably, as a woman promoting the intellectual capacities of women, Willard was known to be prejudiced and proved as much in published textbooks regarding both blacks and Indians.[47]

Willard founded the Willard Association for the Mutual Improvement of Teachers in 1837, which include the alumna of the Troy Female Seminary.[48] Through this organization, Willard worked for educators' career development but also maintained contact with her former students. She also "organized the Troy Society for the Advancement of Education in Greece to raise money for a teacher-training school, which would be supervised by a Troy graduate who, by good fortune, was already in Athens."[49] As an example of Willard's awareness of early nineteenth-century world events in real time, she knew that Greece was in a struggle for independence from the Ottoman Empire. She also knew about the work of missionaries in Greece who were setting up a school, so she lectured and wrote for contributions to fund an opportunity to take a progressive step in training women overseas. With the help of many others, her association raised over $3,000 for the school in Athens. In the process, Willard had also learned much about recruiting, organizing, and leading a large and diverse group of women.[50]

New York Governor DeWitt Clinton, one of those for whom Clinton, Georgia, may have been named, encouraged Willard to move her female seminary to his state and lead in setting up others. The New York legislature, however, refused to give her funding. This caused her to go over their heads and appeal to the public by writing *A Plan for Improving Female Education* which was soon published and sold in New York and Philadelphia and thereby read in every state.[51] This short thirty-five-page book was considered the "Magna Carta" by those champions of higher education for women. In the work, Willard condemned the traditional boarding schools for girls after she learned about the curricula being used in male education. Her main argument in her *Plan* was that the task was too large for the few champions and required the involvement of state governments. Her fight began earlier than Slade's but was similar in its challenges, obstacles, and success, however limited. "By shewing the justice," she wrote, "the policy, and the magnanimity of such an undertaking to persuade [the legislature] to endow a seminary for females, as the commencement of such reformation."[52] While many more nearsighted educators struggled to establish a single school in one community, either for the benefit of students or themselves, Willard and Slade were part of a far more exclusive body of visionaries who imagined thousands of academies in as many towns and cities, open to all, and supported by public funding. In 1837, the year of Slade's visit, Willard was promoting seminaries, through correspondence, to international leaders such as Simon Bolivar, the South American revolutionary and president of Columbia, Peru, and Bolivia.[53]

Willard, more than Slade, never imagined co-educational seminaries. She believed that as men and women were different physically, emotionally, and intellectually, they needed gender-specific institutions. This is not to say she believed females were inferior to males; in fact, she spent her career proving their equality, but she did believe they learned by different methods and required gender-specific instruction. "The business of the husbandman," she wrote, "is not to waste his endeavors in seeking to make his orchard attain the strength and majesty of his forest, but to rear each to the perfection of its nature."[54] Willard masterfully made the case for female education and Republican Motherhood in her well-written plan. She described in detail the causes of the defective mode of female education common in the early nineteenth century and the principles by which female education should be organized. She outlined her plan and laid out the benefits to society from properly established female seminaries.[55] This work was likely how Slade became acquainted with Willard, learned of her work, and determined that her school in Troy was his primary destination on the trip north.

Several points in Slade's speech to the Georgia Teachers' Society in 1832, given five years before meeting Willard in person but fourteen years after her *Plan* was published, and evidently after Slade had read it, appear to be directly influenced by her writing. She argued, for example:

> Civilized nations have long since been convinced that education, as it respects males, will not, like trade, regulate itself; and hence, they have made it a prime object to provide that sex with everything requisite to facilitate their progress in learning, but female education has been left to the mercy of private adventurers; and the consequences has been to our sex, the same, as it would have been to the other, had legislatures left their accommodations, and means of instruction, to chance also.[56]

In his speech to the Georgia Teacher's Society, Slade said, "In every state removed from a state of barbarism, and free from the debasing yoke of tyranny, education holds a prominent station and may with truth and reason be considered the groundwork of every temporal blessing we enjoy."[57] He went on to more fully explain the differences in various cultures education had made and then described how the argument for education of males must also include female education in order to be fully effective in any civilized nation. Willard argued that educational programs, male or female, only prosper with the sponsorship, protection, and support from the best members of any community, state, or civilization.[58] Considering the lack of support from the economic and political leaders in Georgia, Slade said, "When I see the mountains of opposition which this cold neglect throws in the way of the diffusion of knowledge in the State of Georgia, I must candidly own and acknowledge, zeal abates, and thick darkness and despondency seem to brood over the prospect before us."[59]

Willard's description of traditional female boarding schools, the basis of her criticism of them, was too uncomfortable for Slade, who found in her words a physical description of his own Clinton Female Seminary. For lack of funding, for example, his school, based in his home, was too small for adequate housing of students, a library, or other necessary facilities. For these reasons, Willard called them "temporary" and impediments to progress in study.[60] Slade knew this was an issue before reading Willard but struggled to attract enough "paying" students and to maintain his policy of not refusing a girl based on her ability to pay. It is conditions such as Willard described that eventually pushed Slade to accept the offer of the Macon trustees. The Georgia Female College promised to provide all the amenities that Willard described in detailing female education as it should be, to the benefit of the women under instruction. Students at the Clinton Female Seminary lived in Slade's home, their own homes if the family lived nearby, and in private homes throughout Clinton. Trustees in Macon envisioned a grand dormitory where all the students of Georgia Female College would live under one roof with spacious accommodations supported by food and laundry services. Slade, in Clinton, owned precious few teaching aids and fewer scientific instruments. The Georgia Female College provided him funds to purchase the necessary aids and instruments needed, on site in Boston and New York. Thus, by 1836, the offer to merge his seminary with the new Macon female college must have been a dream come true for Slade, and if his ultimate motive was the common good through education of females—as it was—certainly, an offer he could not logically refuse.

As headmaster and the main teacher of the Clinton Female Seminary, Slade disagreed, and likely took offense, with Willard who maintained that females were best taught by their own sex. "Feminine delicacy requires," she wrote, "that girls should be chiefly educated by their own sex. This is apparent from considerations that regard their health and conveniences, the propriety of their dress and manners, and their domestic accomplishments."[61] She went on to include this idea in her criticism of traditional female boarding schools, but Slade, the father of daughters, felt called to his profession. Being a teacher was equal to his ministry as an itinerant Baptist evangelist. Furthermore, he had the assistance of several capable, responsible, and well-educated women on his staff, including his wife Anne and Maria T. Lord, among others. In his speech to Georgia teachers, he spoke, apologizing for his "plainness of speech" specifically to those sitting before him who were also mothers:

> I know there are some selfish, short-sighted, ignorant persons who would degrade your character and delight in casting a sneering contempt upon your influence; who think the female mind unsusceptible to high and rational improvement and unfit for those refined enjoyments which flow from a cultivated intellect. They would assign your lot to the cares of domestic drudgery and make you the degraded instruments of their selfish dispositions. But nature has designed you for purposes of a more exalted character: your duties lie in a more expanded sphere.[62]

Rather than defending his role as a male educator of women, Slade was passionately calling those women in teaching to greater responsibilities in the profession. Instead of arguing with Willard, he was inviting more women to leadership, not only in the classroom but in administration.

Willard did not allow that gender-specific education should justify separate treatment of women in society. The role of women in America was "pathetically unjust" in many ways, according to Willard. This, however, according to headmistress of Troy, resulted from and was reinforced by inequalities in education. She railed against the injustice of brothers being allowed an education while sisters were "drudged at home, to assist in support of the father's family and perhaps to contribute to her brother's subsistence abroad."[63] While supporting much of Republican Motherhood and the need for educated men to have intelligent wives, Willard qualified her position by writing, "Reason and religion teach, that we too are primary existencies; that is for us to move, in the orbit of our duty, around the Holy Centre of perfection, the companions, not the satellites of men."[64] Then, however, in the next paragraph, seemingly afraid lest she go too far, Willard qualified that statement as well by reinforcing the traditional role of wife and mother. She allowed for "obedience to the other sex" in "particular situations." Remember her *Plan* was an attempt to convince an all-male legislature to appropriate funds for her project in female education; Willard may have hinted at a more modern gender equality but stopped short of making a complete argument for full equality.

Willard's overall argument was far further tilted toward demonstrating how educated women were partners for men and essential to the patriarchy than offending the men who had the ability to appropriate for her academy.[65] Indeed, it was common for Troy graduates to marry college presidents, judges, lawyers, and members of Congress. Secretary of State William H. Seward's wife, Frances Miller, was an early 1820s graduate of the Troy Female Seminary. While this may sound "compromising" to a modern reader too eagerly anticipating that the women might be the presidents, judges, and cabinet members in the early nineteenth century, Willard was genuinely authentic in her commitment to the core principles and justification of female education. She was visionary, but she was also an early nineteenth-century realist. Her patience allowed her to plot a course for women and begin a one-thousand-mile march even though she knew that she herself would not live to see its completion. Her first biographer was John Lord, who had access to her personal letters and journals, many of which are lost to history. He affirmed "that she was indeed a proper Christian lady" who was committed "to make women better wives and mothers." He credited her for influencing state legislatures, successfully operating educational institutions, rewriting some scientific theories, and setting public policy.[66] According to Scott, "In 1820 she published a pamphlet, *Universal Peace to be Introduced by a Confederacy of Nations Meeting in Jerusalem*," which was "a proposal for a league of nations a century before the idea became a staple of western diplomacy."[67]

Willard listed the essentials for a "proper" female educational institution as part of *Plan*. In the early nineteenth century, any academy, seminary, or college needed a building according to most educators. These buildings needed to be comfortable for young, female students and to include rooms for lodging and instruction. There must be a library where books could be found on every subject in which the students were being taught. As envisioned by Willard, these libraries should contain musical instruments, paintings, maps, globes, and scientific instruments. A female institute should be governed by a board of trustees, and Willard described their responsibilities. The curriculum was divided into four very general categories: Religious and Moral, Literary, Domestic, and Ornamental, roughly corresponding to the academic divisions of Theology, the Liberal Arts, Home Economics, and the Fine Arts, particularly music, dancing, drawing, and painting. Willard may have included the last two rather reluctantly, after criticizing the boarding schools for being only these, but she listed Religious and Moral first on purpose and knew that the bulk of female education lay in a host of disciplines included under Literary. She promoted the teaching of Christian principles in all classes by adding, "The trustees would be careful to appoint no instructors, who would not teach religion and morality, both by their example, and by leading the minds of the pupils to perceive, that these constitute the true end of all education."[68] Although the Literary division of the curriculum in Willard's plan included history, literature, mathematics, science, and so on, she spent the bulk of her words specifically describing the many branches of science that should be taught in any female educational institution. In true Hartlibian fashion, she wrote, "Natural philosophy has not been taught to our sex. Why should we be kept in ignorance of the great machinery of nature, and left to the vulgar notion, that nothing is curious but what deviates from her common course?" Willard understood that a curiosity about God's creation drives a student of science to discover the secrets the creator had placed in the many elements of nature. She never imagined, like hundreds of educators before her, that there would ever be a perceived conflict between faith and science. To understand natural philosophy for Willard and Slade was to explore what God had made and understand more about Him as a result. Thus, "A knowledge of natural philosophy is calculated," she wrote, "to heighten the moral taste, by bringing to view the majesty and beauty of order and design."[69] Bacon, Hartlib, Milton, Boyle, Newton, or Slade could not have said it any better and all would have applauded her conclusion because they all agreed that scientific research leads to a stronger faith, enabling the mind to more clearly perceive the work of God.

Governor Clinton, who had prompted Willard's New York project in the first place with his invitation to Willard, praised her for the work. In her *Plan*, he saw "the capacity of your sex for high intellectual cultivation."[70] In his next address to the state legislature, he urged the members to initiate new legislation for the improvement of female education in New York State. Although the legislature never acted on this issue in her time, Willard proceeded to start the work on her own with limited assistance from the officials in Troy. Like Slade, Willard admitted "ambitious" women who were unable to pay tuition, but the Troy seminary also assisted them in finding paid employment in town and required them to work as a means of paying for their complimentary education.[71] She also admitted girls of all ages although her plan was to have only students between sixteen and nineteen years old. She allowed single term (one academic year) enrollments, like Slade, even though she wanted all students to commit to a three-year course. She wanted only boarders but was forced to admit day students.[72] These conditions, which were common to the female seminaries, colleges, and academies of Georgia, all serve as examples of the tension between the ideals of the theory of female education and the reality of an early nineteenth-century girls' life and the needs of her family. Many students married young for reasons of economic necessity, and families of every class were keen to save money whenever possible.

Willard's method was to "start where the student is," which was developed based on her study of John Locke and Johann Heinrich Pestalozzi, who founded schools in Switzerland. Thus, in geography, she first had students draw a map of their own hometown. Her methods were indirectly drawn from earlier seventeenth-century educational reformers such as John Amos Comenius, the father of modern education, and his friends John Dury, Hartlib, and Milton, whose book *Of Education*, his most complete work on the subject, was dedicated to Hartlib. Milton believed the purpose of education was twofold. Publicly, it made the individual directly and society indirectly better, and privately, it partially repaired the intellectual damage all humans inherited from their first parents in the Fall, which occurred in the Garden of Eden. Education for Milton and most seventeenth-century Puritans was, thus, the long and difficult process of restoring that which had been lost and returning to the perfect state in which God had originally created humanity. This further explains the Puritan commitment passed down to reformers such as Willard, Pierce, and Slade that drove the founders of the New England colonies to establish colleges so quickly after the charters were issued and the first towns were settled. Comenius, meanwhile, produced forty-three works that established a philosophy of public education, organized principles for educators choosing curricula, and justified public schools funded by government for all children of all classes, male and female. In fact, at one point, "Cotton Mather wrote that Winthrop had been authorized to offer the presidency of Harvard College to Comenius, but the famous educator declined the invitation."[73] Hartlib suggested that Comenius relocate himself and his entire Moravian congregation to New England in 1642 due to the devastating effects of the Thirty Years' War, and John Davenport in New Haven was offering an open invitation. Hartlib and Davenport had Comenius' attention, so John Dury offered to facilitate the migration and provide curriculum resources that Comenius needed to start public schools in America. Dury included books and outlines for history, Latin, grammar, and rhetoric, including a suggestion to have New Haven students translate Comenius' book, *Ianua*, into Greek and Hebrew.[74] The plan never materialized, but the episode demonstrates clearly the connections between the seventeenth-century educational scholars in Europe and the nineteenth-century educators in America. Methods, philosophy, curriculum, theory, and practice were common to both.[75]

Like Slade, Willard took her own journey for educational purposes seven years earlier in 1830. After transferring leadership of the Troy Female Seminary to her sister, Willard and her son traveled east to Europe where she first visited Paris. According to her own journals and letters, she sent back her descriptions of what she saw, including architecture and works of art. Speaking in her limited knowledge of the French language, she met with women in Paris who were working in female education. Of the moment, Willard wrote:

> How differently, at different periods of our lives do similar events affect us. At fifteen I was all in a flutter at the thought of entering on a village ballroom, with plenty of company; how could I then have believed that a time would come when I should enter the court of France alone, pass through a long room . . . without any particular emotion whatever.[76]

Before leaving the country, Willard pronounced that the state of female education in France was "deficient."

Willard also visited Britain, both England and Scotland, where she found the state of female education "equally deficient." The result of her travel was that she was encouraged to believe that the state of female education in America was equal to or better than any other nation. She recorded feeling that the work of female educators was more important than ever. The trip thus provided her with knowledge and encouragement. As she shared her knowledge with Slade, he experienced the same feelings of enhancement. Willard's trip also strengthened her reputation in America. More than before, she "spoke her mind with considerable freedom and one who—after seeing the best the old world had to offer—was happily returning to continue her mission in the new."[77] Slade did not leave Troy or Litchfield feeling that the state of female education in New England was deficient. Quite the contrary. While he may have felt a small "flutter" at the thought of meeting Willard, he must have been inspired, based on his own facilities, pool of students, finances, curriculum, and prospects for the future, that the state of female education in Georgia was healthy and promising. Incidentally, one Troy graduate, Julia Pierpont (1793–1878), had been sent by Willard to Sparta, Georgia in 1819 to open a female seminary there. Pierpont married and had a child but when both died suddenly, she returned to Troy in 1824 to further her education. She later married Elias Marks who had started a female school in South Carolina at Barhamville and who had proposed a plan like Willard's to the legislature of the Palmetto State. Pierpont transformed Marks' school to fit Troy standards and rebranded it as the Barhamville Collegiate Institute.[78] Finally, the abandoned Spata Female Academy in Georgia was renewed and expanded in 1832 by Sereno Taylor of Vermont with the support of Georgia Baptists. Taylor offered "cosmics," "geotics," government, history, languages, mathematics, and philosophy. Madam Salmon Hantute of Paris taught French, piano, and singing there after 1839. Some buildings, originally built in 1815 and expanded in 1831, survive today although the main building is in ruins.

Another of Willard's graduates, Caroline Livy, who began her studies in Troy the same year as Slade's visit, married a minister, J. M. Calwell, and moved with him to Rome, Georgia, where she began the Rome Female Academy in Floyd County.[79] Over 5,000 young women attended this academy, where they too received an education structured according to Willard's standards in Troy. Other Troy graduates were sent to every other state. Some married, but many of those continued to lead their respective seminaries, academies, and colleges. A few, like Sarah R. Foster, for example, founded and ran two schools simultaneously. This represents a pattern of Willard's to send graduates as educational missionaries to points throughout America. "As early as 1832," Scott wrote, "she traveled in a private carriage from Troy to Detroit, spending almost every night in the home of a former pupil."[80] In 1846, she traveled over eight thousand miles to visit every state south and west of New York except for Florida and Texas. "She visited former pupils, collected old debts, and lectured on pedagogy," and always followed up her visits with correspondence.[81] There is no record of her stopping in Columbus, Georgia, to visit Slade and the Slade Academy there, but it is more than likely due to the importance of the school, the prior relationship with Slade, and the location of this major city.

Willard, therefore, constructed, like Hartlib in the seventeenth century, a circle of correspondents. Like the Hartlib Circle, Willard's was a series of concentric circles with the inner circles consisting of those graduates who remained in Troy to become teachers of the seminary in daily contact with the center. One of these, Sarah Lucretia Hudson, married Willard's only son and became headmistress of the seminary when Willard retired just one year after Slade's visit to Troy. The intermediate circle was composed of those alumnae who became teachers away from Troy, founding their own academies, colleges, and seminaries for women. The outermost and largest ring of the Willard Circle was the former students and the daughters of students who became wives and mothers or those who lived single with their families. Although these chose not to not become educators outright, many of them were no less influential in society as organizers and members of local associations, many of these founded to promote common schools.[82]

While still visiting the Troy seminary, Slade was carried by curiosity on Saturday night, August 5, to visit the Union House in Saratoga, New York about 28 miles away, where more than one hundred members of the Quaker church met nightly. "Aged men," he wrote. On invitation, he prayed with them. "I disliked the water," he commented, "but was pleased with the society."[83] These Quakers, also known as The Society of Friends, practiced a simpler version of Christianity, even in 1837, than to which Slade would have been accustomed.[84] They claimed it was a more "authentic" faith but were often persecuted for their lifestyle by "Englishers," though much of that was based on their pacifist conscience in relation to military service. Baptists shared much about the Gospel and religious freedom with early nineteenth-century Quakers but were never shy about volunteering for active duty in the American Revolution, War of 1812, or Seminole Indian Wars. Baptists were also far more evangelical than Quakers and less concerned with social justice. Furthermore, Quakers were always more numerous in the North than the South for these and other reasons. Pennsylvania was founded by Quakers but it was not the Friends who migrated south in the form of the Protestant German migrants of the late eighteenth century. Quakers were among the earliest abolitionists in America. Slade was a slave owner from the slave State of Georgia but he may not have revealed this part of his identity even if he was open about where he was from. Slade may have been speaking literally about the "water" in Saratoga but, more likely, he meant the doctrines and practices though he obviously enjoyed the fellowship he shared with Christian brothers at the Union House.

Returning to the seminary, Slade examined classes and heard lessons in "Arithmetic, French, Philosophy, History, Geometry, etc." and then departed by stagecoach for the train station over the Massachusetts state line to proceed to Boston, passing "through a beautifully cultivated country thickly interspersed with towns and villages." Coming from the rough, agricultural frontier in Georgia, Slade was struck by the settlement patterns he saw from his window across eastern New York State. He visited the Mount Lebanon Shaker Village, the most significant community of Shakers in America, in New Lebanon, New York, where he noted "the neatness of their houses, gardens and farms" but felt compassion for "this deluded race of people."[85] The village covered thousands of acres and was home to hundreds of Shakers who were similar to the Quakers but more extreme to Slade and his Baptist sensitivities. The village is 39 miles east of Troy and very near the border with Massachusetts. They were advocates of gender and racial equality in the early nineteenth century. Slade was impressed by their craftsmanship, musical abilities, and industrial habits. The Mt. Lebanon Village was fifty years old when Slade visited but the movement, originally from Manchester, England, had been in America since 1774. They were initially settled near Albany, New York, by a charismatic but illiterate daughter of a blacksmith named Ann Lee.[86] The father of six in 1837,

Slade found "delusion" in their belief that "heaven" could be created on earth through communal living, gender and racial equality, pacifism, and celibacy.

North Hampton, Pittsfield, Mount Tom, Mount Holyoke, and Amherst, Massachusetts, made the journal only as towns through which Slade passed on his way to Boston. The Boston and Albany Railroad and Western Railroad connected those cities and are the route taken by Slade. The City of Boston turned to rail when threatened by New York City's advantage found in the Erie Canal. The first line was originally chartered in 1831 and fully opened on July 4, 1835, two years before Slade's journey, but the Western line was still under construction as he passed through. This means the New York portion of his journey east was probably by stagecoach.

Just six weeks before Slade's arrival in Boston, the city had experienced a violent uprising known as the Broad Street Riot. Eight hundred Irish-American Catholics and volunteer Yankee Firefighters, mainly Anglo-American working-class Protestants, sacked each other's homes, vandalized, and battered occupants found as ten thousand Boston residents witnessed the event. The fight lasted for three hours and many were injured as the firefighters invaded the homes of the Irish who had taken refuge. Incredibly, there were no immediate deaths from the violence although there were hundreds injured and thousands of dollars in damage to property. The riot was ended only by the state militia and was the inspiration for Mayor Samuel Eliot forming professional police and fire departments in Boston.[87]

Slade spent five days in the capital city, much of it with Joseph Milner Wightman (1812–85) of Claxton and Wightman, originally Codman and Claxton founded by John Codman and Timothy Claxton, makers of philosophical (scientific) instruments. "Though young in age," Slade wrote, "he is old in science."[88] Wightman was twenty-five years old and only twelve years younger than Slade, and he was self-taught but proficient in his knowledge of chemistry, electrical engineering, and mensuration.[89] Slade was in the shop just before Claxton returned to England, and Wightman took full control of the company. He was soon supplying award-winning scientific instruments to educational institutions throughout America.[90] He later became a politician and served as mayor of Boston during the Civil War.

Slade visited the Massachusetts State House and saw a British drum, musket, and sword taken at the *Battle of Bennington* in 1777. On Sunday, August 13, he preached at Baron Alanson Stow's Baldwin Place Baptist Church.[91] Stow (1801–69) was a well-known Baptist pastor, writer, and editor in Boston who published eight books including *The Psalmist*, which was the most widely used Baptist hymnal in America from 1843 until 1873. Stow was only thirty-six years old when the thirty-seven-year-old Slade preached for him in 1837 but had already graduated from Columbian College (now George Washington University) in Washington, DC.[92] Sadly, Slade nor anyone else left a record of his sermon from that day in Boston. A Northern Baptist, Stow held several denominational leadership positions, including third president of the Conference of Baptist Ministers in Massachusetts, and authored several books on missions including *A History of the English Baptist Mission to India* in 1835.[93] Stow was an ardent abolitionist who preached and wrote to end slavery in America yet had no problem inviting the slave-owning Slade to preach at Baldwin Place. We are left to assume Slade did not preach on the topic of slavery in August 1837.

The next morning Slade visited the graves of "Dr. Spurgeim [sic], the phrenologist," whose grave has since been lost to time and records, and Hannah Adams, the "first tenant of this gloomy abode," according to Slade, in Cambridge.[94] He may have seen others but only mentioned these two, representing his complementary interests in female education and science. Adams, who died only six years before Slade's visit, was an early American author of books on comparative religion and early US history. The author of ten published works of history and religion, she was the first female in America to work as a full-time professional writer.[95] German physician Johann Gaspar Spurzheim (1776–1832) had inspired interest in phrenology, and the formation of the Boston Phrenological Society was formed on the day of his elaborate and public funeral, November 17, 1832. The first meeting was held on Spurzheim's birthday with ninety members in attendance, including Rev. John Pierpont (1785–1866), teacher, lawyer, merchant, and Unitarian minister who was the best-known American poet after 1816, because of his poem *The Airs of Palestine*.[96] John was not only the grandfather of industrialist James

Pierpont Morgan but was a second cousin of Troy Female Seminary graduate Julia Pierpont, who founded the female seminary in Sparta, Georgia.

After meeting with classmates, missionaries, and some Georgia friends without giving any further details as to names or places, Slade visited what he called John Pierce Brace's female school in Hartford, Connecticut (now the Litchfield Female Academy). This school was founded in 1792 by Sarah Pierce and became one of the most important institutions in America. Pierce was the daughter of John Pierce and Mary Paterson who were farmers and potters. Her brother John Pierce served as the Assistant Paymaster of the Continental Army during the American Revolution. He became personal friends with Washington and was named Commissioner of the Army after the war. John was responsible for sending Sarah Pierce and her sister Mary to school and assisting them in establishing the female academy in Hartford.[97] Mary managed the school's housing and accounting while James Brace, husband of a third sister, Susan, was a teacher at the academy. Sarah Pierce enrolled over two thousand students within its first thirty years representing seventeen states and territories of the United States, Canada, and the West Indies. Eighty percent of the Litchfield students were housed on campus where the faculty included Rev. Lyman Beecher, the Presbyterian father of Harriet Beecher Stowe but who had moved to Cincinnati, Ohio by the time of Slade's visit, Senator Uriah Tracy, Col. Benjamin Tallmadge, Capt. Julius Deming, and Oliver Wolcott, an American founding father and politician who signed the *Declaration of Independence* and the *Articles of Confederation* as a representative of Connecticut. Pierce would have reinforced Slade's ideas about female education and how it related to ideas of Republican Motherhood. Pierce strongly believed in the intellectual equality of women but also believed the purpose of female education was to prepare young women to be supportive wives for their husbands within the home. Further, like Slade, Pierce believed that the moral principles of Christianity were critical to the success of any educational program.[98]

Understanding the concept of Republican Motherhood is critical to understanding Slade's life and work. Granted, it is a twentieth-century term used to describe the role of women in the early nineteenth-century United States when Americans were busy building their new nation, creating new institutions, and proving the wisdom of republican government. The idea includes a conviction that the daughters of the founding generation carried the responsibility of understanding the principles of republican government and transferring that understanding to the next generation through their children.[99] Joined with this concept was the core value of early Americans that it was the wife and mother's responsibility to maintain the highest moral standards of ethical Christianity and to hold both her children and her husband accountable to these principles, both of which may have been allowed occasional lapses of good judgment not as commonly allowed wives and mothers. They were not allowed equal grace as women were the moral shepherds. Thus, strict expectations were placed on these women and punishments for them were both real and imagined whether pressure to conform was educational, political, religious, or social. Educators like Pierce, Slade, and Willard never thought of Republican Motherhood as being cruel or unfair to women; they were terribly afraid the success of the American experiment depended on it. There was no other way for the American experiment to succeed. On the other hand, it resulted in respectable American society isolating females into only one of three mutually exclusive categories. All women were either virgins, wives, or whores.[100] Women who refused to cooperate were ostracized, shunned, and excluded from mainstream society. The female academies, seminaries, and colleges provided them an education, yes, but it also taught them how to function in a world with these unwritten but powerful expectations. Yet they were written into etiquette manuals, institutional rules, and so on, and they appeared in books, magazines, newspapers, sermons, and lectures. "As evidence that this statement [the important role of educated women in a republic] does not exaggerate the female influence in society," Willard wrote, "our sex need but be considered, in the single relation of mothers."[101] Republican Motherhood was foundational to education, freedom, justice, and liberty. "In a republic like ours," Slade said, "where all power emanates from the people, knowledge should be universally diffused."[102] In the future, Slade envisioned universal public education funded by the state to include all children regardless of class, "rich or poor," he said, "wise or ignorant." In the early nineteenth century, Republican Motherhood was essential to what it meant to be American.[103]

Before the term was coined, therefore, Slade understood Republican Motherhood clearly. "From your hands," he poetically said to the mothers, "the infant often receives those impressions, its impressions which are to determine its everlasting destiny. When the bud of life begins to unfold its native beauty and artlessness, then is the golden opportunity to train the mind to virtue."[104] He then gave his often-quoted anonymous quote about the importance of the first ten years in "the life of a man" before more completely detailing the antisocial and criminal behavior commonly occurring in a man who was not properly trained by his mother. Finally, this led him to detail, once again, the utility and importance of female education.

Much of what Willard was doing in Troy and Pierce was doing at the Litchfield Female Academy, Slade was already doing at the Clinton Female Seminary. The curriculum he had developed was like what students were given in Hartford and found in various degrees of completeness in female academies and seminaries throughout the country, but especially in the North. Slade was a pioneer and exceptional educator in that he had developed a complete classical curriculum in rural Georgia before his model was commonly found in the South. Like Pierce, Slade was already teaching ancient and classical history, geography, arithmetic, English grammar and composition, foreign languages (French, Latin, and Greek), and science (botany and chemistry) to women.[105] Pierce may have been more concerned with proving female intellectual equality. Slade was working to prepare young women, including his own daughters, to become good wives, mothers, citizens, and members of polite society. Slade and Pierce both integrated rigorous classical curricula with the "ornamental" subjects of painting and embroidery to reinforce the most intellectual topics. It also made parents happy who insisted these skills be included. Pierce insisted that the students were encouraged to "read aloud" and have "serious" conversations while practicing the ornamental arts.[106] She and her academy had the advantages of powerful human political connections, geography, forty-five years of experience by 1837, and strong enrollment numbers of students from wealthy and influential families. Slade struggled because of location and low enrollment numbers despite his having established and developed a notable reputation and influential contacts, many of whom were supporters of his project. Pierce benefited from multiple generations of returning students whereas Slade spent seven years in Clinton, twenty months in Macon, and only one year in Penfield. Only in Columbus for forty years was he finally able to establish himself well enough to begin seeing the daughters of alumna among his students.

The students of Litchfield Female Academy did not all come from elite, wealthy, and politically connected families. Records reveal that the student body was economically diverse. Slade's schools were even more diverse in this way. While many wealthy families did seek a "finishing" for their daughters and college-educated fathers often wanted a quality education for their female children, even middle-class families knew that the best education gave a girl the best opportunity to achieve economic stability and social independence whether she married or not. Academies and seminaries equipped a young woman with the possibility of not just being a teacher but the opportunity to teach in or start their own institution of higher and more lucrative education. Twenty graduates of the Litchfield Academy became teachers and fully fifty-eight of them founded their own seminaries after graduation. Unfortunately, similar statistics are not available for the Clinton Female Seminary due to missing manuscripts documenting enrollment and the identity of graduates.[107] Although Slade spent two days at this remarkable institution, he wrote almost nothing in his journal of who he met, what he observed, or how much he learned at the Litchfield Female Academy, quietly moving on to New Haven.

On the northern shore of Long Island Sound, Slade visited his former professor, Denison Olmstead (1791–1859), who had moved from the University of North Carolina, where he taught Slade, to Yale, his own alma mater. Olmstead was a famous physicist and astronomer, but Slade referred to him as "my old friend and faithful teacher."[108] A meteor shower in 1833 inspired Olmstead to study meteors, and he is now known as the father of meteor science. At North Carolina, he was the chair of chemistry, mineralogy, and geology. When a gold rush in North Carolina provoked the state legislature to mandate a geological survey, Olmstead had ridden on horseback over the state collecting samples and publishing maps.[109] "Time had made but few changes in his appearance," Slade wrote of the forty-five-year-old academic, "His manner, as usual, was pleasant and agreeable. He politely showed me his lecture room and other things worthy of notice at Yale College." Olmstead informed Slade of the New Haven female schools [plural] and concluded, "they have long settled the point that females should be equal participants in the advantages of a thorough education. This has long been my opinion and for accomplishment of which I have devoted much time, labor, and expense." Thus, he revealed this critical motivating opinion regarding female education and simultaneously reinforced his own credentials as a highly qualified college professor.

Olmstead was also the first person on record to have used the word "radiator" to refer to a heating device in 1834. He and a colleague were also the first American astronomers to observe Halley's Comet in 1835. In 1836, when the university divided his department, Olmstead chose to remain in natural philosophy (science) rather than mathematics. He was known to have invented several devices to enhance human comfort and convenience but rarely filed for patents on his productions. Olmstead wrote nine textbooks in science, four of them before Slade's visit in 1837, including his *Introduction to Natural Philosophy* in 1831, which was republished in several editions over the next one hundred years, and the *Compendium of Natural Philosophy* in 1832.[110] His *Introduction to Astronomy* (1839) was reprinted in fifty editions.[111] He also wrote some history including biographical sketches of other inventors. One of these, *Memoir of Eli Whitney, Esq.*, included the invention of the cotton gin in Georgia and was published in the *American Journal of Science* just seven years after Whitney's death.[112]

Yale has a particular relationship with the history of science going back to its seventeenth-century foundations. The modern university in New Haven traces its history back to the 1640s when scientifically minded English Puritans founded a college in the New Haven Colony. John Davenport (1597–1670) was a co-founder of the New Haven Colony (with his classmate Theophilus Eaton) as well as the first to propose a college there like the one in Massachusetts. Davenport was also a member of the London-based Hartlib Circle, which was promoting empirical science based on Christian principles in the seventeenth century. Born in Coventry, England, Davenport studied at both Oxford and Cambridge before becoming pastor of the St. Stephen's Church on Coleman Street in London. He reached out to Samuel Hartlib looking for a replacement in 1637 as he prepared to move his entire congregation to America and charter a new colony south of Massachusetts. Davenport set the tone for the colony and the college as an ardent proponent of education, empirical natural philosophy, and Puritanism. As late as 1659 he was still sending papers he had written on chemistry, medicine, and surgery to Hartlib.[113] It was, moreover, through Davenport that Hartlib reconnected with John Winthrop, Jr. All of this reveals not only how the founding of Ivy League schools, particularly Yale, was part of the Hartlibian Empirical Project of Scientific Improvement but that educators such as Olmstead and Slade were a continuation of this same project just two hundred years later.[114]

On the homeward bound transit through New York, Slade bought dozens of twenty-six different academic titles including everything from Homer's *Iliad* to John Playfair and Euclid's *Elements of Geometry: Containing the First Six Books of Euclid with a Supplement on the Quadrature of the Circle and the Geometry of Solids to which are added Elements of Plane and Spherical Geometry*. He bought thirty-six copies of Roswell Chamberlain Smith's *Introduction to Arithmetic* and forty-eight copies of J. Olney's atlas among others. He bought Bibles, hymnals, pencils, plotting instruments, globes, potassium, flexible tubes, saltpeter, indelible ink, a thermometer, chemical instruments, and more. He purchased an accordion and two lined "Fool's cap."[115] These numbers for the most part seem appropriate for a school of thirty students like the Clinton Female Seminary, but the expense is well beyond what Slade could have afforded on his own. The range of subjects and level of instruction more appropriately match the Georgia Female College. Whether he used them in Clinton does not alter the fact they were purchased for Macon by the founders of the female college and undoubtedly moved with Slade and the others who soon merged into the new Bibb County institution. Later, although Slade left Macon for Penfield, Georgia, he left his 1837 New York purchases in Macon at the Georgia Female College, some of which remain on display until today at Wesleyan College where they are known as *Slade's Instruments* [emphasis added]. Able to use valuable tools in Penfield, it remains utterly inconceivable he would have left these expensive scientific instruments in Macon if they had been purchased with his personal funds.

Notes

1 "Clinton Female Academy" and "Music," Georgia Messenger (June 1, 1837), p. 3.
2 Thomas Bog Slade, *Autobiography of Thomas Bog Slade*, Southern Historical Collection 1837–1846, 2683-z, University of North Carolina, p. 1.
3 "Georgia Female College," *Chronicle and Sentinel* (December 13, 1838), p. 2.
4 Thomas Bog Slade, *Autobiography of Thomas Bog Slade*, Southern Historical Collection 1837–1846, 2683-z, University of North Carolina, p. 1.
5 T. Wood Clarke, *Émigrés In The Wilderness* (New York: The Macmillan Company, 1941), p. 51.
6 *Cecil County Directory*, MD (1856).
7 *The Cecil Whig Elkton, MD* (Elkton, MD), 1856.
8 Thomas Bog Slade, *Autobiography of Thomas Bog Slade*, Southern Historical Collection 1837–1846, 2683-z, University of North Carolina, p. 2.
9 Fanny Trollope, *Domestic Manners of the Americans* (London: Whittaker, Treacher, and Co., 1832), pp. 74–5.
10 John S. C. Abbott, *History of Joseph Bonaparte, King of Naples and of Italy* (Harper & Bros., 1869); Owen Connelly, *The Gentle Bonaparte: A Biography of Joseph, Napoleon's Elder Brother* (Macmillan, 1968); Thomas E. Crocker, *Empire's Eagles: The Fate of the Napoleonic Elite in America* (Prometheus, 2021); Michael Ross, *The Reluctant King: Joseph Bonaparte: King of the Two Sicilies and Spain* (Sidgwick and Jackson, 1976); and Patricia Tyson Stroud, *The Man Who Had Been King: The American Exile of Napoleon's Brother Joseph* (Univ. of Pennsylvania, 2014).
11 Thomas Bog Slade, *Autobiography of Thomas Bog Slade*, Southern Historical Collection 1837–1846, 2683-z, University of North Carolina, p. 2.
12 Ibid., p. 3.
13 Arthur Hornblow, *A History of the Theatre in America from its Beginnings to the Present Time* (1919), p. 96.
14 Benjamin Feldman, *East in Eden: William Niblo and His Pleasure Garden of Yore* (New York: Wanderer Press, 2014).
15 Thomas Bog Slade, *Autobiography of Thomas Bog Slade*, Southern Historical Collection 1837–1846, 2683-z, University of North Carolina, p. 3.
16 Ibid.
17 *The History of Sing Sing Prison* (Half Moon Press, 2000) and Guy Cheli, *Sing Sing Prison* (Arcadia, 2003).

18 Stephen E. E. Ambrose, *Duty, Honor, Country: A History of West Point* (Johns Hopkins, 2000); Stephen Ambrose, William F. Buckley, et al., *West Point: Two Centuries of Honor and Tradition* (Grand Central Pub., 2002); John B. Buckley, Bill Patterson, et al., *Born in the Shadow of History: West Point's Early Years and the American Revolution* (Ind. published, 2023); and Robert C. Richardson, Jr, *West Point: An Early History, 1776-1917* (Ind. published, 2019).

19 John K. Mahon, *History of the Second Seminole War, 1835-1842* (Univ. of Florida, 1967), p. 118.

20 Robert Sobel, *Biographical Dictionary of the Governors of the United States, 1789-1978*, vol. iii (Meckler Books, 1978), p. 1121. See also Mark Groen, "The Whig Party and the Rise of the Common Schools, 1837-1854," *American Educational History Journal* 35, no. 1-2 (March 2008): 254.

21 Michael Hill, *The Governors of North Carolina* (NC Office of Archives and History, 2007); and Milton Ready, *The Tar Heel State: A New History of North Carolina* (Univ. of South Carolina Press, 2020).

22 George H. Callcott, *A History of the University of Maryland* (Maryland Historical Society, 1966).

23 See A. W. Winship, "Emma Willard," *The Journal of Education* 109:25 (June 1929): 703; John Lord, *The Life of Emma Willard* (New York: Appleton, 1873); Elizabeth Cady Stanton, "Emma Willard, the Pioneer in the Higher Education of Women," *Westminster Review* 140:1 (January 1852-January 1914): 538; Susan M. Cruea, "Changing Ideals of Womanhood During the Nineteenth Century Woman Movement," *General Studies Writing Faculty Publications* 1 (2005): 188; and Florence Woolsey Hazzard, "Women Pioneers in Democracy," *Pi Lambda Theta Journal* 28:2 (1949): 110.

24 Anne Firor Scott, "What, Then, is the American: This New Woman?" *The Journal of American History* 65:3 (December 1978): 689.

25 Ibid., p. 690.

26 David Gold and Catherine L. Hobbs, *Rhetoric, History, and Women's Oratorical Education: American Women Learn to Speak* (Routledge, 2013).

27 Hamilton Child, *Gazetteer and Business Directory of Rensselaer County, N. Y., for 1870-71* (1870). See also George Baker Anderson, *Landmarks of Rensselaer County* (Syracuse: D. Mason & Co., 1897).

28 Don Rittner, *Legendary Locals of Troy* (Arcadia, 2012), *Remembering Troy: Heritage on the Hudson* (History Press, 2008), and *Troy Through Time* (America Through Time, 2017).

29 Hamilton Child, *Gazetteer and Business Directory of Rensselaer County, N. Y., for 1870–71* (1870).
30 *The Troy Budget*, 1828–1840, newspaper (Troy, NY) January 2, 1837.
31 Don Rittner, *Legendary Locals of Troy* (Arcadia, 2012), p. 98.
32 Florence Fleming Corley, "The Presbyterian Quest: Higher Education for Georgia Women," *American Presbyterians* 69:2 (Summer 1991): 84.
33 Thomas Bog Slade, *Autobiography of Thomas Bog Slade*, Southern Historical Collection 1837–1846, 2683-z, University of North Carolina, p. 4.
34 Anne Firor Scott, "What, Then, is the American: This New Woman?" *The Journal of American History* 65:3 (December 1978): 698.
35 Ibid. See also Diary of Thomas Bog Slade, Southern Historical Collection, University of North Carolina Library (Chapel Hill).
36 Florence Fleming Corley, "The Presbyterian Quest: Higher Education for Georgia Women," *American Presbyterians* 69:2 (Summer 1991): 83.
37 Trudy J. Hanmer, *Wrought with Steadfast Will: A History of the Emma Willard School* (Troy, NY: The Troy Book Makers, 2012), p. 72.
38 Ibid., p. 187.
39 Henry Fowler, "Educational Services of Mrs. Emma Willard," in Henry Barnard, ed., *Memoirs of Teachers, Educators, and Promoters and Benefactors of Education, Literature and Science* (New York, 1861), p. 167.
40 See Alma Lutz, *Emma Willard: Pioneer Educator of American Women* (Boston: Beacon Press, 1967); and John Lord, *The Life of Emma Willard* (New York: D. Appleton & Co., 1873).
41 Anne Firor Scott, "What, Then, is the American: This New Woman?" *The Journal of American History* 65:3 (December 1978): 679–703.
42 Alexis de Tocqueville, *Democracy in America*, Henry Steele Commager, ed. (London, 1946), p. 377.
43 Anne Firor Scott, "What, Then, is the American: This New Woman?" *The Journal of American History* 65:3 (December 1978): 680.
44 Emma Hart Willard, "Letter from George Combe to Emma Willard, in 'Notes', New York State Assembly, Document No. 74, March 4, 1852," in The Papers of Emma Hart Willard.
45 Willard, "Receipt of the American Colonization Society," in The Papers of Emma Hart Willard.
46 Anne Firor Scott, "What, Then, is the American: This New Woman?" *The Journal of American History* 65:3 (December 1978): 702.

47 Lisa Trattner, "The Complexities of a Nineteenth-Century Icon: Emma Hart Willard," PhD diss., Notre Dame of Maryland University, 2021, p. 80; Grant Arndt, "Ho-Chunk Powwows: Innovation and Tradition in a Changing World," *The Wisconsin Magazine of History* 91:3 (2008): 30; and Emma Hart Willard, *Abridged History of the United States; or Republic of America*, new and enlarged ed. (New York: A.S. Barnes & Co., 1855), p. 19.

48 Anne Firor Scott, "The Ever-Widening Circle: The Diffusion of Feminist Values from the Troy Female Seminary 1822–1872," *History of Education Quarterly* 19:1 (1979): 9.

49 Anne Firor Scott, "What, Then, is the American: This New Woman?" *The Journal of American History* 65:3 (December 1978): 693.

50 Edward T. James, Janet Wilson James, and Paul S. Boyer, eds., *Notable American Women, 1607–1950*, 3 vols. (Cambridge, 1971), vol. ii, pp. 191–3.

51 Emma Hart Willard, *An Address to the Public; Particularly to the Members of the Legislature of New York, Proposing a Plan for Improving Female Education* (Middlebury: J. W. Copeland, 1819).

52 Ibid., p. 5.

53 Amherst College Archives and Special Collections, *Emma Hart Willard Family Papers, 1819–1961*.

54 Emma Hart Willard, *An Address to the Public; Particularly to the Members of the Legislature of New York, Proposing a Plan for Improving Female Education* (Middlebury: J. W. Copeland, 1819), p. 5.

55 Ibid., p. 7.

56 Ibid.

57 "An Address," *Georgia Messenger* (June 21, 1832).

58 Emma Hart Willard, *An Address to the Public; Particularly to the Members of the Legislature of New York, Proposing a Plan for Improving Female Education* (Middlebury: J. W. Copeland, 1819), p. 7.

59 "An Address," *Georgia Messenger* (June 21, 1832).

60 Emma Hart Willard, *An Address to the Public; Particularly to the Members of the Legislature of New York, Proposing a Plan for Improving Female Education* (Middlebury: J. W. Copeland, 1819), p. 8.

61 Ibid.

62 "An Address," *Georgia Messenger* (June 21, 1832).

63 Emma Hart Willard, *An Address to the Public; Particularly to the Members of the Legislature of New York, Proposing a Plan for Improving Female Education* (Middlebury: J. W. Copeland, 1819), p. 14.

64 Ibid., p. 15.
65 Ibid., p. 16.
66 John Lord, *The Life of Emma Willard* (New York: Appleton, 1873), p. 46.
67 Anne Firor Scott, "What, Then, is the American: This New Woman?" *The Journal of American History* 65:3 (December 1978): 688.
68 Emma Hart Willard, *An Address to the Public; Particularly to the Members of the Legislature of New York, Proposing a Plan for Improving Female Education* (Middlebury: J. W. Copeland, 1819), p. 18.
69 Ibid., p. 19.
70 Alma Lutz, *Emma Willard: Pioneer Educator of American Women* (Boston: Beacon Press, 1967), p. 644.
71 Anne Firor Scott, "What, Then, is the American: This New Woman?" *The Journal of American History* 65:3 (December 1978): 689.
72 Ibid., p. 691.
73 Cotton Mather, *Magnalia Christi Americana: Or, The Ecclesiastical History of New-England, from its First Planting in the Year 1620, unto the Year of Our Lord, 1698* (London, 1702), p. 14.
74 Child to Hartlib? 24 Dec 1645, *HP* [15/5/1A-2B].
75 For more information on Comenius and his educational reforms specifically, see Johann Amos Comenius, *Conatuum Comeniamorum Praeludia Ex Bibliotheca* (London, 1637), *The Labyrinth of the World and the Paradise of the Heart,* Howard Louthan and Andrea Sterk, trans. (New York, 1998), and *A Reformation of Schools* (London 1642); Daniel Benham, *A Sketch of the Life of J. A. Comenius* (London, 1858); Milada Blekastad, *Comenius: Versuch eines Umrisses von Leben, Werk und Schicksal des Jan Amos Komenský* (Oslo and Prague, 1969); Johannes Radomil Kvacala, "The Educational Reform of Comenius in Germany up to the End of the XVIIth c," Karl Kehrbach, ed., in *Monumenta Germaniae Paedagogica*, Vol. 32 (Berlin, 1904); S. S. Laurie *John Amos Comenius: Bishop of the Moravians* (Cambridge, 1904); Gerhard F. Strasser, "Das Erbe von Johann Amos Comenius und Samuel Hartlib: Tagungen in Bayreuth, Prag und Sheffield," *Berichte zur Wissenschaftsgeschichte* 16:3-4 (1993): 293-5; and George Henry Turnbull, *Hartlib, Dury and Comenius: Gleanings from Hartlib's Papers* (London, 1947) and *Samuel Hartlib: A Sketch of His Life and His Relations to J. A. Comenius* (Oxford, 1920).
76 Willard, *Journal and Letters*.
77 Anne Firor Scott, "What, Then, is the American: This New Woman?" *The Journal of American History* 65:3 (December 1978): 693.

78 Ibid., p. 696.
79 Ibid., p. 697.
80 Ibid., p. 698.
81 Ibid.
82 Ibid., p. 699.
83 Thomas Bog Slade, *Autobiography of Thomas Bog Slade*, Southern Historical Collection 1837–1846, 2683-z, University of North Carolina, p. 4.
84 See Stephen W. Angell, *The Oxford Handbook of Quaker Studies* in Oxford Handbooks in Religion and Theology series (Oxford, 2015); Sydney G. Fisher, *The Quaker Colonies: History of the Early Quaker Settlements in New England and the Delaware River* (Pantianos, 1919); Thomas D. Hamm, *Quaker Writings: An Anthology, 1650–1920* (Penguin, 2011); Robynne Rogers Healey, *Quakerism in the Atlantic World, 1690–1830* in The New History of Quakerism, vol. iii (Penn State Univ., 2022); and Robert Lawrence Smith, *A Quaker Book of Wisdom: Life Lessons in Simplicity, Service, and Common Sense* (William Marrow, 2013).
85 Thomas Bog Slade, *Autobiography of Thomas Bog Slade*, Southern Historical Collection 1837–1846, 2683-z, University of North Carolina, p. 5.
86 See Nardi Reeder Campion, *Mother Ann Lee: Morning Star of the Shakers* (Univ. Press of New England, 1990); Frederick William Evans, *Ann Lee (The Founder of the Shakers): A Biography with Memoirs of William Lee, James Whittaker, J. Hocknall, J. Meachem, and Lucy Wright* (HardPress, 2018); Richard Francis, *Ann the Word: The Story of Ann Lee, Female Messiah, Mother of the Shakers, the Woman Clothed with the Sun* (Arcade, 2013); and Robert Peters, *Shaker Light: Mother Ann Lee in America* (Unicorn, 1987).
87 "The Boston Montgomery Guards, 1837," *Donahoe's Magazine* 18:5 (November 1887): 415–19. See also Patrick Browne, *Boston Street Riot, Boston, 1837* (Historical Digression, 2016); Peter F. Stevens, *Hidden Histories of the Boston Irish: Little Known Stories from Ireland's "Next Parish Over"* (The History Press, 2008); and Jack Tager, *Boston Riots: Three Centuries of Social Violence* (Northeastern, 2001).
88 Thomas Bog Slade, *Autobiography of Thomas Bog Slade*, Southern Historical Collection 1837–1846, 2683-z, University of North Carolina, p. 5.
89 Massachusetts Charitable Mechanic Association, *Annals of the Massachusetts Charitable Mechanic Association, 1795–1892 Printed by Order of the Association* (Boston, Massachusetts: Press of Rockwell and Churchill, 1892), p. 424.

90 Huey B. Long, *Early Innovators in Adult Education* (New York: Routledge, 1991), pp. 60–1.
91 William H. Hutchinson, *A Concise History of the Baldwin Place Baptist Church* (Legare Street Press, 2023).
92 *A History of Rowe Street Baptist Church, Boston, MA, with the Declaration of Faith and the Church Covenant, and List of Members, 1853* (Legare Street Press, 2021), p. 10.
93 Baron Stow, *A History of the English Baptist Mission to India* (American Sunday School Union, 1835).
94 Thomas Bog Slade, *Autobiography of Thomas Bog Slade*, Southern Historical Collection 1837–1846, 2683-z, University of North Carolina, p. 5.
95 "Hannah Adams (1755–1831)," *Women in World History: A Biographical Encyclopedia*, vol. 1 (Pennsylvania State Univ., 1999), p. 49.
96 Anthony Walsh, "The American Tour of Dr. Spurzheim," *Journal of the History of Medicine and Allied Sciences* 27 (1972): 187–205.
97 Lynne T. Brickley, Glee Krueger, Sally Schwager, Theodore Sizer, and Nancy Sizer, *To Ornament Their Minds: Sarah Pierce's Litchfield Female Academy 1792–1833* (Litchfield, CT: Litchfield Historical Society, 1993).
98 See Laurel Thatcher Ulrich, *Good Wives: Image and Reality in the Lives of Women in Northern New England, 1650–1750* (Vintage, 2010).
99 Emma Hart Willard, *An Address to the Public; Particularly to the Members of the Legislature of New York, Proposing a Plan for Improving Female Education* (Middlebury: J. W. Copeland, 1819), p. 5.
100 Louisa May Alcott, *Good Wives* (Roberts Brothers, 1869); Kathleen M. Brown, *Good Wives, Nasty Wenches, and Anxious Patriarchs: Gender, Race, and Power in Colonial Virginia* (Univ. of North Carolina, 1996); and Dilek Kantar, "Virgins, Wives and Whores in the Eighteenth-century Ironic Myths," *Interactions* 23:1–2 (2014): 123.
101 Emma Hart Willard, *An Address to the Public; Particularly to the Members of the Legislature of New York, Proposing a Plan for Improving Female Education* (Middlebury: J. W. Copeland, 1819), p. 6.
102 "An Address," *Georgia Messenger* (June 21, 1832).
103 See Jeanne Boydston, *Home and Work: Housework, Wages, and the Ideology of Labor in the Early Republic* (New York: Oxford University Press, 1994); Anne M. Boylan, *The Origins of Women's Activism: New York and Boston, 1797–1840* (Chapel Hill: University of North Carolina Press, 2002); Mark David Hall,

"Beyond Self-interest: the Political Theory and Practice of Evangelical Women in Antebellum America" *Journal of Church and State* 44:3 (2002): 477-99; Linda K. Kerber, "The Republican Mother: Women and the Enlightenment-An American Perspective," *American Quarterly* 28:2 (1976): 187-205, *Intellectual History of Women: Essays by Linda K. Kerber* (Chapel Hill: University of North Carolina Press, 1997), and *Women of the Republic: Intellect and Ideology in Revolutionary America* (Chapel Hill: University of North Carolina Press, 1980); S. J. Kleinberg, *Women in the United States, 1830-1945* (New Brunswick, NJ: Rutgers University Press, 1999); Mary Beth Norton, *Liberty's Daughters: The Revolutionary Experience of American Women, 1750-1800* (Ithaca, NY: Cornell University Press, 1980); Sarah Robbins, "'The Future Good and Great of our Land': Republican Mothers, Female Authors, and Domesticated Literacy in Antebellum New England," *New England Quarterly* 75:4 (2002): 562-91; and Rosemarie Zagari, "Morals, Manners, and the Republican Mother," *American Quarterly* 44:2 (1992): 192-215.

104 "An Address," *Georgia Messenger* (June 21, 1832).
105 Caroline Winterer, "Women and Civil Society: An Introduction," *Journal of the Early Republic* 28:1 (2008): 23-8.
106 Lynne T. Brickley, Glee Krueger, Sally Schwager, Theodore Sizer, and Nancy Sizer, *To Ornament Their Minds: Sarah Pierce's Litchfield Female Academy 1792-1833* (Litchfield, CT: Litchfield Historical Society, 1993), p. 9.
107 See Barbara P. Atwood, "Miss Pierce of Litchfield," *New England Galaxy* 9 (1967): 32-40; "Litchfield Female Seminary," *Hartford Courant* (Hartford, Connecticut), May 4, 1835, p. 4; Judith Livingston Loto, "One Voice: The Work and Words of Litchfield Female Academy Student Charlotte Hopper Newcomb, 1809-1810," *Dublin Seminar for New England Folklife Annual Proceedings* 27 (July 2002): 65-77; Lisa Roberge Pichnarcik, "On the Threshold of Improvement: Women's Education at the Litchfield Female and Morris Academies," *Connecticut History* 27 (September 1996): 129-58 and *The Role of Books in Connecticut Women's Education in the New Republic: As Examined in Sarah Pierce's Litchfield Female Academy and James Morris' Coeducational Academy,* Master's thesis (Southern Connecticut State University, 1996); Emily Noyes Vanderpoel and Elizabeth C. Barney Buel, eds., *Chronicles of a Pioneer School, from 1792 to 1833 being the History of Miss Sarah Pierce and Her Litchfield School* (Harvard, 1903); and Albert J. Von Frank, "Sarah Pierce and the Poetic Origins of Utopian Feminism in America." *Prospects* 14 (October 1989): 45-63.

108 Thomas Bog Slade, *Autobiography of Thomas Bog Slade*, Southern Historical Collection 1837–1846, 2683-z, University of North Carolina, p. 6.
109 Margaret Martin, *A Long Look at Nature: The North Carolina State Museum of Natural Sciences* (Univ. of North Carolina, 2001), pp. 7, 26–7.
110 Denison Olmstead, *An Introduction to Natural Philosophy; Designed as a Textbook for Students in College* (New Haven: H. Howe, 1831) and *A Compendium of Natural Philosophy: Adapted to the Use of the General Reader, and of Schools and Academies* (New Haven: H. Howe, 1833).
111 Theodore R. Treadwell, "Denison Olmsted an Early American Astronomer," *Popular Astronomy* 54 (1946): 239.
112 Denison Olmstead, *Memoir of Eli Whitney, Esq.* (New Haven: Durrie & Peck, 1846). See also Franklin Bowditch Dexter *Biographical Sketches of the Graduates of Yale College: With Annals of the College History* (New York: Holt, 1885); John M. Parker III, "Denison Olmsted, 18 June 1791–13 May 1859," in William S. Powell, ed., *Dictionary of North Carolina Biography* (University of North Carolina, 1996); and Theodore R. Treadwell, "Denison Olmsted an Early American Astronomer," *Popular Astronomy* 54 (1946): 237–41.
113 John Winthrop to Hartlib, December 16, 1659, *HP* [40/3/1A].
114 See Francis J. Bremer, *Building a New Jerusalem: John Davenport, a Puritan in Three Worlds* (New Haven, CT: Yale University Press, 2012); and Timothy E. Miller, *Gold for Secrets: The Hartlib Circle and The Early English Empire, 1630–1660*, DPhil Thesis (Oxford, 2020).
115 Thomas Bog Slade, *Autobiography of Thomas Bog Slade*, Southern Historical Collection 1837–1846, 2683-z, University of North Carolina, p. 8.

4

Macon and Wesleyan

The mind has no sex.

Mary Wollstonecraft

Bibb County was created by the Georgia legislature, meeting at Milledgeville after 1807, in 1822 and the City of Macon was founded in 1823. The first steamboat docked at Macon, the *S. S. North Carolina*, on the Ocmulgee River in 1829 and the state legislature approved the charter for the Georgia Female College in 1836. In 1838 the railroad was completed between Macon and Atlanta, the first college building was completed for the college up the hill on College Street, and George Foster Pierce (1811–84) was elected first president.[1] The son of Lovick Pierce, the father of Methodism in Georgia, George was only twenty-eight years old when he assumed the presidency of Georgia Female College. Although he later became a Bishop in the Methodist Episcopal Church South and president of Emory University, in 1839 he was young and inexperienced. He was, however, "unusual" in his maturity and judgment.[2] Classes began in January 1839 and the first commencement was held in 1840.[3]

Despite the denominational argument that followed the Georgia Female College's founding, the story of Wesleyan, arguably, begins with the Scots-Irish pioneers who settled in the Southern states during the eighteenth century. Some entered through the ports of Charleston and Savannah while others migrated down from Virginia, Pennsylvania, and further north. Having experienced a difficult reformation in Scotland and "complicated" relationships with the English, these settlers were overwhelmingly Protestant and especially Presbyterian upon arrival with a willingness to consider other evangelical choices such as Baptist and Methodist when convenient.[4] Those who remained within the "orthodox" church had a particular appreciation for education, both male and female, from the beginning. This was so much so that they cost themselves the growth seen among Baptists and Methodists during the First and Second Great Awakenings. Their refusal to send out uneducated (i.e., unqualified) pastors allowed the other denominations, willing to ordain less educated clergy for the sake of expediency, to plant new churches much further afield and more quickly. Granted, the Methodists developed innovative practices such as circuit-riding ministers to mitigate the shortage but the Presbyterians clung to the patient, long-term approach of slow and steady in church planting. Imagine a spectrum of quality and quantity with the various denominations taking a position somewhere in between based on their ordering of evangelical priorities. Despite being, thus, always smaller in numbers, Presbyterians were disproportionately influential in their communities and many of them led the way in promoting female education. According to Corley, the University of Georgia, originally known as Franklin College in the eighteenth century, was "so salted with Presbyterians that from 1819 to 1829, during the presidency of the Rev. Moses Waddel (1770–1840), the Baptist and Methodist communions complained of liberalism, secularism, and denominational favoritism."[5]

These sectarian differences in the state university drove each denomination to organize schools for the students in their respective churches. In 1833, Georgia Baptists organized Mercer College in Penfield, Georgia; in 1835 the Presbyterians founded Oglethorpe College in Midway; and in 1836 Methodists chartered Emory College in Oxford (Newton County).[6] All three of these schools became well-known universities and, for a time, the flagship schools for their respective denominations. Each relocated from their original founding towns: Mercer to Macon (1870), Oglethorpe to Atlanta (1870), and Emory to Decatur (1914). Two have since terminated their denominational connections and established themselves as nonsectarian institutions, Mercer in 2006 and Oglethorpe in the early 1920s. Emory maintains its official affiliation with the United Methodist Church but practically seeks diversity and welcomes students regardless of religion.

There was, however, much cooperation among the leading denominations both in the state and nation during the early days of the Second Awakening. As people gathered in large crowds for the purpose of protracted religious services, the camp meetings were organized and became a staple of the movement, especially along the frontiers of the English-speaking settlements. The Red Bone Camp Ground, for example, was in Marion County, Georgia, where five-day meetings were held annually. Lovick Pierce preached there in 1870 at the age of eighty-five. Other camp meetings were held in or adjacent to towns throughout the South. William Arnold, for example, organized an open-air annual conference near the Walton County Courthouse in Monroe, Georgia, for the preachers of the Athens District in 1825.[7] People traveled to these protracted meetings in wagons, on horseback, and on foot, bringing provisions and bedding. Most literally camped on the ground as others constructed temporary housing. "Presbyterians, Baptists, and Methodists, united together in prayer, exhortation, and preaching, exerting all their energies to forward this good work," wrote Bangs.[8] Not only were people converted to faith in Christianity but many were encouraged to take up the work of reforming American society for the improvement of the common good. This led some to organize abolitionist movements while others focused on education.

Col. Duncan Green Campbell (1787–1828) of North Carolina, a third-generation Scots-American and 1806 graduate of the University of North Carolina who migrated to Washington, Georgia, was the foremost example of Presbyterian leadership in female education. Like Slade, Campbell practiced law, then organized a female academy in his home. Also like Slade, Campbell had daughters whom he believed deserved a formal education. Their curiosity and capacity to learn and understand became the primary motivation for Campbell's life work. As there were no institutions available to Mary, Sarah, and Rebecca Campbell in Wilkes County, Georgia, Campbell created one for them and others like them. Unlike Slade, Campbell left the classroom instruction to the teachers and contributed to his school as a trustee from 1816 until his death in 1828. Campbell read Emma Willard's *Plan,* and it moved him to greater action. He became an enthusiastic activist for female education in Washington, Georgia, and then lobbied in Milledgeville, urging the state legislature to support schools for girls. Unlike Slade, Campbell ran for political office, and by 1825 he was the president *pro tempore* of the Georgia State Senate, a powerful position that gave him particular advantages in the campaign for female education in the early nineteenth century. He introduced a bill "to establish a public seat of learning . . . for the education of females" in Georgia. The bill passed the House of Representatives but was ultimately defeated in the Senate despite Campbell's strong support.[9]

Daniel Chandler (1805–66) was the valedictorian of the Franklin College (University of Georgia) Class of 1826. In 1828 he married Campbell's daughter Sarah, moved to Mobile, Alabama, and became an elder in the Government Street Presbyterian Church. Daniel was handsome, clever, and he was an eloquent and passionate public speaker, especially for causes in which he strongly believed. In 1834 he was invited to address the Demosthenian and Phi Kappa Societies back in Athens and there he delivered the landmark speech promoting state-supported higher education for women in Georgia. He proposed an institution for women comparable to the male-only Franklin College. "There are in these United States in this year, 1835," Chandler declared, "sixty-one colleges, and be it said to the disgrace of the nation, not one is dedicated to the cause of female education."[10] Depending on one's definition of the word "college," Chandler's statement was exaggerated but it did not matter to those enthusiasts in the audience. William A. Mercer of Washington, Georgia, was so moved by Chandler's speech that, at the suggestion of John McPherson of Berrien, Georgia, he printed five thousand copies of the text, *An Address on Female Education*, and distributed them throughout the state.[11]

Senator Benjamin Herbert Rutherford introduced a bill in 1836 to establish a female college in Georgia. State Representative Alexander H. Stephens sponsored the bill in the Georgia House as chairman of the Education Committee. As a result, the bill was passed on December 23, 1836, but due to the poor economy of 1837, no state appropriation was made to fund the bill. While the unfunded bill lingered, separate meetings were being held to organize a female college. Businessmen in Macon with the backing of the Ocmulgee Bank campaigned for a nonsectarian female college to be located specifically in Macon while denominational leaders in the Methodist Episcopal Church Georgia Conference met to plan a college to be specifically Methodist, at first with no predetermined location in mind. Subsequently, Rutherford and Stephens' act was repealed[12] but once the college was founded despite the repeal and proved itself beyond sectarian controversy, Stephens reflected:

> The movement for women's education was the occasion of amusement to some. I may be pardoned in saying that it met with my warm support. The experiment proved successful beyond the expectation of its most sanguine friends, the example became contagious, not only in our own state, but in adjoining states, and we now have a perfect galaxy of these brilliant luminaries, sending forth their cheering beams in every direction[13]

Many other early Georgia residents opposed the idea of educating young women. One solicitor for the Georgia Female College was told, "I will not give you a cent for any such object. I would not have one of your graduates for a wife, for I could never even build a pigpen without her criticizing it and saying it was not put up on mathematical principles." Another said, "No, I will not give a dollar; all a woman needs to know is how to read the New Testament, and to spin and weave clothing for her family."[14] In spite of these sentiments, support for female education continued to grow in the 1830s and whereas most schools for girls were no more than secondary schools where students learned ornamental skills, the visionaries in Macon aspired to more than a seminary.[15] The businessmen of Macon were strategically hopeful that a women's college would attract a similar college for men. Fathers of girls wanted a curriculum equal to that provided to boys, so the college offered Latin and Greek which was enough to qualify the liberal arts curriculum as higher education even though no individual student was required to take ancient languages. There were also tertiary classes in astronomy, botany, chemistry, French, and geography.

Another group of men in Monroe County hoped to establish a college for women in Forsyth under the leadership of B. B. Hopkins, who was already operating a large female school there before 1835. One other member of this organizing group complained that the opportunity had been lost to Macon due to the opposition the idea of a female college had encountered in Monroe County, which, among other objections, included the school possibly being controlled by Methodists. A Presbyterian, the other member dismissed the concern in the *Messenger* by writing, "I cannot see how Methodism can be confused into grammar, philosophy, or chemistry. Our children will be under our roofs more than half their times."[16] The school was lost to Macon, from the Forsyth perspective, but the writer was wrong about the other. Not all students were commuters, and the curriculum was never the issue.

Female writers to the *Messenger* urged the women of Macon to unite despite denominational differences and support the idea for a female college as it was good for women. "No matter whether you be Presbyterians, Methodists, Baptists, or Episcopalian," a writer known only as "Mother" wrote, "united in common cause and united, the opposition of our husbands will dissolve like mist, and we the partners of their bosoms must be heard." An anonymous but obviously well-educated woman herself, the writer continued, "Has God, when strewing this fair land with his choice blessings been niggard to women alone? Has the immoral mind deserted the land of orange, the vine, and the cotton to dwell alone with our northern sisters?"[17] Letters to the editor being what they were in the 1830s, she made a full argument of over 1,600 words for female education in Macon by appealing to necessity, grandmothers, and logic.

A group of men responded in the same year. They were Macon businessmen, fathers of daughters and owners of enslaved persons, and several had previous experience in the field of education.[18] This group was ecumenical and included Robert Augustus Beall, Jerry Cowles, Robert Collins, and Henry Graybill Lamar. Specifically, they represented commercial, financial, and transportation industries in Macon. They were in conversation with John Howard, Elijah Sinclair, and J. W. Talley to secure supervision of the college by the church, but the latter three gentlemen were given the obligation, by the Macon businessmen, "*until it could be referred* [emphasis added] to the annual session which was to meet in Macon on January 14, 1836."[19] Their friends included Simri Rose, Slade's brother-in-law who was also previously of Clinton, and Myron Barlett, editors of the *Georgia Messenger* and *Georgia Telegraph*, respectively, who gave generous attention to their efforts of promotion and progress. A public meeting was held July 8, 1835, to publicize the benefit a college would be to the City of Macon, but the agenda was entangled in a dispute about the advantage a college would be to any denomination which controlled it. Some objected to the donation of two city acres for the college while others argued against the idea of female education in general. The first announcements appeared July 9, 1835, in the Macon newspapers.[20] Rose, understandably, was most enthusiastic for the project. He urged his readers to support the prospect and assured them that the college would be staffed by "able and experienced professors" who would be "nonsectarian."[21]

In September the *Telegraph* published an article extracted from the *Knickerbocker* on the cause of female education. A literary magazine founded in New York by Charles Fenno Hoffman in 1833, the *Knickerbocker*, edited by Lewis Gaylor Clark, regularly promoted the education of women. The article "Female Character" by the anonymous author of *Pulpit Eloquence and the Downfall of Nations,* known only as Intellectual Over Ornamental, wrote, "It is time the mechanism of female education should give place to its philosophy,— that the mind should no longer be a mere receptacle for the dates and facts but a living, active, and thoughtful agent, fulfilling the high designs of its creation in the best and most efficient manner."[22]

In the meantime, the mainline denominations established churches in Macon from the earliest days. Lovick Pierce, Samuel Hodges, and John Howard held a four-day evangelical meeting in a Macon warehouse on Walnut Street in 1825. The response was so good, a Methodist church was built in 1826 on Mulberry Street. Ignatius Few became the first pastor, in just the second year of his ministry. "Dr. Few gave dignity to every place he filled," wrote Historian George G. Smith, "and he soon gathered about him a large and appreciative congregation. Many substantial Methodists from the older parts of the State had already moved to the city, and he found lay members ready to help him in organizing the church for work."[23]

The often-cited Methodist Church meeting that contributed to the founding of the Georgia Female College occurred in November, four months after the first public meeting and six months after the first meeting of the nonsectarian Macon businessmen. Even the Methodist meeting was chaired by Lamar, suggesting the Methodist Church was more a convenient location for the meeting rather than its organizer and sponsor. James A. Nesbit and A. H. Chappell, both local businessmen, led the discussion. As these men stressed the economic benefits of having the school in Macon, Rev. John Howard "gave assurance that the upcoming Conference meeting *would assume responsibility* [emphasis added]" for the college and promised to help raise the needed $150,000.[24] Unfortunately, due to much confusion about the history, explained in detail below, the point needs clarification that while the church was seeking to start a female college in Georgia, the idea of having a female college specifically in Macon was already in motion before the church chose to merge these two ideas. The conference did, in fact, adopt the college unanimously on January 14, 1836, and appointed *half* the trustees for a newly constituted board which met for the first time the next day at the courthouse.[25] According to the minutes of the trustees, these included Bishop James Osgood Andrew (1794–1871), John Wesley Talley (1800–86), Samuel K. Hodges (1809–80), Philip Lovick Pierce (1785–1879), Ignatius Alphonso Few (1789–1845), Alexander Speer (1790–1856), William Arnold (1800–50), Thomas Sanford (1789–1870), William J. Parks (1799–1873), George Foster Pierce (1811–84), and Elijah Sinclair (1788–1846).[26] These were among the most prominent leaders of Methodism in Georgia. Few, Hodges, Parks, and Lovick Pierce were the entire Georgia delegation who represented Georgia Methodists at the General Conference held in Baltimore, Maryland, in 1840.[27]

As described by Smith, 1836 was a good year to start college. The economy was growing and the people, including businessmen, were optimistic about the future of Macon.

> 1836 was one of those which are known as flush. Cotton was high. Speculation was wild. Paper promises were abundant. The new cotton lands of Southwest Georgia were then most productive. Railroads were being projected, and all things seemed to be on the tide to success. To make more cotton, to buy more negroes, to buy more land, to make more cotton, and so on in a vicious circle, seemed to be the ruling aim of the planter. The country was wild in its pursuit after wealth, but God was providing something better than money—a great revival—and to prepare the way for it the rod of a terrible chastisement was lifted, but ere it fell the church suffered spiritually.[28]

Andrew had been a bishop in the Methodist Episcopal Church since 1832. Although he was ordained in South Carolina, as a son of Wilkes County, Georgia, he is known to be the first native Georgian to be a Methodist minister in the state. In his early years of ministry, Andrew gave no indication of his future leadership abilities. "James Andrew was not a promising-looking lad," Smith wrote,

> when he was somewhat reluctantly licensed by the quarterly conference to preach; but he was a good boy, of good parentage, and might make a useful man, they thought. Preachers were needed, and so the conference, on the recommendation of his presiding elder, received him on trial, and he was

sent as second man, on the Saltcatcher Circuit, in Barnwell and Beaufort Districts, S. C. His own estimate of himself was low, but not lower than that of some who composed the quarterly conference which licensed him. It required the entreaties of Epps Tucker to induce them to grant him license. He was required to preach, and after he came out of the church, mortified at his failure, he was comforted by one of the brethren saying to him, "James, I voted for you, but if I had heard that sermon I would not have done it."[29]

Andrew owned "dozens" of enslaved people and this increasingly became a problem for his ministry even after southern Methodists created the Methodist Episcopal Church South.[30] He became the symbol of the abolitionist controversy in the denomination. In his defense, Andrew claimed he had never purchased a slave but that the enslaved he owned were acquired through marriage only. Enslaved ownership was an offense to Methodists nationally by any means and Andrew became the catalyst for the departure of southern Methodists from the General Conference and creation of the Methodist Episcopal Church South. He later moved to Alabama and in 1858 became a founding trustee of Vanderbilt University in Nashville, Tennessee. Andrew College in Cuthbert, Georgia is named for Andrew.[31]

Born in Greensboro, Georgia, in 1800, John W. Talley was sent more than five hundred miles from Columbia, South Carolina to the Pensacola Mission by the church, which was the most remote of the western appointments. He rode from Columbia across the entire State of Georgia and West Florida to the Gulf, and all the comfort he was given "was to be told that it was well to bear the yoke in his youth."[32] Talley's journey was difficult. During a thunderstorm, for example, in Alabama, his horse once ran away and left him with a broken buggy. His journal further notes several other dangers, stretches of hunger, and the isolation he experienced on the way. Once there, "Pensacola had been the most important town in Florida during the time the Spaniards held possession of the country. There were very large trading houses, Scotch and English, which did large business with the Indians of the Creek Nation in Alabama."[33] Pensacola continued to do well until it began to be displaced by Mobile, Alabama. After an outbreak of yellow fever in Pensacola, prospects declined as quickly as they had been increasing. Talley later served as presiding bishop of the Tallahassee District. By the 1840s, "Talley, Parks, Glenn, George

F. Pierce, Payne, Anthony, Key, Lewis, Mann, were now among the leading working men in the conference."[34] Talley continued to serve as trustee for the Georgia Female College in the 1850s but moved to Texas in the 1880s where he is buried. "Jno. W. Talley, G. F. Pierce, Wm. Arnold, Wm. J. Parks, G.A. Chappell, Isaac Boring, Jno. L. Jerry, and Geo. W. Carter were a fine corps of presiding elders," wrote Smith, "some of them young and ardent, some of them old and experienced—all of them gifted and pious."[35]

Samuel K. Hodges was a merchant, minister, presiding elder (P.E.), known today in the Methodist Church as a district superintendent (D.S.), and agent for the Augusta Auxiliary Bible Society originally from Putnam County, Georgia.[36] In 1825 he was the presiding elder of the Milledgeville District where he assigned Methodist ministers to churches in the area. By 1834, however, he was a major stockholder in the Bank of Columbus.[37]

Lovick Pierce, known as the father of Methodism in Georgia, was the father of George Foster Pierce, studied and practiced medicine, and when he died in 1879 was "probably the oldest clergyman in the United States."[38] He was originally from North Carolina and had served as chaplain in the War of 1812.[39]

Ignatius Adolphus Few was the first president of Emory University (1834–41). Originally a lawyer who earned his degree at Wesleyan University in Middleton, Connecticut, he joined the Methodist Church when he became seriously ill. In 1828 he was ordained as a minister in the Methodist Episcopal Church. Few died in Athens, Georgia, of tuberculosis November 21, 1845, and is buried in Oxford, Georgia, where he was considered "the first citizen."

William Speer came from South Carolina and became a Methodist minister. He was appointed to Savannah by Lovick Pierce in 1835 and to Macon by Parks in 1836 when he was also elected by voters in Monroe County to represent them at the railroad convention held in Macon on November 7. The meeting was held at the Methodist Church and was chaired by Henry G. Lamar. Whereas this was not a religious gathering and most of the delegates to the convention were not Methodists, the event illustrates the role of churches as community halls in addition to their denominational functions. Besides his daughter Margaret Amelia, who was among the first graduating class of the Georgia Female College, Speer was the father of three successful sons,

Alexander Middleton (1820–97) who became a Georgia Supreme Court Justice after graduating from the University of Georgia, Algernon Sidney, who became a lawyer, planter, and state representative in Florida, and Eustace Willoughby who became a prominent Methodist minister in Georgia.[40]

William Arnold was a presiding elder in the Georgia Conference assigned to various locations over the years of his ministry including Athens, Macon, and Milledgeville. It was his responsibility to assign ministers to churches within his district, which he did for those including Few, Sinclair, Parkes, and Lovick Pierce, among several others. There were, thus, only four districts in the Georgia Conference at the time and all of them were led by trustees of the Georgia Female College at various times in the 1830s because Lovick Pierce served as presiding elder for the Savannah District in 1835 and Thomas Sanford served the Athens District in 1830. He had occasion to appoint Andrew, Parks, and Sinclair that year to churches in Athens and Madison, Georgia; Walton, Washington, and Lexington counties.[41] In 1825 Hodges appointed Sanford to the Alcovy Church, Newton County, in the Milledgeville District near Covington, Georgia, where the church survives as the Alcovy United Methodist Church. In 1834, Arnold appointed Sanford to the Apalachee Church, Morgan County, in the Athens District near Madison, Georgia where the original school building survives and is listed on the National Register.[42] Granted, the population of Georgia was much smaller in the 1830s and those among the leadership of the Georgia Conference even fewer, but the mutual promotions and the multitude of both professional and personal connections among the founding college trustees are no less remarkable.

Thomas Sanford served as presiding elder of the Athens District in 1830, appointing Andrew and Sinclair to churches in Apalachee and Little River respectively. William J. Parks was a Methodist pastor in Walton County, Georgia, before becoming the presiding elder for the Athens District in 1840 and later served as president of the trustees for Wesleyan in the 1850s. He was away from home, traveling a large circuit of churches in the Macon District, "found his work farther away from home than before. His highest hope was to see his family a few days six times during the year, and such was his industry that he held the plough while he was at home, till he often left blood-stains on it."[43]

Robert Toombs, US senator and secretary of state for the Confederate States of America, once described George Foster Pierce as "The most symmetrical man, the handsomest, the most gifted intellectually, and the purest in life of any man I have ever known." Another anonymous admirer of Pierce's preaching added, after the president's death, "He never failed to fill a house, and never spoke to a listless audience."[44] Smith described him in the early days of his ministry:

> He entered upon the work with enthusiasm. His love for the planting people of Georgia, with their plain and unpretending ways, had always been ardent, and where many a young man of culture and refinement would fret and complain at hardships and want of congenial society, this young preacher found only delight. Travelling his district in a buggy, leaving his fair young wife for weeks at a time; from one quarterly conference to another, from one camp-meeting to another, he went to work with all his strength and ardor. He was laboring for souls, and God crowned his labors with great success.[45]

Finally, Elijah Sinclair (1788–1846) served with Parks in Baldwin County, Georgia, as early as 1804 before the church building was complete and the "stumps were still in the street" of Milledgeville.[46] He was pastor there in 1831. Hodges (1827), Lovick Pierce (1830), and Arnold (1830) also served as pastors of this historic Methodist Church. In the meantime, Methodism came to Amelia Island, Florida, in 1822 when Sinclair arrived, appointed by the South Carolina Conference. Florida was ceded to the United States in 1821 by Spain, but Protestant Scots and English settlers were already settled there to welcome the first Protestant English-speaking minister to East Florida.[47] Both Sinclair and Lovick Pierce labored to share their faith and build Methodism among African Americans who established the African Methodist Episcopal Church in 1816. Sinclair, along with Andrew, Few, and George Pierce, were all pastors of the historic Trinity Methodist Church in Savannah, the oldest Methodist church in the city with a history going back to the 1736 ministry of John Wesley himself. Like Hodges, Sinclair was a merchant as well as a minister, and at the time of his death, this father of eight daughters was engaged in teaching young women in Grovetown, South Carolina.

"Half" of the Georgia Female College trustees, the Methodist ministers outnumbered the local Macon businessmen eleven to ten, but as George Pierce became president, the board was balanced. The local non-Methodist minister faction not appointed by the church included Henry Graybill Lamar (1798–1861), Jerry Cowles (1802–77), Ossian Gregory (1810–62), Robert Collins (1798–1861), Everard Hamilton (1791–1847), a member of the Mulberry Street Methodist Church, George Jewett (1799–1849), Henry Solomon (1791–1847), Augustus B. Longstreet (1790–1870), Walter Colquitt (1799–1855), and James A. Nesbitt (1800–75). The list given by Akers in his *First Hundred Years* lists four names as the "first board of trustees" that are not listed in the more authoritative minutes, and confirmed unchanged by the published list in the *Georgia Messenger* on November 24, 1836, and he also failed to list Nesbitt, Solomon, and Collins, who are listed in the minutes.[48] Akers seems to have the later roster, obviously not having referenced the minute record. General Robert Augustus Beall (1800–36), who had been serving as secretary to the pre-charter group, died on July 16 and was replaced as secretary in the first official meeting by Nesbitt. Of those who signed the charter, only one minister appears to represent those on the board appointed by the Georgia Conference, Samford, who is listed first. The others, Collins, Hamilton, Solomon, and Nisbet, all represent the nonsectarian faction. This may reflect the reality that, even though half the board was appointed by the conference, the businessmen represented more political and financial strength to the legislators in the General Assembly who, even though they were also Christians, were concerned for the long-term financial solvency of the Georgia Female College. Furthermore, they were local, so they were more readily available to respond quickly and regularly to conduct business on behalf of the board.

Henry Graybill Lamar (1798–1861) was born in Clinton, Georgia. A friend of Slade, he served as a trustee of the Clinton Female Seminary and practiced law in Macon. A Jacksonian Democrat, Lamar was elected to the U.S. House of Representatives in 1828, where he served until 1833. Lamar later ran an unsuccessful campaign for governor of Georgia in 1857 but became an associate justice on the Georgia Supreme Court. He was a trustee of the Georgia Female College until he resigned in January 1841. Based on the minutes of the trustees, Lamar was one of the most active supporters of the college, providing his legal and political expertise as well as his respected character in the community and his professional connections from the beginning of the idea as early as 1835. Unfortunately, due to his resignation in the midst of controversy, he was never recognized for the invaluable contributions he made not only to the college but to female education in general. He is buried in the Rose Hill Cemetery of Macon.

Jerry Cowles (1802–77) was president of the Ocmulgee Bank in Macon and instrumental in bringing the railroad to the city. In 1850, he was a "coal dealer."[49] He built the historic Cowles-Bond-Woodruff House, 1836–40, and was its first resident. Cowles also resigned from the board during the denominational conflict and, partly due to personal financial trouble, migrated to New York after 1845 where he died. He is buried, however, in the Rose Hill Cemetery of Macon.

Ossian Gregory (1810–62) was a Presbyterian planter and colonel in the Georgia Militia who wrote a surviving 1836 letter to Georgia Governor William Schley inquiring whether substitutes were allowed for persons drafted into the Seminole Indian War (1835–42) if serving proved to be an unfair hardship on the part of the one drafted.[50] In 1840 he was one of two delegates from Georgia to the Democratic National Convention held in Baltimore, Maryland. Martin Van Buren was nominated for reelection by that convention but was defeated in the general election by William Henry Harrison. Originally from New York, Ossian Gregory was the brother of the physician and minister in West Troy, New York, Oscar Hubert Gregory.[51] Ossian died in Alabama.

Robert Collins (1798–1861) was a Macon physician originally from North Carolina. He was also a banker and assisted in bringing the railroad to central Georgia. He was a wealthy landowner, Macon city father, and entrepreneur. William Smith and Ellen Smith Craft, a slave couple who made their way to New England and then to England where they lobbied for abolition, escaped from the home of Collins, who died in 1861 and is buried in the Rose Hill Cemetery of Macon.

Everard Hamilton (1791–1847) served as the first official chairman of trustees. Originally from Hancock County, Georgia, he was also a colonel in the Georgia Militia. He was a veteran of both the War of 1812 and the Creek Wars of 1813–15. He surveyed the state line between Georgia and Alabama, and he served as Georgia Secretary of State during 1823–33. He was Episcopalian and owned a large plantation in Twiggs County, Georgia. He and his wife Mary Hazzard Floyd are buried in the Laurel Grove Cemetery of Savannah.

George Jewett (1799-1849) was originally from Granby, Connecticut. He was one of the founders and first officers of the Macon Masonic Lodge, moving to the city in 1822. Jewett was also a trustee of the Vineville Academy. He owned George Jewett and Company on Second Street in Macon. The warehouse and commission business, which sold dry goods, groceries, hardware, hats, shoes, and so on, was doing so well in 1836 that Jewett was expanding to add a cotton exchange warehouse.[52] He was eulogized "As a good citizen and exemplary and devoted Christian, he stood pre-eminent; and his memory is embalmed in the hearts of all who knew him."[53] Jewett is buried in the Rose Hill Cemetery of Macon.

Henry Forsyth Solomon Sr. (1791-1847), originally from North Carolina, lived in Twiggs County, Georgia, was a colonel in the Georgia Militia, and was a member of the Macon Lodge. Solomon bought the *Georgia Statesman* newspaper in 1830 at auction and changed the name to *The Federal Union*. The *Statesman* is not to be confused with a white supremacist newspaper of the same name published in 1932-56 by Georgia Governor Eugene Talmadge in Atlanta and Hapeville. Solomon purchased the newspaper first published in 1825 by Elijah H. Burritt and Silas Meacham in Milledgeville. *The Federal Union*, managed by John G. Polhill, was the counter media to the *Southern Recorder* which was sympathetic to the Whig Party. In 1836 he and Lamar were two of only forty-four stockholders in the railroad.[54] Solomon was also a member of the railroad board of directors, elected by the stockholders.[55] He is buried in the Faulk Family Cemetery of Jeffersonville, Georgia, where his gravestone reads, "In all the relations of life, he sustained himself with dignity and honor."

Agustus B. Longstreet (1790-1870) was an author, educator, humorist, journalist, judge, lawyer, planter, politician, and Methodist minister who wrote *Georgia Scenes: Characters, Incidents, etc. in the First Half Century of the Republic* in 1835, published in 1840, which some argue is Georgia's first important literary work. He supported slavery and secession. He once wrote to northern abolitionists, "What you believe to be sinful, we believe to be perfectly innocent." He portrayed blacks as a "tribe of self-infuriated madmen, rushing through the country with the Bible in one hand and a torch in the other—preaching peace, and scattering the flames of civil war," and said that they were creating a "system of warfare against Slavery."[56] Despite owning dozens of slaves, he served, at various times, as president of Centenary College, Emory University, South Carolina College (now the University of South Carolina), and the University of Mississippi. He was the uncle of Confederate General James Longstreet. As a politician, he identified as a Jeffersonian Democrat who was committed to a strict, literal interpretation of the US Constitution and states' rights.

Born in Augusta, Longstreet graduated from Yale University in 1813 and studied law in Litchfield, Connecticut. He met John C. Calhoun as a classmate at Yale and the two remained lifelong friends. Longstreet first practiced law in Augusta but then moved to Greensboro, Georgia, from where he was elected to the Georgia State Legislature in 1821. Beginning in 1822, he also served as a district judge in the Ocmulgee Judicial Circuit. He founded the *August State Rights Sentinel* newspaper. In 1824, Longstreet was running for US Congress but withdrew from the campaign when his son Alfred Emsley Longstreet died. Of his and Frances Eliza Parke's eight children, only two survived into adulthood: daughters Virginia Lafayette and Frances Eliza. The death of Alfred also became the catalyst for Longstreet's conversion experience, although he had not been religious previously. He joined the Methodist Church in Augusta and first felt the "call to preach" in 1828. He was elected to the Georgia Female College Board of Trustees in 1836 on the nonsectarian side of the balance, meaning he was not appointed to the board by the Georgia Conference, but he was, in fact, a Methodist minister after 1838 who frequently contributed articles to *The Methodist Quarterly, Southern Literary Messenger, The Magnolia, The Orion,* and *The Southern Field and Fireside,* which included two of his series entitled "Letters to Clergymen in the Northern Methodist Church" and "Letters from Georgia to Massachusetts."[57] In 1870, Longstreet died at Oxford, Mississippi, an unreconstructed secessionist, and is buried in the St. Peter's Cemetery of that city.[58] His daughter Virginia married US Supreme Court Justice Lucius Quintus Cincinnatus Lamar, who was first cousin to Henry G. Lamar.

Walter Terry Colquitt (1799–1855) was a lawyer and politician. He was born in Halifax, Virginia, but moved to Carroll County, Georgia, as a child. Like Longstreet, he was elected to the board on the businessman side of the trustees, but after 1827, was also a circuit-riding Methodist minister. He was a Princeton student who was later elected to the US House of Representatives (1839–40, 1842–3) and the US Senate (1843–8). He also lived in Sparta, Georgia, and Cowpens in Walton County. He was a state judge in the Chattahoochee Judicial Circuit, and he was a brigadier general in the state militia. Colquitt was a strong supporter of states' rights, especially regarding Georgia's ability to sort out relations with Native Americans. Due to the many hats he wore, it was said of him he was "able to make a stump speech, try a court case and plead another at the bar, christen a child, preach a sermon, and marry a couple—all before dinner."[59] Colquitt died in Macon, but is buried with Slade in the Linwood Cemetery of Columbus, Georgia.

Finally, James Alexander Nesbit (1800–75) was born in South Carolina and became a successful planter near Spartanburg, only moving to Georgia in the last few years of his life. In the Palmetto State, he owned over one thousand acres of land and more than two hundred enslaved persons. Nesbit's South Carolina home has survived. He was a very successful businessman, merchant, planter, textile pioneer, civic leader, and member of the Baptist Church. Nesbit was the first official secretary on the board of trustees for the Georgia Female College, replacing Beall, who had died, in the first recorded meeting on September 19, 1836. He died of pneumonia in Rome, Georgia, on March 24, 1875.

In summary of the profiles of original Georgia Female College trustees, their average age in 1836 was thirty-nine years. Lovick Pierce was the oldest trustee at fifty-one years and George Foster Pierce, his son, was the youngest at twenty-five. There was no age gap among the original trustees and they cannot be divided into groups based on age. All but three of them were in their thirties and forties. They were all fathers of daughters, seventy-four potential college students among them from Julia Elizabeth Pierce, born in 1813, to Ida Lochram Lamar, not born until 1851, thus revealing one motivating reason for each man's interest in founding a college for women. There were at least nine enslavers among them and possibly twelve. Gregory, Jewett, and Solomon were all in businesses that typically used involuntary labor. At least five of the Methodist ministers on the board were slave owners. Nesbit owned the most, two hundred to work his thousand-acre plantation in South Carolina. Incidentally, he is also the only trustee who was not resident in Georgia in the 1830s. The other enslavers included Andrew, "dozens," Lamar, forty-six, Collins, forty-one, Arnold, eight, Longstreet seven, Few, two, and Colquitt, two. Others may have owned slaves but no record was found in a brief search of slave schedules in 1830 and 1840. Therefore, over half the founding trustees were slave owners and, based on sermons, letters, and other opinions recorded, it is safe to conclude that all of them were in agreed support of the institution of slavery, including Cowles who was from New York and returned there in the 1850s. The first of the original trustees to pass was Few, at the age of fifty-six in 1845. Five others died before 1850 but half of them lived until after 1870, three into the 1880s including Hodges, George Foster Pierce, and Talley who was the last living original trustee in 1886 when he passed away at the age of eighty-six. Lovick Pierce, who died in 1779 at the age of ninety-four, was the longest-lived trustee. Two of them, Arnold and Jewett, were only fifty when they died in 1850 and 1849, respectively.

The first trustee meeting in the minutes of the board is dated Monday, September 19, 1836, even though they had been meeting prior to the charter, documented since January 15 and likely since 1835. The charter was not officially granted by the state until December 1836. Hamilton had been serving as chair and treasurer of the meetings and continued without election in the meeting on September 19. After Andrew became chairman in 1838, Hamilton continued as treasurer. Thus, all three officers of the original trustees were elected from the nonsectarian faction of the board in 1836. No comments of debate or vote totals are recorded in the minutes so any possible contention is not revealed. Sinclair, forty-eight, was elected "agent" of the institution with compensation to travel the region as a recruiter. Nesbit was elected secretary to replace Robert Augustus Bealle who had died July 16, 1836, in Macon. Originally from Prince George County, Maryland, he was born in 1800, came to Georgia with his family in 1808 to Warren County, and was thus only thirty-six years old when he passed. He was survived by his wife, Caroline Smith, and a daughter, Florida Jane Bealle, born in 1830. There is no record of Florida Bealle having attended Wesleyan. Bealle was the second mayor of Macon, a brigadier general in the Georgia Militia, a member of the Georgia House of Representatives, part owner of the *Georgia Messenger*, and a celebrated lawyer in Twiggs County, Georgia. He was "considered a genius by everyone who heard him speak," and "a genius of a higher nature," according to Historian Scott B. Thompson Jr.[60] Bealle was ambitious and partisan in his beliefs, engaging in two duels, one of which left his opponent, Thomas D. Mitchell, dead on the ground. He moved to Macon and became a planter but his plantation failed so he sold it. Plagued by chronic health problems and a gambling addiction, Bealle declined physically.[61] At the end of his life, he joined the Methodist Church in 1835. Even at the time of his death, the Southern Recorder considered him a "rising star" with "peculiar talents of high order."[62] Bealle was buried in the Old City Cemetery of Macon with military honors. His funeral drew "a large concourse of citizens." His death was unfortunate, a significant loss for the Georgia Female College in the first year of the charter. Surely the minutes would have included far more color if Bealle had survived.

Plans were made in the inaugural meeting of the trustees to begin construction on a building for the college. The board hired Thomas B. Clark to supervise the work, including the laying of the cornerstone less than one month later, on a Thursday, October 13. Nesbit, as secretary, was directed to place a notice in the "public gazettes" and Sinclair was selected to deliver the address at the ceremony. Although Macon has seen forty-five different newspapers come and go between 1823 and 1904, there were only two publishing in 1836, *The Macon Georgia Telegraph* and *The Georgia Messenger* based at Ft. Hawkins.

Further, in the inaugural meeting, the trustees resolved that Lamar and Collins were elected to serve as a subcommittee to address announcements of the cornerstone ceremony to the state legislature and include the "merits of the Georgia Female College, soliciting their aid in obtaining appropriations from the Legislature for its endowment."[63] They voted to call for the first installment of the pledges that supporters had made leading up to this meeting. A notice was placed in the local newspapers and Sinclair was instructed to call on these sponsors personally. They advertised a call for bids on the construction of the building in the newspapers. Finally, Nesbit was elected to fill Beall's seat on the board, in addition to his office of secretary, and George Foster Pierce was elected to replace John Howard, who had been serving during the unofficial meetings but who died on August 22, 1836. Howard, forty-five, was a Methodist minister who also owned a dozen enslaved persons. The *Telegraph* reported, "With what unshaken confidence did he rely on the all-sufficient merit of his Redeemer, and with that calmness and serenity undergo the bitter pangs of death exclaiming" the twenty-third Psalm. This "testimony abundantly satisfied his surviving friends that he was going to that "sweet, sweet home" about which he loved in health to sing and talk, and to which it was the business of his life to allure his fellow men."[64] Howard is buried in the Rose Hill Cemetery of Macon.

Therefore, based on the full comparison of all surviving records, the best interpretation of these early events indicates the idea for a female college originated simultaneously in two different locations then came together in a joint partnership, one half with the understanding they were founding a nonsectarian educational institution for women with the assistance of the Georgia Conference of the Methodist Episcopal Church and the other half believing they were founding a thoroughly denominational college with the cooperation of several local businessmen. It becomes evidently clear this was a tentative cooperation when, in fact, it unraveled just days after the first commencement, but from the first official days of active trustees, the board reflects an attempt to strike a balance between these two streams. Only after George Foster Pierce pressed the Methodist narrative in the local media did the balance tip and after several resignations, the sectarian faction was able to gain control of the narrative, minimizing the participation of the local businessmen who thus made a loud, reasonable, and ongoing protest.

The charter was granted by the state legislature December 21, 1836, in Milledgeville and plans continued for construction of the building and classes to begin in 1839. Fortunately for the trustees, the legislature took up the charter for the Ocmulgee Bank of Macon on December 22. The owners of the bank, primarily Georgia Female College Trustee Cowles as president, aware that their support among the legislators was weak, pledged $25,000 to the college to strengthen their chance of approval. Opponents of the bank were accused of opposing the college and the bank was, therefore, approved.[65]

The second *recorded* meeting of the trustees did not occur until January 16, 1838, a full fifteen months after the first one, and it was not a meeting of the full board. In the meantime, they had laid the cornerstone and Slade had taken his 1837 trip to the northern female schools. With members of the board required to travel from around the state and Nesbit coming from Spartanburg,

South Carolina, and considering the difficulty of travel in the 1830s, it is understandable why the trustees were not meeting more often. They managed this by having an executive committee which meant more frequently to sort out college business. In July 1838 the board decided to hold annual meetings and the executive committee to meet as needed. Once construction began on the building, the business of the committee was almost entirely management of building contractors. In 1838 this committee was composed of Sinclair, chairman, Cowley, Lamar, and Collins. The group was chaired by a Methodist minister but was two-thirds businessmen due to their proximity in Macon and expertise in the skills needed for the task. It was this committee which resolved on Tuesday, January 16 in Macon to request a report from Sinclair and to express their gratitude to Joseph Moultrie, a Methodist minister, for his services which were not recorded. Sinclair and Collins were appointed to contract for roofing the building with tin. Sinclair was also asked to measure the building and calculate the number of bricks to be needed and to pay with "any money coming into his hands." As Sinclair was then busy with the construction planning, J. L. Stevens was employed to assume his responsibilities of collecting subscriptions to the college. The committee authorized a draft of $5,000 to be paid to the contractor Elam Alexander and $3,000 to Rufus Evans, from the Ocmulgee Bank.

The second full meeting of the trustees was held on Friday, February 16, 1838, in Macon. Andrew served as chairman. A committee of Andrew, Hodges, and Lovick Pierce was appointed to examine the progress of the building. Hodges and Gregory were appointed to examine the finances of the institution. Sinclair, Gregory, Nesbitt, and Lamar were appointed as a third committee "to draft Rules regulation & By Laws for the Government of the Board of Trustees." Andrew was appointed to lead an unnamed committee to design the curriculum of the college.

The executive committee met twice on Saturday, March 3, 1838. Hamilton was then chairman of the entirely nonsectarian committee which also included Lamar, Jewett, and Collins. Clearly until the denominational crisis began, this was not a concern for others on the full board. In the evening meeting, Evans presented a bill for brick work amounting to $19,057.58 which the trustees found to be "extravagant and unreasonable." They refused to accept it. Lamar made the motion to refer the dispute to neutral arbitrators. The committee, however, chose the members of the arbitrating body which were Thomas Hardeman, Alfred Clopton, and William Fort. The meeting ended with the committee electing Peter Solomon (1806–83) member and secretary to replace Nesbit who had resigned. Living in South Carolina, it is reasonable to believe, in 1838, that he was unable to continue traveling to Macon for the infrequent meetings of the trustees. Solomon was cashier for the Monroe Railroad and Banking Company. When he married Martha C. Fort in 1840, George Foster Pierce performed the ceremony.

The committee of Sinclair, Gregory, and Lamar completed the by-laws for the board of trustees in 1838 even though they were never published publicly until 1876. This document formalized many of the practices already in place for the trustees, formulated in practice since January 1836. The fourth article specified that the president would open each meeting of the board with prayer. The seventh article established the fourth Wednesday of each year as the date for an annual meeting of the full board of trustees, beginning in 1838.

The college building was constructed during 1838 by local builders Elam Alexander and Rufus K. Evans. Despite the dispute with Evans regarding his bill, the trustees were pleased with his work. Before the building was completed it was recorded in the minutes to be "one of the most splendid monuments of private munificence and philanthropy that has appeared in our country demanding the approbation of every lover of his race . . ."[66] The building was appreciated as much for its construction as for the rise of female education it symbolized. The college then occupied five acres on the hill between Macon and Vineville "entirely secluded from the noise and bustle of either place."[67] The description gives the modern reader a rural, countryside impression and, in fact, the college was located on the edge of Macon at the time. Historian Eunice Thomson described the location "a commanding eminence. . . . The city is spread out upon the plain below; the surrounding hills are crowned with private mansions of the most tasteful architecture."[68] She poetically spoke of "the majestic pine forests nearby; on the north are the ruins of old Fort Hawkins. Blockhouses and relics of ancient fortifications are remaining, to connect its present peaceful habitations with the stir and clangor of deadly strife." The description reveals more about Thomson and her period (1947), because the main campus had relocated by then, than it does about the site in

1839. The same site, however, almost two hundred years later is quite urban and most Macon residents would consider it to be in the city center. In Spring 1838 the building was "rapidly approaching completion," projected to be November 1, 1838, two months before the commencement of the first semester. It was 160 feet long, 65 feet wide, 4 stories high with wings of 3 stories and covered with a tin roof. It contained 78 rooms for 250 students and was due to be "easily completed" by the self-imposed deadline.[69]

George Foster Pierce clearly had a vision for making the Georgia Female College a higher, more serious academic institution than the several female seminaries operating throughout Georgia in 1839. To this end, he extended the terms and, to deepen the level of study in particular subjects, reduced the number of studies any individual student was required to master. He wrote in the *Southern Ladies' Book*, "We want to make education a thorough, practical, and intellectual preparation for the duties of life, by giving matter the preference over manner. We would not waste time, money, and youth in preparing a frail, filigree fabric and then overloading it by meretricious decorations."[70] Pierce, Slade, and the others wanted to build a college for women that was academically as rigorous as any male school in the nation.

Figure 4.1. Thomas Bog Slade (public domain, from *History of the Baptist Denomination in Georgia*, Atlanta: James P. Harrison & Co., Printers and Publishers, 1881).

Driven by the demographic changes in Clinton and Macon and enticed by an offer too good to refuse, Slade sold his house in Clinton in 1838 and merged his entire enterprise into the proposal for the new Georgia Female College, including two other teachers, his family, and thirty students, most of whom have been identified, some detailed herein, by comparing enrollment lists, the history of Jones County, and census records from Jones and Bibb County.[71] Slade became the college's first professor of science and Miss Maria T. Lord became the *primum* assistant professor of music. The other teacher was Miss Martha Massey, "a beneficiary pupil" who served as Lord's assistant.[72] Lord also gave music lessons at the Macon Female Academy beginning in June 1837. At the time, Slade indicated she had been teaching music in Clinton since 1834 "and her skill as an instructress in music needs no higher recommendation than the proficiency of her pupils."[73] Both were still resident in Clinton as of May of the same year. "Slade moved to Macon ready to teach a rigorous curriculum," wrote historian Florence Fleming Corley.[74] The transferred enrollment of the Clinton Female Seminary made up fully one-third of the Georgia Female College's first student body. As argued in the previous chapters, however, Slade took his fact-finding trip north on behalf of the Georgia Female Academy trustees in 1837 and, according to various documents and circumstances, accepted the offer of the trustees to a faculty position and to merge his female seminary as early as 1836. He was a well-known educator of women by that time and with the support of Lamar and Flewellen, his denominational affiliation was not an issue.

Slade was present for the first matriculation ceremony in January 1839. He, along with Maria Lord and Martha Massey, was already familiar with one-third of the first students, having taught them in Clinton. Many of them had lived in his house, which was the primary boarding site for most of his enrollment. He, Lord, and Massey already knew their parents, their personalities, and their academic strengths and weaknesses. Historian John Campbell Butler described this moment in his *Historical Record of Macon and Central Georgia* by writing:

> After a solemn prayer, ninety young ladies came forward and registered their names as candidates for admission. It was an occasion of deep and thrilling

excitement. A large and respectable number of the citizens of Macon were assembled in the college chapel to witness the opening scene. The hopes and fears of friends, the predictions of its enemies, and the eager delight of the congregated pupils all conspired to invest the service with an interest additional to its intrinsic importance.[75]

The most pressing issue on the first day of class in 1839 was enrollment and budget. With only eighty-eight college students, two less by two already, and forty-three preparatory students committed, the trustees were pressed on every side. To stimulate enrollment, the trustees had already been forced in mid-December 1838 to reduce tuition to $50, cut room and board to $120, and amend faculty and staff salaries.[76] As a result, the president complained that standards had been reduced so low to accommodate admissions; the vision for a quality academic institution was being compromised. He admitted that to have held true to the published catalog, all applicants may have been excluded. The attempt to satisfy parents, compensate faculty, and reduce the pressure on trustees had created a stressful and nearly unfeasible situation.[77] Fortunately for everyone, enrollment climbed to 168 by the end of the first semester due to the appearance of 80 late arrivals. Rather than applying by mail, in those days students turned up at the door with their tuition and baggage in hand to request admission.

A typical day on College Hill began at dawn when resident students were awakened by the ringing of the bell, calling them to the chapel downstairs on the main floor where they joined in "family prayer" led by Pierce. Attendance was mandatory. After chapel, students had time to study before breakfast and were then allowed time for recreation until a second prayer meeting began which included commuting students. The noon lunch was bookended by classes until 5:00 p.m. when all students were dismissed by a third assembly for prayer.[78] According to the catalogs, after dinner, recreation, and further study, at 9:00 p.m. students were allowed to "sleep at will."

Slade was one of the first four professional faculty, all men with the Master of Arts degree (A.M.) which was the early nineteenth century equivalent to the modern PhD, and he was the second highest paid. There were other faculty without advanced degrees. They were all women except for one who taught in the Fine Arts and Domestic Economy divisions.[79] According to one historian, Slade "wrote the first diploma delivered to a woman and arranged the curriculum for the oldest female college in existence."[80]

There is much debate, however, about Wesleyan's historic claim to have been "first for women" since several other female schools, still in existence, were founded well before the Georgia Female College, including the Clinton Female Seminary. For example, the Bethlehem Female Seminary (now Moravian College) was founded as a seminary for girls ninety-four years before Wesleyan, in 1742. Salem College, the alma mater of Anne Jacqueline Blount, Slade's wife, was founded by Moravian Sisters as the Little Girls' School in 1772 and is considered the oldest female educational institution for women in the South. Slade himself had gone north to tour female colleges already open before 1835. One historian excitedly referred to "the first college for women in the world."[81] Wesleyan is, therefore, to be perfectly clear, the first college chartered from its inception as a full four-year *college* exclusively for and awarding the *Bachelor of Arts degree* to *women* whether it grounds its founding in 1839, 1836, or 1821, but it has always been easier, though slightly misleading, for promoters of the college to simplify the qualification into "First for Women." It is, arguably, no higher than the eighth college *for women* in the United States.[82] Further down the list of "in the world." Wesleyan being "First for Women" critically hinges on the definition of the words "first" and "college." Finally, in Griffin's own article, when James Silk Buckingham visited the Georgia Female College in March 1839, just two months after the first classes, he proclaimed the Macon college to be "about the equal of any Northern academy for women."[83] This is not meant to diminish Wesleyan College but to explain the often simplified and exaggerated claim made. Either way, classes began three years after the charter was granted with Slade at the lectern in January 1839. The curriculum included botany as well as mathematics, physics, languages, music, and literature. Slade's first diploma given is dated July 16, 1840, and signed by himself, President George Foster Pierce, and Professor William H. Ellison.[84] This baccalaureate degree was presented to Catherine Elizabeth Brewer (1822–1908) of Augusta purely due to alphabetization of the first nine students' family names.[85] Brewer is remembered on the campus of Wesleyan in the annual alumnae association meeting in the Benson Charge, her married name, taken from a speech she made to the Class of 1888. Benson was the wife of Richard Aaron Benson (1821–77) and mother of William Shephard Benson, America's first chief of naval operations in 1915.

Sarah E. and Sarah Ann Abercrombie of Russell County, Alabama, were members of the junior class in 1839 along with Brewer, but they and eight others, almost half of the cohort, disappeared from the enrollment in 1840. Speculating that the deletions were a direct result of the sectarian debate is not proper research, but since those absent include Marcy S. Griswold and Martha H. Pitts, both of Clinton, the conclusion may be more than speculation.[86] Records proving denominational affiliation for most residents of early nineteenth-century Georgia are rare. This information is not included on the census, most church records have been lost, and unless an individual identified themselves, their church membership remains unclear. However, those records which are found do indicate, in the main, that those students from Methodist families remained at the college until graduation while those students from non-Methodist families dropped out of school. Marriage records indicate that most of that non-Methodist cohort did not transfer to other schools. For example, several of those who graduated chose to have Pierce officiate their wedding ceremonies, while only Martha Childers, married January 14, 1840, in what would have been her last semester before graduation, chose Pierce. The president of the college also performed the wedding of Harriet Matilda Ross, who graduated then married Walter T. Colquitt, father of Georgia Governor Alfred H. Colquitt. Ross became the long-term president of the Women's Missionary Society of the Methodist Episcopal Church South.

Critics of the college exaggerated its exclusivity and cost, so Pierce responded with another article in the *Southern Ladies' Book* in 1840. He pointed out the low cost of $50 for an entire year's tuition and that room and board averaged out to only $15 per month. This price did not include "washing and candles" or "extra" classes, which included music, drawing and painting, Latin, Greek, Italian, or Spanish. "The college has suffered," Pierce wrote, "from the idea entertained throughout some portions of the country that the expenses of this institution exceed those of any other Female School. A simple inspection of the rates will convince any individual to the contrary; for it will be observed that for about $190 per year all the necessary expenses for a thorough education are covered."[87] With the average annual cost of a college education in the United States now more than $30,000, the criticism of the 1840 opponents seems humorous. According to Pierce, some said the students were "extravagant." "Just what we expected," he quoted them. Pierce scolded readers for believing these reports without researching the source. He sarcastically claimed the college had no more to do with any behavior on the part of the students that may or may not be "extravagant . . . than the French Chamber of Deputies." He then gave an extended but most illustrative example that he must have observed many times as president of the college:

> A gentleman brings his daughter to the Institution. He is a very economical gentleman, and the times are hard, and he informs the President that the great drawback to education is its cost. Then he purchases for her room fine furniture, a high post bedstead, bureau of mahogany, a carpet at $1.50 a yard. He goes down town and tells some merchants to give his daughter credit for anything she wants, for he desires that his darling shall be comfortable.
>
> When he goes home he slips a ten or twenty dollar bill in a letter every once in a while that his daughter may buy fruit, ice creams, candy, almonds, raisins, and the like. At the close of the term he adds it all together, throws in stage and tavern bills on the road going and coming, and when it is all figured out, he draws along asthmatic breath and exclaims, "Good heavens! What an extravagant place that female college is!"[88]

The denominational controversy appears to have been devastating when comparing the enrollment before and after the public debate. Of the 115 students enrolled in the college program in 1839, only 36 percent of those remained on campus until their respective graduation. Fully 64 percent of the names enrolled disappeared from the rolls by the Fall of 1840. The college lost 90 percent of the freshman class, 77 percent of the sophomore class, and 48 percent of the junior class. There was no senior class in 1839, the first year of classes. These losses are evident in the graduation numbers during 1841–50. After graduating eleven students in 1840, the Georgia Female College did not graduate more than eleven until 1847. In 1843 and 1844 there were only six in each class. Not until 1850 did the number of graduates surpass the number of juniors studying for graduation in 1839 before the controversy. It is thus clear how sectarianism stunted growth and led to the financial crisis of 1844.

The others who did not graduate in 1840 were Eunice Frances Freeman, Theodosia Parker, and Euphemia Y. Ward of Macon; Sarah A. Munson of Vineville, and Amanda A. Rogers of LaGrange. Those others graduating included Matilda J. Moore and Mary L. Ross of Macon, Elizabeth Flurnoy of Putnam County, Ann Hardeman and Sarah V. Clopton of Vineville, Martha Faulkner Heard of LaGrange, Julia M. Heard of Mobile, Alabama, Sarah M. Holt of Bibb County, and Margaret Amelia Speer of Columbus, daughter of Georgia Female College Trustee and former South Carolina Secretary of State Alexander Speer. Margaret's brothers included Alexander Middleton Speer, a Georgia Supreme Court Justice during the 1880s, Algernon S. Speer, a prominent Florida planter and politician, and Eustace Willoughby Speer, a well-known Georgia Methodist minister. Flournoy was a descendant of a Huguenot family which fled France in 1567, wife of Walter R. Branham, Wesleyan professor of history, and grandmother of Sara Elizabeth Branham Matthews, a senior bacteriologist working in the US Public Health Laboratory. Hardeman was one of Thomas Hardeman's seven daughters who attended Wesleyan. He was the prominent pastor of the Mulberry Street Methodist Church in Macon. Both Ann's daughter, Nell Griswold (1897), and granddaughter, Laura Nell Anderson (1933), were Wesleyan graduates. Heard was noted for wearing the best dress at the 1840 graduation. She became the president of the Protestant Orphan Asylum in Mobile, Alabama, and worked diligently for the welfare of Confederate soldiers during and after the Civil War. Holt was the daughter of Judge Tarpley Holt. Her brother, uncle, and cousin served as Wesleyan trustees. Moore was the daughter of a Macon merchant, though she later lived in Dublin, Georgia. She married Willis S. Breazeal in Macon on June 10, 1847. Her daughters Leila (1881) and Cleone (1882) graduated from Wesleyan.

Griswold and Pitts were among those students who transferred with Slade from the Clinton Female Seminary. Pitts was the daughter of Captain Jack Pitts and Griswold was the daughter of industrialist Samuel Griswold who married General Daniel Newman Smith.

Half of those who dropped from the roster in 1839 and 1840 were married before what would have been their graduation day. They gave up a chance to be among the first graduating class of the Georgia Female College to become wives and mothers only slightly earlier than their peers. Eunice Frances Freeman married George Jewett on November 24, 1839, and her professor, Ellison, a Methodist minister, performed the ceremony. She was quickly followed to the altar by Amanda A. Rogers on December 26, 1839, Martha A. Childers on January 14, 1840, Sarah Ann Abercrombie on March 27, 1840, and Mary Spencer Griswold on May 17, 1840. This cohort represented a quarter of the entire class, two-thirds of which were married by 1849; fifty-seven percent by 1844. Of those who graduated, Martha Faulkner Heard was the first to marry, on April 22, 1841, ten months after graduation, to James M. Beall.

Pierce delivered the first commencement address and despite the college's many ongoing struggles, "waxed eloquent and long, in his paean to the college accomplishments."[89] "Hail ye daughters of the South!" he said,

> I proclaim to-day the restoration of your birth-right; I commit to the flames the warrant of your exile. To your legitimate possession, in the name of the State and the Church, I give to you title and welcome. Hail Georgia! Beacon star in the night of years, we greet thy beams with rapture and hail the sign of promise.... The first to rise on Woman's destiny, shine on undimmed and bright, nor set 'till earth is childless and time's no more![90]

Under Pierce's leadership in cooperation with Slade, Ellison, the professor of math and astronomy, and Adolphus Maussinett, the professor of languages, the college was grounded in the highest level of academic integrity from the beginning. Students were required to obtain mastery in a rigorous course of arts and sciences, yet due to the leadership, cultural context of the late 1830s, and the alliance with the Methodist Episcopal Church, there was also an equally strong theme of evangelical Christianity on campus. "The Bible has been too long excluded from the republic of letters," Pierce wrote, "He who would prolong this banishment, forbid the alliance of learning and religion, is a moral madman, more fit for the confinement of a lunatic asylum than for the immunities of society."[91] In context, the comment delivered a more powerful sting to readers in 1840 whereas the Georgia State Lunatic, Idiot, and Epileptic Asylum had been chartered by the state legislature in 1834 and admitted its first patients in 1842 at Milledgeville as Georgia's first public psychiatric hospital. Eventually, this institution became the largest of its kind in the world and "send you to Milledgeville" became a pejorative comment commonly used in the state against anyone behaving or advocating opinions outside the boundaries of the "normal" social expectations.

An ordained Methodist minister and son of the "Father of Methodism in Georgia," Lovick Pierce, it was not surprising that Pierce added:

> We repudiate and denounce the principle of compromise and exclusion. With education, divorced from Christian morals, we hold no fellowship, and unto the assembly of its advocates we would not unite our honor. No; let the Bible be to our colleges what the shekinah was to the Temple of the olden time, at once the symbol of the presence and the worship of God.[92]

Whether Pierce was speaking for himself in third person, on behalf of the college trustees, the faculty, or for the church, his comments reflected the philosophy the trustees and faculty imposed upon the college in the form of strict rules for students and reassurance for parents concerned for the physical and spiritual safety of their daughters, some as young as twelve years old, living away from home. As for the relationship between science, which was suddenly personified as female and no longer known as natural philosophy, and religion, Pierce concluded, "Science itself is blind to the true interests of man until her eyes are opened by washing in the waters of Siloam's pool."[93] Pierce was referring to the pool of the same name in the Bible located in the Old City of Jerusalem where Jesus sent a blind man to complete his healing.[94]

According to Pierce's description of the one Wesleyan building in 1839, Slade had an office along with other faculty in what was called the "basement" floor. Most classrooms were also on this floor, which was underneath the main floor where students attended chapel and ate their meals. The library was also on the main floor. Students lived four per room on the third and fourth floors. Student rooms were fully 324 square feet each, approximately 16 feet by 20 feet.[95] Many described the college building as one of the most beautiful examples of architecture in the state. It was demolished after the college moved to what is now called the Rivoli Campus on Forsyth Road in 1928. A telephone company in a far less appealing structure now occupies the original site on College Street.

Unfortunately, the leadership Slade provided at the Georgia Female College in administration and as faculty in the classroom is overshadowed by a sectarian divide that erupted soon after his arrival. His work as an instructor and the details of his teaching, sharpening his skills for the benefit of female college students, are lost in the flood of documents detailing the denominational crisis. Evidence of the brewing crisis appears in print as early as August 24, 1839, just as the first full academic year had commenced, in an article written for the *Southern Post* by an anonymous author identified only as "Justice."[96] The author was concerned regarding who deserved credit for the Georgia Female College. "A jealous Southerner of Southern rights" was annoyed by an article read recently in the July issue of the *Ladies Garland* of Philadelphia, Pennsylvania. It was, for "Justice," "A most glaring effort made to tear the laurels from the brows of the founders of our institution and transfer them across the Potomac, to be worn by the Victoria of American Literature."[97] The *Garland* article was a printing of an address delivered at West Chester Seminary as a eulogy to the late Mrs. Willard Yates. The offense to "Justice" was not that the speaker quoted from Yates' poem, "The Eye," but that she gave credit for the Georgia Female College entirely to Duncan Campbell. Clearly, Campbell was part of the college's history, but "Justice" was adamant that the college was entirely the product of the Methodist Episcopal Church. "Justice" questioned whether Campbell had seen Yates' pamphlet about the Troy Female Seminary and dismissed his vision to establish a similar school in Georgia. "Justice" argued that "Any individual at all acquainted with the origin of this institution will at once perceive the injustice of these remarks."[98]

Clearly unaware of Slade's visit to Troy, New York on behalf of the trustees in 1837 for the benefit of organizing the Georgia Female College, of Campbell's foundational and essential work of lobbying the state legislature for the charter of this same institution, the true injustice is that "Justice" also claimed Willard Yates" seminary model "was subsequently examined and had been rejected."[99] "Justice" continued to unnecessarily degrade the Troy Female Seminary and its founder although their claim is patently false, unfair, and blatantly sectarian. Emma Willard's record of life and work needs no defense and is above reproach but to the uninformed sectionally partisan readers of *Southern Post* it may have been a convincing argument necessitating a rebuttal from those who knew better. "However great her name may be at the North, as a literary giantess" "Justice" continued, we of the South are not willing that the authoress of that most wretched doggerel poem called *The Eye*, and that most sickly *Journal to France and England*, should have the credit of founding an institution, the first of its kind in the world which originated in the matured judgment and exalted wisdom of some of the noblest worthies of our State.[100]

Any individual at all acquainted with Willard must have, at once, felt the bitter and divisive malice of these hurtful claims especially since they were made against a deceased person and under a fictitious name.

Finally, "Justice," in defense of the Methodist Episcopal Church, attacked those who credited the Georgia State Legislature for the founding of the college. "So far from this being true," "Justice" wrote, "if I mistake not, there was a mighty effort made to get a loan from the State, but all to no purpose." Then the mistaken and unfortunate tirade mercifully ended with, "In conclusion, we would say to the instigators of this thing, however degraded Georgia may be as a State, in their estimation; and however unworthy the Methodist Episcopal Church may be in the promulgation of science and literature in the world, it is but sheer justice, according to the old adage, to 'let the devil have his due.'"[101] Nonetheless, the incident illustrates, perhaps, the beginning of the controversy over the founding of the Georgia Female College which almost destroyed it completely within the next twelve months. As no record has been found to indicate Slade's relationship with "Justice" or his opinion of the same, we can only imagine how he, an admirer of Willard, must have received these remarks.

There is significant evidence in the records that Slade and others resigned from the faculty of the Georgia Female College, within eighteen months of opening, over these denominational differences. Although the trustees had taken great pride in publicizing the fact that the first four faculty members represented the three largest denominations in Georgia, Slade and others, including the president who resigned on July 6, 1840, and several trustees, resigned when the church membership of students became an issue in Spring 1840. Just three semesters after classes began, this crisis of identity almost closed the college as soon as it was opened. The controversy erupted when Pierce wrote an article detailing the history of the college and implied, according to the Presbyterian and Baptist supporters of the college, that the college had been founded by, and only by, the Methodist Episcopal Church.[102] He stated that the idea for the college originated exclusively with Elijah Sinclair, which, to many, displayed a denominational preference for the Methodist Church to the exclusion of several local businessmen who were supporters of the college and members of various local churches of all three denominations.[103] "Sinclair was among the first who adopted, (if not *the very man* [emphasis added] who originated the whole scheme,) and devoted himself to the work . . .," Pierce wrote. This claim is remarkable whereas almost everyone who had contributed to the founding was still alive and knew that Pierce's claim, as given, was patently false and, at least, far more complicated. That he would attempt to establish the narrative of the founding so early in the college's history, knowing there were dozens of individuals able to rebut, reveals either irresistible pressure put upon him by partisan denominational leaders or a brazen bias in his own mind to favor his preferred ecclesiology even at the offense of several non-Methodists who gave sacrificially over several years to help bring the college into being.

There was little enthusiasm for sectarianism as late as 1826 in Georgia, but since then, religious revivals had occurred at various locations around the state. According to several sources, "In 1827 a remarkable revival commenced in July, at Eatonton, then in the Ocmulgee Association under the ministry of Adiel Sherwood."[104] Sherwood's student, J. H. Campbell, was Slade's pastor in Jones County. These events provide the details of the historical context for Pierce's attempt to establish the history of the college, but it further explains the pejorative reaction he provoked. Sherwood preached in the open air due to the number of those in attendance at the Antioch Church in Morgan County that year, and more than four thousand responded to his invitation. "The Holy Spirit descended with mighty power," one witness reported.[105] Suddenly, people felt competitive denominationally and resentful when other denominations were growing faster than their own.

Over the next decade, this type of revival meeting multiplied and spread to other denominations. Though all involved credited the Holy Spirit and were comforted that so many were embracing the Christian faith, denominational partisans were more than a little motivated by sectarianism and revealed a selfish envy when others were observed reaching more or growing faster than their own church. As the Baptists celebrated 708 baptisms in 1830, the organization of both temperance and tract societies, $3,000 subscribed for

Columbian College, one leadership report nevertheless lamented, "We regret to learn that in the Ocmulgee and Flint River Associations there are divisions and contentions; and religion, of course, is at a low ebb [there]." Macon is in the Ocmulgee Association, but as the decade progressed, the religious tide began to turn. Church membership, the number of ministers, and the number of churches across the spectrum more than doubled in Georgia between 1834 and 1835. Yet, "it was a time of chaos and confusion; of bitter animosity and dissension."[106] Denominational distinctives grew sharper, and churches moved to tighten qualifications of membership, expanded reasons for exclusion, and more narrowly defined what it meant to be in good standing. Rules were adopted regulating how to handle those who joined a church from another denomination. On July 7, 1836, a Baptist meeting chaired by Jesse Mercer was held in the Presbyterian Church of Forsyth, Georgia, "which is kindly offered," to not interrupt the revival that was ongoing in the local Baptist Church. Sherwood served as clerk. Slade and eight other men were licensed to preach in this same meeting.[107]

Near the end of his life, Slade reflected on what turned out to be a historic meeting at Forsyth by writing:

> I think the meeting was held in the Methodist Church, near the railroad. Though there were a great number of ministers present, I have a distinct recollection of only Jesse Mercer, Vincent Thornton, Jonathan Davis, and Granby Hillyer. I remember that Mr. Mercer was moderator; and that he, Mr. Davis, and Mr. Thornton figured as speakers and that the meeting was occasioned by an unhappy feeling among some of our denomination. Arminian sentiments were gaining ground, contrary to our Calvinist opinions. No doubt this assemblage of ministers was productive of good as it led to a better understanding among the brethren.[108]

Not only does Slade's attendance reveal that he was active in denominational work during the period of his employment at the Georgia Female Academy, but it also provides evidence of the theological context for denominational differences. Slade and Campbell were listed among the "No nobler men, no men more pious, able and zealous [who] who have graced our denominational history than those who guided Baptist affairs" from the 1830s through the 1850s.[109] Baptists, who are often labeled Arminian in the twenty-first century, were clearly more nearly aligned with the Calvinist Presbyterians in the early nineteenth century while the Methodists were, and have always been, the true representatives of American Arminianism in the South. The difference is rooted in the difference between the sixteenth-century theologies of John Calvin and Jacobus Arminius and involves how each individual believer views salvation, missions, and the relationship between a believer and God. Occasionally adherents, and sometimes ministers, switched denominations and this was always criticized by the losing church as a loss of faith or "backsliding" in the convert but met with great rejoicing and a work of Providence in the church that received the convert. Those who did switch were almost always labeled permanently with the name of the denomination from whence they came and there was more than a little controversy over whether converts baptized according to the practice of the new sect. For example, when an indigent Baptist minister was acknowledged in 1827 as one qualified to receive financial support, his name was given as "Thomas Walsh, lately a Methodist." Originally an Irish printer, Walsh joined the Methodist Church but having read several books about baptism, he expressed "scruples" regarding sprinkling. An unnamed "distinguished Methodist minister, who represented the Calvinist faith in most horrible colors" attempted to dissuade Walsh but after corresponding with his wife and reading Andrew Fuller's work, *A Narrative of Surprising Baptisms*, he left the Methodists and eventually became a leading minister among the Baptists. When James Hutchinson, a Methodist minister, sought membership in the Baptist Church, "Many were not well pleased with such a course, and therefore it led to strife and confusion," even though, as a Methodist, Hutchinson had been baptized by immersion, was an eloquent speaker, he gave up the Methodist discipline and doctrines, and embraced fully those of the Baptist denomination.[110]

A later example from 1853 illustrates that 1830s tensions between denominations continued through the decades when competition arose between Methodists and Baptists to establish a female college in southwest Georgia on 41 acres of land near Cuthbert, Georgia. James Clark of Lumpkin, Georgia reported that the Baptist Female College of Southwestern Georgia was being incorporated, construction was about to begin, and the Methodists "had been caught napping."[111] Jesse Campbell was one of the trustees. The

Methodists soon raised "opposition" by founding a college of their own in the same town.

Bishop James O. Andrew was a distinguished Methodist minister who served as a Georgia Female Seminary trustee. "He was sublimely eloquent," according to Robert Fleming, a Presbyterian, who heard him preach at a Methodist camp meeting in Columbia County. "It was this which first engaged my attention," he wrote, "his reasoning seemed to me irresistible."[112] Fleming had been a teacher since the War of 1812 and was known to be an "excellent English scholar and good teacher." Partly because of Andrew's preaching, Fleming became a Christian but then joined the Baptist church in which he was ordained a minister.

In another example of sectarian rivalry, faith and race converged as early as 1789 when an unnamed enslaved man was converted to the Baptist faith at Black Swamp on his own plantation. He was baptized by his stepfather and later ordained in 1805. An educated African American, the anonymous black Baptist minister wrote a book on baptism and engaged in debates with a certain Mr. Russell, a Methodist, who was surprised to find the enslaved "displays a sound mind and respectable talents."[113]

In this context, many strongly attacked Georgia Female College President Pierce's poorly worded claims of college history and his reputation as the president, offering their own versions of what they remembered of the founding. Letters, insults, and threats were cast back and forth in the local newspapers, but the effect was that support for the college in the community and among the parents of the students declined in the second year of the college's existence. Simultaneously, Pierce reported that thirty-five Georgia Female College students, about 21 percent of the entire student body, had joined a particular local church which he called "the Church of Christ," which was not the modern church of that denomination but the Methodist Church, during a particular emotional evangelistic meeting.[114] Pierce called it "a genuine work of the spirit of grace," while others suspected inappropriate evangelistic pressure with emotional manipulation on the part of the Methodist president working in cooperation with local church leaders. Soon after, when young sisters Mary and Martha Soullard died suddenly, the *Southern Ladies' Book* noted, "Mary was a student of the Georgia Female College. She joined the Methodist Church while at college."[115]

Pierce had provoked complaints from many parents, understandably concerned that their daughters had been sent to Macon for an education but were being emotionally and spiritually manipulated by denominational sectarians to the benefit of a particular church without the permission of their parents, many of whom were Baptist and Presbyterian. The initial backlash may even be Pierce's first motivation for writing the very early history of the college, hoping to explain his position. Fearing the students' commitment to return to the college and the motivation of parents to send them back for Fall Semester, however, might evaporate during the college's first summer vacation in 1839, Pierce was pleased to note, as classes resumed, the fervor among the girls, despite their return to home churches and the influence of parents, was "undiminished over the two-month break."[116] This comment is, unbelievable but well documented, a blatant admission by Pierce that his goal of winning the students of the college to Methodism was contrary to the wishes of many parents.

Sensing these encouraging words to the college's Methodist supporters might possibly cause others unnecessary alarm, Pierce hedged his sectarian enthusiasm and concluded his controversial narrative by assuring the non-Methodists:

> There is nothing sectarian in the design, organization, or management of the college. It is denominational in that, it is under the control of the Georgia Annual Conference and has been sustained, thus far by funds raised from voluntary contributions of the members and adherents of the Methodist Episcopal Church; yet the board of trustees includes men of the world, not only not members of the ecclesiastical body, but whose church predilections are against it. The three most prominent denominations in the state are represented in the faculty of the college, and perfect harmony prevails in all their councils. Parents of every religious persuasion patronize the Institution.[117]

The elucidation was insufficient to prevent the resulting protest in the community, and Pierce was forced to retract his initial statements about the history and status of the college. Many Baptists and Presbyterian supporters of the college perceived that the new college had become "so salted" with

Methodists that they complained of denominational favoritism and threatened to withdraw their support and their daughters. "It is a state college," Pierce wrote in his weak defense to mitigate the damage, "although the state has done nothing for it," but then he hedged this statement as well by defensively declaring, "We are not bigots to build up a party—to disseminate a sectarian belief—a denominational creed."[118] Minimizing the charter granted by the state, Pierce's statement also clarified his earlier first-person plural which, by this quote, cannot possibly include the "men of the world" or those with "predilections . . . against it."

These two issues combined to cause one great concern for the college trustees who were forced to issue a statement to minimize the damage to reputation done by the president in the community and enrollment on campus. The financial deficit of the college grew to $46,668.20 and enrollment fell to less than 60 percent of capacity within a year directly because of this sectarian, or denominational, controversy.[119] In June, Pierce accepted responsibility for causing the turbulence but doubled down on his argument. "From the tenor of several articles lately published, it seems I am to be burdened with the responsibility of the whole controversy," he wrote, "unfair as it is . . . my publications have been regarded passionate—uncharitable, the result of irritation."[120] Then,

> The Georgia Annual Conference had taken the subject of Education, under practical consideration some three or four years before this Institution was projected . . . preparation for the creation of Emory College. The necessity and expediency of a female college was discussed by Bishop Andrew and Mr. Sinclair in a private conversation nearly or quite two years before any citizen of Macon had moved or was interested in the subject at all.[121]

He cited the community meeting at the Methodist Church in Macon and that Gen. Elias H. Beall, a Methodist, had argued for Macon as the site of the college. He conveniently excluded many non-Methodists who had worked diligently to have a female college in Macon and who had given great sums of money and time to make the college a reality. He seems unaware that local businessmen were meeting in neutral locations downtown about the possibility of founding a school for girls simultaneously to the conversations in the Methodist meetings and that these plans had not included any anticipated affiliation with any denomination. To the great offense of the local leaders, he further appears to have been unaware of how two streams eventually merged to complete the independent intentions of both parties. A very denominationally diverse group of sponsors, for example, had raised over $9,000 for the college in 1835.[122] Therefore, his comments, regardless of how sincerely they may have been made, did nothing to mitigate the controversy which intensified denominational differences and created enemies out of former friends.

The controversy provided incidental cover for many who had made financial pledges to the college to suddenly cancel their commitment, citing the dispute. Pierce accused them of using the opportunity to disguise the fact that many were unable to meet their obligation.[123] Either way, those pledges were never paid and the financial difficulties of the college grew worse. Sympathy for subscribers caused supporters of Pierce to attack Simri Rose, who had long been a strong supporter of the college. A well-qualified and capable president, Pierce's divisive comments, especially those in print, caused serious and irreparable damage to the college and the community.[124]

Remarkably, this denominational debate escalated to involve most Macon residents, including persons otherwise unrelated to the college, as it was fought on the battlefield of the city's several newspapers, in the shops, and on the street. Many, fearing hostile reactions against their person, family, or businesses, participated anonymously by using pseudonyms in print such as "Justice," *Multus in Uno* or C*****.[125] Pierce took obvious satisfaction in exposing *Multus in Uno* as James Corson Edwards and C***** as Jerry Cowles, but it did not prevent others from attacking Pierce's argument by presenting strong opposing counterarguments supported by significant evidence. Cowles effectively appealed to The Scottsboro Institute, The Sparta Female Model School, a college for females in Granada, legislative journals of 1821, columns printed in Macon and Milledgeville newspapers, an address delivered at Athens in 1835, and the American Annals of Education printed in 1832 and 1833 to undermine Pierce's argument with a logical and well-researched rebuttal.[126] Cowles was a financier who served as president of the Ocmulgee Bank and was responsible for bringing the railroad to Macon from Knoxville, Tennessee. His home, which survives as the Cowles-Bond-Woodruff House on Coleman

Hill in Macon, was built in 1836 by Elam Alexander, the same builder who constructed the building for the college. Personal financial trouble, partially related to the controversy over the college, drove Cowles to relocate his family to New York in 1844. His home was sold and later used as a headquarters by Union General James H. Wilson during Sherman's infamous March to the Sea. The Bond Street house is now owned by Mercer University.

Clearly the need for an accurate history of Macon's female college was of great importance to the generation of its founding and neither side was close to conceding or compromising in 1840. Edwards accused Pierce of "willful misrepresentation."[127] "He was well aware," Edwards wrote, "Mr. Sinclair had *nothing* to do with the origin of the scheme, and it would moreover accuse him of a design to place the honor upon his own particular sect." He credited Cowles as having been "the very man" who originated the scheme as he appealed to a Monroe Rail Road Bank meeting which took place well before the community gathered at the Methodist Church in Macon.

In July, some trustees were complaining "that this institution is assuming a sectarian character by interfering with the religious predelectiory [sic] of students."[128] They argued this assumption was "an injury" to the students and a "manifest injustice to the faculty," some of whom were not Methodist. They agreed, half of them appointed to the board by the Georgia Conference of the Methodist Episcopal Church, over the objection of the president, that all students wishing to join a local church while resident in Macon would be required to secure their parent or guardian's permission in the future. The student's desire was thereafter to be communicated to the president of the college, whose responsibility it would be to inform the parents of the student's request and then honor the parents' decision. The policy was published in the *Southern Christian Advocate*, the official newspaper of the Methodist Episcopal Church in the South, then published in Charleston, South Carolina.[129] In the same meeting, however, trustee, judge, and State Representative Alexander Middleton Speer (1820–97), a Methodist, resigned in protest and was replaced the next day by Rev. William H. Ellison, a Methodist minister and member of the faculty.[130] Speer agreed with Pierce and the direction he was taking in defining the college so clearly along denominational lines, supported evangelizing the students, and resigned in protest of the policy passed by the board to involve the parents. Clearly the nonsectarians were losing the battle despite the resolution and Speer's resignation.

Pierce also resigned on July 6, and Ellison was elected the second president of the college to replace him. Pierce, however, continued to serve on the board. Slade, not present in the trustee meeting as a non-trustee member of the faculty, resigned later that same day and quickly had his resignation accepted by the trustees an hour later in their 3:00 p.m. session. He received a gracious reply as the exhausted board resolved on a very busy day:

> that the Board of Trustees of the Geo. Female College entertain a deep sense of the faithful, able and devoted manner in which the Rev. Mr. Slade has discharged the duties of the professorship of natural science and acquitted himself in all his relations to the college during his connexion with the same, & that their best wishes for his happiness & prosperity follow him in his retirement from the Institution.[131]

The denominational conflict within the college and community seems to have been rooted specifically in the evangelizing of students without parents' permission and, perhaps, more generally in regional tension resulting from the events and results of the Second Great Awakening. It did not result from arguments over slavery, which each denomination had in the 1830s with their northern brothers. Presbyterians split over involuntary servitude in 1838. Methodists and Baptists divided in the 1840s, although the controversy was already present in the 1830s due to questions over the appointment of slave-owning missionaries. Each denomination, however, was united in the South in support of slavery and would not have divided within the board of trustees over the issue. The Great Awakening, however, a period of unprecedented denominational growth in the South, gave rise to sectarian competition. As stated, the Baptist willingness to ordain uneducated ministers allowed them to start churches as fast as a congregation was organized. Presbyterians were hindered by their unwillingness to ordain uneducated ministers, so the number of their churches kept them third in both membership and numbers of churches. The Methodists managed to maintain the middle ground, resentful of Baptist growth but justly critical of their lack of appreciation for academics in minister qualifications. Many Baptists were content to concede, if God called a man to preach, the minister did not need formal theological training.

Presbyterians were also limited by their doctrine of predestination, which was increasingly unpopular among the preachers of all denominations in the period in favor of a far freer will of the believer theological interpretation. Unlike the colonial First Great Awakening, the Second Great Awakening emphasized personal religious experience and/or social reform. In the North, this reform included abolition and rights for women, but in the South, it was far more about temperance, orphans, and mental health. Large-scale revivals and camp meetings featured emotional preaching, public altar calls, and visible conversion experiences, which were manifested by weeping, shouting, testimonies, or convulsions. Religious fervor grew so strong during the 1830s and 1840s that new denominations were founded for the religious community to keep up with the masses of new converts. These included a wave of African American churches as well as Adventists and Mormons with their own unique doctrines and theories of education. Some have argued that, because Southern ministers "reflected a broader social sentiment and were intellectually closer to their parishioners than their New England counterparts . . . they aimed at individual moral reformation rather than broader social transformation."[132]

Slade was only forty years old and on July 16 had resigned with no contingency plans or means of support as the husband and father of his family. The board expressed their "anguish" over his departure but attempted to replace him in the same meeting with 61-year-old J. W. Armstrong, a local educator who was head of the Vineville Seminary. Originally of Troy, Alabama, Armstrong was an 1879 graduate of the University of Georgia with a degree in Literature but was chosen by the trustees to replace the resigned botanist. Aware of the controversy and concerned about the "fit," Armstrong, who ordinarily would have been honored to take up a position at the new college, refused the offer.[133] This brief episode illustrates how desperately and quickly the college trustees desired to resolve the controversy and begin rebuilding the community's confidence in the institution. Ultimately John Gould Darby, A.M. (1804–77), of Williams College of Williamston, Massachusetts, accepted the position of professor of natural science and took the place of Slade.[134] Darby was a self-taught botanist who later published a botany of the Southern States but who taught at Wesleyan less than four years, perhaps only one. Records are conflicting as to how long Darby remained on the faculty of the

Georgia Female College. Historian Schuyler Medlock Christian documented Darby's return to Williams College by 1844 to teach math at his alma mater, but the alumni directory of Williams placed him still living in Macon in the same year.[135] His house in Monroe County, attached to the Culloden Female Seminary, was foreclosed on August 26, 1841, and sold at public auction, but by 1845 he was back in Monroe County as the headmaster of the "Sigourney Institute," a female academy in Culloden, Georgia.[136] Christian judged Darby's botany a useful textbook although it was "not very original" and he "made a few errors." It was, however, the best textbook of the period for the study of plants in the southern states. Darby wrote articles on botany and religion and contributed at least one article to *DeBow's Review*. Christian claimed he taught in Culloden for the last thirty years of his life, but that is exaggerated since Darby was living in Macon County, Alabama by 1860, in 1869 was elected president of Wesleyan College of Kentucky, resigned in 1875, moved to New York where he manufactured chemicals, and died in Brooklyn in 1877. Incidentally, Darby's wife, Julia Pierpont Sheldon, was the niece and namesake of Julia Pierpont who graduated from Emma Willard's Troy Female Seminary and founded the seminary in Sparta, Georgia in 1819 only to end up in South Carolina.

The departing Pierce was invited to publish his final commencement address in the *Advocate* but then two other trustees walked out of the eventful meeting.[137] Altogether five trustees resigned or had their seats declared vacant on July 16, including Charter Member Ossian Gregory.[138] By January of the next year, 1841, Henry G. Lamar, arguably the most important and influential founder and trustee of the college to that date, resigned along with Abner H. Flewellen, both of whom had been trustees of the Clinton Female Seminary and longtime supporters of Slade. Lamar was a two-term US Congressman, associate justice of the Georgia Supreme Court, and one-time gubernatorial candidate. Subsequently, he was also the grandfather of Walter D. Lamar who married Wesleyan Graduate and longtime Wesleyan Trustee Eugenia Dorothy Blount, an eleventh cousin of Slade's wife Anne Jacqueline Blount. Willingness of the 1841 trustees, however, to lose such men as Lamar and Flewellen illustrates the depth of the desire among the Methodists on the board to solidify the college's denominational affiliation. To be fair, those on the board who were members of Methodist churches were also being unduly pressured to do so by denominational officials both in Macon and on the national level.

Later in the month, the only remaining non-Methodist member of the original faculty, Adolphus Maussinett, a Presbyterian, resigned along with trustee Everard Hamilton. The purge was over but the denominational controversy continued to cost the college dearly in reputation, students, finances, leadership, and personnel. As non-Methodists were replaced with Methodists, the college grew more and more sectarian despite continuing public announcements to the contrary. In July the board also lost Judge Augustus Baldwin Longstreet, lawyer, Methodist minister, educator, humorist, and 1813 graduate of Yale and the Litchfield, Connecticut School of Law. A former president of four universities, including the University of Mississippi (twice), South Carolina College (now the University of South Carolina), and Emory, his resignation was the excruciating final straw of casualties in the denominational controversy. Granted, Longstreet had been president of Emory, the flagship boys' college for Methodists in Georgia, since 1839 but the attachment of his name to the Georgia Female College gave them significant academic and political credibility. He was succeeded at Emory by Pierce. In Macon, an unusual number of resignations continued, enrollment declined, and revenue evaporated until the college was "sold" on July 10, 1844, and the board was dissolved.[139] The trustees confessed they were "irretrievably bankrupt" and unable "to pay ten cents in the dollar." Most who had supported the college dismissed the institution "as an entire failure."[140] The college had no money for operations and could not guarantee that salaries would be paid. Facing a deficit of $46,668.20 in 1841, trustees soon leased the college property to a newly created independent and private firm, headed by President Ellison and Professor John Gould Darby who proposed the plan. The building, which was foreclosed upon since the original construction cost had never been paid in full, was sold to the builder, Elam Alexander. The Friends of the College bought it from him and then James Everett loaned a newly constituted board of trustees $8,000 to purchase the same in 1843. For his magnanimous generosity, the trustees established the James Everetts Scholarships in Everett's honor and these were given to students of Wesleyan from 1843 until 1907.

Only with the help of private financing and the sheer determination of the denomination was the college able to reorganize and continue. Only then did the college come under exclusive control of the church. That is when the institution was rechartered as Wesleyan Female College to honor John Wesley, founder of the Methodist denomination. Legally, therefore, it may be argued that the college founded in 1836 was an entirely different institution than the one chartered in 1844. Incidentally, this was the same year the Methodist Episcopal Church South was organized as Methodists in the southern states formally separated from the national Methodist Episcopal Church.

As late as August 15, 1842, the remaining faculty of the college issued another clarification independent of the trustees. "Although the college was placed, by a public meeting under the control of the Georgia Conference of the Methodist Episcopal Church," the statement read, "yet as a faculty we utterly banish all sectarian peculiarities or influences from its operations. No young lady will be permitted to join any church, while under our charge, without a written permission from her parent or guardian."[141] Finally, the last example of evidence proving why Slade left Macon after only three semesters of teaching is that when Slade left the Georgia Female College, he moved to Penfield, Georgia, the center of Georgia Baptist activity and home of the recently founded Mercer Institute (now Mercer University) (1837–71) and *The Christian Index*, the state Baptist newspaper. It was the most Baptist town he could have gone to but because he remained there for such a short time, it indicates a hasty decision made purely on frustrated emotions aggravated by sectarian prejudice. Pierce, on the other hand, became president of Emory University in Decatur, Georgia. The other former trustees and faculty of the Georgia Female College all likewise took refuge in safe denominational havens.

Slade generally avoided going on record to reveal his opinion during the dispute. A Baptist minister and an academic with the highest qualifications, he continued to do his job at the college with complete professionalism until the day he resigned. In December, however, after safely settling in Penfield, he revealed his thoughts in a report given to document his review of the Vineville Academy. Slade attended an examination of the pupils there, one class in fractions, and it gave him "pleasure" to state that he had "never seen any . . . of the same age answer more promptly" or "more correctly the sums" he gave them.[142] Then he concluded his report by subtly tying the size of the academy to the decline at the college and "denominational prejudices and jealousies" which were "unbecoming as they are Christian." He magnanimously urged, however, all denominations to support the college nonetheless, perhaps because several of the students who had enrolled with him in Clinton and had transferred with him to the Georgia Female College were still studying in Macon.

Therefore, and in conclusion, while the founding and history of the Georgia Female College, apart from Slade's involvement, is beyond the scope of this paper, suffice it to say that the history has since been firmly established. While the Methodist Episcopal Church was invited, very early in the college's history, to sponsor and appoint trustees to the college's board, the initial organization of the idea which became the college was instigated by local Macon businessmen, some of whom, including Henry G. Lamar, the first chairman, were also trustees of the Clinton Female Seminary. The issue was complicated because several of the businessmen were Methodists, the church had been discussing a female college to be somewhere in Georgia, and the first organizational meeting open to members of the community was held at the Methodist Church of Macon in November 1835. The Methodist Conference voted, on invitation of the community, to adopt the college on January 14, 1836, but the college did not come under the direct control of the church until its fourth year in 1843 when the name was changed. The first meeting of the trustees, composed of half local businessmen and half appointees of the church, met the next day at the Bibb County Courthouse for the first time. Therefore, the fullness of records proves that both sides of the denominational controversy over the early history of Wesleyan were partially correct. Unfortunately, once the fight began, insults were launched, and relationships were broken; neither side was willing to allow any space in the history to the other. Friendships were lost, careers were damaged, reputations were destroyed, and relationships were permanently broken only to make the early days of Wesleyan more difficult and its ultimate long-term growth far more limited. Although some won the battle for "quality" over quantity, from the Methodist point of view, by the late twentieth century few trustees, faculty, alumna, or students gave much thought to the college's denominational affiliation. In 1835, affiliation mattered. Macon had only been settled for twelve years and had almost already lost a college. Clinton was thirty-three years old by 1840 and, although already in decline due to the opening of Creek land in West Georgia, was still, and would be for a little while, larger than the county seat of Bibb. The college and the city had a long way to go, more divisive issues to face, and a history still being clarified in the twenty-first century.

Meanwhile, female schools proliferated throughout Georgia in the 1850s as the Methodists founded six additional colleges for women, Presbyterians three, and the Baptists organized five. This budding trend, however, was extinguished by the local chaos of the Civil War. Only Wesleyan, LaGrange, and Andrew College have survived.[143]

Notes

1 Samuel Luttrell Akers, *The First Hundred Years of Wesleyan College: 1836–1936* (Macon, GA: The Stinehour Press, 1976), p. 16.

2 Eunice Thomson, "Ladies Can Learn," *The Georgia Review* 1:2 (Summer 1947): 192.

3 The first Wesleyan building, completed in 1838, was located at 451 College Street in Macon, across College from Washington Park, where the US post office is located today. The post office was somewhat designed to reflect the history of the former college building in its architectural design.

4 Florence Fleming Corley, "The Presbyterian Quest: Higher Education for Georgia Women," *American Presbyterians*, 69:2 (Summer 1991): 83.

5 *Ibid*. See also Thomas G. Dyer, *The University of Georgia: A Bicentennial History, 1785–1985* (Athens: Univ. of Georgia, 1985), pp. 31, 40 and Ernest Trice Thompson, *Presbyterians in the South*, vol. i (Richmond: John Knox Press, 1963), p. 263.

6 Florence Fleming Corley, "The Presbyterian Quest: Higher Education for Georgia Women," *American Presbyterians* 69:2 (Summer 1991): 85.

7 "Notice," *The Missionary* (August 1, 1825).

8 Nathan Bangs, *A History of the Methodist Episcopal Church*, vol. iv (New York: Carlton and Phillips, 1853), p. 103.

9 See Samuel Luttrell Akers, The First Hundred Years of Wesleyan College, 1836–1936 (Macon: Beehive Press, 1976), p. 4 ff.; John Campbell Butler, *Historical*

Record of Macon and Central Georgia (Macon: J. W. Burke & Co., 1879), pp. 115–21; Stephen F. Miller, *The Bench and Bar of Georgia: Memoirs and Sketches*, vol. i (Philadelphia: J. P. Lippincott & Co., 1858), pp. 115–39; Dorothy Orr, *A History of Education in Georgia* (Univ. of North Carolina, 1950), p. 389; Robert Marion Willingham, Jr., *We Have this Heritage: The History of Wilkes County, Georgia, Beginnings to 1860* (Washington: Wilkes Pub. Co., 1969).

10 Eunice Thomson, "Ladies Can Learn," *The Georgia Review* 1:2 (Summer 1947): 190.
11 Florence Fleming Corley, "The Presbyterian Quest: Higher Education for Georgia Women," *American Presbyterians* 69:2 (Summer 1991): 85.
12 L. E. Roberts, "Educational Reform in Ante-Bellum Georgia," *The Georgia Review* 16:1 (Spring 1962): 68–82.
13 Eunice Thomson, "Ladies Can Learn," *The Georgia Review* 1:2 (Summer 1947): 189. See also Mary Wollstonecraft, *A Vindication of the Rights of Woman* (Boston: Peter Edes for Thomas and Andrews, 1792).
14 Joan Elizabeth Barbour, "College Education for Women in Georgia Before the Civil War" (Honors Paper in History, Emory College, 1972), pp. 23, 90, in Special Collections, Woodruff Library, Emory University.
15 Florence Fleming Corley, "The Presbyterian Quest: Higher Education for Georgia Women," *American Presbyterians* 69:2 (Summer 1991): 86.
16 L. E. Roberts, "Educational Reform in Ante-Bellum Georgia," *The Georgia Review* 16:1 (Spring 1962): 76.
17 "Female Education," *Georgia Messenger* (August 27, 1835), p. 3.
18 Multus in Uno, "The Origin of the Georgia Female College, Macon," *Georgia Messenger* (April 23, 1840).
19 *Georgia Messenger* and *Georgia Telegraph* (July 9, 1835) each quoting personal letters of July 6, 1835.
20 Richard W. Griffin, "Wesleyan College: Its Genesis, 1835–1840," *Georgia Historical Quarterly* 50:1 (Mar 1966): 54–73.
21 *Georgia Messenger* (July 9, 1835).
22 Intellectual Over Ornamental, "Female Character," *The Knickerbocker* 6:3 (September 1835): 209.
23 George G. Smith, *The History of Georgia Methodism from 1786 to 1866* (Atlanta: A. R. Caldwell, 1913), pp. 357–8.
24 *Georgia Messenger* (December 3, 1835).
25 *Georgia Messenger* (January 21, 1836).

26 Wesleyan College, "Minutes of the Board of Trustees of the Georgia Female College and the Wesleyan Female College (from 1838), 1836–1844," *Wesleyan College Archives*, The Lucy Lester Willet Memorial Library, p. 1.
27 Nathan Bangs, *A History of the Methodist Episcopal Church*, vol. iv (New York: Carlton and Phillips, 1853).
28 George G. Smith, *The History of Georgia Methodism from 1786 to 1866* (Atlanta: A. R. Caldwell, 1913), p. 225.
29 Ibid., pp. 119–20.
30 *Population Slave Schedules of the Sixth Census of the United States, 1840*, roll 48, GA, vol. 7, 1–151, The National Archives and 1860, AL, Dallas Co., schedule 2, "Slave Inhabitants," reel 29.
31 Rossiter Johnson and John Howard Brown, eds., "Andrew, James Osgood," *The Biographical Dictionary of America*, vol. 1 (Boston: American Biographical Society, 1906), pp. 114–15. See also George Gilman Smith, *The Life and Letters of James Osgood Andrew* (Southern Methodist Pub. House, 1882), pp. 311–12 and Brian D. Lawrence, The *Relationship between the Methodist Church, Slavery and Politics, 1784–1844* (Rowan University, 2018).
32 George G. Smith, *The History of Georgia Methodism from 1786 to 1866* (Atlanta: A. R. Caldwell, 1913), p. 191.
33 Ibid., p. 192.
34 Ibid., p. 243.
35 Ibid., p. 222.
36 "Executive Department Georgia," *The Constitutionalist* (October 29, 1829), p. 1.
37 "Bank of Columbus," *Georgia Courier* (November 21, 1834), p. 3.
38 "Rev. Lovick Pierce, D.D.," *New York Daily Herald* (November 11, 1879), p. 4.
39 Zach C. Hayes, "Bishop George Foster Pierce," *The Georgia Review* 7:2 (1953): 156–63.
40 "Eustace Willoughby Speer," *The Macon Telegraph* (October 22, 1899), p. 6.
41 "Georgia Conference," *Augusta Chronicle and Georgia Advertiser* (February 20, 1830).
42 "Georgia Conference," *Southern Banner* (February 8, 1834).
43 George G. Smith, *The History of Georgia Methodism from 1786 to 1866* (Atlanta: A. R. Caldwell, 1913), pp. 221–2.
44 Eunice Thomson, "Ladies Can Learn," *The Georgia Review* 1:2 (Summer 1947): 192.
45 George G. Smith, *The History of Georgia Methodism from 1786 to 1866* (Atlanta: A. R. Caldwell, 1913), pp. 222, 225.

46 Anna Maria Green Cook, *History of Baldwin County, Georgia* (Anderson, SC: Keys-Hearn Printing Company, 1925), p. 124.
47 Florida Heritage Site Marker F-371, The General Duncan Lamont Clinch Historical Society of Amelia Island and The Florida Department of State, 1996.
48 Samuel Luttrell Akers, *The First Hundred Years of Wesleyan College: 1836–1936* (Macon: The Stinehour Press, 1976), p. 16 and "Georgia Legislature," *Georgia Messenger* (November 24, 1836).
49 1850 US Census, National Archives and Records Administration.
50 Letter, 1836 January 27, Macon, Georgia [to] W[illia]m Schley, Gov[ernor of Georgia], Milledgeville, [Georgia] / Col[onel] Ossian Gregory, Hargrett Rare Book and Manuscript Library, The University of Georgia Libraries, presented in the Digital Library of Georgia.
51 *Deaths Published in the Christian Intelligencer of the Reformed Dutch Church from 1830 to 1871*, Ray C. Sawyer, ed., vol. v. (1933), p. 28.
52 *Georgia Messenger* (October 6, 1836), p. 4.
53 "Died," *Georgia Journal and Messenger* (March 28, 1849).
54 "Monroe Rail Road," *Georgia Messenger* (May 26, 1836).
55 Ibid (November 3, 1836).
56 Elizabeth R. Varon, *Longstreet: The Confederate General Who Defied the South* (New York: Simon & Schuster, 2023).
57 Lewis M. Purifoy, "The Southern Methodist Church and the Proslavery Argument," *The Journal of Southern History* 32:3, Southern Historical Association (August 1966): 325–41.
58 John Soward Bayne, "Augustus Baldwin Longstreet," *Gravely Concerned: Southern Writers' Graves* (Clemson, 2012), pp. 24, 25.
59 Richard Carwardine, "Methodists, Politics, and the Coming of the American Civil War," *Church History* 69:3 (2000): 584.
60 Scott B. Thompson Jr, "The Prentiss of Georgia," in *Pieces of Our Past* (Dublin, GA: Scott B. Thompson Jr, 2014).
61 W. H. Sparks, *The Atlanta Constitution* (June 25, 1881).
62 "Robert Augustus Beall Obituary," *The Southern Recorder* (July 26, 1836), p. 3.
63 Wesleyan College, "Minutes of the Board of Trustees of the Georgia Female College and the Wesleyan Female College (from 1838), 1836–1844," *Wesleyan College Archives*, The Lucy Lester Willet Memorial Library.
64 "Obituary," *Macon Georgia Telegraph* (August 25, 1836).
65 "A Lobby Member," *Georgia Telegraph* (December 22, 1836).

66 Wesleyan College, "Minutes of the Board of Trustees of the Georgia Female College and the Wesleyan Female College (from 1838), 1836-1844," *Wesleyan College Archives*, The Lucy Lester Willet Memorial Library.
67 Eunice Thomson, "Ladies Can Learn," *The Georgia Review* 1:2 (Summer 1947): 190.
68 Ibid., pp. 190–1.
69 Ibid., p. 190.
70 Thomas Woody, *A History of Women's Education in the United States* (New York: The Science Press, 1929).
71 "Georgia Female College," *Chronicle & Sentinel* (December 13, 1838), p. 2 and Thomas Bog Slade, *Autobiography of Thomas Bog Slade*, Southern Historical Collection 1837–1846, 2683-z, University of North Carolina, p. 2.
72 Frank M. Abbott, "History of the People of Jones County, Georgia," vol. v., *Genealogies* (Lineage Unlimited, 1977) and *Annual Catalogue of the Wesleyan Female College, Macon, Georgia: 1879-1880* (Macon: J. W. Burke & Co., 1880), p. 35.
73 "Music," *Georgia Messenger* (June 1, 1837), p. 3.
74 Florence Fleming Corley, "The Presbyterian Quest: Higher Education for Georgia Women," *American Presbyterians*, 69:2 (Summer 1991): 86.
75 John Campbell Butler, *Historical Record of Macon and Central Georgia, Containing Many Interesting and Valuable Reminiscences Connected with the Whole State, Including Numerous Incidents and Facts Never Before Published and of Great Historical Value* (Middle Georgia Historical Society, 1969), p. 298.
76 *Georgia Messenger* (December 25, 27, 1838).
77 Richard W. Griffin, "Wesleyan College: Its Genesis, 1835–1840," *Georgia Historical Quarterly* 50:1 (Mar 1966): 65.
78 Eunice Thomson, "Ladies Can Learn," *The Georgia Review* 1:2 (Summer 1947): 193.
79 Florence Fleming Corley, "The Presbyterian Quest: Higher Education for Georgia Women," *American Presbyterians*, 69:2 (Summer 1991): 86.
80 Gale White, "A Town Progress Passed By," *The Atlanta Journal and Constitution Magazine* (22 June 1975): 20.
81 Richard W. Griffin, "Wesleyan College: Its Genesis, 1835–1840," *The Georgia Historical Quarterly* 50:1 (March 1966): 70.
82 Consider Bethlehem (1742), Salem College, NC (1772), Bradford (1803), Elizabeth (1818), Clinton (1821), Lindenwood (1837), and Columbia (1833). Salem and Columbia are still in existence under these same names.

83 Richard W. Griffin, "Wesleyan College: Its Genesis, 1835–1840," *Georgia Historical Quarterly* 50:1 (Mar 1966): 65.
84 "An Interesting Momento," *The Weekly Sun* (July 22, 1873), p. 3.
85 Ibid.
86 *Catalogue of the Officers and Pupils of the Georgia Female College with the Statutes of the College and the By-Laws of the Faculty* (S. Rose & Co., Printers, 1839), p. 6.
87 Eunice Thomson, "Ladies Can Learn," *The Georgia Review* 1:2 (Summer 1947): 193.
88 George F. Pierce, "An Address on Female Education," *Southern Ladies' Book* 1:1 (January 1840): 3–14.
89 Richard W. Griffin, "Wesleyan College: Its Genesis, 1835–1840," *Georgia Historical Quarterly* 50:1 (Mar 1966): 68.
90 George F. Pierce, *An Address on Female Education* (Macon, 1839), p. 19.
91 George Foster Pierce, "An Address on Female Education," *The Southern Ladies' Book* 1:1 (January 30, 1840): 3–14.
92 Ibid.
93 Ibid.
94 *Gospel of John*, chapter 9.
95 George Foster Pierce, "The Georgia Female College: It's Origin, Plan and Prospects," *The Southern Ladies' Book* 1:2 (February 1840): 67.
96 The Georgia Female College and Mrs. Willard Yates, *Southern Post* (Macon, GA, August 24, 1839), p. 3.
97 Ibid.
98 Ibid.
99 Ibid.
100 Ibid.
101 Ibid.
102 Ibid. See also Richard W. Griffin, "Wesleyan College: Its Genesis, 1835–1840," *Georgia Historical Quarterly* 50:1 (Mar 1966): 60.
103 George Foster Pierce, "The Georgia Female College: It's Origin, Plan and Prospects," *The Southern Ladies' Book* 1:2 (February 1840): 65–6.
104 *History of the Baptist Denomination in Georgia: with Biographical Compendium and Portrait Gallery of Baptist Ministers and other Georgia Baptists* (Atlanta: J. P. Harrison & Co., 1881), p. 178.
105 Ibid., p. 180.

106 Ibid., p. 181.
107 Ibid., p. 186.
108 Ibid., p. 192.
109 Ibid., p. 217.
110 Jesse H. Campbell, *Georgia Baptists: Historical and Biographical* (Macon: J. W. Burke & Co., 1874), pp. 57-8.
111 Ibid., pp. 161-2.
112 Ibid., p. 423.
113 Ibid., p. 184.
114 George Foster Pierce, "The Georgia Female College: It's Origin, Plan and Prospects," *The Southern Ladies' Book* 1:2 (February 1840): 71.
115 "Death of Sisters," *The Southern Ladies' Book* 2:3 (September 1840).
116 Ibid.
117 Ibid., p. 80.
118 George Foster Pierce, *The Southern Ladies Book* 1:3 (March 1840).
119 Wesleyan College, "Minutes of the Board of Trustees of the Georgia Female College and the Wesleyan Female College (from 1842), 1836-1844," *Wesleyan College Archives*, The Lucy Lester Willet Memorial Library.
120 George Foster Pierce, "Letter to the Editor," *Georgia Messenger* (June 25, 1840).
121 Wesleyan College, "Minutes of the Board of Trustees of the Georgia Female College and the Wesleyan Female College (from 1838), 1836-1844," *Wesleyan College Archives*, The Lucy Lester Willet Memorial Library, p. 1.
122 L. E. Roberts, "Educational Reform in Ante-Bellum Georgia," *The Georgia Review* 16:1 (Spring 1962): 76.
123 *Georgia Messenger* (April 23, 30; May 14, 21; June 4, 25, 1840).
124 Richard W. Griffin, "Wesleyan College: Its Genesis, 1835-1840," *Georgia Historical Quarterly* 50:1 (Mar 1966): 70.
125 "Origin of the College," *Telegraph* (June 2, 1840).
126 Ibid.
127 *Multus in Uno, Georgia Messenger* (April 23, 1840).
128 Wesleyan College, "Minutes of the Board of Trustees of the Georgia Female College and the Wesleyan Female College (from 1838), 1836-1844," *Wesleyan College Archives*, The Lucy Lester Willet Memorial Library, p. 49.
129 Ibid.
130 Ibid., p. 53. See also *Semi-Centennial Exercises: Memorials of Methodism in Macon, Georgia, 1828-1878* (J. W. Burke & Co., 1878); and "Judge A. M. Speer Dies at Madison," *The Atlanta Constitution* (March 29, 1897), p. 4.

131 Wesleyan College, "Minutes of the Board of Trustees of the Georgia Female College and the Wesleyan Female College (from 1838), 1836–1844," *Wesleyan College Archives*, The Lucy Lester Willet Memorial Library, p. 57.

132 John A. Andrew, "Review of *Southern Evangelicals and the Social Order, 1800–1860*, by A. C. Loveland," *Journal of the Early Republic* 1, no. 4 (1981): 429–31.

133 Ibid., p. 56; "Literary," *Georgia Messenger* (June 9, 1836), p. 3; and *Catalogue of the Trustees, Officers, Alumni and Matriculates of the University of Georgia at Athens, Georgia, 1785–1906* (Athens: E. D. Stone Press, 1906), from the Hargrett Rare Book & Manuscript Library, p. 126.

134 John C. Butler, *Historical Record of Macon and Central Georgia, Containing Many Interesting and Valuable Reminiscences Connected with the Whole State, Including Numerous Incidents and Facts Never before Published and of Great Historical Value* (Macon, J. W. Burke & Co., 1879), pp. 114, 295; Schuyler Medlock Christian, "A Sketch of the History of Science in Georgia," *The Georgia Review* 3:1 (Spring 1949): 60; The National Archives in Washington, DC; Record Group: *Records of the Bureau of the Census*; Record Group Number: 29; Series Number: M432; Residence Date: 1850; Home in 1850: Division 60, Monroe, Georgia; Roll: 78; Page: 81b, Series Number: M653; Residence Date: 1860; Home in 1860: Northern Division, Macon, Alabama; Roll: M653_14; Page: 876; Family History Library Film: 803014, and *1870 US Census*; Brooklyn Ward 9, Kings, NY; Roll: M593_950; Page: 190A; John Darby, *Botany of the Southern States: Structural and Physiological Botany and Vegetable Products and Descriptions of Southern Plants* (New York: A. S. Burnes & H. L. Burr, 1860); and James Grant Wilson and John Fiske, eds., *Appleton's Cyclopedia of American Biography, 1600–1889*, vol. ii (New York: Appleton, 1887), p. 76.

135 *Greenfield Gazette and Franklin Herald*, newspaper (Greenfield, MA), October 4, 1831 and *Triennial Catalogue of the Philo Technian Society of Williams College, 1844* (Troy: J. C. Kneeland & Co., 1844).

136 Schuyler Medlock Christian, "A Sketch of the History of Science in Georgia," *The Georgia Review* 3:1 (Spring 1949): 60; James Grant Wilson and John Fiske, eds., *Appleton's Cyclopedia of American Biography, 1600–1889*, vol. ii (New York: Appleton, 1887), p. 76; and *Georgia Journal and Messenger*, August 26, 1841 (Macon, GA), p. 4.

137 Wesleyan College, "Minutes of the Board of Trustees of the Georgia Female College and the Wesleyan Female College (from 1838), 1836–1844," *Wesleyan College Archives*, The Lucy Lester Willet Memorial Library, p. 57.

138 Ibid., p. 58.
139 Ibid., p. 92.
140 *Annual Catalogue of the Wesleyan Female College, Macon, Georgia: 1879–1880* (Macon: J. W. Burke & Co., 1880), p. 36.
141 Ellison and Darby, *The Southern Ladies Book* (S. Rose & Co., 1842): 10–11.
142 Thomas Bog Slade, *Georgia Messenger* (December 31, 1840).
143 Joan Elizabeth Barbour, "College Education for Women in Georgia Before the Civil War" (Honors Paper in History, Emory College, 1972), p. 21f.

5

Penfield

A copious Providence this, which founds a Christian College on Jewish cornerstones.

H. R. Bernard

Slade's resignation from the Georgia Female College in Macon and his new position with the Penfield Female Academy in Penfield, Georgia was announced two weeks later in the *Georgia Messenger* on August 6, 1840.[1] He had accepted the position of "rector" at the female academy in Penfield, Greene County, Georgia. He assumed his new responsibilities as quickly as he was able to move his family of ten 70 miles northeast or 35 miles south of Athens, then consisting of eight children, ages one through fifteen. The Penfield Female Academy was six years old in 1840. Penfield was founded in 1829 and named for Josiah Penfield (1785–1828), a Savannah merchant, silversmith, and Baptist deacon originally from Connecticut who gave $2,500 to create the town and issued a challenge to the Georgia Baptist Convention, organized in 1822, to match his gift for educational purposes. Thanks to the generous contributions made by several leading Georgia Baptists including William Flournoy, Jesse Mercer, Billington Sanders, Adiel Sherwood, and Thomas Stocks, the convention met Penfield's challenge by matching his donation and founding a vocational school which they named Mercer Institute (now Mercer University) in 1833 in honor of Mercer (1769–1841), a resident of Wilkes County who gave the largest amount toward the challenge. Mercer eventually gave over $40,000, in the earliest days, to the university that continues to bear his name even after severing all legal ties to the convention in 2005, after a 172-year-old relationship. Jesse Mercer was disappointed when Greene County was chosen to be the site of the town and campus,

Figure 5.1. Thomas Bog Slade (public domain, Ancestry.com. Originally shared by cironwolf1, Panama City Beach, FL, and Findagrave.com. Originally shared by Jeff Donaldson).

having lobbied for Washington, Georgia, instead. He nevertheless relocated and is buried there in the Penfield Cemetery behind the old campus. Mercer's wealth came from his second wife, Nancy Mills, formerly the wealthy widow of Abraham Simons of Wilkes County, Georgia. Simons was a successful Jewish entrepreneur who owned an inn, tavern, cotton plantation, and horse-racing track near Washington, Georgia. He was a captain in the American Revolution and a state legislator from Wilkes County. After he died in 1824 and Mills inherited his fortune, Mercer, the man she married in 1827, and the university became the ultimate beneficiaries. "She was a beautiful little dark-eyed and dark-haired woman," Rice wrote, "and often wore yellow ribbons on her bonnets and caps. She was refined and cultured and smoothed out the rough spots of Jesse's social manners."[2] Mills died in 1834 and Mercer in 1841. Mills died "after a year of paralysis, not speaking a word or making a step."[3] Mercer historian H. R. Bernard said, "Mercer University is largely indebted to the skill and enterprise of a Jewish financier for much the larger part of its life and power. A copious Providence this, which founds a Christian College on Jewish cornerstones."[4] Simons is buried in the Simons Cemetery of Wilkes County.

"Four hundred and fifty acres of land, just seven miles north of the courthouse, were purchased by Georgia Baptists and Penfield was founded." The Penfield Female Academy was founded in 1834, six years before Slade arrived to take control. Penfield, today a shadow of its former self, was then the center of the Baptist denomination in Georgia and of culture in Greene County. It was home to *The Christian Index*, *The Temperance Banner*, *The Georgia Illustrated Magazine*, and *The Orion*, which were all published there.[5] In Penfield there were five Baptist churches, primarily Penfield Baptist, two Presbyterian, but no Methodist.[6]

Greene County was created by the Georgia legislature on February 3, 1786, from land ceded by the Creek Indians and was named for Revolutionary War General Nathanael Greene (1742–86) who died in the year of the creation. Greene is buried in Savannah but not in Greene Square, named for him; rather, he is in Johnson Square, which was named for Robert Johnson, a colonial governor of South Carolina and friend of General James Oglethorpe. The county seat of Greene County has been Greensboro since 1802. In 1840, the county was dominated by cotton plantations. Situated along the fall line of Georgia, Greene County was ideal for cotton production and thus produced a population of a few wealthy landowning whites and many enslaved African Americans. Georgia Female College Trustee Augustus Baldwin Longstreet lived there for several years.[7] The first school in Greene County was the Greensborough Academy, founded for boys in 1786. This early institution was followed by the Brockman United Academy in 1826, the Lafayette Hall Academy in 1827, the Thornton Academy in 1831, the White Plains Academy, and the Penfield Female Academy, the first school in Greene County for girls, in 1834.[8] A second female academy was established in Greensboro in 1852 by Presbyterians. One of the teachers there was Louisa May Alcott, author of *Little Women*.[9] According to Rice, the population of Greene County was only 5,405 in 1790 but doubled to 10,761 by 1800 and 11,690 in 1840.

The Baptist Convention for the State of Georgia (now Georgia Baptist Convention) was first organized in 1822 and was one of nine state Baptist conventions that organized the Southern Baptist Convention in 1845. It followed an earlier attempt at organization, which was the General Committee of Georgia Baptists in 1803, but this group failed in 1810 due to concerns raised regarding the inclusion of pedobaptists. The convention represents those Baptist churches in Georgia that chose to affiliate but certainly does not include every church with Baptist in the name. Georgia Baptist churches, especially in the nineteenth century, included those Baptist churches that supported missionary work in America and in foreign countries, believer's baptism, priesthood of the believer, autonomy of the local church, as well as many forms of education including Sunday School, colleges, and universities. The convention organization was first proposed by Adiel Sherwood of Greene County through Charles J. Jenkins at a meeting of the Sarepta Baptist Association in 1820. Prior to this date, Baptist churches were only linked by their voluntary membership in local associations. Far more autonomous than either Methodist or Presbyterian churches, Baptist churches were organized only for fellowship and cooperative mission work. Like the other denominations, they believed in camp meetings and church revivals but placed less emphasis on the formal education of ministers, trusting in the "calling of God" and the "anointing of the Holy Spirit." The Georgia Baptist Convention does not include the Primitive Baptist churches that chose to organize separately in 1835. Primitive Baptists do not support mission work or formalized religious education. Jesse Mercer served as the first president of the Georgia Baptist Convention.[10]

Penfield, which Slade described in 1840 as a "country village," demonstrated incredible promise in the early nineteenth century because of its affiliation with Georgia Baptists, but is today not mentioned among the "largest communities" of Greene County, which include Siloam, Union Point, White Plains, and Woodville. In the 1830s, however, "Covington-Oxford had followed the lead of Penfield, and established a religious school for boys; Clinton was being sapped to death by Macon."[11] When Slade was there, Penfield had a bank, several boarding houses, cotton warehouses, a hosiery mill, hotel, mercantile shops, a post office, and print shops. The Mercer campus featured a science hall, a brick dormitory, two literary society halls, a baseball field, and several administrative buildings, besides the chapels, both old and new. The faculty included Joseph E. Willet, a Yale graduate who taught Chemistry and Natural

Science (1847–93) and who married Billington Sander's daughter Emily. Many of the trustees lived in Penfield and were a constant help to the health and growth of the university. According to Rice, Greensboro was "second fiddle" to Penfield in the 1840s, and the "tradespeople" in the county seat considered relocating to one of the fastest-growing towns in Georgia.[12]

Adiel Sherwood, a Baptist minister in Greene County, was a major contributor to the Josiah Penfield Fund and had founded his own "private school." He was pressured in 1832 to "give up his private school . . . in favor of Mercer Institute" by the Mercer trustees, but the request was later withdrawn, presumably because Sherwood agreed to merge. Penfield, therefore, began to grow after 1833 when the institute was founded and in 1837 when the name was changed to Mercer University. The first faculty included J. W. Attaway, W. D. Cowdry, J. F. Hillyer, Ira O. McDaniel, Billington Sanders, S. P. Sanford, and A. Williams. They were all Baptists and there was never any pretense that Mercer would be anything other than a sectarian university. In 1838, the village was governed by the trustees of Mercer and Penfield was the cultural center of Greene County. The status of the community, however, plateaued and declined through the 1850s and 1860s until the Georgia Baptist Convention moved the university from Penfield to Macon in 1871 after the Civil War. "The War Between the States so impoverished the people that it was impossible to maintain a university, and the best that the trustees of Mercer could possibly do was to operate an academy until such time as sufficient funds could be raised to re-establish the University."[13] Thus Georgia Baptists in Macon and Atlanta began to argue that it would be impossible to reestablish Mercer in Penfield or any other remote location in the state. They, therefore, petitioned to have the university reestablished in their own city. After much bitter debate, the "Heart of Georgia" won the argument with the help of James Hyde Porter, a Macon Methodist who gave $150,000 toward relocation. Although a few university buildings survive in Penfield, the village all but disappeared and is today considered part of Union Point.

Georgia Baptists initially intended to locate a Southern Female College in Washington, Georgia, but the first plan never materialized even though "thousands of dollars had been pledged for its establishment."[14] Men were hired by the convention to solicit funds for the college in 1837, but then on

August 25 of that year, a resolution was adopted to establish the Penfield Female "Institute" in Greene County and to secure funding by selling lots in the village.

The *Christian Index* also moved to Penfield from Washington, Georgia in 1840 after being originally founded in Washington, DC, by Luther Rice in 1822. The *Index*, not to be confused with a Methodist magazine published by the Christian Methodist Episcopal Church, is the oldest continuously published religious newspaper in the country. Rice created the *Index* to promote the work of several friends who had gone to be missionaries in foreign countries. One of those missionaries was Adoniram Judson, the legendary minister of Burma, but another, lesser known, was Thomas Bowen of Greensboro, Georgia, who alphabetized the Yoruba language and mapped that section of Nigeria. W. T. Brantley, a Baptist minister from Augusta, Georgia, became editor of the *Index* in 1831 when it was based in Philadelphia, Pennsylvania, and he moved it to Washington, Georgia, in 1833. With Jesse Mercer as editor, the *Index* grew to be primarily concerned with Baptist work in Georgia. The newspaper eventually moved to Macon in 1856 and Atlanta in 1865, where it became the official news outlet of the Georgia Baptist Convention. Among several editors of *The Christian Index*, Henry Holcombe Tucker (1819–89) served the newspaper before and after being the chancellor of the University of Georgia (1874–8). Tucker was also president of Mercer University from the Civil War until he resigned to go to Athens.

Jesse Mercer was also publisher of *The Temperance Crusader*, one of the oldest and longest surviving temperance newspapers in the country. Founded in 1834, it was published out of the same office as *The Christian Index*, at first advocating for moderation in the consumption of alcohol but then evolving to become an advocate for abstinence from all intoxicating drinks in 1835. The *Crusader* practically came to Penfield as a package deal along with the *Index*. It was later purchased by Col. John H. Seals, who moved publication to Atlanta in 1857, where it died in the 1860s.[15]

The Orion, a classical nineteenth-century national magazine, was founded in 1842 and published by William Carey Richards in Penfield to establish and develop a literary culture in the South.[16] Richards was adamant that the magazine was not about *Southern* literature but that it happened to be published in the South. He also denied any similarity to the *Knickerbocker*, popular in the 1840s, although the two magazines looked much the same.[17] Thus the *Orion* had no denominational affiliation and published a diversity of literary genres from a national pool of contributors. In 1844, Richards relocated *The Orion* to Charleston, South Carolina, but then ended publication just six months later.[18]

Penfield Baptist Church was organized in 1839 by teachers and students of both Mercer and the female academy after the older Shiloh Baptist Church was destroyed by a tornado. The present church meets in the Mercer Chapel in Penfield, but before Mercer relocated to Macon, they occupied a wooden structure on the south side of the campus, opposite the location of the female academy. This is the church Slade and his family attended after arriving in Penfield in 1840. In those days, men and women sat on opposite sides of the church, separated by the center aisle. Although no record is found of the Slades joining Penfield Baptist until April 10, 1841, Slade's name appears in the minutes of the church when he was appointed with two others as early as Tuesday, February 9, 1841, to correspond with Thomas Curtis, formerly of Bangor, Maine, about being head of Mercer's Department of Theology and pastor of the church. On Saturday, February 13, this committee was dissolved, and Slade was appointed to another committee, the only non-deacon so appointed, to procure a "Bible and hymn book for the pulpit," and he was appointed a "correspondent" with Attaway to the Greensboro Baptist Church."[19] The church was meeting in conference as needed, separate from the regular religious services.

On Monday, March 29, William Carey Richards, publisher of *The Orion*, joined the Penfield Baptist Church in the same service that welcomed Thomas Curtis to be the new pastor. Richards transferred his church membership from Hamilton Institute, New York. He immediately offered to assist the church clerk, Benjamin Brantley, in compiling an updated list of all members of the church. On Saturday, April 10, nine months after resigning from the Georgia Female College, Slade, wife Anne, and daughter Janet, sixteen, formally presented letters of dismissal from "the Macon church" and officially joined the Penfield Baptist Church.[20] Presumably the other children were too young to have joined the church in Macon, although Mary was fifteen and "Annie" was twelve. Baptist churches in the nineteenth century were strict about church membership and not only worked diligently to be sure members of the church had made a genuine commitment of faith but that they were members of only one church at a time. Letters were given and received by churches when members moved to a new church, signed by the respective clerks of the sending and receiving church. They were equally strict regarding church discipline, as members were regularly dismissed for unexcused absences or reports of immoral behavior such as "profane language" or "drinking." The clerk of the church often noted in the church minutes that the roll of members was called in meetings. In fact, in the same meeting the Slades joined the Penfield Baptist Church, "Bro. E. Randale . . . after investigation and deliberation, on motion, he was excommunicated." Some members, so dismissed, were defiant in protesting the discipline of the church. E. L. H. Johnson, for example, who had been dismissed in May, reappeared when he sought to join a church in Upson County, Georgia, and a letter from there addressed the charges against him. Johnson, who had been accused of "drinking wine" in a "grocery on the Sabbath," declared that if he was not given a letter of dismission from Penfield "he would relate his experience and be re-baptized," and then added that "Baptists were not all the people in the world, for he could join others." Since he had already been excommunicated, the church encouraged members to avoid him and consider him unworthy of fellowship. Words such as these and this approach to individuals seem harsh to the modern Christian reader but were common in churches of the nineteenth century. Such declarations in a time when church attendance was almost universal could be devastating to one's career and ability to circulate in the local social circles.

Usually when new members joined the Penfield Baptist Church, the pastor presented them to the congregation and gave them "the right hand of Christian fellowship." When Curtis, the new pastor, joined, however, on Saturday, May 1, 1841, it was Slade who represented the congregation to present and welcome him. Curtis transferred his membership from the First Baptist Church of Bangor, Maine. Fully $760 was pledged by resident members and students toward the new pastor's salary, but by September 4, only $356 had been received. Interestingly, seven percent of the pledged amount was committed by students, while less than two percent of the amount received was given by students.

On Friday, July 2, Slade, Greene, and Brantly were appointed to investigate a "difficulty" between members Davant and Chase.[21] This was settled on July 31. That Slade became a respected leader in the Penfield church so quickly speaks of his reputation and character. That he maintained these qualities is evidence of his integrity and good behavior as a minister and school administrator. On July 17 the church, then meeting in the Mercer chapel, voted to build their own building. Slade and others were appointed to "apply for a location, raise funds and proceed as a building committee, in furtherance of the object, and that they report progress at the next conference."[22] On July 31 this committee was instructed to propose a joint venture with the university to build a multi-purpose building to serve the needs of the church but also be available for use by Mercer. On August 7, however, after negotiations with the trustees, the church respectfully withdrew from the proposal.

On Saturday, October 2, Curtis resigned as pastor after serving only five months but gave up to a three-month notice before his departure. It is not known whether he was unsatisfied as pastor of the church or as a professor of theology at Mercer since he was serving in both positions. Slade and others were appointed to a pastor search committee. Curtis did not give a reason for his departure, but the minutes of the church indicate that he was never paid the subscribed amount determined upon his arrival, and then the church was unable to pay even the discounted amount that was given. Despite the healthy membership made up of professors, teachers, businessmen, etc., the church accepted Curtis' resignation early to avoid increasing the debt that was owed to him. He was officially dismissed on Sunday, October 17 after the morning service.

Writing from Penfield to his brother, Slade said the cost of living was cheaper in Penfield although he paid $5,000 for a house. He was still hiring out his "negroes" for money but still asked William, who was still in debt to his brother, for $500 owed. Although Slade did not start the Penfield Female Seminary, several "members of the Senior Class [transfer students from Macon]—they have followed me to this place."[23] The surviving academy building is located on West Main Street (now Penfield Road), down the hill from the Mercer campus. Whereas Maria Lord and Martha Massey did not follow Slade to Penfield from Macon, music was taught by Mariah Frances Dickerman, the wife of Shelton

Palmer Sanford who taught mathematics and astronomy at Mercer. They were married in 1840, just as Slade arrived. Their grandson was later president of the University of Georgia and is the namesake of Sanford Stadium in Athens. As educators, the Sanfords nevertheless owned five enslaved persons.

Up the street north, behind the Penfield Female Academy, was the site of the James Davant House along the west side of Mercer Circle between the surviving Greens-Martin House and the existent home of Rev. Billington M. Sanders who was one of the principal donors to the Josiah Penfield Fund in 1829. Sanders was principal of the Mercer Institute in 1833–8 and first president of Mercer University. Lemuel Greene and James Davant were trustees of Mercer in 1838–42 and the Penfield Female Academy in 1839, respectively. Slade would have known Sarah Northern, the wife of Rev. Thomas Martin, as she was the daughter of Peter Northern of Jones County. The female academy faced south, next door to the A. M. Lansdell House and diagonally positioned to face both the William B. Johnson home and the C. A. Lawrence Boarding House.

Slade was the fourth principal of the Penfield Female Academy, following Rev. Smith (1838), William C. Richards (1838), and Benjamin O. Pierce (1840). In what almost seems to be an annual appointment, Slade (1840–2) was followed by Rev. Iverson L. Brooks (1843–4), Rev. Shaler Hillyer (1845), George Y. Browne (1848), P. S. Whitman (1850–2), and Richard T. Asbury (1853–5). According to Rice, the academy became a town school after 1855 and by the mid-twentieth century was a private home.[24]

On Saturday, December 4, 1841, after only three semesters at the Penfield Female Academy, Slade requested and was granted letters of dismission from the Penfield Baptist Church. As when they joined the church eight months earlier, only Slade, his wife Anne, and daughter Janet are mentioned.[25] Clearly by then, Slade had made the decision to leave Penfield and make his last move, this time to Columbus, Georgia, more than 185 miles southwest, a journey, in the winter of 1841–1842, that would have taken up to a week and perhaps longer when traveling with children. By this time Slade was forty-one years old and was the father of nine children including Janet, sixteen, Mary, fifteen, "Annie," twelve, "Jery," ten, "Coon," nine, Thomas Jr., eight, Martha, four, Stella, two, and Helen, who was born in Penfield, was ten months old. With two more children to be born, Slade packed a wagon for the last time and again headed for his longest lasting educational adventure.

Additional research is needed regarding Slade's brief stay in Penfield because it is not clear why he left so quickly after taking the position in Greene County. He excitedly wrote of possibilities that arose because of forced Indian removal in 1836 and the governor's provision of new lands by lottery for the expansion of Georgia and white settlement to the Chattahoochee River and the border of Alabama. After only one year, Slade resigned from the Penfield Female Seminary and migrated with the *Southern School Journal*, the mouth of the Georgia Teachers Association, to Columbus, Georgia, founded in 1828.[26] Whatever seemed clear to Slade in 1841 was evidently not visible in 1840, so it seems more likely that Penfield was a safe landing spot until Slade and his family could sort out the more permanent plan for his life and work. Slade kept a close watch on Penfield events, however, even after moving to Columbus despite the brief residency there. There is evidence he maintained his subscription to *The Temperance Banner* at least until 1855.[27] Having resigned from the faculty of the Georgia Female College during a denominational controversy and spending only one year in Penfield, the center of Baptist life in Georgia, Slade may have experienced his most uncertain days in 1840–1 but the incident illustrates his strength of principle even at the risk of his family's financial security.

Slade traveled back to Penfield in 1855 and conducted the wedding of Thomas Jefferson Neal and Margaret J. McKay on November 18. Slade's relationship with Neal, a farmer, and McKay is not certain but she may have been his student from Columbus since the couple have ties to Harris County, Georgia and may also have named one of their seven children for Slade. Thomas McCormick Neal was born June 9, 1861, in Talbot County. The Neals are buried there. Neal's gravestone inscription, of 1899, reads, "He died as he lived, a pure, upright man." McKay's stone, however, from 1903, says, "Blessed are the pure in heart for they shall see God. A light from our household's gone. A voice we loved is stilled. A place is vacant in our hearts that can never filled."

Hannah O. Slade was married to William J. Gallimore of Twiggs County, Georgia, on December 16, 1855, but Hannah, the daughter of Ollyphair Slade of Washington County, seems to be of no relation to Thomas Bog Slade. Neither is Lavinia B. Slade of Pike County, Georgia, who married Henry F. Turner on November 20, 1855. Their wedding was conducted by Rev. James B. Hanson.[28]

Notes

1. *Georgia Messenger* (August 6, 1840).
2. Thaddeus Brocket Rice and Carolyn White Williams, *History of Greene County, Georgia, 1786–1886* (Wilkes Publishing Co., 1973), p. 254.
3. Thaddeus Brocket Rice and Carolyn White Williams, *History of Greene County, Georgia, 1786–1886* (Wilkes Publishing Co., 1973), p. 254.
4. Leon Huhner, "Captain Abraham Simons of the Georgia Line in the Revolution," *Publications of the American Jewish Historical Society*, No. 33 (1934), p. 236 and Lucian Lamar Knight, *Georgia's Landmarks, Memorials, and Legends*, vol. ii (Atlanta: Byrd Printing Company, 1914), pp. 1042–5. See also H. R. Bernard, *The Work Once Delivered to the Saints* (Macon: J. W. Burke, 1906).
5. Thaddeus Brocket Rice and Carolyn White Williams, *History of Greene County, Georgia, 1786–1886* (Wilkes Publishing Co., 1973).
6. "Baptist Denomination in Georgia: With Biographical Compendium and Portrait Gallery of Baptist Ministers and Other Georgia Baptists," *The Christian Index* (1881) and J. C. Bryant, "Antebellum Years in Penfield," in the *New Georgia Encyclopedia* (Mercer University, 2006).
7. Thaddeus Brocket Rice and Carolyn White Williams, *History of Greene County, Georgia, 1786–1886* (Wilkes Publishing Co., 1973).
8. Thaddeus Brocket Rice and Carolyn White Williams, *History of Greene County, Georgia, 1786–1886* (Wilkes Publishing Co., 1973), p. 220. See also p. 202 which incorrectly states the founding of the Penfield Female Academy as 1840.
9. Thaddeus Brocket Rice and Carolyn White Williams, *History of Greene County, Georgia, 1786–1886* (Wilkes Publishing Co., 1973), p. 202.
10. Chad Brand and David E. Hankins, *One Sacred Effort: The Cooperative Program of Southern Baptists* (B&H Publishing Group, 2006), pp. 120–1; Jarrett Burch, *Adiel Sherwood: Baptist Antebellum Pioneer in Georgia*. Baptists Series (Mercer University Press, 2003), pp. 85–8; Jesse Harrison Campbell, *Georgia Baptists: Historical and Biographical* (Richmond: H. K. Ellyson, 1847), pp. 197–201; and Julie Whidden Long, *Portraits of Courage: Stories of Baptist Heroes* (Mercer University Press, 2008), p. 35.

11 Thaddeus Brocket Rice and Carolyn White Williams, *History of Greene County, Georgia, 1786-1886* (Wilkes Publishing Co., 1973), p. 103.
12 Ibid., p. 253.
13 Ibid., p. 255.
14 Ibid., p. 248.
15 John H. Seals, ed., *Temperance Crusader*, newspaper, Penfield, GA (1856-1857).
16 Ernest C. Hynds, "William Carey Richards," in Sam G. Riley, ed., *American Magazine Journalists, 1741-1850*, vol. 73 (1988): 252-7.
17 Bertram Holland Flanders, *Early Georgia Magazines: Literary Periodicals to 1865* (Athens: University of Georgia Press, 2010), pp. 68-88.
18 Edward L. Tucker, "Two Young Brothers and Their *Orion*," *The Southern Literary Journal* 11:1 (1978): 64-80 and Kate Esary Russell, "William Carey Richards and the Orion" (thesis, University of Georgia, 1987), 132, World Cat (17464386). See also, Beth Abney, "The Orion as a Literary Publication," *The Georgia Historical Quarterly* 48:4 (December 1964): 411-24.
19 *Penfield Baptist Church Book of Minutes, 1839-1892*. Archival material, Mercer University Libraries, p. 25.
20 Ibid., p. 27.
21 Ibid., p. 30.
22 Ibid., p. 31.
23 Thomas Bog Slade, Letter to William Slade, undated, Slade Family Papers (1841).
24 Thaddeus Brocket Rice and Carolyn White Williams, *History of Greene County, Georgia, 1786-1886* (Wilkes Publishing Co., 1973), p. 259.
25 *Penfield Baptist Church Book of Minutes, 1839-1892*. Archival material, Mercer University Libraries, p. 40.
26 Nancy Telfair, *A History of Columbus, Georgia, 1828-1928* (Historical Publishing Company, 1929).
27 Tad Evans, *Greene Co., GA Newspaper Clippings, 1852-1873*, vol. I (Savannah: Tad Evans, 1995), pp. 1, 53, 108, 134-5.
28 Ibid., p. 165.

6

Columbus

Thou'rt gone to the grave, and its mansions forsaking,
Perhaps thy tried spirit in doubt lingered long;
But the sunshine of Heaven beamed bright on thy waking,
And the song that thou heard'st, was the Seraphim's song.
Thou'rt gone to the grave, but 'twere wrong to deplore thee,
Where God was thy ransom, thy guardian and guide;
He gave thee, and took thee, and soon will restore thee,
Where death has no sting, since the Savior has died.

Reginald Heber (1783–1826)

The town of Columbus, Georgia, was chartered by the state legislature December 27, 1827, when Slade was only in his second year teaching at the Clinton Male Academy. As he noted in his letters to North Carolina, the land designated had been recently ceded by the Creek Indians in the 1827 Land Lottery and 1830 *Indian Removal Act* as signed by President Andrew Jackson. Previously known as Coweta Falls, prior to the charter, Columbus was named to honor Christopher Columbus, the Portuguese navigator of 1492. The town, like Augusta and Macon, was situated at the northernmost navigable point on one of Georgia's major rivers, in this case, the Chattahoochee. Columbus was also on the federal road just before it passed into Alabama. Across the river, in Alabama, the Indians continued to live as before until 1836. The falls at Columbus were ideal for the generation of power for manufacturing and the river allowed for both import and export trade to Mobile, New Orleans, the Caribbean, the East Coast of America, and Liverpool, England. Columbus was ideal for textile production and thus the need for labor prompted a migration of Americans to this new town. By 1830, there were almost one thousand people living in Columbus. By 1860, Columbus was known as the "Lowell of the South."[1]

When Georgia Governor John Forsyth signed the act to create the town of Columbus on Christmas Day, 1827, there was only a trading post where one of Georgia's largest cities would appear. Once the sale of lots began on July 10, 1828, white settlers began migrating to the Georgia side of the lower Chattahoochee River in Muscogee County. Forsyth appointed five commissioners to lay out the town on December 27 in what was named the Coweta Reserve. These commissioners chose a plot of 1,200 acres on February 7, 1828. By the time they offered lots for sale, the first settlers were already there. In the original plan, called the Plelan Plan of Columbus, still on file at the Columbus Government Center, two blocks were set aside for academies. These map squares were 600 by 300 feet between north-south avenues, 132 feet wide, and east-west streets, 99 feet wide. One street, named Broad, was 164 feet wide. In the beginning, the avenues were named for Georgia politicians such as Thomas, Baldwin, Forsyth, and Troup but are today only known by their numbers, consecutive beginning at the river. Thus, Forsyth is now Fourth Avenue, Troup is Third, Baldwin is Eighth, Thomas is Ninth, Crawford is Tenth, and St. Clair is Eleventh. Although Slade's school was a leading academy in Columbus for many years, it was not located in the designated block because the Columbus Female Institute began in a private home purchased by Slade.[2]

According to the *Columbus Enquirer*, there were teachers in Columbus from the beginning, "drawn by the lure of a new frontier community with its opportunities and challenge."[3] Even Slade had given evidence to his brother in a personal letter of his interest in Columbus as early as 1825, more than two years before the charter.[4] The first known teacher was John Randolph Page (1804–64) of Fairfield, Virginia, who was there in 1828. Page was the son of William Byrd Page and Anne Elizabeth Lee, sister of Founding Father and American Revolutionary War hero Henry "Lighthorse Harry" Lee and thus the aunt of Robert E. Lee. Page was a single teacher until he married Maria L. Williamson of Putnam County, Georgia, on June 4, 1832, in Harris County, Georgia. They had eight children between 1833 and 1846, during which time they moved to Russell County, Alabama, where Page became a small farmer. Page, sixty, died on October 26, 1864, in Opelika, Alabama, and is buried there in the Old Lebanon Methodist Church Cemetery. Page's son, William Byrd Page (1833–95) was also a teacher, and his grandson, Rinaldo William Page (1862–1920) was the owner and publisher of the *Columbus Ledger* from 1892 until his death. The combined *Columbus Ledger-Enquirer* is today the fourth-oldest newspaper in Georgia in continuous publication, originally founded in 1828 by Mirabeau B. Lamar. From 1874 to 1920, the *Enquirer* was known as the *Columbus Enquirer-Sun*, having purchased the other large newspaper of nineteenth-century Columbus, and was absorbed by the *Ledger* in 1930. The owner was then known as the R. W. Page Corporation.

Other early educators living in Columbus included Jane L. Marks (1786–1851) of Augusta, Georgia, who was also a charter member of the First Presbyterian Church in 1829.[5] A certain teacher "Mrs. Kingsbury" was there in 1830 and was joined by Frances Eudora Gunby (1805–1858) and Garrett Hallenbeck (1797–1868) of Albany, New York, in 1831. Frances came to Columbus single but married "General" James Neil Bethune in 1832, a lawyer and publisher who was one of the first Southerners to call for secession. Bethune founded and edited several Columbus newspapers, including a term as owner of the *Enquirer* in 1833 and editor of the *Columbus Times* during the 1840s. He is most known for his management of "Blind" Tom Wiggins (1849–1908), an African American musical prodigy he acquired as one of several enslaved persons purchased in 1850 from the Wiley Edward Jones Plantation in Harris County. The Bethune daughters taught Wiggins how to play piano and soon he was writing his own songs. Bethune hired him out as an entertainer. Wiggins played for President James Buchanan at the White House. Bethune then took Wiggins on a European tour after the Civil War and reportedly earned over $750,000 from the talents of Wiggins.[6] Hallenbeck came to Columbus after the death of his first wife in 1826. He married Martha Trotter in 1838 and became a Columbus merchant.

By 1830 there were ten academies in Muscogee County and by 1832 there were "quite a number of new schools" in Columbus, but none for females.[7] Columbus also had a theater by 1832 and there was a horse-racing track built there in 1834. Most of the schools had one teacher and most were taught in private homes. Unsuccessful attempts were made by Frances Bethune and John Baker, a Presbyterian minister and principal of the male academy in 1833, to start female academies in Columbus. Teachers were in demand, however, to teach males in Columbus. One *Enquirer* advertisement sought "A man who is well qualified to teach the languages and can give satisfactory evidence of his moral and sober habits, can get a good school, in a good neighborhood, at fair prices. Apply to Robert S. Hardaway, in Harris County, near the road leading from Columbus to Hamilton on the Sowhatchie Creek."[8] Teachers such as William Stogner were looking for jobs in 1834 even as Moses Butt, Josiah Grimes, and E. E. Spivey wanted to hire a teacher. Several Columbus teachers offered specific education such as Mrs. E. J. Smith of Sparta, Georgia, who gave Columbus classes in only music and drawing at the Columbus Hotel in 1833. Edward Lee announced another music school in the same year.[9] A Mrs. H. Blome advertised classes in French, English, drawing, painting, and needlework before Slade's arrival. In 1834, Mrs. Ticknor opened "one of the first schools for young ladies." No identification has been found to determine whether this was the Clinton, Georgia teacher, Harriot Coolidge, who was known by the same name.

Some Columbus students from the upper class attended schools outside Muscogee County. Thomas Fielding Scott founded the LaGrange Female Academy in January 1833 and another school for males and females opened in Meriwether County under the direction of Fleming Penfield who proudly advertised his possession of a "celestial and terrestrial globe, Philadelphia chemical apparatus, and oyrometer tide dial." Tuition in that year was $14 per term. There were other schools including an Infant Academy and an Indian School.[10]

The national economic depression, however, of 1837 hurt Columbus as much as any other newly struggling city, especially one on the "frontier" of early nineteenth-century settlement. Two railroad proposals, for example, which would have connected Columbus to the rest of the state, were postponed because of the economy. The first train did not arrive in Columbus until 1853. Before that year, however, forty-three different steamboats regularly arrived and departed in Columbus, importing every supply imaginable and mostly exporting cotton.[11] In the early days, land was inexpensive, housing was affordable to working-class residents, and unemployment was low. Life in Columbus was rough; however, some recorded "gunplay, barroom stabbings" through the 1850s.[12]

As Columbus began to emerge from the Panic of 1837, a certain Mrs. Leigh and Jeanne McNair reopened the Muscogee Female Academy in 1838. They accepted students to study French, drawing, painting, and music on the corner of Forsyth and St. Clair (Fourth Avenue and Eleventh Street). Later in the same year, McNair married Joseph Daniel Bethune (1812-40), the brother of James Neil Bethune, and gave up teaching as many single women did. A certain Mrs. Seaman, however, opened a female seminary on January 9, 1838, teaching French with "a true Parisian pronunciation" in a French class held between two and four o'clock daily.[13] Other female academies are mentioned in 1838 including the Wynnton Female Academy which featured Lovic Pierce among its board of trustees. Most of these schools changed leadership frequently and closed after only a few years. Most female teachers were single and socially expected to quit their careers once they were married. Other schools appeared to replace those that closed but then those too ended for a variety of reasons. There was no public funding for these private schools which depended entirely on the tuition collected from students. Some parents paid by bartering with so much firewood, for example, in exchange for an education. Some schools burned, closed because of disease, or were suspended after the death of the teacher. Most of these were never rebuilt or reopened for lack of funds, students, or teachers.[14]

Having migrated 186 miles southwest to Columbus in December 1841, Slade's school along the Chattahoochee was open by January 1842 as the first tertiary or college-level female academy in the city and known as Slade Female Institute and sometimes called The Female Institute or even Columbus Female Institute even though there was an earlier secondary school known by that name.[15] It was the second female school he founded and the fourth of which he was the administrator. It proved to be his final and longest tenure as an educator. Advertisements, placed even before leaving Penfield, began to appear, soliciting enrollment in the new Columbus school, announcing the qualifications of the faculty and the institute, and listing prices that amounted to only $50 without the optional courses in music, drawing, etc. The first faculty included Slade, his wife Anne, and three daughters, Janet, Mary, and Ann.[16] Slade may have been duplicating the cost, structure, organization, and curriculum of the Georgia Female College or it may have been that the cost, structure, organization, and curriculum of the Georgia Female College was originally designed with Slade's influence.

Slade's tenth child, his third son, John Henry Slade, was born January 11, 1843, just one year after Slade's arrival in Columbus. The last addition to the Slade children was Fanny Blount Slade, born May 31, 1845, one month before Slade's first Columbus graduation ceremony at the Female Institute. Like all the Slade children, these two were also born at home. By 1845, however, Anne had the assistance of Janet, then twenty, Mary, nineteen, Anne, sixteen, and Emma, twelve, besides any others who may have been called to assist. Preparing the birth room in the early nineteenth century was important to doctors and midwives who insisted the room be kept dimly lit and no visitors be allowed. It was common for physicians to advise mothers not to read anything until at least three days after the birth.[17] Sadly, Fanny, two years and eleven months, only lived until April 29, 1848. She was the first of three Slade children who died before her parents.

The first commencement of the Slade Female Institute was held in 1845 at the First Baptist Church, where the Slades were members and where Slade served at various times as interim pastor and in supply for the pastor. Various speeches were given at graduation by students Lucy Ann Pitts, Sophia H. Shorter, Amanda Jernigan, Mary L. Rose, and Lucy A. Barnett on various topics including "Benevolence," "Wisdom and Knowledge," "Difficulty of Originating a Thing," "He Labors in Vain Who Strives to Please All," and "When I Leave School." The commencement address was given by Lemuel Tyler Downing (1814–82), a local Columbus attorney practicing with Grigsby E. Thomas, Slade's son-in-law, as Thomas & Downing after Downing was admitted to the Georgia Bar on June 3, 1841. Slade knew Downing through the temperance association and his partnership with Martha Bog Slade's husband. Although he was born in Connecticut, Downing graduated from Yale in 1838 as a student from Columbus, Georgia.[18]

Lucy Ann Pitts (1828–75) was only seventeen years old in 1841. The daughter of Henry Pitts and Hannah Singleton Lassiter, Pitts was from Houston

County, Georgia. One of six children, she had four sisters who may have also attended Slade's institute. Pitts attended the Georgia Female College in Macon before transferring to study with Slade again in Columbus. She married John Nathaniel Barnett (1818–1889) just three months after graduation in Columbus where they settled and where Barnett became a successful grocery wholesaler. According to the *Macon Telegraph*, he was also "one of the most prominent and popular citizens of Columbus and has held the office of city treasurer since 1872."[19] Pitts' death also appeared in the *Telegraph* but only as the wife of Barnett, further reinforcing the theory that female education in early nineteenth-century Georgia was primarily meant to prepare the daughters of wealthy white families to be complementary wives for successful men.

Oddly enough, Pitts graduated with a colleague named Lucy A. Barnett (1829–61) who was the sister of John, both children of William Barnett Jr. (1793–1886) and Lucy Barnett (1794–1886). They were residents of Russell County, Alabama, before moving west to Mississippi. Lucy, the student, married Algernon Sidney Glen, a farmer, on October 20, 1853, in Russell County.

Sophia Herndon Shorter (1830–50) was the daughter of planter and physician Reuben Clark Shorter Sr. and Mary Butler Gill of Eufaula, Barbour County, Alabama. They owned sixteen enslaved persons in 1850. Reuben founded the First Baptist Church in Eufaula. They were previously living in Monticello, Jasper County, Georgia. Sophia had ten siblings, including her brother Eli Sims Shorter (1823–79), not to be confused with the Columbus judge of the same name who died in 1836 and was married to another Sophia H. Shorter. Eli, son of Reuben, was a US Congressman during 1855–9 representing Alabama's Second Congressional District. John Gill Shorter, another brother, served as governor of Alabama during 1861–3 during the Civil War.[20] Sophia, daughter of Reuben, married Tennent Lomax, a lawyer, in 1849. She died just five years after graduation and only one year after her wedding. Lomax went on to marry a second time and become a colonel in the Confederate States Army. He was killed in battle on June 1, 1862, at Seven Pines in Virginia. General John B. Gordon told the story that Lomax prophesied his own death.

> As he rode into the storm of lead, he turned to me and said: "Give me your hand, Gordon, and let me bid you goodbye. I am going to be killed

in this battle. I shall be dead in half an hour." I endeavored to remove this impression from his mind, but nothing I could say changed or appeared to modify it in any degree. I was grieved to have him go into the fight with such a burden upon him, but there was no tremor in his voice, no hesitation in his words, no doubt on his mind. The genial smile that made his face so attractive was still upon it, but he insisted he would be dead in half an hour, and that it was "all right." The half-hour had scarcely passed when the fatal bullet had numbered him with the dead.[21]

Sophia is buried in Barbour County, Alabama, and Tennet Lomax is buried in Montgomery in the Oakwood Cemetery with his second wife, Caroline Ascenath Virginia Billingslea, who was first married to another brother of Sophia, Reuben Clark Shorter Jr., further illustrating the small social and familial circles of the time and place. Caroline was also a first cousin once removed of Slade's friend Abner Holloway Flewellen (1800–49).

Amanda C. Jernigan first married Madison Troup Key (1826–52), of Lee County, Alabama, his second, in Columbus on March 4, 1852, seven years after graduation. Possibly orphans, Amanda and three siblings were previously living with the family of her sister Ann Eliza Jernigan, who was married to Nat M. Robison, a brick mason, from Columbus.[22] Sadly, Key died three months after the wedding, so Amanda remarried George W. Turner (1820–99) on December 19, 1854, also in Columbus. Turner was known to have been a strong proponent of slavery and a supporter of states' rights. He served in three wars, including the Second Seminole War in Florida (1835–42), the Mexican War (1846–8), and the Civil War (1861–5). He was said to be the "first to enlist and served with credit."[23]

Mary Lavinia Rose (1829–99) was the oldest child of Simri Rose and Lavinia Helen Elizabeth Blount, of Macon and born in Clinton, Georgia. She married George Beavers Carhart (1812–1905) of New York on March 1, 1851, and moved to Brooklyn. They had one son, Amory Sibley Carhart (1851–1912) who was educated in Hanover, Germany and worked as director of the Union Trust Company of New York and the People's Trust Company of Brooklyn.[24] Mary and George are buried in the Greenwood Cemetery of Brooklyn, New York. Thomas Bog Slade Jr. noted her sister's death in 1865, Leila Foote Rose, seventeen, of typhoid, in Macon. "Very beautiful," he added, "and amiable. She was engaged to a Lieutenant Evans of the Army of Tennessee. It was a heavy affliction to Aunt Lavinia and to us all, for she was to us like a sister."[25]

Teaching classes in his home, Slade purchased a larger, sixteen-room house in Columbus in 1847 as he was also preparing to build a separate construction specifically for the school. This was a 4,416 square foot building 48 feet by 46 feet, two stories high located at 1417 Fourth Avenue in Columbus.[26] Slade purchased a second building there because, "the prospects of the school for the next term are very good."[27] At the age of forty-seven he acknowledged, "It would seem that after so long employment in teaching my energies might fail ... I am enobled to hold out." He could not have known that he was, in 1847, only five years past the midpoint of his life and not yet to the midpoint of his career. He was still building in that year, not satisfied to simply maintain where he was and long from seriously slowing down or reducing his responsibilities. Not only was he advertising for students in all the local newspapers but also in statewide publications such as *The Christian Index*, for example, where he presented a curriculum similar to that being offered in Macon at the Wesleyan Female College. Tuition was $50 for a scholastic year and board was $10 per month with electives available in art and piano.[28]

As Slade's brother, James Bog Slade (1803–47) was on his way to service in the Mexican War, Slade wrote to him on June 12, 1847, acknowledging James' letter from New Orleans where he had been for at least five years prior.[29] Oddly enough, a runaway slave, Isham, was captured in Warren County, Mississippi on August 4, 1842. He escaped from Charles D. DeWees of Madison County, Mississippi, a physician, who identified Isham to be a 5-foot 9-inch tall, slender man of about twenty-six years of age. When captured by Warren County Sheriff E. B. Scarbrough, Isham identified James Bog Slade of New Orleans as his owner. It is unclear how James was to have seen the notice in the Vicksburg newspaper or whether he responded to "prove property, pay charges and take [Isham] out of jail." James was a surgeon in New Orleans and in 1847 attached to the 15th Regiment, US Army, from his enlistment that year on March 3, just twenty days after the regiment was formed. Slade sent James $130 which was owed. "I cannot say that I have no objection to the position," Slade wrote, "However, much I might desire your personal comfort, I am glad that your skill and ability as a surgeon are devoted to your country and the relief of suffering humanity. I trust that a kind providence may watch over you, preserve your life and health and that you may be abundantly found in the responsible position you occupy."[30] James was then killed in action on November 30, 1847, in Mexico City. He was reburied January 19, 1849, in the Vicksburg National Cemetery of Vicksburg, Mississippi.

In a letter to William on June 21, 1847, after responding to the latter's report about his wife's health, Slade informed his brother that he intended for his oldest son, James Jeremiah, sixteen, to be educated at the University of North Carolina "next June" (1848) because it cost less than having him study in Georgia.

In 1849, Slade sold a negro man, "the husband of Bertha" for $1,000, and used the money to buy the lot where he was living. He spent another $5,000 to enlarge his house and rebuild "an academy" of fifteen rooms "neatly furnished."[31] Apparently the investment was successful as enrollment reached 109 within a year, approximately one-third of students boarding "on campus."[32] In May, Slade informed a cousin in North Carolina, "We have plenty of girls here."[33] According to the US Census of 1850, thirty female students were living at Slade's "Boarding School" and identified by name, age, and home state.[34] Georgia, Alabama, Florida, and North Carolina were represented as were ages fourteen to eighteen and the average age was fifteen years and six months. There were three sets of sisters which included Emma, sixteen, Sarah, fifteen, and Elizabeth, fourteen, Russ, daughters of John Green Russ Sr. and Rebecca Charlotte Russ of Cottondale, Jackson County, Florida; Betty, seventeen, and Mary, sixteen, Hendison from North Carolina; and Sarah, sixteen, and Martha, fourteen, Lurvis of Alabama. These ages were those of college-level students in the early nineteenth century because women typically married young. By necessity, they were forced to complete their education early so it was made available to them. The same was true at Wesleyan.

In 1860, there were only fourteen young women boarding "on campus" but others were living at "the orphanage" just three doors away from the school and as they were not all orphans were likely affiliated with the Institute; the orphanage being used as an overflow dormitory. These students were almost all from Georgia and the average age was fifteen. The oldest student was twenty-four but by 1860, Slade was admitting girls as young as twelve just as the Georgia Female College was allowing in Macon. Fanny Randolph Eley (1844–80) of Florida was the only non-Georgian living in the main building that year. The daughter of Francis Roulhac Ely and Frances Adalaide Randolph, Fanny was a first cousin once removed to Anne Jacqueline Blount which is an example of Slade relatives coming to receive their education in Columbus from North Carolina. Francis Luminack, a seventeen-year-old living in the orphanage, was from South Carolina.

Although Slade knew the success of public schools in Georgia would have undermined the purpose of his own institute, with the long view in mind he continued to work tirelessly for the common good of all Georgia children on the state level. He was confident that he could hold his own as a proper college, if necessary, for those young women prepared for tertiary studies once public schools were established. Slade was always helpful to other schools, not focused on the competition but on the common good, throughout his career. He trained other teachers, sent his graduates to be teachers, and assisted in founding and building academies, institutes, and seminaries at his own expense and with no personal financial incentive. For example, he regularly attended the examinations of other schools to give his endorsement of their curriculum and product. He was known for this in Macon and Columbus. Schools coveted his endorsement as an authoritative confirmation of their own product. On July 21, 1849, for example, he was "permitted" to attend the examination of Shoal Academy near Ellerslie, Georgia, just eighteen miles northeast of Columbus, probably an overnight trip. "It gives me pleasure to express my unqualified approbation of the exercises," Slade stated to the *Columbus Enquirer*, "While they exhibited the proficiency and mental training of the pupils, they reflected the highest honor on the knowledge, efficiency, and energy of the instructor," who was James B. Huff.[35]

The graduation ceremonies of Slade's school were always covered by the local newspapers. In 1850, for example, the *Weekly Columbus Enquirer* published a detailed account of the ceremonies held that year. The graduation drew "a large and intelligent audience" from the community to the "flourishing school" on a Thursday night, July 11.[36] "Former experience had taught us to expect on this occasion something of more than ordinary interest," the editor wrote, "and we were not disappointed." Well-written compositions were "read with a propriety of voice and manner which indicated to every hearer that there was nothing superficial in their instruction." These unsolicited comments were high praise for the students but also for the quality teaching and leadership provided by Slade nine years after moving his career to the city. Four students, Martin, Pride, Mahon, and Mangham, were singled out by the *Enquirer* for special recognition. Slade had asked that there be no applause after the piano and voice recitals, but the newspaper noted how his request was ignored due to the overwhelming appreciation felt for the performances. Slade himself gave the commencement address and was "worthy of himself and the occasion." The editor could not remember having heard "more good practical advice, more that was worthy to be remembered, embodied in an address of the same length." Sadly, the *Enquirer* did not choose to print the text of Slade's speech.

The Slades were very busy maintaining the school, but both Thomas and Anne found time to be active in the community. Slade continued to preach throughout the region of southeast Alabama and southwest Georgia, while Anne was active in the Temperance Movement, along with others who took the Temperance Pledge, and met with temperance supporters at the Catholic Church under the direction of "Fr. Matthews."[37] The identity of this priest is unclear, whereas the Catholic priest in Columbus from February 1841 until July 17, 1844, the period covering Slade's arrival, was Fr. Thomas Molony of Limerick City, Ireland.[38] Other priests in Columbus during Slade's time included Timothy Bermingham, Edward Barron, John Gillespie, and Michael Cullinan. Matthews was either a temporary mission pastor, such as were common in Columbus after 1857, or Slade's reference may be a distant, general, impersonal one to Theobald Mathew (1790–1856), an Irish Catholic priest known for his advocacy of the temperance movement and known as Father Mathew.[39] *The Knights of Father Mathew*, an abstinence society, were founded in 1838 and within a year had recruited over 150,000 members representing various religious sects. Not simply a fight against the consumption of alcohol, the Knights were motivated by a vision of improving the lives of the working class in Ireland and America, who were often impoverished by their purchase and consumption of beer and whiskey. Slade was known to be a teetotaler, so his willingness to work with Catholics and his support of the Knights chapter in Columbus is easy to understand. Mathew visited the United States from

1849 until 1851, but there is no record of him traveling to Columbus. His reputation, however, was tainted among Southerners by his having taken a pledge against slave ownership.[40] On the other hand, he refused to publicly condemn slavery and was thus snubbed by abolitionists, including Frederick Douglass.

The history of Catholicism in the South has been too little researched whereas there were so few Catholics there as compared to the mainline Protestant denominations. Slade's relationship with Catholics, especially in Columbus, is complicated. He left the Georgia Female College because of a sectarian debate with Methodists, fled to Penfield because it was the center of Baptist life in Georgia, and then was united with Catholics in Columbus by the issue of temperance. The current Church of the Holy Family on Fourth Avenue in Columbus dates only to 1880, but it was a replacement for an earlier building constructed in 1829. Catholics organized a parish in Columbus in the early nineteenth century named for Saints Philip and James.[41] This was only the fourth Catholic parish established in Georgia after Locust Grove (1793–5), Savannah, which had originally banned Catholics along with slavery and lawyers (1733–53) (1796), and Augusta (1811).[42] The parishes were geographically large in those days due to the number of Catholics living in the South. The Columbus parish ran from Montgomery, Alabama, to Milledgeville, Georgia, and included only about two hundred adherents. The state granted a half block to Catholics in Columbus as they did the three Protestant denominations. The first Catholic priest, John Healy, arrived in 1835. Most Columbus Catholics were Irish and many of them were foreign born.[43] As long as the economy was growing and residents were prospering economically, relations based on class, race, and religion were good. When the economy regressed, however, tension between classes, races, nationalities, and religious sects increased. There is, of course, a well-documented history of anti-immigrant and anti-Catholic sentiment in American history.

Catholics opened their first parish school in Columbus in January 1851. John Coffey was the founder and principal instructor until 1862. This late date may be the result of Slade's reputation among the Catholics of Columbus and the fact that some Catholic women were attending Slade's female institute.

The Temperance Society did not only meet at the Catholic Church. On August 11, 1841, the Society, then known as the Reform Association of Columbus, met at the Methodist Church. It was a gathering of "all friends of temperance" and included the Slades along with Abner Flewellen, Lemuel Downing, Grigsby Thomas, their son-in-law, and others. The stated purpose of this group was to devise "some effective means of discouraging the evil of the habitual and ruinous indulgence in intoxicating drinks."[44] Lovick Pierce, pastor of Columbus' Second Methodist Church on Troup and Bryan Streets, prayed the invocation. In the subsequent meeting on August 21, a committee consisting of Pierce, Thomas, Flewellen, and two others, the Society agreed that

> intemperance is an evil, the wide sweep of which has been seen and felt in almost every family of our great and happy country; and, in many, has left in the track of its desolating progress, mortified friends and relatives, impoverished widows and beggared children; necessarily involving in those ruinous and disastrous results innocent and deserving individuals.[45]

At this meeting, members officially adopted the Reform Association of Columbus as their name, leaving open the possibility of adopting other reform issues. Focused on temperance only, however, in 1841, the association committed to hold regular meetings on the last Friday night of each month at "such place as may be determined upon at each preceding meeting." Every meeting was opened with prayer and each meeting included the reading of essays on the topic of temperance. Members decided against requiring a pledge of members but chose to rely on self-enforcement of those "favorable to sobriety and the happiness of their fellow men," those who were "unfriendly to intemperance, and alarmed at its dangerous influences upon the community." Their mission was to convince the intemperate to abandon the consumption of alcohol and join the Reform Association. Flewellen and Downing, secretary of the association, were appointed to a recruiting committee along with several others, and the next meeting was committed to the Presbyterian Church.

As early as July 31, 1850, Thomas Bog Slade Jr., in Columbus, wrote to his brother Jeremiah Slade in North Carolina regarding the possibility of war. "There is a great deal of excitement here," he explained:

concerning politicks the democrats down here in Georgia seem determined to dissolve the union they think of nothing less than this and I have no doubt if they had to decide the question that we would be immediately involved in a civil war with the north. But happy for our country that there are yet left a few more patriots to check such dangerous measure.[46]

The census was taken on Fourth Avenue in Columbus on November 22, 1850 by Assistant Marshall John Henry Rutherford. This snapshot finds Slade with his family and twenty-nine boarding students of the Slade Female Institute. All his living children were still at home with him including Janet, twenty-five, Mary, twenty-three, Anne, twenty-one, Jeremiah, nineteen, Emma, seventeen, Thomas Jr., sixteen, Martha, thirteen, Stella, eleven, Helen, nine, and John Henry, seven. All of them were either students at the Institute or were working as faculty or staff in some capacity.

Promoting educational improvement in Georgia was difficult as state legislators were happy to speak in favor of education throughout the nineteenth century; they only began to vote for improvements with public funding after the war.[47] Coulter wrote in 1925 that most Georgians of the nineteenth century regarded public funded education as "some other kind of Yankee notion—to be peddled around and hawked about by wandering nondescripts, often referred to as pedagogues." Thus, schools such as Slade's academy were functioning as independent commercial businesses competing with other academies, institutes, and seminaries for students and achieving success by giving value for money and pointing to the enrollment as proof of success. "It was no more the right nor duty of the state to set up schoolhouses and license teachers than it was to build factories and determine the qualifications of workmen."[48] Slade obviously did not agree with the majority, and neither did the teachers association. They argued that state-supported schools should be erected in each county of the state. This was debated as early as 1777 in Georgia but was consistently rejected until 1868.[49] A Poor School Fund, to pay for poor students to attend private schools, was established in 1817, but it was always inadequate.[50] In 1852, for example, $23,096 was appropriated for 38,536 students. A local grand jury determined who was poor enough to receive these funds but annually kept the number low, as some have estimated the actual qualified number in 1852 to have been over 50,000 or about fifty cents per poor student per year. In that year, there was not one state-owned schoolhouse in Georgia, and none of 1,313 teachers in Georgia were paid by the state.

Thus, the teachers' association decided to bypass the state temporarily and appealed to individual counties. As a result of Slade's work, Muscogee County was the first county in the state to levy a 20 percent school tax on the state tax to be used for education. Jackson County followed with a 10 percent school tax and Clarke County limited funds to no more than eight cents per student per day.[51] "Elementary education in the state was a farce," Coulter wrote, "It was worse than a farce; it was a mean trick played upon the ignorant masses, for as a uniform system it was non-existent." Because 98 percent of Georgia counties had no school tax, and up to 1,000 "communities" had no school, two-thirds of the state's children received no education. Georgia was "too busy to do anything for general education."[52] Undeterred, Slade and the other members of the teachers' association resolved to organize the "teachers and friends of education of every county into 'County Associations.'" Muscogee, Talbot, located adjacent to Muscogee, and Bibb were the only counties where this effort was successful before it ultimately collapsed for lack of support.

Already established as a leading educator in Georgia, and in 1850 at the age of fifty, a leading resident of Columbus, a well-known and respected itinerant Baptist minister, and an expert botanist, Slade decided to learn French.[53] It was his first attempt to learn a foreign language other than the Latin he studied at the University of North Carolina thirty years earlier. As his motivation seems simply to have been purely for reading and correspondence, it demonstrates his ongoing drive for self-improvement even at the midpoint of his career.

The last of Slade's brothers, William, died in 1852, of typhoid fever at his home in North Carolina. Subsequently, the correspondence preserved in the Slade Family Papers fell dramatically thereafter with only Slade's daughters occasionally writing to their Tar Heel cousins. William's death was especially difficult for Slade to manage. "The death of my Brother has been and still is a profound reflection to me," he wrote to a nephew in North Carolina.[54]

In 1853, Slade was again president of the then Georgia State Teachers' Association meeting that year at the Griffin Baptist Church of Spalding County.[55] Invitations to meet in Griffin from twenty-five leading Georgia educators appealed to teachers throughout Georgia in all the major newspapers. The association sought to awaken a "deeper interest in the cause of Education" and they planned to accomplish this goal by "promoting a greater degree of system and efficiency among Teachers, and a better appreciation of their professional labors among the people generally, and by affording to those engaged in this important work the means of counsel, instruction and encouragement."[56] That was the first year the association drafted and ratified a constitution to define and regulate their state educational improvement project. Member Thomas F. Scott declared, in the journal of the association, that Georgia needed "a common school system 'more than railroads, canals and manufactories.'"[57] The association urged support for education, organization of county associations, and called for greater minimum qualifications for teachers.[58] They called for all interested persons to meet in Macon, the center of the state, for the next convention. The appeal was signed by notable men from around the state, including Slade of Columbus. The Macon meeting was later canceled, however, for lack of support. Sadly, for the cause of education, the teachers' association died a natural death just three years after it had built its greatest level of support. Slade refused to give up, however, and, along with others, organized a meeting to be held in Milledgeville on November 30, 1853. This was an attempt to build a state-based organization to lobby the legislature for public schools in Georgia. At the meeting, Slade, James P. Waddell, and Thomas F. Scott presented a plan which included the formation of a state board of education which would create and supervise a statewide system of elementary schools.[59] The bold and forward-thinking proposal was presented to the Georgia Senate but was never read. It was read in the House but was then lost in committee. No further action was taken by either house to the frustration of Slade and the others.

Still undeterred, advocates for public education in Georgia met again on July 9, 1854, in Madison, Georgia, where Slade and others promoted a system of normal schools in which future Georgia teachers would be trained. Slade was back in Macon on August 8, 1855, for the fourth meeting of this latest advocacy group, which drew only seven members. Whereas the group's own constitution required a minimum of ten members to conduct business, the meeting failed for lack of a quorum in a city, at that time, of over three thousand white citizens.⁶⁰ Slade and the others gave up in frustration but not fully understanding how much they had laid a foundation for improvements to be realized after the war. "Public agitation had been aroused."⁶¹ Three years later, in 1858, there was enough public pressure on the legislature that a bill was passed to appropriate $100,000 annually for a public school system to be funded by rents collected from the Western and Atlantic Railroad. Implementation was delegated to the counties, some of which began programs during the three years before the Civil War, but most counties took no action until after the end of the war.

On December 18, 1856, Slade performed the wedding of his nephew, William's son, James Bog Slade, and Mary Elizabeth Denson, the daughter of Joseph W. Denson and Mary Moon, just four years after William's death. The couple were married in the Denson's Harris County home.⁶² James moved to Columbus after his father's death and after having graduated from the University of North Carolina in 1852. He and Mary became prominent citizens of Columbus and the parents of five children. James was a plantation overseer in Harris County before running a cotton warehouse in Columbus. In 1880, Mary's father lived with them along with the boarder Julia Crawford, a student at the Slade Female Institute. James died November 1, 1886. Mary lived until June 17, 1920. She died at the home of her daughter, Helen Janet Slade Farish, on Fourth Avenue in Columbus. *The Atlanta Journal* recognized her as the widow of James Bog Slade and one of "pioneer residents" of Columbus. She was "prominently identified with the early history of Columbus," the newspaper reported.⁶³ James and Mary are buried in the Linwood Cemetery of Columbus.

Anne Louisa Slade died on February 16, 1858, the second of Slade's three children to die before the parents. "Annie" was the third child and only twenty-eight years old at the time of her passing. She was married only seven months earlier to Captain Roswell Ellis, the junior editor of the *Times* and *Sentinel* newspaper of Columbus. No explanation is found as to her cause of death, but her passing was devastating for her family and newlywed husband. Her Linwood Cemetery gravestone simply reads:

Here in the tomb the mortal members rest.
The glorious resurrection morn they wait

To rise again to an immortal state.
Her soul unharmed by death divinely blest
Awaits our advent to that land of Love,
God's Paradise, the home of saints above.

Roswell remarried in 1868 to Elizabeth Rutherford, the creator of Confederate Memorial Day through the Ladies' Memorial Association of Columbus. He died in Greenville, Georgia, and is buried in LaGrange, Georgia.

In 1859, Slade's Female Institute in Columbus, the oldest school in the city, was the only one mentioned in the city directory. The building Slade built was, for many years, alternately used by boys and girls, one time for both in the same year, and was known as Sladeville Hall, which was partially demolished in 1890 but remodeled by Slade's daughter Stella in 1891 and her husband Hockley C. McKee, who inherited the home after Slade's death in 1882. Slade was not, however, without competition as there were twenty-seven Columbus male and female teachers advertising education in their homes in 1859.[64] Granted, five of these were named Slade and attached to the Slade Female Institute, located on Forsyth Street (Fourth Avenue) between Bridge Street and Franklin Street, including Slade himself, whose occupation was "teacher."[65] Anne Jacqueline Slade and daughters Helen, eighteen, and Martha, twenty-two, were assistant teachers in the same school, and daughter Janet, thirty-four, still unmarried until 1863, was teaching music. James Jeremiah Slade, twenty-eight, was working as a lawyer, a partner with Martin, Martin, and Slade at 116 Broad Street. Widowed after the death of his first wife, Annie Gertrude Graham, in 1856, he was living with his parents. Thomas Bog Slade Jr., twenty-five, was employed with *The Columbus Daily Times* and, unmarried until 1871, was also living at the institute. Slade's "female college" had a reputation in Columbus "of long and fine character."[66] Above reproach within the social context of the time, "in most cases, men taught boys and women taught girls," according to the newspaper.[67]

By 1860, Columbus was the major city in the lower Chattahoochee Valley region. There were nineteen factories, mostly engaged in textile production. The largest, Eagle Mill, founded in 1851, had 500 employees and 282 looms. Male workers there earned one dollar per day while female workers were paid

Figure 6.1 The Slade Female Institute, Columbus, Georgia (public domain, John S. Lupold Collection (MC 197) Columbus State University Archives, Columbus, GA).

fifty cents. The population of the city by then was almost 10,000 including 5,674 whites, 3,265 enslaved persons, and 100 free blacks.[68] There were, however, almost 17,000 living in Muscogee County. This number decreased slightly due to the war in 1870 but was over 19,000 by 1880. Columbus was still larger than Atlanta in 1860 and followed only Savannah and Augusta as Georgia's third-largest city. The number of steamboats on the lower Chattahoochee decreased in the 1850s, but the coming of the railroad more than made up the difference. Besides the textile mills, Columbus had two iron foundries, a paper factory, two flour and corn mills, two sash and blind makers, a carriage manufacturer, multiple artisans, blacksmiths, carpenters, and wheelwrights, both black and white.[69]

Slade continued to own ten enslaved persons in 1860 although most of these were not with him in Columbus. Fifty-one percent of all slave owners in Columbus before the Civil War owned less than five persons. Twenty-five percent owned between five and ten. It was common for one's slaves to be involuntarily working elsewhere. The enslaved of Henry H. Epping, a Columbus banker, cotton broker, part owner of a steamboat, and owner of multiple properties in the city, for example, were working in the cotton fields of Russell County, Alabama.[70] John L. Mustain, who combined farming and railroad and was a part owner of the Palace Flour and Meal Mill, employed an overseer to supervise sixty enslaved persons. Once the war began, industries in the South quickly converted to supply the Confederate war effort. During the war, crime increased exponentially as theft, arson, street fighting, and the number of murders increased.[71]

Once the war began, Columbus residents became increasingly suspicious of transient workers, refugee whites, and free blacks. *The Daily Sun* attacked this "dangerous element" in 1860 whereas one-third of the city's population was enslaved. Five slaves were hung and their bodies burned in 1862, accused of murdering their master. "Idle negroes are public curses," the *Sun* reported. This continued, of course, after the war ended. As late as September 28, 1865, orders were issued for all "unemployed negroes" to leave the city. This order was ignored and the *Sun* complained about the number of "idle negroes doing nothing on the pavements" of Columbus. The newspaper struggled to reconcile how the military authorities in Macon and Montgomery were able to hire their formerly enslaved persons to planters while similar authorities in Columbus were unable to do so.[72] By November, military authorities were forcing "idle negroes" into "chain gangs" which were used to level fortifications around Columbus which remained from the war.[73] Some freedmen chose to migrate north after the war and many arrived in New York. This was equally alarming to northerners who were afraid of the impact of this growing labor supply on local wages. "Negroes can live cheaper than white men," *The New York News* editorialized, "Their wants are fewer and they have no idea of refinement. Hence there are many branches of trade in which the white man cannot compete with the negro, and the manufacturers will employ that labor which is cheapest."[74]

Blacks were excluded from white schools, including the female institute, but there were two Sabbath schools available to the children of free blacks in Columbus, housed in two of the city's black churches.[75] According to laws passed in 1829 and 1833, whites like Slade were forbidden, under the threat of punishment, to teach enslaved persons to read or write.[76] In a state where Georgians gave so little support to the education of whites, it is unreasonable for a modern reader to expect educators to have done more for blacks. On October 17, 1865, the *Sun* wrote of "two negroes" who attempted to "set the court house on fire."[77] Originally arrested for gambling at the Cook Hotel where they were employed, Albert and Fred were attempting to escape imprisonment by setting the building on fire. They were handed over to the Freedmen's Bureau. In the same issue of the Sun, local police reported that as many as "forty idle negroes" had been arrested and held in an idle railroad caboose.[78] Because the city refused to feed them, "the darkies were dismissed with a caution of what would be done to them if they were caught a second time." Without fail, however, some of them were arrested the next day as the police were attempting to "clean out a den on the East Commons who have been pilfering for some time." Freedmen were also concentrated on the North Commons near the old Confederate Arsenal. A reporter from the *Sun* counted twenty-five freedmen there on December 1, 1865, "who were either basking in the sunlight, gabbing or wandering idly about. They were living in mean hovels, appeared to have nothing, were doing nothing and seemed vastly pleased with the occupation."[79] The *Sun* questioned how they survived without stealing and called upon local authorities to act. In December, the Sun was terrified that "idle negroes" would flock to Columbus during Christmas.[80]

Slade was invited on January 27, 1861, to join the ordination presbytery of Jesse Montreville Lafayette Burnett (1829–83) of North Carolina, who was being ordained a Baptist minister by the Fort Gaines Baptist Church in Georgia after his graduation from Union University in Jackson, Tennessee. Burnett grew up in Tennessee, was converted to Christianity, and called to preach during the Second Great Awakening at the age of thirteen in Cocke County during a "meeting" held by Joseph Manning and Ephraim Moore at the Clay Creek Church. He preached his first sermon in Tennessee, but he was ordained in Georgia as the pastor of the Fort Gaines Church. Adiel Sherwood, who knew Slade from Penfield, was on the presbytery along with Richard Thornton and Edmund Cody, Baptist ministers. Fort Gaines is approximately 72 miles south of Columbus in Clay County, Georgia, also on the Chattahoochee River. Burnett married Henrietta Sarah Cody (1843–1927), his second wife, the daughter of Edmund. The Codys were living in Henry County, Alabama, at the time, which is across the Chattahoochee River from Fort Gaines. Henrietta, who was described as "a woman of refined tastes and consecrated life," seems to have been one of Slade's students at the Columbus Female Institute during the late 1850s.[81]

Before his marriage to Henrietta, Burnett wrote to Edmund, her father and his mentor in the ministry, regarding the coming of the war in Jonesville, Tennessee. Due to family ties, he was visiting there on July 18, six months after his ordination. "Detained a full week in getting home," he was unhappy with the enthusiasm for war he was witnessing in the Volunteer State. "I have not enjoyed one moment of real pleasure," he wrote, "Distrust and hate among the more violent; and an awful sense of impending peril among the reflecting portion of the people—these are the all prevalent feelings here."[82] Burnett was distressed that families were divided in every community. "Father crying long live the Union, and death to traitors," he wrote, "the son cheering, 'Liberty and the South.'" He was attempting to "soothe this frantic people" but compared his task to stopping a tempest on an angry sea. He was unable to find a single moderate man and he was "disgusted" with human nature. He related that all the Baptist ministers were secessionists but many churches would not allow them to preach. "The Devil is let loose on the earth," he wrote and identified Jonesville, Tennessee to be capital of his evil empire. His own family, however, was more reasonable though they were outnumbered at least "five to one."

After the war began in 1861, Slade and others were opposed to Georgia Governor Joseph E. Brown, who was unpopular with many for not supporting the Confederate government of Jefferson Davis more enthusiastically. Brown was a strict states' rights politician, incidentally in the tradition of Governor Troup, and was withholding men and supplies. While Slade had been a strong supporter of states' rights in the Indian wars of the 1820s and 1830s, he apparently believed that there would be no independence for Georgia unless the Confederate States could collectively win their secession from the Union. Therefore, he signed his name to appeals for Col. James M. Chambers of Columbus gubernatorial campaign against Brown.[83] Statewide, seven candidates opposed Brown in 1862, including Judge E. A. Nisbet of Macon, a trustee of, by then, Wesleyan Female College. The anti-Brown voters finally consolidated behind either Nisbet or Chambers, and Slade, who knew Nisbet personally, chose to continue his support for Chambers. Nisbet won the Democratic nomination at Milledgeville on September 11 but ultimately lost to the incumbent governor in the general election.[84] Thus, Slade, who was dismissive of secession before it passed, called for support of "independence" after it passed.[85]

Slade continued classes at the Female Institute in Columbus throughout the war. Advertisements appeared in the local newspapers in every issue during the months before the beginning of a new term. While the boys marched off to battle, the girls maintained their studies. At the same time, Anne received a letter from "a Virginia lady" asking for donations of cotton so volunteers in the Commonwealth State could make "comforters" or blankets for the Confederate sick and wounded.[86] Therefore, on Anne's behalf, Slade appealed to the residents of Columbus for donations of cotton. "Beg a bale of cotton from some planter near Columbus," he wrote, "and have it sent to Frederick's Hall Depot, Louisa County, Virginia, directed to me." Within three days, Slade was expressing his gratitude to two local planters Thacker B. Howard and James Cook for "promptly and generously" contributing a bale each for the comforter appeal.[87] Although girls did not go to war like their brothers, enrollment at the female institute declined during the war because many Southern families were forced to divert funds away from education for their daughters. With attitudes of parents strongly biased against "free" school, Slade found it difficult to keep students enrolled even after offering significant discounts and delayed payment options. Tuition fell at the Columbus Female Institute to as low as $17.50, but this made it difficult for Slade to buy books, furniture, and other supplies.[88]

The war years took two more of the Slade children and six of their grandchildren. John Henry Slade, Slade's tenth child and youngest son, nineteen, was killed in action at the *Battle of Sharpsburg*. He enlisted in the Second Georgia Infantry, Company G, on April 16, 1861, only four days after the Civil War began with the firing at Fort Sumter, South Carolina. Also known as the *Battle of Antietam*, Sharpsburg was a conflict between troops led by Confederate General Robert E. Lee and Union General George McClellan as part of Lee's attempt to take the fighting into the Union State of Maryland. There was a total of 23,000 casualties, including 3,600 fatalities in one day, September 17, 1862. Shots began early in the morning and the action was intense throughout the day. The casualties were unusually high because of new, more accurate rifles then recently introduced and used against traditional battle formations. The Sunken Road became a trap and is thus known as Bloody Lane.

The company from Columbus arrived on the battlefield two days before the clash. Colleagues of John Henry recounted camping in a meadow near Antietam Creek. On the day of the battle, the 2nd Georgia Infantry and part of the 20th Georgia Infantry faced the Union's Ninth Corps under General Ambrose Burnside and successfully kept them in position while inflicting heavy casualties. Outnumbered more than two-to-one, however, the Georgia troops began to give way after several hours. Theodore Turner Fogle, a friend of John Henry, later wrote to his own parents,

> Poor Johnnie Slade, he was a splendid soldier. He did his duty well before he fell. He had nearly shot away all his cartridges & was standing up watching the effect of his last shot when a ball passed through the third finger of his right hand and into his stomach and liver. It came out at his back (and) he was carried off to a safe place.[89]

Henry was being taken four miles by ambulance to a Confederate hospital in Shepherdstown, West Virginia, but died in transit before reaching the Potomac River. He was thus buried near a brigade hospital on the farm of David Smith near Sharpsburg and southwest of the battlefield. Slade, his father, however, later arranged to have John Henry reinterred on March 23, 1869, in the Slade Family Plot at Columbus in the Linwood Cemetery where he lies today. Fogle was later promoted to first lieutenant but was also killed on May 6, 1864, on the second day of the three-day *Battle of the Wilderness* in Virginia, the first battle that featured Lee against Union General Ulysses S. Grant. Fogle is also buried in the Linwood Cemetery.[90]

Sharpsburg was the single bloodiest day in American history and is the event that prompted President Abraham Lincoln to issue his preliminary *Emancipation Proclamation*, his intention to free all enslaved people in the Confederate States. The battlefield is now a national park under the management of the National Park Service.[91]

Mary Lavinia Slade, thirty-six, died one year later on Valentine's Day in 1863. She was Slade's second child and the fourth of four to pass before her parents. Mary never married but worked with her parents at the institute. She was a student of the Georgia Female College in the first freshman Class of 1839 when her father was a member of the faculty there.[92] Her cause of death was not given and she was buried with "Annie" in the Slade Plot of Linwood Cemetery.

Thomas Bog Slade Jr. also served in the war, enlisting in September 1861 as a sergeant in the Georgia Light Artillery (Terrell's Artillery), Brooks Company but later transferring to the Third Cavalry. He survived the war to become a teacher in Carroll County, Georgia despite remaining on active duty until the end of the war on April 18, 1865, when his company was informally disbanded in North Carolina.[93] He visited family in North Carolina on the way home from the war, within days of the surrender, and must have been struck by his cousin Ann Janet Slade (1834–1901), the daughter of William, who was recently married to John A. Mautsby in Hillsboro, North Carolina. He wrote to her several times after returning to Columbus between July and December 1865 discussing the war and their family. Far from being anything inappropriate, the correspondence seems to be mainly driven by Ann's desire to know more about Thomas' experience in the war, the circumstances of his travel, and events in Columbus. The relationship is complicated, however, because he never asked about Mautsby or referred to her marriage. The affection in his letters is explained by the formality of writers in letters during the nineteenth century. He began the first letter, "Though it has been near three months since I saw you all at Hillsboro, my thoughts often revert to my short visit there. After since, have I longed to know what has been your fortune and what treatment you have had at the hands of the Federals."[94] Because the postal service had not yet been reestablished in July 1865, Thomas Jr had his brother-in-law, Hockley McKee, the husband of sister Stella Blount Slade, deliver his letter. McKee was on his way to Philadelphia, Pennsylvania to visit his mother Elizabeth Ballinger Atkinson (1812–86) for the first time since his father, Hockley Cloyd McKee Sr, had died two years earlier during the war. Stella and Hockley were married at the institute, her home, on July 16, 1861. Slade performed hundreds of wedding ceremonies for his former students over fifty years but he never

Figure 6.2 The Slade Family Plot, Linwood Cemetery, Columbus, Georgia (photo by author).

conducted the weddings of his own daughters. Isaac T. Tichenor (1825–1902), thirty-six years old in 1861, joined Stella and Hockley just three months after his own wedding to Emily C. Boykin.[95] He was pastor of First Baptist churches in Montgomery, Alabama and Memphis, Tennessee before becoming president of the Agricultural & Mechanical College (now Auburn University) in 1872–81. Tichenor was thereafter secretary (now president) of the Home Missions Society of the Southern Baptist Convention (now the North American Mission Board) after 1882. He was "one of the best-known clergymen of the South."[96] Tichenor was also a planter, slave owner, and consistent proponent of slavery from the pulpit. Slade's relationship with Tichenor and others illustrates the high level of national leadership who were among his friends and associates and the reputation he had within and outside the state. Janet, Anne, Martha, Helen, and even Tichenor were all married by James Howard DeVotie who lived in Harris County, Georgia before becoming the agent for Howard College in Marion, Alabama during the 1840s and 1850s. In 1856 he was pastor of the

First Baptist Church of Columbus. He served as chaplain in the Civil War and then lived in Spalding County, Georgia. He was also friends with Slade's cousin Marmaduke Slade who had moved to Tuscaloosa, Alabama where he worked as a printer.

Thomas Jr. revealed to Ann that the Slade Female Institute was not damaged during the war and that his parents had remained physically healthy despite the loss of children and grandchildren in and outside the conflict. "In the defense of Columbus Pa although sixty-five years of age shouldered his musket and was probably the last one that fired a shot at the enemy here."[97] Slade did contract a fever in late 1865 while visiting his newborn granddaughter, Helen Mary Gignilliat, in Thomas County, Georgia, about 150 miles south. Slade was accompanied by his married daughter Martha, twenty-seven, who contracted the same fever. Thomas Jr. wrote that the illness was so serious "they despaired at one time of reaching home again." Both recovered, however, and were home in time for Christmas.

In the midst of war, which was enduring longer than expected, Slade announced his retirement. Sixty-three years old, he was no longer "enobled to hold out" as his physical energies were failing.[98] The war had two more years to go and although Slade lived eighteen more besides, he offered his residence and school for sale in 1863, "located in a most desirable part of the city." Whereas his daughter inherited the property after his death, the advertisements were obviously not successful and, in the meantime, school operations continued despite the announcement and the war. In fact, once the war ended, Slade was not retired and opened a school for boys in Sladeville Hall on October 1, 1867.[99] He and his sons, James Jeremiah Slade, who had earned his own Master of Arts degree, and Thomas Bog Slade Jr. along with C. P. Willcox, A.M. were listed as instructors.[100] It was advertised to be a preparatory school for boys intending to enroll in a "standard" university. Tuition began at $75 per year, payable half in advance and the balance due by March 1 of the following year. For this expense, students were required to take classes in arithmetic, ancient languages, French and German, English composition, mathematics separate from arithmetic, and others.[101]

Thomas Bog Slade Jr. revealed to Ann Janet Slade that he had also committed to teach at a school "about a mile from Pa's place beginning the 1st of August." At the time of the letter, however, he was growing corn and potatoes in Russell County, Alabama. Although many Southerners were struggling with the food supply after the war, Thomas Jr. wrote, "We have plenty of nice fruit and vegetables, making a most enjoyable change to the rough fare of a Confederate soldier." He further declared defiantly of the entire experience, "It has not killed our spirit." It is unclear who he meant by the first-person plural pronoun because he then stated, "The family is now very much divided and in transitions when we have no mails we hear but seldom from each other." He concluded by writing, "Mother as well as the rest of the family send much love to you all. Please write and let me know how you have fared since I left, for I am very anxious to hear all. I cannot begin to express the love I have for you all and must sincerely pray that the misfortunes of these evil times may not press too heavily upon you."[102]

He signed his letters, "Your affectionate cousin." By December, postal service was reestablished between Columbus and North Carolina, so Thomas Jr. wrote to Ann again, still not certain that his first letter had come to her. He had received no letter from her. He had been "looking in vain for an answer," but gave up and concluded his first letter had been lost. Hockley had passed it to someone in Nashville, Tennessee, since his route had not passed nearer to Hillsboro, North Carolina. Thomas Jr. was still processing his active duty during the war. "From being the proud defier of the enemy," he shared with his "dear cousin,"

> the Confederate soldier had become a fugitive before the overpowering force of the enemy; instead of being a terror to his enemies he had truly become one to his friends, whom he was in a fair way to starve. Valor had accomplished much, but then the force of circumstances had combined against it. I had been sad before at leaving defenseless women and children to the mercy of the foe; but this sadness came with redoubled force upon me, when I thought of the ones I was then leaving. I have anxiously thought of you since, and wondered what were the accidents that befell you in that trying hour.[103]

Speaking for many Southerners of all classes, genders, races, and sects, Thomas Jr. described the period after the war as "dark days" and prophesized the darkest of them were yet to come to "our unhappy land" even though the military exercises had ended eight months before. "We are no longer freemen," he wrote, "we merely submit to what is imposed upon us. Our position is a most degrading one, and my only consolation is that I did all that I could in my contracted sphere to avert it."

Despite having contracted to teach school in Columbus away from the Slade Female Institute, Thomas Jr was living at his father's school in December 1865. He was both teaching and farming. "This is the best I can do for the present," he informed Ann, "I live very quietly and happily because I am always busy and relieve Pa of all the annoyance of business himself." At that time, Thomas Jr expected to remain with his parents for the remainder of their lives. "I feel it a duty," he said, "to relieve them as far as possible of all care in their old age."[104] He could not have known that Slade would live seventeen years more and his mother twenty-six. By 1871, just six years later, he married Almarine Cowdrey (1848–1926) and moved to Lee County, Alabama, where he was when Slade died. By the time his mother passed away, he was teaching school 85 miles north in Carroll County, Georgia.

With the war ended, Slade's work for a statewide system of public schools made significant progress when Georgia Governor Charles J. Jenkins (1805–83) signed *An Act to Provide for Education and to Establish a General System of Georgia Schools* on December 12, 1866. With the addition of new leadership, a new group created a statewide association of educators who met in Atlanta on August 21, 1867, with Slade, sixty-seven, in attendance. There were twenty-five professors, college presidents, and several private school teachers present in what is considered the first meeting of the Georgia Teachers Association, which became the modern Georgia Education Association. Henry Holcombe Tucker, elected president of the association, was there from Penfield along with President John Mitchell Bonnell and C. Schwartz, professor of modern languages and Latin, from Wesleyan College.[105] This meeting turned out to be the last statewide meeting related to education Slade attended. The association, however, came to him in 1871 when they held their fifth annual meeting in Columbus. Seventy-one years old by that time, there is no indication Slade attended the meetings in Columbus but surely several of its leaders, not least among them, President Gustavus J. Orr, Jr., made their way to visit Slade and his institute on Fourth Avenue. Slade's vision of a free school in each county was established. Unfortunately, the law only provided for the education of white children, but that disparity was soon addressed by the period of Reconstruction and, over time, several decisions of the US Supreme Court.

The Columbus Female Seminary continued as well after the war. A granddaughter of Slade (Emma's daughter) and a student, eleven-year-old Annie Prescott, however, was studying at Miss Sallie Michell's school, too young for the seminary, and described her experience to her fifteen-year-old cousin Helen M. Gignilliat in 1870.[106] "I am not studying as many books as you are," she wrote with an impressive hand for her age, "I am studying *Rays Arithmetic, Parley's Universal History, Cornell's intermediate Geography, Scholar's Companion,* and *Pineo's primary Grammar.*" A young white female such as Annie was obviously influenced toward the profession of teaching by her family and with few career choices open to women, Southern white women in large numbers chose to be teachers as a means of livelihood after the war. Those who became teachers were taught in local colleges, institutes, normal schools, and seminaries like the Columbus Female Institute.[107] In 1860, 43 percent of all teachers in Columbus were women. In 1870, it was 78 percent including one black female teacher and one mulatto.[108]

After the war, competition for students increased from many sectors. A convent of four Catholic nuns finally arrived in Columbus after 1870 and soon there were fourteen nuns teaching up to three hundred Columbus students. The textile mills opened the Columbus Free School targeting the "children of the poor" and "the children of soldiers" as early as 1864. This, of course, meant the children of mill employees such as those who worked for The Eagle Mill, which managed to earn "enormous profits" during the war.[109] This mill school, however, exposed sharp class distinctions in Columbus. Over one thousand men, women, and children worked in the Columbus mills at the beginning of the war and although they may have desired an education for their children, they were so sensitive about a charitable education that many refused to allow their children to attend.[110] Furthermore, municipal leaders in Columbus debated moving the mills across the river into Alabama to remove factory workers from downtown. Some considered mill workers "worse than a nigger" and removing them equivalent to "moral and social uplift."[111] *The Daily Times,* however, with Thomas Bog Slade Jr. on staff, wrote, "Hundreds of poor children in our midst who have hitherto been neglected and permitted to run wild, can now be brought within the pale of civilization, and led on in the useful, virtuous and honorable paths of human existence."[112] The school, meeting in "the church on the river," opened with only forty-five students. Expecting parents to soften to the idea of a free school and enrollment to climb to more than 200, mill executives made plans to construct a building solely for the Columbus Free School. Once the permanent building opened, there were 120 boys and 97 girls, 60 of them children of factory workers, 45 children of widows, 42 children of war veterans, 36 of them children of fathers killed in the war, and thirty-five others from the families of "citizens."[113] The *Times* became the school's chief promoter. On April 26, 1864, Editor James Warren wrote;

> Let these children see and feel that the community looks upon them as human beings worthy of notice, and not as outcasts and beggars, too contemptible to attract the attention and sympathy of the public . . . let them feel that poverty does not necessarily entail disgrace, and that moral and virtuous action will prove the key which will admit them to public favor and public esteem.[114]

Others were hopeful the school would finally eliminate vagrancy in Columbus, reduce crime, and bring order to the city. Before the war ended, the *Times* expressed great fear for the future of the Confederacy due to "the evil generation of boys now coming on." Hopeful, and urging readers to take positive action, the newspaper lamented, "these are demoralizing times"[115] "Not only boys but girls in the city were observed dipping snuff, and the use of profanity, tobacco, and alcohol was reportedly on the rise." The free school was thus supported by many as the solution to these social ills.

Other new schools opened after the war to teach black children. Partly because Southern whites did not support teaching the children of freedmen and partly because these schools were founded and led after September 1865 by missionaries from the North, they were opposed, sometimes violently, by a significant number of residents over time. "Yankee" teachers were often ostracized and, arguably, the movement further undermined support for public schools in the state.[116] The newspapers argued that the greatest objection of Columbus whites to black schools in Columbus stemmed from the role of Yankee teachers. Tension increased in 1866 when the federal government stationed a garrison of black troops in Columbus who built a school for the children of freedmen. After a white citizen was killed, whites in Columbus burned the school. The newspapers blamed the Yankee "missionaries" for "stirring up trouble." "We won't have them teaching the black to hate us," one wrote, "and to fight us."[117] Ultimately, poor whites chose no school at all rather than send their children to the missionary schools. The Columbus Free School was then burned by federal troops in retaliation for the burning of the colored school. Eagle Mills rebuilt it across the river in Alabama. Parents were interested but absolutely refused mixed-race schools of any kind. Some were said to have told the missionaries that they wished their own children "had the advantages the niggers were enjoying" but also added, "I never will get so low as to have my children learning with nigs."[118] Thus, educational progress was severely restricted by gender, class, and race. It took another one hundred years to seriously begin to unravel the complexity of these social restraints.

The Slades were in Columbus when they celebrated their golden wedding anniversary, fifty years, Wednesday, April 1, 1874, with forty children and grandchildren and numerous guests. This is where the local newspaper described them by publishing that they were, "Two lives beautifully blended, as the rays of the setting sun, lighting and purpling the crystal clouds, until sun and clouds are mingled in one mass of crimson beauty."[119] By comparing sources and consideration of the Slade chronology, it is possible to determine the "forty children and grandchildren" who were present for the anniversary gathering. It is, of course, impossible to know the identity of the "numerous guests." None of the grandchildren had married by April 1, 1874, and there were no great grandchildren to be present. Those, besides Slade, seventy-four, and his wife Anne, sixty-nine, in attendance were: Janet Elizabeth Slade, forty-nine, the oldest child, her husband William Robert Gignilliat Sr, sixty, and their children Helen, nine, and Anna, six. William's three sons from his first marriage, William, thirty-five, Gilbert, thirty-two, and Thomas, thirty-two, were apparently there even though they were required to travel from Darien, Georgia to be in Columbus for this special occasion. Mary Lavinia Slade passed away in 1863. She was not married and had no children. Anne

Louisa Slade passed away in 1858 but her widowed husband, Roswell Ellis, fifty-one, attended with his new wife, Elizabeth Rutherford, forty-one. James Jeremiah Slade, forty-three, was there with his second wife Leila Birchett Bonner, thirty-three, and their children William Bonner, fifteen, Mary Janet, thirteen, Thomas Bog Jr., eleven, Norah Hermione, seven, James Jr., five, Seymour Bonner, three, and Leila Rose, two. Leila Bonner was nine months pregnant with their ninth child Charles on April 1, 1874. Child John Henry, 1867, had already passed away. Leila, who was present, died just five months after the celebration. Emma Jacqueline Slade, forty-one, was there with her husband Alfred B. Prescott, forty-eight, and their children Fanny Slade, eighteen, the oldest living grandchild, Anne Bemis, seventeen, Helen Malvina, thirteen, William Roulhac, seven, Stella Warren, four, and Alfred Brackett, two. Children Henry Slade, 1856, George Thomas, 1862, John Henry, 1864, and Isabella Bacon, 1867, had already passed away. Thomas Bog Slade Jr., forty, was there with his wife Almarine Cowdrey, twenty-six, and their child John Henry, two. Cowdrey was four months pregnant with their second child Lester Cowdrey on April 1, 1874. Martha Bog Slade, thirty-seven, was there with her husband Grigsby Eskridge Thomas, forty-two, and their children Emma Jacqueline, seven, Hockley McKee, five, Slade, three, and Helen Martha, nine months. Children Annie Slade, 1864, John Grisby, 1862, Grisby Eskridge, 1863, Jennett Elizabeth, 1865, and John Grigsby, 1873, had already passed away. Stella Blount Slade, thirty-five, was there with her husband Hockley Cloyd McKee Jr., thirty-five. The McKees had no children. Helen Roulhac Slade, thirty-three, was there with her husband John Bright Lindsey, thirty-four, and their child Johnie Bright, nine.

It was typical in the nineteenth century for significant anniversaries such as this one to include gifts. Although no specific details of the celebration were recorded, it is reasonable to expect Thomas and Anne exchanged gifts with one another. There may have been a theme and there were decorations. Cameras were invented before 1874 whereas many photographs survive from the Civil War but, if one was taken, no photo remains of Slade's golden anniversary.

The public school system in Columbus began in October 1867 and its charter passed by the state legislature December 28, 1866, but, since the transition to common public schools was slow due to the public's acceptance of the idea, several private schools, including the Slade Female Institute continued strong into the late nineteenth century.[120] By 1874, the combined Columbus schools (male and female) were cited as "Capt. J. J. Slade's school" in *The Columbus Daily Times*, although Slade himself was seventy-four years old and still living. Slade the father, now apparently officially retired and in the last eight years of his life, was recognized in "memoriam," equivalent to a professor *emeritus*.[121] In the same year, however, advertisements for the schools in the newspapers continued to read, "Rev. T. B. Slade's School," one for "Young Ladies" and one for "Boys."[122] Tuition for the boys was $60, twice the amount charged for young ladies.

By 1877, the new school headmaster was Slade's son, James Jeremiah Slade. Slade, the father, was seventy-seven years old. Graduation exercises were being held in the Springer Opera House. "Declaration Exercises" were held separately by gender, the enrollment of the male institute then up to fifty students.[123] The event drew a large crowd of students, parents, and otherwise unaffiliated residents of the area. The students were found to be "among the most intelligent and influential of our citizens," according to the newspaper. *The Columbus Times* reported, "a host of expectant sweethearts filled the house, and cheered by their presence, the efforts of the embryo orators, and those who, trained to the exact modulation of the voice, their poise of the body, and their grace of gesture effectively riveted the attention of their large and enthusiastic audience."[124] Jeremiah introduced each student speaker but himself gave a political commentary, entertaining to the partisan crowd of unreconstructed Southerners present, on the history of the carpetbagger, which he graphically illustrated with an actual buzzard. He "followed his lineage from the flood through the intervening centuries down to the present day, where in this Southern country, he has been at last overpowered and returned crest-fallen to his proper home—the North." Fifteen years later, Jeremiah was elected mayor of Columbus (1892–4), partially based on his years of experience as administrator and teacher at the Slade schools. The student speakers and their topics in 1877 included Lonie Gibson, who delivered "Georgia State Pride"; George E. Glen, who presented "Altering the Virginia Constitution"; Harry T. Hall, "Farewell to Hungary"; L. Walter Cowdery, "Value of Reputation"; George R. Golden, "Charles DeMoore's Remorse"; John S. Roberts, "Foundation of

National Character"; Charles M. Webster, "Our Country"; George Garrett, "An Appeal to Texas Patriotism"; Kie E. Wynne, "The War Inevitable"; Hilton Howard, "Geneva"; Albert Sidney Woolfolk, "Caesar's Triumph"; J. Norman Pease, "The Contrast"; John D. Pou, "Daniel Webster on Trial of John K. Knap"; Thomas L. Ingram, "Rienzi to the Romans"; and Leonidas W. Lamar, "Supposed Speech of an Indian," before the carpetbagger presentation which served as an intermission. Those who followed were Charles D. Preer, "Anthony's Oration Over Caesar's Body"; J. Edward Daniel, "Marie Antoinette"; Charles J. Joseph, "The Immortality of Patriots"; Frank J. Dudley, "Development of Southern Resources"; Moses A. Prather, "Leonidas to His Brave Three Hundred"; George W. Radcliff, "American Literature"; Nolan L. Dudley, "Regulus to the Roman Senate"; Owen M. Brady, "Declaration of Irish Rights"; Albert S. Dozier, "Death of General Lee"; Henry B. Woolfolk, "Spartacus to the Roman Envoys in Etruria"; Earnest Woodruff, "Caesar's Passage Over the Rubicon"; Thomas B. Slade, son of Jeremiah and grandson of Thomas, the subject of this book, gave "In Memorium"; William C. Bradley, "Our Duty to the Republic"; Felder Pou, "Spartacus to the Gladiators at Capua"; and James E. Borders, "Robert Emmet at Close of His Trial for High Treason."

The time given to each speaker was not revealed by the *Times*, but the exercises, as indicated by the newspaper, were a lengthy event, as a modern reader may imagine. The audience was not fatigued, however, despite thirty-one presentations. Even if given only five minutes each, along with Jeremiah's presentation, prayers, and hymns, the commencement could have easily taken over four hours. The entire list of presentations is given here to illustrate the range of topics, heavy in classical and "modern" history, researched by the students, the magnitude of students who became significant contributors to the history of Columbus, and to demonstrate that even though these were male students in the Slade school, they were sons and grandsons of those women who had been taught by Thomas Bog Slade Sr from 1842 until 1877. Space does not allow a detailed description of these connections, but these young men were not only a testimony of their own studies but of the education given to them at home by educated mothers and grandmothers; and all this after these same students had participated in similar exercises just six months earlier with different topics.

In 1880 an item appeared in the *Columbus Daily Enquirer-Sun* that the home of Thomas B. Slade "of Ashville" was burned on January 6 and "nothing was saved to amount to anything."[125] This was certainly not the home of Thomas B. Slade the educator because his home was in Columbus and clearly survived beyond 1880, but the identity of the person affected is not clear. There is no Ashville, Georgia. There is only Asheville, North Carolina and Ashville, Alabama but the latter is located north of the modern highway Interstate 20 in St. Clair County. Thomas Bog Slade, Jr. was living and farming in Lee County, Alabama in 1880 so if there was a small community, then known as Ashville, this may have been his home or the home of Jeremiah's son, recently graduated. As of June 14, 1880, however, he was still in Columbus with his family, making it less likely that it was his home which was destroyed by fire. By 1890 he was living in Carroll County, Georgia.

By the time Slade died in 1882, Reconstruction was over and Georgia had adopted a new state constitution in 1877 which authorized a state school tax. Not without controversy, the amount collected by the collection of this tax steadily grew each year as Georgia's population increased. Free public schools were in the process of being established in every Georgia county by 1873 with support from the legislature. While there was always a place for private schools, the vision of universal education was being realized. Slade was part of refining the argument in Georgia for tax-supported schools. Conservative in his politics, traditional in his cultural views, and a general conformist to his social context, Slade was calculating in his philosophy of justifying mandatory collection of taxes for public education. According to the *Columbus Times*, "He was a gentleman of the old school."[126] As one who would not take such government power lightly, it demonstrates his deep commitment to and realistic appreciation for the great importance of education for both males and females. With others, for example, he argued, while also dismantling fifteen common objections against tax-supported schools, that education tend to prevent pauperism and crime, it reduces poverty, increases production, and corrects wrong ideas about the distribution of wealth. Public schools, he argued, eliminate class distinctions which threaten the stability of a republic. As he admitted, though he had spent his life attempting to prove otherwise, that religious and private schools had failed to meet the needs of a changing society in a rapidly changing nation such as the United States. One to understand the larger context and able to see the future clearly, Slade agreed, "A state which has the right to hang has the right to educate."

Slade died on Friday, May 5, 1882, at 5:00 p.m. in the afternoon at his Forsyth Street home in Columbus "without a murmur or a struggle."[127] Recognizing Slade's lingering memory in Macon, the newspaper there wrote, "Mr. Slade was one of the pioneers of female education in Georgia and the good influence of himself and his most charitable wife runs like a thread of gold through many lives that bless our country." They further described him as a charitable, benevolent, kind, patriotic, useful, and liberal gentleman. The spring semester was still in session on the day of his death, so all the current students were there to mourn his loss and attend the funeral. "A good man has gone to rest," wrote the *Daily Times* in the city.[128] Slade was acknowledged for having educated "a number of the mothers of Columbus and the vicinity" who "received their early instruction from him and his aged companion," his work in the ministry, especially through First Baptist Church. Because of his ministerial work, in addition to his work as an educator, "many souls have been won to Christ." Slade was given credit for having done "great vast good in the community" of Columbus, Georgia.

Slade was buried the next day on Saturday, May 6, in the Linwood Cemetery of Columbus, in the family plot (Section 1, Lot 201) with his children Mary, Anne, and John Henry, two grandchildren, a son-in-law, daughter-in-law, and niece Amelia, daughter of his brother, James Bog Slade. He was survived by his wife of fifty-eight years, seven children, and thirty-five of his forty-nine grandchildren. According to the *Columbus Daily Enquirer-Sun*, "A large number of friends and acquaintances were present to pay the last tribute of respect to the deceased."[129] Jesse Harrison Campbell (1807–88), the author of *Georgia Baptists: Historical and Biographical*,[130] and a lifelong friend of Slade's, conducted the service. Slade had also been baptized by Campbell in Clinton, Georgia, almost fifty years earlier. It may thus be said, Campbell, his lifelong pastor, buried Slade in the water of Clinton then buried him in the earth of Columbus. He had been living in Columbus with his son, also a Baptist minister, since 1876. Campbell was an original trustee of Mercer University and founder of both the Masonic Female College in Lumpkin, Georgia, and the Baptist Female College at Cuthbert,

Georgia. His remarks at Slade's funeral, according to the *Times*, were "most impressive." Slade's pallbearers were Dr. E. C. Hood, Dr. N. J. Busey, Jacob E. Appler, Banker Henry H. Epping Sr., Insurance Executive Robert B. Murdock Sr., Judge W. H. Brannon, and I. J. Strupper.

In his will, Slade left the house and school building to Anne, his wife and executrix, along with all the furniture, instruments, and 81 acres he owned in Russell County, Alabama.

The Slade Female Institute ended with Slade, but the male academy continued under the leadership of his son. In fact, graduation ceremonies were held there only one month and four days after Slade was laid to rest.[131] The announcement appeared in the column next to a similar announcement regarding graduation at the colored schools. Female education in Georgia did not die, for as public education was established, both movements grew together. Eighty years later, they even merged with the colored schools, thus erasing educational division in not only class and gender but also race.

Notes

1 Christopher J. Manganiello, *Southern Water, Southern Power: How the Politics of Cheap Energy and Water Scarcity Shaped a Region* (Chapel Hill: University of North Carolina Press, 2015), p. 23.
2 Katherine Hines Mahan and William Clyde Woodall, *A History of Public Education in Muscogee County and the City of Columbus, 1828–1976* (Muscogee Co. Board of Education, 1977), p. 3.
3 *The Columbus Enquirer* (May 1828).
4 Thomas Bog Slade, Letter to William Slade, April 3, 1825, Slade Family Papers, Box 3 (1825) and Thomas Bog Slade, *Autobiography of Thomas Bog Slade*, Southern Historical Collection 1837–1846, 2683-z, University of North Carolina, p. 2.
5 John H. Martin, "The Making of a Modern City: Columbus, Georgia, 1827–65," II (1875): 53.
6 "How a Blind Autistic Slave Boy Made White House History," *Columbus Times* (February 4, 2009). See also Deirdre O'Connell, "The Ballad of Blind Tom" (Overlook Press, 2009).

7 Katherine Hines Mahan and William Clyde Woodall, *A History of Public Education in Muscogee County and the City of Columbus, 1828–1976* (Muscogee Co. Board of Education, 1977), p. 5.
8 Ibid., p. 7.
9 Ibid., p. 8.
10 Ibid., p. 10.
11 Michael J. McNally, "Catholic Parish Life in the Antebellum South: Columbus, Georgia, 1830–60," *American Catholic Studies* 113:1/2 (Spring-Summer 2002): 14.
12 Victoria MacDonald Huntzinger, "The Birth of Southern Public Education: Columbus, GA, 1864–1904," PhD thesis (Harvard, 1992), p. 12.
13 Katherine Hines Mahan and William Clyde Woodall, *A History of Public Education in Muscogee County and the City of Columbus, 1828–1976* (Muscogee Co. Board of Education, 1977), p. 13.
14 Ibid., p. 16.
15 Thomas Bog Slade, *Autobiography of Thomas Bog Slade*, Southern Historical Collection 1837–46, 2683-z, University of North Carolina, p. 2.
16 "Female Institute," *The Christian Index* (August 5, 1847), p. 256.
17 See Laurel Thatcher Ulrich, *A Midwife's Tale: The Life of Martha Ballard, Based on Her Diary, 1785–1812* (Vintage, 1990) and Helen Varney and Joyce Beebe Thompson, *A History of Midwifery in the United States* (Springer, 2015).
18 *The Columbus Times* (June 3, 1841), p. 2 and *Catalogue of the Linonian* Society, Yale (New Haven: B. L. Hamlen, 1841), p. 62.
19 "Barnett of Columbus Dead," *The Macon Telegraph* (July 11, 1889), p. 3.
20 Mike Bunn, *The Eufaula Regency: Alabama's Most Celebrated Secessionist Faction* (Eufaula: Eufaula Heritage Association, 2009); Lewy Dorman, *Party Politics in Alabama from 1850 Through 1860* (Tuscaloosa: University of Alabama Press, 1995); and J. Mills Thornton III, *Politics and Power in a Slave Society: Alabama, 1800–1860* (Baton Rouge: Louisiana State University Press, 1978).
21 John B. Gordon, *Reminiscences of the Civil War* (New York: Charles Scribner's Sons, 1904), p. 60.
22 Record of Wills, 1834–1964; Georgia, Court of Ordinary (Muscogee County).
23 *The National Tribune*, Washington, DC (July 13, 1899), p. 7.
24 *The New York Times* (March 19, 1912).
25 Thomas Bog Slade Jr to Ann Janet Slade, personal letter (December 17, 1865), *Ruffin-Roulhac-Hamilton Papers, 1784–1957*, no. 643, in the Southern Historical Collection at UNC Chapel Hill, NC.

26 W. C. Woodall, "The First of the Slades," *The Columbus Ledger* (January 6, 1964), p. 13.
27 Thomas Bog Slade, Letter to William Slade, June 21, 1847, Slade Family Papers, Box 2.
28 "Female Institute," *The Christian Index* (August 5, 1847), p. 256.
29 "Academy for Young Gentlemen," *The Times-Picayune* 7:25 (February 21, 1843): 1 and "Committed," *The Vicksburg Daily Whig* (August 16, 1842), p. 3.
30 Thomas Bog Slade, Letter to James Bog Slade, June 12, 1847, Slade Family Papers, Box 2.
31 Thomas Bog Slade, Letter to William Slade, January 25, 1849, Slade Family Papers, Box 2.
32 Affectionate Brother, Letter to Anne, April 18, 1850, Slade Family Papers, Box 2.
33 Thomas Bog Slade, Letter to Jeremiah Slade, May 27, 1850, Slade Family Papers, Box 2.
34 The National Archives in Washington D.C., Records of the US Bureau of the Census, 1850, Columbus, Muscogee, Georgia, M432.
35 "Shoal Academy," *The Columbus Enquirer* (July 31, 1849), p. 3.
36 "Columbus Female Institute," *Weekly Columbus Enquirer* (July 16, 1850), p. 2.
37 Elizabeth Slade Henderson, Letter to Anne Slade, February 22, 1850, Slade Family Papers, Box 2.
38 Michael J. McNally, "Catholic Parish Life in the Antebellum South: Columbus, Georgia, 1830–60," *American Catholic Studies* 113:1/2 (Spring-Summer 2002): 16.
39 Patricia Curtin-Kelly, *An Ornament to the City: Holy Trinity Church and the Capuchin Order* (Dublin: The History Press Ireland, 2015), pp. 21, 29.
40 Brian Dooley, *Black and Green: The Fight for Civil Rights in Northern Ireland & Black America* (London: Pluto Press, 1998).
41 Michael J. McNally, "Catholic Parish Life in the Antebellum South: Columbus, Georgia, 1830–60," *American Catholic Studies* 113:1/2 (Spring-Summer 2002): 1–30.
42 Douglas K. Clark, *A History of the Cathedral of Saint John the Baptist, Savannah* (Savannah, GA: Diocese of Savannah, 1999) and *English Catholics at Locust Grove* (Savannah, GA: Diocese of Savannah, 1999); Anthony R. Dees, "Georgia, Catholic Church In," in Michael Glazier and Thomas J. Shelley, eds., *The Encyclopedia of American Catholic History* (Collegeville, MN: Liturgical Press, 1997), 566–8; and John England, "The Early History of the Diocese of

Charleston," in Sebastian G. Messmer, ed., *The Works of the Right Reverend John England, First Bishop of Charleston*, vol. iv (Cleveland, OH: Arthur H. Clark, 1908), 298–327.

43 Michael J. McNally, "Catholic Parish Life in the Antebellum South: Columbus, Georgia, 1830–60," *American Catholic Studies* 113:1/2 (Spring-Summer 2002): 5.
44 "Reform Association of Columbus," *Columbus Enquirer* (September 1, 1841), p. 3.
45 Ibid.
46 Thomas Bog Slade, Jr., Letter to Jeremiah Slade, July 31, 1850, 926.3, Slade Family Papers, Box 1.
47 E. Merton Coulter, "A Georgia Educational Movement During the Eighteen Hundred Fifties," *The Georgia Historical Quarterly* 9:1 (March 1925).
48 *The Southern Eclectic* (February 1854).
49 Denise Mewborn, "Public Education," *The New Georgia Encyclopedia* (2020).
50 E. Merton Coulter, "A Georgia Educational Movement During the Eighteen Hundred Fifties," *The Georgia Historical Quarterly* 9:1 (March 1925): 2.
51 Ibid., p. 4.
52 Ibid., p. 11.
53 W. C. Woodall, "The First of the Slades," *The Columbus Ledger* (January 6, 1964), p. 13.
54 Thomas Bog Slade, Letter to Dear Nephew, November 23, 1852, Slade Family Papers, Box 1.
55 E. Merton Coulter, "A Georgia Educational Movement During the Eighteen Hundred Fifties," *The Georgia Historical Quarterly* 9:1 (March 1925): 18.
56 "To the Teachers of Georgia," *The Central Georgian* (July 26, 1853), p. 2.
57 *Georgia Home Gazette* in *Southern School Journal* (February 1853), p. 35.
58 "To the Teachers of Georgia," *The Central Georgian* (July 26, 1853), p. 2.
59 Peggy S. Steelman, "Growth and Development of the Georgia Education Association" (PhD, diss., University of Georgia, 1966), p. 35.
60 Ibid., p. 36.
61 Ibid.
62 "Married," *The Columbus Daily Enquirer* (December 18, 1856), p. 3.
63 "Mrs. Mary Slade Buried," *The Atlanta Journal* (June 18, 1920), p. 13.
64 *The Columbus Directory for 1859–1860* (Mears & Company, 1859).
65 Katherine Hines Mahan and William Clyde Woodall, *A History of Public Education in Muscogee County and the City of Columbus, 1828–1976* (Muscogee Co. Board of Education, 1977), p. 3.

66 *R. G. Dun Reports*, vol. 23, Muscogee County, GA 1847–1885 (R. G. Dun & Co.), p. 79.
67 Victoria MacDonald Huntzinger, "The Birth of Southern Public Education: Columbus, GA, 1864–1904," PhD thesis (Harvard, 1992), p. 19.
68 Joseph B. Mahan, *Columbus: Georgia's Fall Line "Trading Town"* (Northbridge, CA: Windsor Publications, 1986), pp. 31–49.
69 Victoria MacDonald Huntzinger, "The Birth of Southern Public Education: Columbus, GA, 1864–1904," PhD thesis (Harvard, 1992), p. 13.
70 Ibid., p. 14.
71 William Standard Diffee, *Columbus, Georgia in the Confederacy: The Social & Industrial Life of the Chattahoochee River Port* (New York: William-Frederick Press, 1954).
72 "Idle Negroes in Columbus," *The Daily Sun* (September 28, 1865), p. 3.
73 "The Chain Gang Ready," *The Daily Sun* (November 1, 1865), p. 3.
74 "The Negro and White Laborer in New York," *The New York News* (September 1865).
75 Victoria MacDonald Huntzinger, "The Birth of Southern Public Education: Columbus, GA, 1864–1904," PhD thesis (Harvard, 1992), p. 20.
76 W. E. B. Du Bois, *The Negro Common School* (Atlanta, 1901), p. 18.
77 "Two Negro Prisoners Endeavor to Set the Court House on Fire," *The Daily Sun* (October 17, 1865), p. 3.
78 "Still Arresting Idle Negroes," *The Daily Sun* (October 17, 1865), p. 3.
79 "Idle Negroes on the Commons," *The Daily Sun* (November 2, 1865), p. 3.
80 "Keep Negroes from the City," *The Daily Sun* (December 15, 1865), p. 3.
81 Edmund Cody Burnett, "Some Confederate Letters: Alabama, Georgia, and Tennessee," *The Georgia Historical Quarterly* 21:2 (June 1937): 188–203 and the 1860 US Federal Census, M653, Bureau of the Census (Henry Co., AL), p. 122.
82 Ibid., p. 193.
83 "Correspondence—Gubernatorial," *Southern Confederacy* (August 30, 1861), p. 3.
84 James Horace Bass, *Georgia Historical Quarterly* 17:3 (September 1933).
85 Thomas B. Slade, "Letter to the Editor," *The Daily Sun* (October 12, 1861), p. 3.
86 Ibid.
87 Thomas B. Slade, "Letter to the Editor," *The Daily Sun* (October 15, 1861), p. 3.
88 Victoria MacDonald Huntzinger, "The Birth of Southern Public Education: Columbus, GA, 1864–1904," PhD thesis (Harvard, 1992), p. 22.

89 Theodore Turner Fogle to John Jacob Fogle, personal letter (October 1, 1862).
90 "Killed," *Columbus Daily Times* (May 19, 1862), p. 2.
91 Stephen W. Sears, *Landscape Turned Red: The Battle of Antietam* (Mariner Books, 1993); Steven Cowie, *When Hell Came to Sharpsburg: The Battle of Antietam and Its Impact on the Civilians Who Called it Home* (Savas Beatie, 2023); D. Scott Hartwig, *I Dread the Thought of the Place: The Battle of Antietam and the End of the Maryland Campaign* (Johns Hopkins, 2023); Bradley M. Gottfried, *The Maps of Antietam: An Atlas of the Antietam (Sharpsburg) Campaign, including the Battle of South Mountain September 2–20, 1862* (Savas Beatie, 2012); and James M. McPherson, *Crossroads of Freedom: Antietam* (Oxford, 2002).
92 "Georgia Female College," *Georgia Journal and Messenger* (July 11, 1839), p. 3.
93 Georgia, US, Confederate Pension Applications, 1879–1960.
94 Thomas Bog Slade Jr to Ann Janet Slade, personal letter (July 9, 1865), *Ruffin-Roulhac-Hamilton Papers, 1784–1957*, no. 643, in the Southern Historical Collection at UNC Chapel Hill, NC.
95 "Married," *The Daily Sun* (July 18, 1861).
96 "Doctor Tichenor Died," *Indian Citizen*, Atoka, OK (December 4, 1902), p. 3.
97 Thomas Bog Slade Jr to Ann Janet Slade, personal letter (December 17, 1865), *Ruffin-Roulhac-Hamilton Papers, 1784–1957*, no. 643, in the Southern Historical Collection at UNC Chapel Hill, NC.
98 Thomas B. Slade, "For Sale," *The Daily Sun* (April 7—May 26, 1863), p. 1, 2.
99 "Sladeville Hall," *The Daily Sun* (September 10–26, 1868), p. 2.
100 "Slade's School, For Boys," *The Daily Sun* (September 11–October 9, 1867), p. 3.
101 "Slade's School For Boys," *The Daily Sun* (September 13—October 1, 1871), pp. 2, 3.
102 Ibid.
103 Thomas Bog Slade Jr to Ann Janet Slade, personal letter (December 17, 1865), *Ruffin-Roulhac-Hamilton Papers, 1784–1957*, no. 643, in the Southern Historical Collection at UNC Chapel Hill, NC.
104 Ibid.
105 *Catalogue of the Trustees, Faculty and Students of the Wesleyan Female College, Macon, Georgia, 1867–1868, Including the Curriculum Terms, etc.* (Macon: J. W. Burke & Co., 1868), p. 4.
106 Annie Prescott, Letter to Dear Cousin Helen, Slade Family Papers, 1870.
107 Mary Elizabeth Massey, *Bonnet Brigades* (New York, 1966), pp. 108–23 and Anne Firor Scott, *The Southern Lady* (Chicago, 1970), pp. 110–18.

108 U.S. Federal Census, 1860 and 1870, Muscogee Co., GA.
109 Victoria MacDonald Huntzinger, "The Birth of Southern Public Education: Columbus, GA, 1864-1904," PhD thesis (Harvard, 1992), p. 24.
110 Frederick Law Olmstead, *A Journey in the Seaboard Slave States* (New York: Dix & Edwards, 1856), p. 190.
111 Victoria MacDonald Huntzinger, "The Birth of Southern Public Education: Columbus, GA, 1864-1904," PhD thesis (Harvard, 1992), p. 27.
112 "The Free School," *The Columbus Daily Times* (January 20, 1864), p. 2.
113 Victoria MacDonald Huntzinger, "The Birth of Southern Public Education: Columbus, GA, 1864-1904," PhD thesis (Harvard, 1992), p. 28.
114 James Warren, *The Columbus Daily Times* (April 26, 1864), p. 3.
115 Leon Basile, "Soiled Dresses Are Better Than Soiled Modesty: Decency and Delinquency in Columbus, Georgia, 1864-1865," *Lincoln Herald* 4 (1981): 574.
116 Victoria MacDonald Huntzinger, "The Birth of Southern Public Education: Columbus, GA, 1864-1904," PhD thesis (Harvard, 1992), p. 30.
117 *Lucy Chase to Miss Stevenson*, personal letters, June 1, 1866, Freeman's Record, 7 (July 1866): 131-2.
118 Sarah E. Chase to Mr. May, April 12, 1866, personal letter, in Henry Lee Swint, *Dear Ones at Home: Letters from Contraband Camps* (Vanderbilt, 1966), p. 202.
119 *The Columbus Ledger* (1874).
120 Etta Blanchard Worsley, *Columbus on the Chattahoochee* (Columbus Office Supply Co., 1951), p. 334.
121 "Declamation Exercises," *Columbus Daily Times* (June 16, 1877), p. 4.
122 "Rev. T. B. Slade's School," *Columbus Daily Times* (September 6—October 3, 1877), pp. 1, 2, 3.
123 "Declamation Exercises," *Columbus Daily Times* (June 16, 1877), p. 4.
124 Ibid.
125 *Columbus Daily Enquirer-Sun* (January 18, 1880), p. 3.
126 "Death of Rev. Thos. B. Slade," *The Times* (May 6, 1882), p. 4.
127 "Death of a Good Man," *The Georgia Weekly Telegraph, Journal & Messenger* (May 12, 1882), p. 8 and "Death of Rev. Thos. B. Slade," *The Times* (May 6, 1882), p. 4. See also "Local Leaflets," *The Marietta Journal* (May 18, 1882), p. 3; *The Gainesville Eagle* (May 12, 1882), p. 2; "Georgia News," *The Summerville Gazette* (June 1, 1882), p. 2; "Georgia Affairs," *Savannah Morning News* (May 8, 1882), p. 1; and *The Home Journal*, Perry, GA (May 11, 1882), p. 2.
128 "Death of Rev. Thos. B. Slade," *The Times* (May 6, 1882), p. 4.

129 "Funeral of Rev. Thomas B. Slade," *The Columbus Daily Enquirer-Sun* (May 7, 1882), p. 3.
130 J. H. Campbell, *Georgia Baptists: Historical and Biographical* (Macon: J. H. Burke and Company, 1874).
131 "Slade's School," *Columbus Daily Times* (June 10, 1882), p. 4.

Conclusion

While preaching regularly, ministering to the sick, administering two schools in Columbus, Thomas Slade managed to travel the State of Georgia as he had in Clinton, Macon, and Penfield, campaigning for a state-supported system of public schools. He died in Columbus on May 5, 1882, and is buried there, still writing, teaching, and advocating for public education until the end of his life. He is an underappreciated figure in the long struggle to establish government-supported public schools in Georgia. His work, combined with others, ultimately led to the passage of universal, state-supported education in Georgia. He changed the educational landscape in the Empire State and his students, primarily young women from all across the Southeastern states, multiplied his influence by becoming teachers, authors, reformers, poets, highly educated wives, and bilingual mothers who in turn valued education and passed this appreciation on to their children and grandchildren. Georgia ultimately became a stronger state economically because of Slade's work in education and ministry over six decades.

Finally, it is crucial to realize that just as it had been Slade's vision of the future, his support for the educational project was above all a spiritual project as much as it was an effort to support the comprehensive training and certification of teachers, and the construction and maintenance of educational infrastructure from taxes to buildings. Perhaps Milton would say of the visionary Slade, as he did of Samuel Hartlib, who was also motivated from the beginning of his work by a desire to improve the common good, "with what difficulty he passes through, directed by the power of that place, to the sight of this new world which he sought."

Bibliography

Abbott, Frank M. *History of the People of Jones County, Georgia*, vol. v., *Genalogies* (Lineage Unlimited, 1977).

Abbott, John S. C. *History of Joseph Bonaparte, King of Naples and of Italy* (Harper & Bros., 1869).

Abney, Beth. "The Orion as a Literary Publication," *The Georgia Historical Quarterly* 48:4 (December 1964): 411–24.

Akers, Samuel Luttrell. *The First Hundred Years of Wesleyan College: 1836-1936* (The Stinehour Press, 1976).

Alabama Department of Archives and History; Montgomery; Various Files, Boxes and Film, 1824-1882.

Alcott, Louisa May. *Good Wives* (Roberts Brothers, 1869).

Ambrose, Stephen E. E. *Duty, Honor, Country: A History of West Point* (Johns Hopkins, 2000).

Ambrose, Stephen E. E., William F. Buckley, et al., *West Point: Two Centuries of Honor and Tradition* (Grand Central Publishing, 2002).

Anderson, George Baker. *Landmarks of Rensselaer County* (D. Mason & Co., 1897).

Andrew, John A. "Review of *Southern Evangelicals and the Social Order, 1800-1860*, by A. C. Loveland," *Journal of the Early Republic* 1:4 (1981): 429–31.

Angell, Stephen W. "The Oxford Handbook of Quaker Studies," in *Oxford Handbooks in Religion and Theology series* (Oxford, 2015).

Annual Catalogue of the Wesleyan Female College, Macon, Georgia, multiple years (J. W. Burke & Co., 1880).

Arndt, Grant. "Ho-Chunk Powwows: Innovation and Tradition in a Changing World," *The Wisconsin Magazine of History* 91:3 (2008): 30.

Arnold, Linda. *The Mexican-American War and the Media, 1845-1848* (Virginia Tech University, 2003).

Athenian, The, 1827-1832, newspaper (Athens, GA).

Atwood, Barbara P. "Miss Pierce of Litchfield," *New England Galaxy* 9 (1967): 32–40.

Augusta Chronicle and Sentinel. 1837-1838, newspaper (Augusta, GA).

Autobiography of Thomas Bog Slade, Southern Historical Collection 1837-1846, 2683-z, University of North Carolina.

Bangs, Nathan. *A History of the Methodist Episcopal Church*, vol. iv (Carlton and Phillips, 1853).

Banks, Charles Edward, and Elijah Ellsworth Brownell. *Topographical Dictionary of 2885 English Emigrants to New England, 1620-1650* (The Bertram Press, 1937).

Barbour, Joan Elizabeth. "College Education for Women in Georgia Before the Civil War" (Honors Paper in History, Emory College, 1972), 23, 90, in Special Collections, Woodruff Library, Emory University.

Bartram, William. *Travels of William Bartram* (New Haven, 1958).

Basile, Leon. "Soiled Dresses Are Better Than Soiled Modesty: Decency and Delinquency in Columbus, Georgia, 1864-1865," *Lincoln Herald* 4 (1981): 574.

Bass, James Horace. "The Georgia Gubernatorial Elections of 1861 and 1863," *Georgia Historical Quarterly* 17:3 (September 1933): 167–88.

Bayne, John Soward. "Augustus Baldwin Longstreet," in *Gravely Concerned: Southern Writers' Graves* (Clemson, 2012).

Benham, Daniel. *A Sketch of the Life of J. A. Comenius* (London, 1858).

Bernard, H. R. *The Work Once Delivered to the Saints* (J. W. Burke, 1906).

Berton, Pierre. *War of 1812* (Anchor Canada, 2011).

Blekastad, Milada. *Comenius: Versuch eines Umrisses von Leben, Werk und Schicksal des Jan Amos Komenský* (Oslo and Prague, 1969).

Bonner, James C. *Milledgeville: Georgia's Antebellum Capital* (Athens, 1978).

Borneman, Walter R. *1812: The War that Forged a Nation* (Harper Perennial, 2005).

"Boston Montgomery Guards, The, 1837," *Donahoe's Magazine* 18:5 (November 1887): 415–19.

Bouge, Virgil T. *Bogue and Allied Families* (Virgil T. Bogue, 1944).

Boydston, Jeanne. *Home and Work: Housework, Wages, and the Ideology of Labor in the Early Republic* (Oxford University Press, 1994).

Boylan, Anne M. *The Origins of Women's Activism: New York and Boston, 1797-1840* (University of North Carolina Press, 2002).

Bragg, William, "Jones County," in the *New Georgia Encyclopedia* (University of Georgia, 2024).

Brand, Chad and David E. Hankins. *One Sacred Effort: The Cooperative Program of Southern Baptists* (B&H Publishing Group, 2006).

Brawley, Benjamin. "Lorenzo Dow," *The Journal of Negro History* I (1916): 265–75.

Brickley, Lynne T., Glee Krueger, Sally Schwager, Theodore Sizer, and Nancy Sizer. *To Ornament Their Minds: Sarah Pierce's Litchfield Female Academy 1792-1833* (Litchfield Historical Society, 1993).

Brown, Kathleen M. *Good Wives, Nasty Wenches, and Anxious Patriarchs: Gender, Race, and Power in Colonial Virginia* (University of North Carolina, 1996).
Brown, Russell. "David Emanuel," *New Georgia Encyclopedia* (September 2, 2016).
Browne, Patrick. *Boston Street Riot, Boston, 1837* (Historical Digression, 2016).
Bryant, J. C. "Antebellum Years in Penfield," in the *New Georgia Encyclopedia* (Mercer University, 2006).
Buckley, John B., Bill Patterson, et al., *Born in the Shadow of History: West Point's Early Years and the American Revolution* (Ind. published, 2023).
Bunn, Mike. *The Eufaula Regency: Alabama's Most Celebrated Secessionist Faction* (Eufaula Heritage Association, 2009).
Burch, Jarrett. *Adiel Sherwood: Baptist Antebellum Pioneer in Georgia*. Baptists Series (Mercer University Press, 2003).
Bureau of Land Management, General Land Office Records. Washington, DC, Federal Land Patents, State Volumes.
Burnett, Edmund Cody. "Some Confederate Letters: Alabama, Georgia, and Tennessee," *The Georgia Historical Quarterly* 21:2 (June 1937): 188–203.
Butchko, Thomas Russell. "Slade Tenant Houses," in *Martin Architectural Heritage: The Historic Structures of a Rural North Carolina County* (Martin County Historical Society, 1998).
Butler, John Campbell. *Historical Record of Macon and Central Georgia, Containing Many Interesting and Valuable Reminiscences Connected with the Whole State, Including Numerous Incidents and Facts Never before published and of Great Historical Value*, vol. iv (J. W. Burke & Co., 1879).
Callcott, George H. *A History of the University of Maryland* (Maryland Historical Society, 1966).
Campbell, Jesse Harrison. *Georgia Baptists: Historical and Biographical* (H. K. Ellyson, 1847).
Campion, Nardi Reeder. *Mother Ann Lee: Morning Star of the Shakers* (University Press of New England, 1990).
Carwardine, Richard. "Methodists, Politics, and the Coming of the American Civil War," *Church History* 69:3 (2000): 584.
Catalogue of the Linonian Society, Yale (B. L. Hamlen, 1841), 62.
Catalogue of the Members of the Dialectic Society, Instituted in the University of North Carolina, June the Third 1795, A. (North Carolina Standard, 1841).
Catalogue of the Trustees, Faculty, Alumni and Students of the Wesleyan Female College Macon, GA, 1850-1915, annual eds. (Benjamin F. Griffin, 1851-1915).

Catalogue of the Trustees, Officers, Alumni, and Matriculates of the University of Georgia at Athens, Georgia, 1785-1906 (E. D. Stone Press, 1906), from the Hargrett Rare Book & Manuscript Library.

Cawthon, William Lamar Cawthon. *Clinton: County Seat on the Georgia Frontier 1808-1821*, MA Thesis (University of Georgia, 1984).

Cecil County Directory, Maryland (1856).

Cecil Whig Elkton, MD, The. newspaper (Elkton, MD), 1856.

Cheli, Guy. *Sing Sing Prison* (Arcadia, 2003).

Child, Hamilton. *Gazetteer and Business Directory of Rensselaer County, N.Y., for 1870-71* (1870).

Christian Index, The, 1833-1840, newspaper (Washington, GA) and 1840 (Penfield, GA).

Christian, Schuyler Medlock. "A Sketch of the History of Science in Georgia," *The Georgia Review* 3:1 (Spring 1949): 57–69.

Chronicle and Sentinel, The, 1838-1838, newspaper (Augusta, GA).

Clark, Douglas K. *A History of the Cathedral of Saint John the Baptist, Savannah* (Diocese of Savannah, 1999).

Clark, Douglas K. *English Catholics at Locust Grove* (Diocese of Savannah, 1999).

Clarke, T. Wood. *Émigrés In The Wilderness* (The Macmillan Company, 1941).

Clayton, Augustin Smith. *A Compilation of the Laws of the State of Georgia, 1800-1810* (Adams and Duyckinck, 1813).

Coleman, Kenneth, ed. *A History of Georgia* (University of Georgia, 1977).

Coleman, Kenneth, and Charles Stephen Gurr, eds. "David Emanuel," in *Dictionary of Georgia Biography* (University of Georgia Press, 1983).

Columbian Centinel, 1790-1840, newspaper (Boston, MA).

Columbus Daily Times, The, 1875-1876, newspaper (Columbus, GA).

Columbus Enquirer, The, 1828-1861, newspaper (Columbus, GA).

Columbus Ledger, The, 1841-1882, newspaper (Columbus, GA).

Columbus Times, The, 1841-185?, newspaper (Columbus, GA).

Comenius, Johann Amos. *A Reformation of Schools* (London, 1642).

Comenius, Johann Amos. *Conatuum Comeniamorum Praeludia Ex Bibliotheca London* (1637).

Comenius, Johann Amos. *The Labyrinth of the World and the Paradise of the Heart*, trans. Howard Louthan and Andrea Sterk (New York, 1998).

Connelly, Owen. *The Gentle Bonaparte: A Biography of Joseph, Napoleon's Elder Brother* (Macmillan, 1968).

Cook, Anna Maria Green. *History of Baldwin County, Georgia* (Keys-Hearn Printing Company, 1925), 124.

Cook, James F. *The Governors of Georgia, 1754-2004*, 3rd ed. (Mercer University Press, 2005).

Corley, Florence Fleming. "The Presbyterian Quest: Higher Education for Georgia Women," *American Presbyterians* 69:2 (Summer 1991): 83–96.

Coulter, E. Merton. "A Georgia Educational Movement During the Eighteen Hundred Fifties," *The Georgia Historical Quarterly* 9:1 (March 1925): 1–33.

Cowie, Steven. *When Hell Came to Sharpsburg: The Battle of Antietam and Its Impact on the Civilians Who Called it Home* (Savas Beatie, 2023).

Crocker, Thomas E. *Empire's Eagles: The Fate of the Napoleonic Elite in America* (Prometheus, 2021).

Cruea, Susan M. "Changing Ideals of Womanhood During the Nineteenth Century Woman Movement," *General Studies Writing Faculty Publications* 1 (2005): 188.

Curtin-Kelly, Patricia. *An Ornament to the City: Holy Trinity Church and the Capuchin Order* (The History Press Ireland, 2015).

Daily Sun, The, 1855-1873, newspaper (Columbus, GA).

Darby, John. *Botany of the Southern States: Structural and Physiological Botany and Vegetable Products and Descriptions of Southern Plants* (A. S. Burnes & H. L. Burr, 1860).

Daughan, George C. *1812: The Navy's War* (Basic Books, 2011).

Dawson, William E. *Compilation of the Laws of the State of Georgia Passed by the General Assembly Since the Year 1819 to the Year 1829 Inclusive*, no. 10 (Grantland and Orme, 1831).

Dees, Anthony R. "Georgia, Catholic Church," in *The Encyclopedia of American Catholic History*, ed. Michael Glazier and Thomas J. Shelley (Liturgical Press, 1997).

Diffee, William Standard. *Columbus, Georgia in the Confederacy: The Social & Industrial Life of the Chattahoochee River Port* (William-Frederick Press, 1954).

Dodenhoff, Donna. "Jeremiah Slade Plantation," Survey Form and File (MT-415), North Carolina State Historic Preservation Office, Raleigh, NC, 1992.

Dooley, Brian. *Black and Green: The Fight for Civil Rights in Northern Ireland & Black America* (Pluto Press, 1998).

Dorman, Lewy. *Party Politics in Alabama from 1850 Through 1860* (University of Alabama Press, 1995).

DuBois, W. E. B. *The Negro Common School* (Atlanta, 1901).

Dyer, Thomas G. *The University of Georgia: A Bicentennial History, 1785-1985* (University of Georgia, 1985).

Ellison, William H., and John Darby. "The Georgia Female College: Its Origin, Plan and Prospects," *The Southern Ladies' Book* 1:2 (1840): 3–14.

England, John. "The Early History of the Diocese of Charleston," in *The Works of the Right Reverend John England, First Bishop of Charleston*, vol. iv, ed. Sebastian G. Messmer (Arthur H. Clark, 1908).

Evans, Frederick William. *Ann Lee (The Founder of the Shakers): A Biography with Memoirs of William Lee, James Whittaker, J. Hocknall, J. Meachem, and Lucy Wright* (HardPress, 2018).

Evans, Tad. *Greene Co., GA Newspaper Clippings, 1852-1873*, vol. I (Tad Evans, 1995).

Feldman, Benjamin. *East in Eden: William Niblo and His Pleasure Garden of Yore* (Wanderer Press, 2014).

Fisher, Sydney G. *The Quaker Colonies: History of the Early Quaker Settlements in New England and the Delaware River* (Pantianos, 1919).

Flanders, Bertram Holland. *Early Georgia Magazines: literary Periodicals to 1865* (University of Georgia Press, 2010).

Fowler, Henry. "Educational Services of Mrs. Emma Willard," Henry Barnard., ed., *Memoirs of Teachers, Educators, and Promoters and Benefactors of Education, Literature and Science* (New York, 1861), 167.

Francis, Richard. *Ann the Word: The Story of Ann Lee, Female Messiah, Mother of the Shakers, the Woman Clothed with the Sun* (Arcade, 2013).

Fredriksen, John C. *American Military Leaders*, vol. 1. (Bloomsbury, 1999).

Friedman, Jean E., and Rachel Mordecai Lazarus. *Ways of Wisdom: Moral Education in the Early National Period* (University of Georgia, 2001).

Gaeke, Robert A. *A History of the Narragansett Tribe of Rhode Island: Keepers of the Bay in American Chronicles*, series (The History Press, 2011).

Georgia Constitutionalist, The, newspaper (Augusta, GA).

Georgia Courier, The, 1826-1837, newspaper (Augusta, GA).

Georgia Department of Health and Vital Statistics; Atlanta, Georgia.

Georgia Historical Commission, "Clinton Female Seminary," 1956, Bronze Plaque, Clinton, GA.

Georgia Journal, The, 1812-1820, newspaper (Milledgeville, GA).

Georgia Journal and Messenger, newspaper, August 26, 1841 (Macon, GA).

Georgia Messenger, The, 1823-1847, newspaper (Ft. Hawkins, GA).

Georgia, Office of the Governor. Returns of qualified voters under the Reconstruction Act, 1867. Georgia State Archives, Morrow, Georgia.

Georgia State University Law Review, *Education HB 797* 29:1 (Fall 2012): 1–69.

Georgia Statesman, The, 1826, newspaper (Milledgeville, GA).

Georgia Telegraph, 1832-1835, newspaper (Macon, GA).

Georgia, U.S. *Central Register of Convicts, 1817–1976*. Series 21/3/27. Georgia State Archives.

Georgia, U.S. *Property Tax Digests, 1793-1892* [various years]. 140 volumes. Georgia Archives.

Georgia, U.S. *Returns of Qualified Voters and Reconstruction Oath Books, 1867-1869*. The Georgia Archives.

Gillentine, Flora Myers, ed. *Lineage Book*, vol. 110 (National Society of the Daughters of the American Revolution, 1929).

Goff, John. *Placenames in Georgia* (University of Georgia, 1975).

Gold, David, and Catherine L. Hobbs, *Rhetoric, History, and Women's Oratorical Education: American Women Learn to Speak* (Routledge, 2013).

Goldstein, Dana. *The Teacher Wars: A History of America's Most Embattled Profession* (Anchor, 2015).

Goloboy, Jennifer L. "Charleston and the Emergence of Middle-Class Culture in the Revolutionary Era," in the *Early American Places Series* (University of Georgia, 2016).

Gordon, John B. *Reminiscences of the Civil War* (Charles Scribner's Sons, 1904).

Gottfried, Bradley M. *The Maps of Antietam: An Atlas of the Antietam (Sharpsburg) Campaign, including the Battle of South Mountain September 2-20, 1862* (Savas Beatie, 2012).

Graham, George Washington. *The Mecklenburg Declaration of Independence, May 20, 1775 and Lives of its Signers* (University of Michigan, 1905).

Greenfield Gazette and Franklin Herald, newspaper (Greenfield, MA), October 4, 1831.

Griffin, Richard W. "Wesleyan College: Its Genesis, 1835-1840," *The Georgia Historical Quarterly* 50:1 (March 1966): 55.

Groen, Mark. "The Whig Party and the Rise of the Common Schools, 1837-1854," *American Educational History Educational Journal* 35:1–2 (March 2008): 254.

Guelzo, Allen C. *Gettysburg: The Last Invasion* (Vintage/Random House, 2014).

Hall, Mark David. "Beyond Self-interest: The Political Theory and Practice of Evangelical Women in Antebellum America," *Journal of Church and State* 44:3 (2002): 477–99.

Hamm, Thomas D. *Quaker Writings: An Anthology, 1650-1920* (Penguin, 2011).

Hanmer, Trudy J. *Wrought with Steadfast Will: A History of the Emma Willard School* (The Troy Book Makers, 2012).

"Hannah Adams (1755-1831)," in *Women in World History: A Biographical Encyclopedia*, vol. 1 (Pennsylvania State University, 1999).

Hargrett Rare Book and Manuscript Library, The University of Georgia Libraries.

Hartford Courant, newspaper, "Litchfield Female Seminary" (Hartford, CT), May 4, 1835.

Hartwig, D. Scott. *I Dread the Thought of the Place: The Battle of Antietam and the End of the Maryland Campaign* (Johns Hopkins, 2023).

Hassell, Cushing Biggs. *History of the Church of God, From the Creation to A.D. 1885: Including Especially the History of the Kehukee Primitive Baptist Association* (G. Beebe, 1886).

Hayes, Zach C. "Bishop George Foster Pierce," *The Georgia Review* 7:2 (1953): 156–63.

Hazzard, Florence Woolsey. "Women Pioneers in Democracy," *Pi Lambda Theta Journal* 28:2 (1949): 110.

Healey, Robynne Rogers. "Quakerism in the Atlantic World, 1690-1830," in *The New History of Quakerism*, vol. iii (Pennsylvania State University, 2022).

Hedge, Levi. *Elements of Logick, and Summary of General Principles of Different Modes of Reasoning* (Kessinger, 1824).

Hickey, Donald R. *The War of 1812: A Forgotten Conflict* (University of Illinois Press, 2012).

Hill, Michael. *The Governors of North Carolina* (North Carolina Office of Archives and History, 2007).

Hillhouse, Albert M. *A History of Burke County, Georgia, 1777-1950* (Spartanburg, 1950).

Historical Guide to Clinton, Georgia: An Early Nineteenth Century County Seat (Old Clinton Historical Society, 1975).

History of Rowe Street Baptist Church, Boston, MA with the Declaration of Faith and the Church Covenant, and a List of Members, 1853 (Legare Street Press, 2021).

History of Sing Sing Prison, The (Half Moon Press, 2000).

History of the Baptist Denomination in Georgia: With Biographical Compendium and Portrait Gallery of Baptist Ministers and other Georgia Baptists (J. P. Harrison & Co., 1881), 188.

Holt, Keri. *Reading These United States: Federal Literacy in the Early Republic, 1776-1830* (University of Georgia, 2019).

Hornblow, Arthur. *A History of the Theatre in America from its Beginnings to the Present Time*, 2 vols. (J. B. Lippincott Co., 1919).

Houston Home Journal, The, newspaper, 12 February 1914 (Perry, GA).

Huhner, Leon Huhner. "Captain Abraham Simons of the Georgia Line in the Revolution," *Publications of the American Jewish Historical Society*, No. 33 (1934).

Hull, A. L. *A Historical Sketch of the University of Georgia* (The Foote and Davies Co., 1894).

Huntzinger, Victoria MacDonald. "The Birth of Southern Public Education: Columbus, GA, 1864-1904," PhD thesis (Harvard, 1992).

Hutchinson, William H. *A Concise History of the Baldwin Place Baptist Church* (Legare Street Press, 2023).

Hynds, Ernest C. "William Carey Richards," in Sam G. Riley, ed., *American Magazine Journalists, 1741-1850* 73 (1988): 252-7.

Inman, Natalie R. "Brothers and Friends: Kinship in Early America," in the *Early American Places Series* (University of Georgia, 2017).

Intellectual Over Ornamental. "Female Character," *The Knickerbocker* 6:3 (September 1835): 209.

James, Edward T., Janet Wilson James, and Paul S. Boyer, eds. *Notable American Women, 1607-1950*, 3 vols. (Cambridge, 1971), vol. ii, 191–3.

Johnson, Rossiter, and John Howard Brown, eds. "Andrew, James Osgood," in *The Biographical Dictionary of America*, vol. 1 (American Biographical Society, 1906), 114–15.

Jones, Robert C. *History of Georgia Railroads* (History Press, 2017).

Jones County Court Records, various, 1824-1839.

Jones County News, newspaper (Clinton, Georgia, 1908).

Kantar, Dilek, "Virgins, Wives and Whores in the Eighteenth-century Ironic Myths," *Interactions* 23:1–2 (2014): 123.

Keith, Patrick. *Through Colonialism and Imperialism: The Struggle for Tuscarora Nationhood in Southeastern North Carolina*, M.A. Thesis (University of Arizona, 2005).

Kerber, Linda K. *Intellectual History of Women: Essays by Linda K. Kerber* (University of North Carolina Press, 1997).

Kerber, Linda K. "The Republican Mother: Women and the Enlightenment--An American Perspective," *American Quarterly* 28:2 (1976): 187–205.

Kerber, Linda K. *Women of the Republic: Intellect and Ideology in Revolutionary America* (University of North Carolina Press, 1980).

Kleinberg, S. J. *Women in the United States, 1830-1945* (Rutgers University Press, 1999).

Klepp, Susan E. *Revolutionary Conceptions: Women, Fertility, and Family Limitation in America, 1760-1820* (University of North Carolina, 2009).

Knight, Lucian Lamar. *Georgia's Landmarks, Memorials, and Legends* (Byrd Printing, 1913).

Kokomoor, Kevin. "Creeks, Federalists, and the Idea of Coexistence in the Early Republic," *Journal of Southern History* 81:4 (2015): 803–42.

Krakow, Kenneth K. *Georgia Place-Names: Their History and Origins* (Winship Press, 1975).

Kvacala, Johannes Radomil. "The Educational Reform of Comenius in Germany up to the End of the XVIIth c," Karl Kehrbach, ed., in *Monumenta Germaniae Paedagogica*, Vol. 32 (Berlin, 1904).

Lamar, John E., and Ben Yarborough. *Reminiscences of John E. Lamar: Early History of Columbus, Georgia* (Sunshine, 2013).

Larson, John Lauritz. *Internal Improvement: National Public Works and the Promise of Popular Government in the Early United States* (University of North Carolina, 2001).

Lathrop, Sallie B. Comer. *The Comer Family Goes to Town* (Birmingham Printing Co., 1942).

Laurie, S. S. *John Amos Comenius: Bishop of the Moravians* (Cambridge, 1904).

Lawrence, Brian D. *The Relationship between the Methodist Church, Slavery and Politics, 1784–1844* (Rowan University, 2018).

Lawson, John. *A New Voyage to Carolina; Containing the Exact Description and Natural History of that Country: Together with the Present State thereof and a Journal of a Thousand Miles Traveled through Several Nations of Indians, Giving a Particular Account of their Customs, Manners, etc.* (London, 1709).

Levasseur, Auguste, *Lafayette in America: 1824 and 1825*, trans. Alan R. Hoffman (Lafayette Press, Inc., 2006).

Long, Huey B. *Early Innovators in Adult Education* (Routledge, 1991).

Long, Julie Whidden. *Portraits of Courage: Stories of Baptist Heroes* (Mercer University Press, 2008).

Lord, John. *The Life of Emma Willard* (D. Appleton & Co., 1873).

Loto, Judith Livingston. "One Voice: The Work and Words of Litchfield Female Academy Student Charlotte Hopper Newcomb, 1809-1810," *Dublin Seminar for New England Folklife Annual Proceedings* 27 (July 2002): 65–77.

Lucas, S. Emmett. *The Third or 1820 Land Lottery of Georgia* (Southern Historical Press, 2005).

Lutz, Alma Lutz. *Emma Willard: Pioneer Educator of American Women* (Beacon Press, 1967).

Macon Advertiser and Agricultural and Mercantile Intelligencer, The, 1831-1832, newspaper (Macon, GA).

Macon Georgia Telegraph, 1836-1844, newspaper (Macon, GA).

Mahan, Joseph B. *Columbus: Georgia's Fall Line "Trading Town"* (Windsor Publications, 1986).

Mahan, Katherine Hines, and William Clyde Woodall. *A History of Public Education in Muscogee County and the City of Columbus, 1828-1976* (Muscogee County Board of Education, 1977).

Mahon, John K. *History of the Second Seminole War, 1835-1842* (University of Florida, 1967).

Manganiello, Christopher J. *Southern Water, Southern Power: How the Politics of Cheap Energy and Water Scarcity Shaped a Region* (University of North Carolina Press, 2015).

Marriage Records from Select Counties, 1811-1828, State of Georgia Archives, Morrow, Georgia, County Marriage Records, Jones County, Book 11, 244.

Martin, John H. "The Making of a Modern City: Columbus, Georgia, 1827-65," vol. II (1875).

Massachusetts Charitable Mechanic Association. *Annals of the Massachusetts Charitable Mechanic Association, 1795–1892 Printed by Order of the Association* (Press of Rockwell and Churchill, 1892).

Massey, Mary Elizabeth. *Bonnet Brigades* (New York, 1966).

Mather, Cotton. *Magnalia Christi Americana: or, The Ecclesiastical History of New-England, from its First Planting in the Year 1620. unto the Year of Our Lord, 1698* (London, 1702).

McCarthy, Jr., J. Patrick. "Commercial Development and University Reform in Antebellum Athens: William Mitchell as Entrepreneur, Engineer, and Educator," *The Georgia Historical Quarterly* 83:1 (Spring 1999): 1–28.

McInnis, Edward, "The Spartan Woman: Symbol for an Age?" *American Educational History Journal* 43:1/2 (2016): 195–210.

McNally, Michael J. "Catholic Parish Life in the Antebellum South: Columbus, Georgia, 1830-60," *American Catholic Studies* 113:1/2 (Spring-Summer 2002): 1–30.

McPherson, James M. *Crossroads of Freedom: Antietam* (Oxford, 2002).

Mewborn, Denise. "Public Education," *The New Georgia Encyclopedia* (2020).
Miller, Stephen F. *The Bench and Bar of Georgia: Memoirs and Sketches*, vol. i (J. P. Lippincott & Co., 1858).
Miller, Timothy E. *Gold for Secrets: The Hartlib Circle and The Early English Empire, 1630-1660*, DPhil thesis (Oxford, 2020).
Miller, Timothy E. *Pleasure, Honor, And Profit: Samuel Hartlib in His Papers 1620-1662*, MA thesis (Georgia State University, 2015).
Muster Rolls of the soldiers of the War of 1812: Detached from the Militia of North Carolina in 1812 and 1814 (C. Raboteau, 1851).
National Archives, Washington, DC, Records of the United States Census.
National Tribune, The, newspaper (Washington, DC).
Neem, Johann N. *Democracy's School: The Rise of Public Education in America* (Johns Hopkins, 2017).
New Orleans Times-Picayune, newspaper (New Orleans, LA).
New York Daily Herald, newspaper (New York, NY).
New York Times, newspaper (New York, NY).
Newnan Herald, The. newspaper, 1865-1887 (Newnan, GA).
North Carolina Land Grants. Microfilm publication, 770 rolls. North Carolina State Archives, Raleigh, North Carolina.
North Carolina, U.S., State Census, 1784-1787.
Northern, William J. *Men of Mark in Georgia*, 7 vols. (Spartanburg, 1907).
Norton, Mary Beth, *Liberty's Daughters: The Revolutionary Experience of American Women, 1750-1800* (Cornell University Press, 1980).
O'Connell, Deirdre. *The Ballad of Blind Tom* (Overlook Press, 2009).
Olmstead, Frederick Law. *A Journey in the Seaboard Slave States* (Dix & Edwards, 1856).
Original Will Records (Mobile County, Alabama), Ca. 1813-1961; Index, 1813-1957, Alabama. Probate Court, Probate Place: Mobile, Alabama.
Orr, Dorothy, *The History of Public Education in Georgia* (n.p., 1950).
Penfield Baptist Church Book of Minutes, 1839-1892. Archival material, Mercer University Libraries.
Peters, Robert. *Shaker Light: Mother Ann Lee in America* (Unicorn, 1987).
Pichnarcik, Lisa Roberge. "On the Threshold of Improvement: Women's Education at the Litchfield Female and Morris Academies," *Connecticut History* 27 (September 1996): 129–58.
Pichnarcik, Lisa Roberge. *The Role of Books in Connecticut Women's Education in the New Republic: As Examined in Sarah Pierce's Litchfield Female Academy and James*

Morris' Coeducational Academy. Master's thesis (Southern Connecticut State University, 1996).

Pierce, George Foster. *The Southern Ladies' Book*, magazine, various issues (1840).

Pierson, John Bennett. *A Journey of Slades: From England to Ravenswood Plantation, Washington County, Alabama* (2015).

Plattes, Gabriel. Printed Pamphlet, *A Description of the Famous Kingdome of Macaria* (Samuel Hartlib, 1641). The Hartlib Papers.

Plumer, Richard. *Charlotte and the American Revolution: Reverend Alexander Craighead, the Mecklenburg Declaration and the Foothills Fight for Independence* (The History Press, 2014).

Polhill, John G. "Pleadings and Evidence in The Trial of Elijah Barber, Otherwise Called Jesse L. Bunkley, for Cheating and Swindling," in *The Making of the Modern Law: Trials, 1600-1926*. Milledgeville, Georgia (The Federal Union Office, 1838).

Pulliam, John D., and James J. van Patten. *History of Education in America*, 9th ed. (Pearson, 2006).

Purifoy, Lewis M. "The Southern Methodist Church and the Proslavery Argument," *The Journal of Southern History* 32:3, Southern Historical Association (August 1966): 325-41.

Raleigh Minerva, The, newspaper (Raleigh, NC).

Randall, Willard Sterne. *Unshackling America: How the War of 1812 Truly Ended the American Revolution* (St. Martin's Press, 2017).

Ready, Milton. *The Tar Heel State: A New History of North Carolina* (University of South Carolina Press, 2020).

Rees, Frances. "A History of Wesleyan Female College from 1836 to 1874," M.A. thesis (Emory University, 1935), 11.

Rice, Thaddeus Brocket, and Carolyn White Williams. *History of Greene County, Georgia, 1786-1886* (J. W. Wilkes Publishing Co., 1973).

Richardson, Jr., Robert C. *West Point: An Early History, 1776-1917* (Ind. published, 2019).

Rittner, Don. *Legendary Locals of Troy* (Arcadia, 2012).

Rittner, Don. *Remembering Troy: Heritage on the Hudson* (History Press, 2008).

Rittner, Don. *Troy Through Time* (America Through Time, 2017).

Roberts, L. E. "Educational Reform in Ante-Bellum Georgia," *The Georgia Review* 16:1 (Spring 1962): 68-82.

Robbins, Sarah. "'The Future Good and Great of our Land': Republican Mothers, Female Authors, and Domesticated Literacy in Antebellum New England," *New England Quarterly* 75:4 (2002): 562-91.

Roosevelt, Theodore. *The Naval War of 1812* (G. P. Putnam's Sons, 1882).

Ross, Michael. *The Reluctant King: Joseph Bonaparte: King of the Two Sicilies and Spain* (Sidgwick and Jackson, 1976).

Ruffin-Roulhac-Hamilton Papers, 1784-1957, in the Southern Historical Collection at the University of North Carolina, Chapel Hill.

Russell, Kate Esary. "William Carey Richards and the Orion," Thesis (University of Georgia, 1987), World Cat (17464386).

Sawyer, Ray C., ed. *Deaths Published in the Christian Intelligencer of the Reformed Dutch Church from 1830 to 1871*, vol. v. (1933).

Semi-Centennial Exercises, "Memorials of Methodism" in Macon, GA, 1828-1878 (J. W. Burke and Company, 1878).

Schmitt, Sunya Kirstin Slade. Email, August 8, 2024.

Scott, Anne Firor. "The Ever-Widening Circle: The Diffusion of Feminist Values from the Troy Female Seminary 1822–1872," *History of Education Quarterly* 19:1 (1979): 9.

Scott, Anne Firor. *The Southern Lady* (Chicago, 1970).

Scott, Anne Firor. "What, Then, is the American: This New Woman?" *The Journal of American History* 65:3 (December 1978): 679–703.

Scot, Anne Firor, Lucy T. Townsend, and Barbara Wiley, eds., *The Papers of Emma Hart Willard, 1787-1870*. ProQuest Research Collections in Microform (Ann Arbor, MI, 2005).

Sears, Stephen W. *Landscape Turned Red: The Battle of Antietam* (Mariner Books, 1993).

Simpson, Richard V., *Historic Tales of Colonial Rhode Island: Aquidneck Island and the Founding of the Ocean State* in American Chronicles, series (The History Press, 2012).

Skewarkee Lodge, *Minutes*, 1873-1895, Williamston, NC.

Skewarkey Primitive Baptist Church Records, 1785-1950, Martin County, North Carolina Church Records.

Slade Family Papers, 1751-1929, David M. Rubenstein Rare Book and Manuscript Library, Duke University.

Slade, Richard Taylor. "Slade Family," in Francis M. Manning and W. H. Booker, eds., *Martin County History*, vol. 1 (Williamston Enterprise Publishing Co., 1977).

Slade, Thomas Bog. various personal letters, 1819, Columbus State University Archives, Columbus, Georgia, donated by Seymour Slade Dozier, October 15, 1933.

Slappey, George H. "Early Foundations of Georgia's System of Common School Education," *The Georgia Historical Quarterly* 14:2 (June 1930): 139-49.

Smith, George Gilman. *The History of Georgia Methodism from 1786 to 1866* (A. R. Caldwell, 1913).

Smith, George Gilman. *The Life and letters of James Osgood Andrew* (Southern Methodist Publishing House, 1882), 311-12.

Smith, Robert Lawrence. *A Quaker Book of Wisdom: Life Lessons in Simplicity, Service, and Common Sense* (William Morrow, 2013).

Sobel, Robert. *Biographical Dictionary of the Governors of the United States, 1789-1978*, vol. iii (Meckler Books, 1978).

Solomon, Barbara Miller, *In the Company of Educated Women: A History of Women and Higher Education in America* (Yale, 1986).

Southern Confederacy, 1861-1865, newspaper (Macon, GA).

Southern Eclectic, The, newspaper (Augusta, GA).

Southern Post, newspaper (Macon, GA).

Southern Recorder, 1820-1872, newspaper (Milledgeville, GA).

Spady, James O'Neil. *Education and the Racial Dynamics of Settler Colonialism in Early America: Georgia and South Carolina, ca. 1700-ca. 1820* (Routledge, 2020).

Sparks, W. H. *The Atlanta Constitution* (June 25, 1881).

Stacy, James. *A History of the Presbyterian Church in Georgia* (Elberton, 1912).

Stanley, C. M. "The Petite Mother of Six Distinguished Sons," *The Alabama Journal* (Montgomery, 1889-1993).

Stanton, Elizabeth Cady. "Emma Willard, the Pioneer in the Higher Education of Women," *Westminster Review* 140:1 (January 1852-January 1914): 538.

Steelman, Peggy S. "Growth and Development of the Georgia Education Association," PhD dissertation (University of Georgia, 1966).

Stevens, Peter F. *Hidden Histories of the Boston Irish: Little Known Stories from Ireland's "Next Parish Over"* (The History Press, 2008).

Stow, Baron. *A History of the English Baptist Mission to India* (American Sunday School Union, 1835).

Strasser, Gerhard F. "Das Erbe von Johann Amos Comenius und Samuel Hartlib: Tagungen in Bayreuth, Prag und Sheffield," *Berichte zur Wissenschaftsgeschichte* 16:3-4 (1993): 293-5.

Stroud, Patricia Tyson. *The Man Who Had Been King: The American Exile of Napoleon's Brother Joseph* (University of Pennsylvania, 2014).

Sullivan, Buddy, *Georgia: A State History* (Arcadia, 2010).

Swanton, John R. "The Indians of the Southeastern United States," Smithsonian Institution, *Bureau of American Ethnology Bulletin 137* (Washington, DC, 1946).

Swint, Henry Lee. *Dear Ones at Home: Letters from Contraband Camps* (Vanderbilt, 1966).

Tager, Jack. *Boston Riots: Three Centuries of Social Violence* (Northeastern, 2001).

Taylor, Alan. *The Civil War of 1812: American Citizens, British Subjects, Irish Rebels, and Indian Allies* (Vintage, 2011).

Telegraph, The. 1824-1840, newspaper (Macon, GA).

Telfair, Nancy. *A History of Columbus, Georgia 1828-1928* (Historical Publishing Co., 1929).

Temperence Crusader, The. 1834-1861, newspaper (Penfield, GA).

Thompson, Ernest Trice. *Presbyterians in the South*, vol. i (John Knox Press, 1963), 263.

Thompson Jr., Scott B. "The Prentiss of Georgia," in *Pieces of Our Past* (Scott B. Thompson, 2014).

Thomson, Eunice. "Ladies Can Learn," *The Georgia Review* 1:2 (Summer 1947): 189–97.

Thornton III, J. Mills. *Politics and Power in a Slave Society: Alabama, 1800-1860* (Louisiana State University Press, 1978).

Throwbridge, Francis Bacon. *The Champion Genealogy: A History of the Descendants of Henry Champion of Saybrook and Lyme, CT Together with Some Account of Other Families of the Name*, vol. I (1891).

Times-Picayune, The, newspaper (New Orleans, LA).

Tocqueville, Alexis de. *Democracy in America*, ed. Henry Steele Commager (London, 1946), 377.

Torrey, Clarence A. *New England Marriages Prior to 1700* (Genealogical Publishing Co., 2004).

Trattner, Lisa Trattner. "The Complexities of a Nineteenth-Century Icon: Emma Hart Willard," PhD dissertation (Notre Dame of Maryland University, 2021).

Triennial Catalogue of the Philo Technian Society of Williams College, 1844 (J. C. Kneeland & Co., 1844).

Trigger, Bruce G., ed. *Northeast*, vol. 15 of *Handbook of North American Indians*, ed. William C. Sturtevant (Smithsonian Institution, 1978).

Trollope, Fanny. *Domestic Manners of the Americans* (Whittaker, Treacher, and Co., 1832).

Troy Budget, The. 1828-1840, newspaper (Troy, NY), January 2, 1837.

Tucker, Edward L. "Two Young Brothers and Their *Orion*," *The Southern Literary Journal* 11:1 (1978): 64-80.
Turnbull, George Henry. *Hartlib, Dury and Comenius: Gleanings from Hartlib's Papers* (London, 1947).
Turnbull, George Henry. *Samuel Hartlib: A Sketch of His Life and His Relations to J. A.Comenius* (Oxford, 1920).
Ulrich, Laurel Thatcher. *A Midwife's Tale: The Life of Martha Ballard, Based on Her Diary, 1785-1812* (Vintage, 1990).
United States Census 1790-1900 (United State Census Bureau).
U.S. Congress, Senate and House of Representatives. *American State Papers, Indian Affairs* (Gales and Seaton, 1832).
U.S., *Pardons Under Amnesty Proclamations, 1865-1869* (National Archives).
Vanderpoel, Emily Noyes, and Elizabeth C. Barney Buel, ed. *Chronicles of a Pioneer School, from 1792 to 1833 being the History of Miss Sarah Pierce and Her Litchfield School* (Harvard, 1903).
Varney, Helen, and Joyce Beebe Thompson. *A History of Midwifery in the United States* (Springer, 2015).
Varon, Elizabeth R. *Longstreet: The Confederate General Who Defied the South* (Simon & Schuster, 2023).
Vicksburg Daily Whig, The, newspaper (Vicksburg, MS).
Von Frank, Albert J. "Sarah Pierce and the Poetic Origins of Utopian Feminism in America," *Prospects* 14 (October 1989): 45-63.
Walker, Anne Kendrick. *Backtracking in Barbour County: A Narrative of the Last Alabama Frontier* (The Dietz Press, 1941).
Walker, Anne Kendrick. *Braxton Bragg Comer: His Family Tree* (The Dietz Press, 1947).
Wallace, Anthony F. C. "The Modal Personality Structure of the Tuscarora Indians," Smithsonian Institution, *Bureau of American Ethnology Bulletin 150* (Washington, DC, 1952).
Wallace, Anthony F. C. *Tuscarora: A History* (SUNY Press, 2012).
Walsh, Anthony. "The American Tour of Dr. Spurzheim," *Journal of the History of Medicine and Allied Sciences* 27 (1972): 187–205.
Watchtower, alumnae newspaper, 1924-1946 (Wesleyan College).
Watson, Marston. "Royal Families: Americans of Royal and Noble Ancestry," vol. 2. *Reverend Francis Marbury and Five Generations of the Descendants Through Anne (Marbury) Hutchinson and Katherine (Marbury) Scott* (Genealogical Publishing Co., 2004).

Weekly Chronicle and Sentinel, 1824-1840, newspaper (Augusta, GA).

Weekly Standard, The. 2 January 1839. newspaper (Raleigh, NC).

Weekly Sun, The, 1841-1882, newspaper (Columbus, GA).

Weeks, Stephen B., ed. *Index to the Colonial and State Records of North Carolina* (Nash Brothers, 1909).

Weissman, Rebecca, "The Role of White Supremacy Amongst Opponents and Proponents of Mass Schooling in the South during the Common School Era," *Paedogogica Historica* 55:5 (October 2019): 703–23.

Wesleyan College. "Minutes of the Board of Trustees of the Georgia Female College and the Wesleyan Female College (from 1842), 1836-1844," Wesleyan College Archives, The Lucy Lester Willet Memorial Library.

White, Gale, "A Town Progress Passed By," *The Atlanta Journal and Constitution Magazine* (June 22, 1975): 12–14, 19–20.

White, George. *Historical Collections of Georgia* (Heritage Papers, 1854).

Wiggins, Elizabeth Slade. *Family Bible*.

Willard, Emma Hart. *Abridged History of the United States; or Republic of America,* new and enlarged ed. (A.S. Barnes & Co., 1855).

Willard, Emma Hart. *An Address to the Public; Particularly to the Members of the Legislature of New York, Proposing A Plan for Improving Female Education* (J. W. Copeland, 1819).

Willard, Emma Hart. Family Papers, MA. 00308. Amherst College Archives and Special Collections. Amherst College Library.

William Letcher Mitchell Papers, Southern Historical Collection, University of North Carolina Library, Chapel Hill.

Williams, Carolyn White. *The History of Jones County, Georgia, 1807-1907* (J. W. Burke, 1957).

Wills, 1774-1867, County Court of Pleas and Quarter Sessions (Martin County, NC), Book 1 and 2.

Wilmington Morning Star, The. November 28, 1876. newspaper (Wilmington, NC).

Wilson, James Grant, and John Fiske, eds. *Appleton's Cyclopedia of American Biography, 1600-1889,* vol. ii (Appleton, 1887), 76.

Winship, A. W. "Emma Willard," *The Journal of Education* 109:25 (June 1929): 703.

Winterer, Caroline. "Women and Civil Society: An Introduction," *Journal of the Early Republic* 28:1 (2008): 23–8.

Wollstonecraft, Mary. *A Vindication of the Rights of Woman* (Peter Edes for Thomas and Andrews, 1792).

Wood, Gordon S. *Empire of Liberty: A History of the Early Republic, 1789-1815* (Oxford, 2011).

Woodall, W. C., "The First of the Slades," in Jones – Muscogee Counties, Georgia Biographies, *Columbus Ledger* (January 6, 1964).

Woody, Thomas. *A History of Women's Education in the United States* (The Science Press, 1929).

Worsley, Etta Blanchard. *Columbus on the Chattahoochee* (Columbus Office Supply Co., 1951).

Zagari, Rosemarie. "Morals, Manners, and the Republican Mother," *American Quarterly* 44:2 (1992): 192–215.

Index

Adams, Hannah   125
Adams, John Quincy   67, 90
Adventists   183
Alcott, Louisa May   199
Alexander, Ashton   107, 108
Alexander, Elam   162, 185
American Colonization Society of the City of New York   112
American Journal of Science   130
American North Carolina House of Commons   9
American Revolution   12, 15, 198
Andrew, James Osgood   148-9, 151-2, 158, 161, 177
Anglican Church in North Carolina   12
Antoinette, Marie   103
Arminius, Jacobus   176
Armstrong, J. W.   183
Arnold, William   143, 148, 151, 152, 158
Articles of Confederation   126
The Atlanta Constitution   70
The Atlanta Journal and Constitution   74
The Augusta Chronicle   81
Azilum   103

Bacon, Francis   79
Baker, John   214
Baldwin, Abraham   37
Baldwin County   43, 152
Barbary pirates   103
Barber, Elijah   56
Barhamville Collegiate Institute   121
Barnett, John Nathaniel   217
Barnett, Lucy A.   217
Barnum, P. T.   105
Battle of Alamance   12
Battle of Atlanta   70
Battle of Bennington   125
Battle of Churubusco   23-4
Battle of Griswoldville   73

Battle of Padierna   23-4
Battle of Sharpsburg   234-5
Battle of Stoney Point   107
Battle of the Wilderness   235
Battle of Yorktown   107
Beall, Elias H.   179-80
Beall, James M.   170
Beall, Robert Augustus   146, 153, 157-9
Beecher, Lyman   126
Beman, Carlisle Pollock   75-7, 81
Bennett, Robert G.   83
Bernard, H. R.   197-9
Bethlehem Female Seminary   166
Bethune, Frances Eudora Gunby (1805-1858)   213
Bethune, James Neil   213, 215
Bethune, Joseph Daniel   215
blacks
    education   231-2
    exclusion from white schools   231
    black schools   242-3
        Yankee teachers   243
Blount, Elizabeth   87
Blount, Eugenia Dorothy   184
Blount, Henry Benjamin, Jr.   15
Blunt, Tom   16
Bog, Hannah Blount   15
Bog, Thomas (1740-77)   4, 15
Bogue, Virgil T.   15
Bogue and Allied Families (Bogue)   15
Bonaparte, Joseph   104-5
Bonaparte, Napoleon   104-5
Booker, W. H.   4
Boston   124
Boston Phrenological Society   125
Bowen, Thomas   202
Brace, John Pierce   126
Brantley, W. T.   202
Britain   120-1
Broad Street Riot   124

Brockman United Academy 199
Brown, Joseph E. 233-4
Brown, Robert C. 75
Buchanan, James 213
Buckingham, James Silk 166
Bullock, Charles 41
Bunkley, Elizabeth Flewellen Slatter 55, 56
Bunkley, Jesse Lucas 55-6
Bunkley, William Dawson, Jr. 55
Bunkley, William Dawson, Sr. 55-6
Burnett, Jesse Montreville Lafayette 232-3
Burr, Aaron 68, 106
Butler, John Campbell 73, 164-5

Calvin, John 176
Calwell, J. M. 121
Campbell, Duncan G. 38-9, 143-4
Campbell, Jesse Harrison 83, 176, 248-9
Carhart, Amory Sibley 218
Carhart, George Beavers 218
Catherine L. Comer Chair of Fine Arts 72
Cawthon, William Lamar 44
Chambers, James M. 233-4
Chandler, Daniel 144
Chappell, A. H. 147
Child, Hamilton 109-10
Christian, Schuyler Medlock 184
The Christian Index 186, 199, 202, 219
Church, Alonzo 75, 81
Clark, John 38
Clarke, John 57
Claxton, Timothy 124
Clinton (Boys) Academy 3, 42, 47, 53-4, 57-62, 83, 85
Clinton (Georgia) Boys Academy 3
Clinton, DeWitt 113, 118-19
Clinton Female Seminary 42, 54, 59-64, 68-9, 74, 101-2, 128-9, 131
   academic term 64
   boarding 62, 115
   closure 89
   controversy 89
   curriculum 128
   moral integrity rules 64

   physical description 115
   prayer (song) 64-5
   students 62, 115
   tuition 62-3
   vision 62
Clopton, Alfred 162
Clower, Peter 57
Codman, John 124
Cody, Edmund 232-3
Cody, Henrietta Sarah 232-3
Collins, Robert 146, 153, 154, 158, 159, 161
Colquitt, Alfred H. 167
Colquitt, Walter 153, 156-8, 167
Columbia Garden 105
Columbian College 175
Columbus, Christopher 211
Columbus, Georgia 211-49
   economic depression of 1837 214-15
   Plelan Plan 212
   population 212, 230
   schools 213-14
   teachers 212-14
   textile production 212, 229-30
Columbus Daily Enquirer-Sun 248
Columbus Enquirer 212, 221
Columbus Enquirer-Sun 213
Columbus Female Institute; *see* Slade Female Institute
Columbus Female Seminary 241
Columbus Free School 241-3
Columbus Ledger 213
Columbus Times 213, 247
Combe, George 112
Comenius, John Amos 119-20
Comer, Bragg 70, 71
Comer, Catherine Lucinda Drewry "Lizzie" 69-72
Comer, Edward Trippe 72
Comer, George Legare 71
Comer, Hugh Moss 70
Comer, John Fletcher 69, 71
Comer, John Wallace 70-1
Comer Loan Fund 72
Committee on Public Education and Free Schools 39
common schools 39

Compendium of Natural Philosophy
  (Olmstead) 130
Cook, James 234
Cook, Samuel 57
Corley, Florence Fleming 111, 142, 164
cotton 14
  donations of 234
Cowles, Jerry 146, 153, 154, 158, 160, 180–1
Creek Indians 90, 211; *see also* Muscogee (Creek) Indians
Cunningham, Russell M. 71
Curtis, Thomas 203–5

The Daily Sun 231
Daily Times 248
Darby, John Gould 183–5
Davant, James 206
Davenport, John 120, 130–1
Dearborn, Henry 16, 43
Declaration of Independence 126
Deming, Julius 126
Denson, Mary Elizabeth 86
De Russy, René Edward 107
de Tocqueville, Alexis 111
Dickens, Charles 104
Dickerman, Mariah Frances 205–6
Downing, Lemuel Tyler 216
Dudley, Edward Bishop 107–8
Dury, John 119, 120

Eagle Mill 229, 241, 243
Eaton, Amos 108–9
Eaton, Theophilus 130
Eldred, Elisabeth Miller 13
Eldred, Samuel 13
Elim Baptist Church 83, 102
Ellis, Roswell 228–9, 243–4
Ellison, William H. 166, 170, 181–2, 185
Emancipation Proclamation 235
Emory College, Oxford 142, 185
Epping, Henry H. 231
Evans, Rufus K. 162
Everett, James 185

Female Institute; *see* Slade Female Institute
female teachers 215, 241

Few, Ignatius 147, 148, 150–2, 158
First Baptist Church of Columbus 216, 238, 248
First Great Awakening 142, 183
Flewellen, Abner H. 89, 164, 184, 218, 224
Flewellen, William 50
Florence, Italy 105
Flournoy, William 197
Fogle, Theodore Turner 235
Forsyth, John 212
Fort, Martha C. 162
Fort, William 162
Foster, Sarah R. 122
Franklin, Benjamin 75
Franklin College 75, 142, 144
Freedmen's Bureau 232
Freeman, Eunice Frances 169–70
free public schools 247
Friends of the College 185
Fuller, Andrew 176

Gainer, Benjamin 12
Gainer, Edward 15
Gaines, Edmund P. 67–8
Gautier, Théophile 101
gender-specific education 116
Gentry, David C. 65
George III 15
Georgia Baptist Convention 197, 199–202
Georgia Baptists: Historical and Biographical (Campbell) 248
The Georgia Constitutionalist 75
Georgia Female College 3, 106, 131, 141–88, 216
  accommodations 115
  aids and instruments 115
  amenities 115
  building 162–3
  classes 88
  foundation 88
  matriculation ceremony 164–5
  solicitor 145
  trustees 58, 152–64
The Georgia Illustrated Magazine 199
Georgia Journal 57–8

Georgia Journal and Messenger 40
Georgia Messenger 41, 87, 89, 101,
   145–6, 153, 158–9, 197
Georgian architecture 12
Georgia Teachers Association 1
Georgia Teachers Convention 75–82, 87–8
Georgia Teachers' Society 81, 114
Georgia Telegraph 146–7
Gignilliat, Helen M. 241
Gordon, John B. 217–18
Grant, Ulysses S. 235
Great Awakening 182–3
   First 142, 183
   Second 142, 182, 232
Greece 112–13
Greene, General Nathanael 199
Greene, Lemuel 206
Greene County, Georgia 199–200
Greensborough Academy 199
Gregory, Ossian 153, 154, 157, 161, 162, 184
Griswold, Marcy S. 167, 169, 170
Griswold, Samuel 48, 53, 58–61, 73, 169

Hallenbeck, Garret (1797–1868) 213
Halley's Comet 130
Hamilton, Alexander 68, 106
Hamilton, Everard 153, 154, 158, 161, 185
Hamilton, Thomas 47, 57
Hancock, Chief 16
Hanson, James B. 208
Hantute, Madam Salmon 121
Hardaway, Robert S. 214
Hardeman, Thomas 162, 169
Hartlib, Samuel 78, 82, 118, 119–20, 122, 130–1, 257
Hartlib Circle 78, 122, 130
Hartlibian Empirical Project of Scientific Improvement 131
Hassell, Cushing Biggs (1809–80) 21–2
   History of the Church of God 22
Hassell, Martha Biggs 21
Havemeyer, Henry O. 106
Hawkins, Benjamin 42
Heber, Reginald 211
Henderson, Mary Ann 22–3
Henderson, Maurice 65–6

Henderson, William F. 22–3, 66
Hendrick, Gustaves 58
Historical Record of Macon and Central Georgia (Butler) 164–5
History of the Church of God (Hassell) 22
A History of the English Baptist Mission to India (Stow) 125
Hodges, Samuel K. 147, 148, 150–2, 158, 161
Hoffman, Charles Fenno 147
Hopkins, B. B. 145
Howard, John 146, 147, 159–60
Howard, Oliver Otis 60–1
Howard, Thacker B. 234
Howell, Clark 70
Hudson, Sarah Lucretia 122
Huntington, Rufus 58
Hyde, J. L. 58

Ianua (Comenius) 120
Indian Removal Act 211
institutions/organizations 111–13
Introduction to Arithmetic (Smith) 131
Introduction to Astronomy (Olmstead) 130
Introduction to Natural Philosophy (Olmstead) 130
Ireland 82

Jackson, Andrew 45, 68, 108, 211
James Everetts Scholarships 185
Jefferson, Thomas 16
Jenkins, Charles J. 200
Jernigan, Amanda C. 216, 218
Jernigan, Ann Eliza 218
Jewett, George 153, 155, 157–8, 161, 170
Johnson, Andrew 25
Johnson, E. L. H. 204
Johnson, Robert 199
Jones County, Georgia 28, 40, 42–61, 63, 69, 73–4, 83, 85, 164, 174
Josiah Penfield Fund 206
Judson, Adoniram 202

Kehokee Primitive Baptist Association 21–2
Kellogg, Gardner 75, 76, 81

Kells, Elias M.   70
Key, Madison Troup   218
Kilpatrick, Hugh Judson   60-1
Knickerbocker   147, 203

Lafayette, Marquis de   103
Lafayette Hall Academy   199
LaGrange Female Academy   214
Lamar, Henry G.   58, 59, 73, 87, 146, 147, 150, 153-6, 184, 187
Lamar, Ida Lochram   157
Lamar, John T.   59
Lamar, Mirabeau B.   213
Lamar, Walter D.   184
Land Lottery   211
Lathrop, Sallie Comer   69, 71
Lawson, John   17-18
Lee, Henry "Lighthorse Harry"   212
Lee, Robert E.   212, 234
liberal arts curriculum   2
Lincoln, Abraham   235
Lincoln, Almira Hart   109
Litchfield Female Academy, Connecticut   108, 126, 128-9
Little Girls' School   166
Livy, Caroline   121
Locke, John   119
Lomax, Tennet   217-18
Longstreet, Augustus Baldwin   185, 199
Lord, Frances   106
Lord, John   117
Lord, Maria T.   101, 106, 116, 164
Louis XVI   103
Lowther, Samuel   58
Lumpkin, Wilson   75

Macon Advertiser   74, 75
Macon Female Seminary   88, 164
Macon Messenger   62, 81-2
Macon Telegraph   217
Manning, Francis M.   4
Manning, Joseph   232
Marie, Louis   103
Marks, Elias   121
Marks, Jane L. (1786-1851)   213
Marshall, John   108
Martin, Josiah   12

Martin, Thomas   206
Martin County   1, 4, 9-13, 15, 18-19, 21-2, 25-9, 39, 40, 66
Martin County History (Manning and Booker)   4
Massachusetts State House   125
mass executions   23
Maultsby, Bessie Rhodes   30
Maultsby, Bessie Rhodes (1872-1909)   30
Maussinett, Adolphus   185
McClellan, George   234
McDonald, Charles J.   58
McIntosh, William   43, 90
McKay, Margaret J.   207
McKee, Hockley C.   229
McNair, Jeanne   215
McPherson, John   144
Memoir of Eli Whitney, Esq. (Olmstead)   130
Mercer, Jesse   197-200, 202
Mercer, William A.   144
Mercer University, Penfield   142, 181, 186, 197-8, 200-6
meteor science   129
Methodist Episcopal Church Georgia Conference   144
Methodists   21-2, 24, 48-9, 59, 76, 111, 141-61, 167-88, 199-202, 223-4
Mexican-American War   23-4
Miller, Frances   117
Mills, Nancy   198
Milton   78, 118, 119
Mitchell, William Letcher   75-8, 80, 82
Moore, Ephraim   232
Moravian Sisters   166
More, Thomas   79
Morgan, James Pierpont   125-6
Mormons   183
Moultrie, Joseph   161
Mount Lebanon Shaker Village   123
Murphy, Thomas H.   41-2
Murphy, William   41
Muscogee (Creek) Indians   16, 19, 42-3, 52, 66-7
Muscogee Female Academy   215
Mustain, John L.   231

Index

A *Narrative of Surprising Baptisms* (Fuller) 176
Neal, Thomas Jefferson 207
Nesbit, James A. 147, 153, 157–62
New Atlantis (Bacon) 79
Newcastle and Frenchtown Railroad 104
New Orleans Times-Picayune 24
New York 105–6
The New York News 231
Niblo, William 105
Niblo's Garden 105–6
Niblo's Theatre 105–6
Nisbet, E. A. 233–4
North Carolina 1–5, 9–31, 39–42, 50–2, 57, 64–6, 76, 84–6, 101, 107–8, 129, 143, 150, 154–5, 211, 220–1, 224, 226, 228, 232, 236, 239, 247
Northern, Peter 206
Northern, Sarah 206

Ocmulgee Association 174–5
Ocmulgee Bank 144
Oglethorpe, James 199
Oglethorpe University 75, 76, 142
Olmstead, Denison 129–31
open-air annual conference 143
The Orion 199, 202–3

Page, Anne Elizabeth Lee 212
Page, John Randolph (1804–64) 212–13
Page, Maria L. Williamson 212–13
Page, Rinaldo William 213
Page, William Byrd, Jr. (1833–95) 213
Page, William Byrd, Sr. 212
Palisades 106
Penfield, Fleming 214
Penfield, Georgia 197–208
  Baptist Convention 199–200
  country village 200
  religious school 200
Penfield Baptist Church 203–4, 206
Penfield Female Academy 197, 199, 202
  foundation 199
  principals 206
  as town school 206
Perry, John 85
Pestalozzi, Johann Heinrich 119

Phelps, A.; *see* Lincoln, Almira Hart
Philadelphia 104–5, 113
phrenology 125
Pierce, George Foster 141, 148, 150, 152, 157, 163
Pierce, John 126
Pierce, Mary Paterson 126
Pierce, Philip Lovick 141, 143, 148, 157, 158, 173–4, 170–171, 177–80, 215
Pierce, Sarah 108, 126–9
Pierpont, John 125–6
Pierpont, Julia 121, 126
Pitts, Lucy Ann 216–17
Pitts, Martha H. 167
Plan (Willard) 143
A Plan for Improving Female Education (Willard) 113
plantation economy 2, 11
plantations in North Carolina 10
planter aristocracy 11
Plattes, Gabriel 78
Plelan Plan of Columbus 212
Point Breeze 105
Polhill, John G. 56
Porter, James Hyde 201
Pratt, Daniel 48
prayers 102
Presbyterian Educational Society 75
Prescott, Annie 241
Prescott, Helen Malvina (1861–1946) 15
private schools 247–8
The Psalmist (Stow) 125
public education; *see* education
Pulpit Eloquence and the Downfall of Nations 147

Quakers 122–3

R. W. Page Corporation 213
radiator 130
Red Bone Camp Ground 143
Regulator Movement (1768–71) 12
religious schools 247–8
Rensselaer Polytechnic Institute 108
Republican Motherhood 114, 116, 126–8
Rhodes, William Slade 30

Rice, Luther 202
Rice, Thaddeus Brocket 198, 199, 201, 206
Richards, William Carey 202–3, 206
Robison, Nat M. 218
Rome Female Academy 121
Rose, Lavinia E. Blount 3
Rose, Mary Lavinia 216, 218
Rose, Simi 3
Rubenstein Library of Duke University 9–10
Rutherford, Benjamin Herbert 144
Rutherford, Elizabeth 229, 244

S. S. Fox 103
S. S. George Washington 103
S. S. North Carolina 141
Sabbath schools 231
Salem College 166
Sanders, Billington 197, 201, 206
Sanford, Camilla Dorinda 55
Sanford, Shelton Palmer 205–6
San Patricio Battalion 23–4
Sarepta Baptist Association 200
Savill, J. B. 65
school tax in Georgia
 collection 247
 constitution (1877) 247
Scotland 82
Scots-Irish 141
Scott, Anne Firor 110, 112, 117
Scott, Thomas Fielding 214
Seals, John H. 202
Second Great Awakening 142, 182, 232
Second Seminole Indian War 107
Second Treaty of Indian Springs 67, 90
Seward, William H. 25, 117
Shannon, James 75–8, 80, 82
Sherwood, Adiel 174, 175, 197, 200, 201, 232
Shiloh Baptist Church 203
Shorter, Eli Sims 217
Shorter, John Gill 217
Shorter, Mary Butler Gill 217
Shorter, Reuben Clark, Jr. 218
Shorter, Reuben Clark, Sr. 217
Shorter, Sophia H. 216–18

Simons, Abraham 198–9
Sinclair, Elijah 146, 148, 151–2, 158–9, 161–2, 174
Sing Sing (Ossining, NY) 106
Skewarkey Primitive Baptist Church 21
Slade, Agnes McNare (1720–1800) 11
Slade, Alfred M. 10, 16, 18, 22, 26–8, 30, 36, 40–1
Slade, Almarine Cowdrey 4
Slade, Anne Jacqueline Blount 3, 28, 40, 102, 184
Slade, Anne Louisa 228, 243–4
Slade, Cordelia Hassell (1849–1915) 21
Slade, Dawson 14–15
Slade, Dewitt Bowen 5
Slade, Ebenezer (1715–87) 10–12
Slade, Elisabeth Eldred 13
Slade, Elizabeth Ann Sutton 22
Slade, Elizabeth Bennett 4
Slade, Emma Jacqueline 5
Slade, Fanny Blount 216
Slade, Frances Abigail Sylvester 11
Slade, Hannah Loveridge 11
Slade, Hannah O. 207
Slade, Henry Blount (1762–1821) 4, 16, 28
Slade, Henry Wickman (1655–1730) 11
Slade, James Bog (1803–47) 23, 219
Slade, James Jeremiah (1775–1824) 9–11, 20–1
 death 28–9, 40–1
 law practice 9
 maternal side 13
 paternal side 11–12
 property and wealth 28–9
 Tuscarora Indians 9
 will 28–9
Slade, James Jeremiah, Sr. (1831–1917) 4, 23
Slade, Janet Bog (1774–1831) 9, 27, 29
Slade, John Henry 216, 234–5
Slade, Lavinia B. 208
Slade, Marmaduke Johnson 40
Slade, Martha Bog 102
Slade, Mary Janet 5
Slade, Mary Lavinia 236, 243
Slade, Myrtle Matthews 5

Slade, Nancy Ann Gainor   12
Slade, Ollyphair   207
Slade, Primus   21
Slade, Thomas Bog (1800–82)
  as an adolescent   3
  books   28
  death and burial   248–9
  discipleship   85
  education   9
  financial struggle   4
  letters   26–7
  life motto   28
  marriage   3, 28
  mission   3
  philosophy of education   85
  property and wealth   28, 29
  will   249
Slade, Thomas Bog (1816–35)   4
Slade, Thomas Bog, IX (1931–2021)   5
Slade, Thomas Bog, Jr. (1834–1926)   4, 54, 86, 218–19
Slade, Thomas Bog, Sr. (1845–1929)   4, 14, 15
Slade, Thomas Bog, V (1863–1942)   4
Slade, Thomas Bog, VI (1891–1956)   4, 5
Slade, Thomas Bog, VII (1906–71)   4–5
Slade, Thomas Bog, VIII (1915–78)   5
Slade, Thomasine Bog (1952)   5
Slade, William (1745–91)   4, 9–15
  will   13–14
Slade, William (1807–52)   14, 21, 22
Slade, William (1841–1919)   21
Slade family   2
  girls   5
  land-based wealth   11
  numbers   4
  reusing names   4–5
Slade Family Cemetery   29–30
Slade Female Institute   215–16
  commencement   216
  graduation ceremony   216
Slade-Gainer House on Slade Farm Road   14–15
Slade's Instruments   131
Sladesville   11
Slappey, George H.   39
slave owners   10

slavery   218
  Hassell on   22
Slave Schedule   25
Smith, David   235
Smith, E. J.   214
Smith, James   58
Smith, Roswell Chamberlain   131
Solomon, Henry Forsyth, Sr.   153, 155, 157
Solomon, Peter   162
South Carolina College   185
Southern Ladies' Book   163, 167, 177
Southern School Journal   207
Spata Female Academy in Georgia   121
Speer, Alexander Middleton   169, 181–2
Speer, Algernon S.   169
Speer, Margaret Amelia   169
Speer, William   150–1
Spurzheim, Johann Gaspar   125
Stanley, C. M.   69–70
Stephens, Alexander H.   1, 144–5
Stogner, William   214
Stoney Point   107
Stow, Alanson   125
Stowe, Harriet Beecher   126
Sylvester, Hannah Leonard   11
Sylvester, Richard William   11

Talley, J. W.   146, 148–50, 158
Tallmadge, Benjamin   126
Taney, Roger B.   108
taxes   12
Taylor, Sereno   121
Telegraph   3
The Temperance Banner   199, 207
The Temperance Crusader   202
Thigpen, Jane   68–9
Thomas, Grigsby E.   216
Thornton, Richard   232
Thornton Academy   199
Ticknor, Francis Orray   57
Ticknor, Orray   57
Times   249
tobacco   14
Toombs, Robert   152
Tracy, Uriah   126
Treaty of Fort Wilkinson   42–3

Treaty of Washington   67
Trollope, Fanny   104
Trotter, Martha   213
Troy, New York   108
Troy Baptist Church   110
Troy Female Academy   49, 108–26, 128, 172, 184
Troy Society for the Advancement of Education in Greece   112
Tryon, William   12
Tryon's Palace   12
Tucker, Henry Holcombe   202
tuition   214
Turner, George W.   218
Turner, Henry F.   208
Tuscarora Indians   9, 16–18, 20, 29
  Lawson on   17–18
  removal from North Carolina to New York   16
  split (northern and southern tribes)   16
Tuscarora War (1711–13)   16–17

United Methodist Church   142, 151
Universal Peace to be Introduced by a Confederacy of Nations Meeting in Jerusalem (Willard)   117
University of Georgia   37
University of North Carolina (UNC)   1, 9, 40

Vineville Academy   155, 183, 186

Waddel, Moses   142
War of 1812   9
Warren, James   242
The Watchtower   69
waterworks   104
Weathers, Jack   65
Wesleyan Female College   58, 186; *see also* Georgia Female College
  Slade's Instruments   131
West Point Military Academy   107–8
White, George   75
White Plains Academy   199
Wiggins, "Blind" Tom   213
Wiggins, Elizabeth Slade   24–5, 31, 66–8
Wiggins, Mason Lee   24, 66
Wightman, Joseph Milner   124
Wilkes County, Georgia   198
Willard, Emma   143
Willard, Emma Hart   49, 108–22, 127, 128, 143, 172–3, 184
Willard, John   111
Willard Association for the Mutual Improvement of Teachers   112
Willet, Emily   201
Willet, Joseph E.   200–1
Williams, William   25
Williamston Library Association   21
Winthrop, John, Jr.   131
Wolcott, Oliver   126
Wynnton Female Academy   215

Yale College   129–30

About the Author

Timothy E. Miller is an assistant professor of history and Latin and curator of a historic village at Brewton-Parker Christian University in Mt. Vernon, Georgia, and a 2021 DPhil graduate of the University of Oxford in Oxford, England. Originally from Dallas, Georgia, he now lives in Dublin, Georgia. The author's interests include the early modern history of science, especially the Hartlib Circle, and the intersection of science and faith. He has published and presented at historical conferences several articles on Hartlib, education, transportation in Ghana (West Africa), the Scots-Irish, and just-war theory. The author was formerly curator of the Abingdon Abbey Buildings in Abingdon, England, a seventh-century Benedictine monastery. "Tim" has three children, including Ben, Eli, and Sara.

www.ingramcontent.com/pod-product-compliance
Lightning Source LLC
Chambersburg PA
CBHW070938230426
43666CB00011B/2478